Psychoanalytic Method in Motion

Psychoanalytic Method in Motion identifies and examines varied controversies about how psychoanalysts believe treatment should be conducted. Irrespective of their particular school of thought, every analyst builds up a repertoire of his or her favored ways of working, which they often come to regard as the most efficacious approach to treatment available. While such differences of opinion are unsettling, and may even threaten to tear the field asunder, this book sees these differences as benefitting psychoanalysis by challenging and improving the ways in which psychoanalysts and psychoanalytic psychotherapists practice their craft.

In this book, Richard Tuch covers the waterfront by examining controversies that further the field and by raising questions that help evolve the treatment, challenging every analyst to rethink what they are doing in the consulting room...and why. Some of the chief controversies explored include:

- the enactment debate – unparalleled tool or regrettable folly?
- whether analysts can be "objective" enough to justify the offering of interpretations
- the advantages and disadvantages of the analyst's use of his authority
- the ways in which theory influences the analyst's search for data – blinding him to evidence he implicitly discards as irrelevant
- whether any given treatment approach is more efficacious than others
- the legitimacy of psychoanalysis itself – whether it can truly be considered scientific
- whether certain methods of supervision are more effective than others
- whether free association can be considered therapeutic in and of itself
- the extent to which an analyst's preferred clinical theory is a product of his personality

Drawing on ideas from a range of different analytic perspectives, this book is an essential and accessibly written guide to working toward best practice in the analytic setting. *Psychoanalytic Method in Motion* will appeal greatly to both students and practitioners of psychoanalysis and psychoanalytic psychotherapy.

Richard Tuch is Training and Supervising Analyst at the New Center for Psychoanalysis and the Psychoanalytic Center of California. He is Clinical Professor of Psychiatry at the David Geffen School of Medicine, UCLA. He has written and co-written books and chapters, and his papers appear in all three major psychoanalytic journals. He received the Karl A. Menninger Memorial Award for Psychoanalytic Writing, the Edith Sabshin Award for Teaching, and the Leo Rangell Essay Contest. He is presently Head of Scholarship Section of the Department of the Department of Psychoanalytic Education at the American Psychoanalytic Association.

Psychoanalytic Method in Motion

Controversies and Evolution in Clinical Theory and Practice

Richard Tuch

Routledge
Taylor & Francis Group
LONDON AND NEW YORK

First published 2018
by Routledge
2 Park Square, Milton Park, Abingdon, Oxon OX14 4RN

and by Routledge
605 Third Avenue, New York, NY 10017

Routledge is an imprint of the Taylor & Francis Group, an informa business

British Library Cataloguing in Publication Data
A catalogue record for this book is available from the British Library

Library of Congress Cataloging in Publication Data
Names: Tuch, Richard, author.
Title: Psychoanalytic method in motion : controversies and evolution in clinical theory and practice / Richard Tuch.
Description: Abingdon, Oxon ; New York, NY : Routledge, 2018. |
Includes bibliographical references and index.
Identifiers: LCCN 2017026392 | ISBN 9781138098558 (hardback : alk. paper) |
ISBN 9781138098565 (pbk. : alk. paper) | ISBN 9781315104355 (Master) |
ISBN 9781351597852 (Web PDF) | ISBN 9781351597845 (ePub) |
ISBN 9781351597838 (Mobipocket/Kindle)
Subjects: | MESH: Psychoanalytic Therapy–methods | Psychoanalytic Theory
Classification: LCC RC506 | NLM WM 460.6 | DDC 616.89/17–dc23
LC record available at https://lccn.loc.gov/2017026392

ISBN: 978-1-138-09855-8 (hbk)
ISBN: 978-1-138-09856-5 (pbk)
ISBN: 978-1-315-10435-5 (ebk)

Typeset in Times New Roman
by Out of House Publishing

This book is dedicated to Jim Grotstein
Who lapped up life
Like a dog does his water
Who lived his life
Like there was no tomorrow
Who loved us all
Like mama does her baby
And left us all
Much wiser though heart achy

Contents

Acknowledgments ix

Introduction 1

SECTION I
The duties of analyst and analysand **17**

1 Daring to let go: The therapeutic benefits of free association 19

2 The analyst's activity and his search for evidence: Theory-determined salience and selective perception 40

3 The analyst's way of being: Method as a function of the analyst's personality 61

4 Questioning the analyst's use of authority: For better and for worse 78

SECTION II
Treating certain sorts of patients **95**

5 Thinking with, and about, patients too scared to think: Can non-interpretive maneuvers stimulate reflective thought? 97

6 Thinking outside the box: A metacognitive perspective on the treatment of concrete thinking 116

SECTION III
Psychoanalytic schools of thought **135**

7 The interpersonalist's handling of enactments: The effect of comparative theories on technique 137

8 Beyond empathy: A wrinkle in self psychology theory 156

9 Learning from Middle School theorists: Technique from a Middle School perspective 171

SECTION IV
Passing the baton: From generation to generation **191**

10 Learning how to think like an analyst: Teaching technique to psychotherapy students 193

11 The effect of style on the quality of supervision: Should the details of treatment be left to the treating clinician? 216

12 What is scientific about psychoanalysis?: Truth comes in many colors 239

References 256
Index 278

Acknowledgments

Writing a book robs important people in the writer's life of his more regular presence; if one hungers to write, it's hard to know how to solve this regrettable dilemma. So my first acknowledgment goes to my wife, Sunnye, who has had to put up with my absence while I fashioned yet another volume. My psychiatric training at the Neuropsychiatric Institute at the University of California at Los Angeles was rich with clinical supervision provided by psychoanalysts who generously donated their time and shared their expertise, which much enriched my education and convinced me of the value of the psychoanalytic approach to treatment. Joel Yager headed the residency training program and, while not an analyst himself, was nevertheless open-minded enough to welcome, include, and promote psychoanalysis in the psychiatric residency program. If only heads of training programs nationwide followed his lead, the field of psychiatry would be much better as a result. Aside from those who supervised me at UCLA, others I wish to acknowledge are my supervisors and mentors at the Los Angeles Psychoanalytic Society and Institute, which – after merging with the Southern California Psychoanalytic Institute and Society – now exists as the New Center for Psychoanalysis. I would like to deeply thank all who contributed to my psychoanalytic education, in particular (in alphabetical order): Dan Borenstein, Rudi Ekstein, Sid Fine, Len Gilman, James Grotstein, Mike Leavitt, Albert Mason, Arthur Ourieff, Leo Rangell, Norman Tabachnick, Larry Warwick, and Robert Zaitlin. If I've failed to mention anyone, please forgive my oversight. I also wish to acknowledge those at the New Center for Psychoanalysis who were supportive when I served as Dean of Training, as well as others who, throughout the years, have been a joy to know. Certain names immediately spring to mind (in alphabetical order): Richard Baker, Jill Model Barth, Barton Blinder, Alan Compton, Van Dyke DeGolia, Helen Desmond, Susan Donner, Morris Eagle, Rina Freedman, Michael Gales, Linda Goodman, Ken House, Robin Jacobs, Robin Kissell, Lynn Kuttnauer, Joan Lachkar, Mel Lansky, Doryann Lebe, Peter Loewenberg, Regina Pally, Jim Perkins, Myra Pomerantz, Dahlia Nissan Russ, Martha Slagerman,

Janet Smith, Julie Tepper, Jeff Seitelman, Sheri Siassi, Heather Silverman, Mark Thompson, Lisa Vitti, and Samuel Wilson. Again, please forgive any oversights. I also wish to acknowledge members at my other institute – the Psychoanalytic Center of California – who have also been quite helpful to me, including David Brooks, Jennifer Kunst, John Lundgren, Barnet Malin, and Leigh Tobias. I am also indebted to many who have contributed to the psychoanalytic literature whose ideas have greatly stimulated my own thinking. Those who I feel particularly affectionate towards include (in alphabetical order): Salman Akhtar, Fred Busch, Darlene Ehrenberg, Henry Friedman, Larry Friedman, Glen Gabbard, Jay Greenberg, Larry Josephs, Otto Kernberg, Joe Lichtenberg, Bob Michaels, Jack and Kerry Kelly Novick Tom Ogden, Warren Poland, Owen Renik, Arnie Richards, Bob Stolorow, Donnel Stern, and Mitchell Wilson. I have little doubt that I have left worthy names out, and I beg your forgiveness for my failure. Particularly helpful was Susan L. Orbach, who got me thinking about the interpersonal approach to enactments, and P.J. Bonavitacola, a resident-supervisee who provided material for the supervision chapter. Others I owe a debt of gratitude to for contributing to my intellectual education include Ron Britton, Michael Feldman, Arnie Modell, Tom Ogden, and John Steiner. Assuredly I have left names out, which I will regret the day the book leaves the print shop. Finally, I wish to acknowledge my long-term friend Bruce Gainsley, who has been in my life for over 40 years, as well as my children, Alex and Zachary. Thank you, one and all, for all you've provided me all these years.

Permissions acknowledgments

Chapter 1 contains significant passages from 'Shifting between alternate modes of cognition: Can free association, in and of itself, prove therapeutic?', *The Psychoanalytic Quarterly*, 86(2): 269–96, April 2017. Reprinted by permission of the journal and John Wiley & Sons, Ltd.

Chapter 3 first published as 'The analyst's way of being: Recognizing separable subjectivities and the pendulum's swing', *The Psychoanalytic Quarterly*, 84(2): 363–88, April 2015. Reprinted by permission of the journal and John Wiley & Sons, Ltd.

Chapter 4 first published as 'Questioning the psychoanalyst's authority', *Journal of the American Psychoanalytic Association*, 59(4): 765–89, August 2011. Reprinted by kind permission of SAGE Publications, Ltd.

Chapter 5 first published as 'Beyond empathy: Confronting certain complexities in self psychology theory', *The Psychoanalytic Quarterly*, 66(2): 259–82, May 1997. Reprinted by permission of the journal and John Wiley & Sons, Ltd.

Chapter 6 first published as 'Thinking outside the box: A metacognitive/theory of mind perspective on concrete thinking', *Journal of the American*

Psychoanalytic Association, 59(4): 765–89, August 2011. Reprinted by kind permission of SAGE Publications, Ltd.

Chapter 8 first published as 'Thinking with, and about, patients too scared to think: Can non-interpretive maneuvers stimulate reflective thought?', *The International Journal of Psychoanalysis*, 88(1): 91–111, February 2007. Reprinted by permission of the journal and John Wiley & Sons, Ltd.

Introduction

Psychoanalysis is an exciting and dynamic field of study as well as a compelling method of treatment, and it has been my privilege, over the last 20 years, to have been able to participate in a dialogue – through the publication of papers and the delivery of talks – about the controversies that rage whenever experienced, well-trained psychoanalysts gather together in the same room and futilely try to reach agreement about how psychoanalysis should be practiced. The degree of disagreement may be seen by some as a sign of weakness in the field and may set in motion a search for "common ground" (Wallerstein, 1988) that establishes that analysts are more alike in how they actually practice than controversy would lead one to believe.

When the debate about technique becomes rancorous – as it often does – some analysts may dispute whether the technique used by certain other analysts deserves to be called by the same name as what they themselves do in their own practices. The charge that often gets leveled – "what you do isn't analysis" – is highly presumptuous and runs counter to how most analysts appear to feel about unwarranted certainty and the recognized value of maintaining an "unknowing stance" when considering clinical material that requires open-mindedness rather than dogmatic insistence about what one imagines to be true. Assuming the right to speak authoritatively on what constitutes superior treatment may develop as a result of various factors: a) from an old-fashioned, know-it-all brand of narcissism that is accompanied by unwavering certainty that one's perspective trumps all others; b) from one's affiliation with a given school of thought – leading one to argue vocally about the superiority of that school's theories or approach to treatment or, alternately, to come to the aid of a like-minded colleague who'd been felled by the harsh criticism of an analyst who hails from an opposing camp against who one retaliates by taking issue with his thinking; or c) from becoming convinced by one's clinical experiences that a given perspective stands the best chance of shedding the most light on the largest segment of a patient's psychopathology and, furthermore, that this perspective provides the greatest amount of guidance about how best to approach the case from a clinical perspective. Whatever the cause, a lack of civility when dealing with colleagues and an expression of mean-spiritedness, which is never justified, should be called out and challenged at every turn. Freud's (1930) concept of the "narcissism of minor differences" helps account for such developments – the idea that slight differences between groups of people who are otherwise very much alike are taken to represent critiques of one's own way of being or beliefs, the reaction to which binds the group in angry and aggressive opposition to the other group.

Given such conditions, offering one's views about the psychoanalytic method risks placing one in the thick of it, with enough analysts lying in wait to pick apart whichever expressed positions fail to conform to their own ways of thinking. Don't get me wrong – I am not speaking about the way in which most analysts act, but rather how a small handful of vocal critics have been known to act as they assert and/or defend their own brand of psychoanalysis with a passion. Such is the environment into which I walk as I offer a book exclusively focused on the matter of technique.

Contentiousness can lay bare an existing schism that can easily cast doubt on the legitimacy of the field. If psychoanalysis is scientific, as some claim it to be, then analysts might be expected to reach a semblance of consensus. But as potentially divisive and undermining as controversy can be, it propels change by challenging analysts to collectively examine, question, and rethink certain of their most essential assumptions to see whether they still hold water or, rather, should be discarded to make room for theories and perspectives that are more consistent with evolving knowledge coming not just from the consulting room, but from other fields of study as well: from infant observation, neuroscience, social psychology, academic psychology, and the like. Many of Freud's original hypotheses have fallen by the wayside – dismissed by Freud himself as no longer adequate to account for phenomena he came to see as being more complex than he had at first imagined. After all, do we still believe that syphilitic fathers beget hysterics? Aren't we past believing that conflicts around issues of control are strictly born of anal phase pathology? A more recent example includes the effect infant observation has had on our former belief about infantile symbiosis, which has been all but banned as a legitimate developmental construct.

Not everyone appreciates just how dynamic the field of psychoanalysis can be. Its critics would have you believe that analysts practice in precisely the same way as Freud did over a century ago – that psychoanalysis is an arcane method of treatment practiced by a dwindling group of aging doctors who are stuck in their ways, deaf to the changing world about them that has essentially left them behind. Better they get their noses out of books and wake up to changes taking place in the outside world – a world that hasn't the patience for analysis, given the pace of life and clamor for instantaneous relief and immediate gratification. Against the backdrop of this portrayal is reality – close examination leaves little doubt that psychoanalytic technique is indeed evolving.

While the psychoanalytic method that Freud discovered is remarkable in its original iteration, it must continue to evolve to stay relevant. Though psychoanalysis has been dismissed by many – particularly in the United States – as antiquated and passé, such conclusions aren't warranted given how far the field has come – the result of dedicated analysts doing their best to work out the kinks and find alternate ways to conceptualize how and why patient's fall ill and what methodologic changes might make the psychoanalytic approach to treatment more effective. Therapeutic failures are studied with an eye toward discovering what went wrong – was it the theory? The technique? A poor match between patient and therapist? Maybe the countertransference? Maybe the patient's pathology lies beyond the field's ability to treat? Psychoanalysts give due consideration to such matters, grappling with how to improve our methods. Psychoanalytic technique has changed, and continues to change, as psychoanalysts study not just what went wrong, but why certain treatments work as well as they do. Yes – people are getting treated and people are getting better, people for whom psychoanalysis appears to have been the most efficacious treatment available, as scientific studies have now shown it to be. But we've gotten ahead of ourselves insofar as the topic of the scientific basis of psychoanalysis doesn't appear until the tail end of the book.

This book is about the controversies that have swirled around the topic of technique for the last several decades. It is also about the evolution of the psychoanalytic method – how psychoanalysis, as it is practiced today, differs markedly from how it had been practiced in days gone by. The process by which the development of psychoanalytic technique evolves over time often involves a swing from one accepted position to its opposite (from thesis to antithesis). This sometimes involves an overstatement of the flaws of the original position (throwing the baby out with the bathwater based on a straw-man argument that over-simplifies standard operating procedure) and a celebration of the benefits of the new position that, for a time, fills many with hope that an answer has finally been found that solves the shortcoming of the "old" method. Finally, clarity reigns with the development of a new tool that many hope will prove infinitely better. Detractors grunt dismissively about "old wine in new bottles," while the most fervent followers of the new method declare that "we've arrived," forgetting that "arrived" implies a final destination, which this new method can't possibly be. Its limitations and flaws will be discovered sooner or later, but for a time, the celebration continues.

The way in which psychoanalysis has evolved can be thought to exist on a macro and a micro level, which is best illustrated by a line graph that appears at first glance to be on an unrelenting uphill course when viewed from a distance. This belies the ups and downs that are noticeable upon closer inspection. Such micro-trends represent a pendulum swing that moves in an extreme direction before the situation rights itself through a process of moderation. This is one of the two main points made in Chapter 3, in which I argue that the "enactment movement" – if we dare call it that – has gone too far, to the extent some act as if countertransference enactments are the gold standard – the new "royal road to the unconscious" – leading some analysts to conclude that any analyses devoid of stark enactments are poorer as a consequence in comparison to analyses in which powerful enactments are seen as propelling analytically facilitated change in a way nothing else can. Controversy developed when Steiner (2006) issued a sobering reminder that enactments, while inevitable and unavoidable, represent a breach in the analyst's duty to contain the patient's material, rather than become swept up in the material (even *swept away* by it), raising concern about whether the analyst will, first, catch on in a timely fashion to the fact he's lapsed into enacting, and then, will find ways to successfully make effective clinical use of his realization of what the enactment means. Steiner's warning runs counter to Boesky's (1990) bold assertion that "If the analyst does not get emotionally involved sooner or later in a manner that he had not intended, the analysis *will not proceed* to a successful conclusion" (p. 573, italics added). Furthermore, it seemingly ignores the clinical problems that could develop if an analyst fails to be "role responsive" to a patient's attempts to assign him a given role consistent with the patient's transference (Sandler 1976), or – put in other terms – when the analyst fails to accept the role assignment and interpretively counters something the patient has attributed to the analyst that the patient needs for the two of them to "live with" for the time being (failure to "*wear the attribution*," Lichtenberg, Lachmann, & Fosshage, 1992, 1996 – touched on in Chapters 3, 7, and 9). I liken such situations (failure to be role responsive or to wear the attribution) to a "block at the net" (when, in volleyball, the ball is kept from making its way across the net to the opposing side's court), which can represent the analyst's refusal or unwillingness to "play ball" for the sake of the treatment. A dialectic develops between the position taken by Steiner and those taken by these other authors – a dialectic that moderates the concerns raised by each party – thus illustrating one of the many controversies raised in this book.

When looked at from a macro level, the enactment movement seemed headed in a direction diametrically opposed to the one commonly held a half century ago, when countertransference was seen as a sign that the analyst needed a bit more analysis himself to "work out" his countertransference inclinations that ran the risk of contaminating the analyses he was conducting. Nowadays, certain analysts are of the opinion that analysts who are characterologically disinclined to lapse into acting out their countertransference feelings are essentially robbing their patients of a clinical experience that might prove to be amongst the most powerful and mutative of all the tools analysts now have to offer.[1] Note how the hero–villain structure of discourse is retained in spite of the swing; all that's changed is which of the two types of analyst – enacter versus container – is thought to be providing their patients with the most optimal therapeutic environment. Today, analysis of the analyst's countertransference reaction (his total emotion reaction to the patient, *not* his idiosyncratic reaction to the patient that is relatively independent of the particulars of the patient) has taken center stage in many analyses, to the extent such data is not theoretic and, accordingly, less likely to generate interventions or interpretations that are more intellectual and speculative in nature. Furthermore, there is a heightened emphasis on the part of certain analysts to consider their own personal contribution to the countertransference, which reminds them to remain aware of who is who. "I think it is fair to say," notes Kernberg (1993), "that all analysts utilise the exploration of their own affective responses to their patients in a consistent and much freer way than earlier clinicians did." (p. 662). Kernberg also advances the idea that "projective identification" has also become widely accepted as a legitimate and useful clinical phenomenon.

Sometimes, evolving theory takes our field too far afield before eventuating in a synthesis between extremes that is not nearly as hyperbolic. Renik (1993) provides a particularly good example of an analyst who's inclined to bolster his arguments using such absolute words as "always" and "never" – doing so eleven different times in this one paper alone (e.g., "awareness of countertransference is *always* retrospective, preceded by countertransference enactment" which he declares to be "*invariably* the case," p. 556). While some readers might feel reassured by statements that are made in no uncertain terms, the absoluteness of such statements should give us pause. Renik not only made absolute statements about his contention that analysts only know their countertransference reactions after the fact, he also argued that analysts cannot be said to possess anything approximating objectivity. Renik may not have recognized at the time that he was going too far out on a limb when he wrote "the fact that we still use the term *interpretation* would seem to indicate the extent to which we retain a conception of analytic technique as potentially objective, rather than inherently subjective" (p. 559), which led Renik to call upon analysts to cease referring to their interventions as "interpretations." To his credit, five years later, Renik (1998) came to the realization that he'd gotten dangerously close to disclaiming the scientific basis of psychoanalysis, which caused him to backpedal, restoring the analyst's right to claim to be objective by employing a most interesting and contorted argument that helped him retain, in part, his original position: analytic objectivity is possible, noted Renik, if – by that term – one means the analyst's acceptance of the fact that his subjectivity is an insurmountable factor in interpretation. The ongoing debate about the analyst's use of authority (see Chapter 4) and the legitimacy of his claim to have something authoritative to say about the patient's psyche rages on.

One can identify certain macro trends in the way in which analysts of varying stripes and colors conduct psychoanalysis today in comparison to how it was practiced decades ago (see Kernberg 1993). One of the most noteworthy changes is a de-emphasis on attempts to genetically reconstruct the patient's past (recover lost memories), in line with doubt that's developed about the analyst's capacity to do just that. Reconstructions of the sort Freud offered the Wolf Man about his dream ("*He had been sleeping in his cot, then, in his parents' bedroom, and woke up, perhaps because of his rising fever, in the afternoon, possibly at five o'clock, the hour which was later marked out by depression…When he woke up, he witnessed a coitus a tergo [from behind], three times repeated; he was able to see his mother's genitals as well as his father's organ; and he understood the process as well as its significance*," Freud, 1918, p. 37) seem highly doubtful if not downright absurd in retrospect, and have given way to the construction of narratives more reflective of a central focus on the here-and-now transference, which can involve an emphasis on narrative truth over historical truth (Spence, 1982; Schafer, 1976, 1992), thought to capture a given patient's "story" about who he is, why he acts as he does, why he's developed the symptoms he has, etc. No longer are analysts willing to settle for a patient's "buying" the analyst's reconstruction on the basis of "an *assured conviction* of the truth of the construction" (Freud, 1937, p. 266, italics added) in the absence of the patient's failure to be able to recollect such a hypothesized occurrence. This isn't to say that reconstruction has entirely been set aside; it is only to note that reconstruction takes a back seat to an examination of the here-and-now unconscious aspects of the transference.

The depth at which analysts attempt to work with a patient's material has also changed. Whereas Kleinians of yesteryear had been inclined to focus on the deepest level of anxiety (Segal, 1973), Kernberg (1993) notes that Hanna Segal "now stresses interpretation at the most active – not deepest – level of anxiety, and with the patient's current level of mental functioning" (pp. 661–662), which is very much in line with the long-standing tendency of modern ego psychologists (Busch, 1995; Gray, 1994) to work from surface to depth, calling the patient's attention to evidence of defenses in action before setting out to determine what those defenses aim to defend against, in line with Fenichel (1945). There has been a comparable shift away from the analysis of specific symptoms or parapraxes to a more holistic analysis of the patient's character and character resistances as manifest in repetitive behavior patterns. Kernberg (1993) also notes an increased tendency, even on the part of ego psychologists, to think in terms of object relations, though he notes a distinction between how analysts who remain chiefly wedded to classic drive theory conceptualize object relations relative to those who are more inclined to focus on the patient's affects separate and apart from how those affects may arise due to wishes to gratify, or in reaction to a frustration of, the patient's drives. We have also seen a diminution in the central role of dream analysis – which isn't to suggest that it hasn't any place; rather, it is to emphasize "the multiplicity of 'royal roads' to the unconscious" (Kernberg, 1993, p. 663) – verbal content, nonverbal content, and the qualities of the relationship that develops between analyst and analysand. Concern has also been widely expressed about the analyst's reliance on his authority – something analysts were more inclined to do in the past, which analysts these days worry may indoctrinate the patient into the analyst's ways of thinking (his theory). Such concerns have led some analysts to take such care to avoid imposing their ideas on the patient that they have all but abdicated their responsibility to provide patients with an alternate point of view on the patient's situation (yet another example of a pendulum shift), a topic discussed in depth in Chapter 4.

Psychoanalytic technique in focus

Freud's legacy is rich, but of all his gifts, the one I personally am most thankful to have received is his development of a method of treatment – an approach that has benefitted mankind more than many realize. The particular component of psychoanalytic technique that comes closest to constituting "common ground" is that of free association, which remains in effect worldwide in the form of a widespread, unshakable belief on the part of analysts in the clinical value of the fundamental rule, and a corresponding reliance upon free association, which steers every analysis. The first section of the book – "The duties of analyst and analysand" – contains four chapters that outline some of the current controversies involving the clinical method. In Chapter 1, we examine patients' difficulties free associating from two vantage points: one having to do with a patient's difficulty switching between alternate modes of cognition – between "making happen" and "letting happen," between "doing" and "being" – and the other having to do with the patient's difficulty recognizing that he has a mind of his own that's become lost in the shuffle because the patient's "as if" tendencies (Deutsch, 1942), which have him adapting to the object world in a chameleon-like fashion, effectively hiding his true self *even from himself*. While free association provides a glimpse into the patient's unconscious, revealed in his difficulties in daring to "let go" (let happen), there is reason to believe that free association, in and of itself, may prove therapeutic to the extent patients who seek treatment are often plagued not only by symptoms, but also by impairments in their ability to freely navigate the inner passages of their mind without experiencing persistent pressure and dread that keeps them from wandering into psychic spaces where frightening skeletons may be hanging or painful memories may be lurking. Slowly gaining the ability to think in a more free-ranging fashion is typically thought to solely develop as a function of interpretation that helps reveal resistances/defenses, which then get worked through to such a degree that the patient becomes better able to move about in his mind without dreading what he might encounter. How one comes to be able to more freely associate may prove to be a bit more complicated than was just outlined. While making the unconscious conscious remains a vital, essential, and laudable goal, it may not be the sole way in which psychic flexibility develops. Exercising the mind and developing a heightened capacity to, for example, shift more nimbly between passive and active modes of cognition might be an added way in which one improves overall psychic functioning. The same might be said of patients for whom free association may be a way to find their lost selves buried beneath the rubble of their attempts to protect the self from being exposed to the danger of being discovered, invaded, and negated. These two alternate modes by which a patient may gain a heightened capacity to free associate – making the unconscious conscious and exercising the use of one's mind by surrendering to the task of free associating – needn't be considered an either/or proposition, and both mechanisms may contribute their share to what is achieved clinically.

Chapter 2 addresses how theory determines what the analyst deems as salient and how an analyst's particular analytic theory directs his search for "evidence" – thus demonstrating the extent to which theory functions by implicitly[2] alerting one to be on the lookout for certain sorts of evidence, which necessarily blinds one from noting other types of clinical data. As much as analysts pride themselves on being remarkably open-minded and unflinchingly observant, there is sufficient reason to doubt such claims. Theories function like polarizing filters that "let in" only a certain select segment of the data – that which is noted because it's deemed salient (relevant) in accordance with one's particular theory. Without the aid of theory, psychoanalysts wouldn't have a clue about the sorts of clinical data that should be prioritized as they search for evidence that goes on to become the data upon which to base their understanding of the patient. For example, an analyst who subscribes to modern ego psychology will be apt to "closely monitor" the patient's associations with an eye toward noting shifts in the patient's associations (Busch, 1995; Gray, 1994) – shifts that alert the analyst to the fact that a defense is afoot. This results in selective attention that keeps the analyst from noticing *other types of data*, given the fact that minds have a limited amount of "RAM" with which to work. A noted failure on the patient's part to stay with a given train of thought wherever it may lead is, for the ego psychologist, a "selected fact" – evidence of a defense in action – which the analyst will then use to help determine what the patient might be defending against in accordance with the goal of defense analysis. A selected fact, which may be born of one's theory and, in turn, may be used to support one's theory about a given patient, differs from an "overvalued idea" (Britton & Steiner, 1994) that runs the risk of leading the analytic couple astray when the analyst and/or the analysand come to accept the selected fact as if it represented the long-awaited answer that now satisfactorily solves the patient's problem. This chapter also examines the belief that the analyst's clinical activities (e.g., his interventions) are the result of conscious, careful deliberation that weighs the pros and cons of the options under consideration. While many interventions may in fact be the result of such conscious, willful deliberation, more and more analysts are willing to admit to instances when something just "blurted out" of their mouth unthinkingly or to instances when they'd found themselves acting in ways without being quite sure what had gotten into them. A particularly illustrative example of this is provided by Jody Davies (1999), who describes her actions during a given session with a patient named Daniel:

> The next thing I knew, I was standing next to Daniel's chair wrapping a blanket around his shoulders, *not quite sure how I ended up there.* I remembered reaching with a disembodied arm into the cabinet where I kept the blanket for my own occasional use, and then getting up out of my chair, *but these were not considered actions.* (p. 193, italics added)

Davies' description will surely spook certain analysts who find it impossible to imagine acting in such a way, but that doesn't mean they don't engage in more subtle forms of the same type of unwitting activity. Finally, in this chapter, we consider the question of whether insight itself is what is mutative or, rather, whether it is the *process by which insight comes about* – whether it's the journey more than the final destination that is of greatest value.

We have already touched on one of the two chief themes of Chapter 3 – the matter of how the evolution of psychoanalytic theory sometimes takes place in extreme pendulum swings. While I agree with the movement that finds great value in the analysis of countertransference enactments, I take issue with those who believe in the hierarchical importance of enactments as if they now constitute – and should constitute – *the* essential component of treatment – another hyperbolic swing of the pendulum in a direction I believe will eventually prove undefendable and unsustainable. The other issue addressed in this chapter has to do with the relationship between the analyst's personality and how it influences the way in which he goes about practicing analysis (Tuch, 2015). Journal reviewers who commented on this paper during the submission process were concerned with the idea espoused in an earlier version of the paper (since removed given their objection, though hints of it remain) that the theory a given psychoanalyst ends up adopting oftentimes proves to be a function of that analyst's personality. Such thinking is in line with what Stolorow and Atwood (1979) proposed in *Faces in a Cloud*, in which they correlated the particular theories promoted by some of our earliest psychoanalytic pioneers (Freud, Jung, Reich, and Rank) with their personalities, convincingly establishing the role personality plays in theory development. These reviewers were concerned that such a claim on my part could be seen as calling into question the scientific basis of our field. I don't see why that would be so, and I remain a firm believer in the science of psychoanalysis, though I do feel that the theory one relies upon is a personal, though unconscious, choice that goes on to help determine what the analyst finds salient in the patient's material (Chapter 2). At the same time, I believe that whatever is chosen as salient becomes grist for the mill – that analysts should not believe they are aiming to discover *the* essential truth of a patient's life when, in fact, there are a host of varied essential truths from which to pick, all of which I believe could prove fruitful when explored. We should not have to worry that one psychoanalytic theory leads to the truth, tossing all other theories into the hopper labeled "also ran."

Chapter 4 addresses a controversy about the pros and cons of the analyst's use of authority when he takes a stand about what he thinks he sees reflected in the patient's behavior, which he fashions into an interpretation that's offered for the patient's consideration. Some analysts believe interpretations, backed with the power of the analyst's authority, run the risk of creating the impression that the analyst is denying or negating the patient's perspective about the matter at hand, leaving the patient feeling wiped out in the process, as if he'd been told that he doesn't know the first thing about his own psyche. It probably goes without saying – but had nevertheless best be said – that this is the last thing any analyst wishes to convey to a patient as a result of offering an interpretation meant to be helpful rather than hurtful. But, assuredly, there are instances when patients nevertheless feel diminished, dismissed, assaulted, and so on when the analyst offers an alternate perspective to the one held by the patient about the patient's situation or condition. Such dangers aren't always avoidable, though they may prove surmountable to the extent a vigilant analyst quickly notes that the offered interpretation has made matters worse, resists the urge to see the matter as one of a negative therapeutic reaction, and sets himself to the task of exploring with the patient what it was about the analyst's interpretation – or, maybe more to the point, the experience of being interpreted – that had so affected the analysand. Certain analysts are adamant that the attendant dangers of interpreting are so great as to make the act of interpreting counter-therapeutic either for certain sorts of patients or for all patients (a subject illustrated in Chapters 5 and 6). Chapter 4 examines the debate about whether analysts can consider their interpretations "objective," given the influence of the analyst's "irreducible subjectivity" (Renik, 1993), which some believe to be so contaminating as to challenge the analyst's claim to have anything approximating expert knowledge about the patient's mind. In yet another pendulum swing, some analysts have taken to privileging the *patient's* perspective over the *analyst's* perspective, which, as I argue, gets analysts into a pickle if analysts wish to retain the claim of having something worthwhile to offer patients.

The widening scope of psychoanalysis – how treatment might be modified to accommodate patients who are too scared to think (Chapter 5) or who exhibit thinking that is primarily concrete (Chapter 6) – is addressed in Section II of this book – "Treating certain sorts of patients." Chapter 5 describes the sorts of difficulties encountered, and the technical modifications required, when treating patients whose separation anxiety makes it exceedingly hard for them to be able, in particular, to tolerate evidence of differences between themselves and others. The intensity of this anxiety makes it nearly impossible for such patients to permit their analysts to do anything that might draw attention to the ways in which the two differ because the evident gap is not one the patient can easily live with, which causes him to react violently – for example – when the analyst is caught thinking to himself about the patient (or, if he relies on reverie, letting himself drift away momentarily), rather than being fully present with the patient in the room – which precludes the analyst from being able to relax. Instances when the analyst appears to be thinking to himself (or shows evidence of having done so, given the interpretation he brings back from such acts of introspection) can trigger intense anxiety and rage, since these instances are experienced by the patient as a betrayal of the analyst's imagined pledge to remain *fully present* with the patient in the here-and-now, with the analyst's thinking representing a failure to do just that. This idea borrows heavily from a paper by Britton (1989), in which he described his treatment of Miss A., the woman who responded to his interpretations by screaming her demand that he "stop that fucking thinking" (p. 88) because she experienced his interpretations as if "*I was eliminating my experience of her in my mind*" (pp. 88–89, italics added). Britton's interpretations left the patient feeling excluded *to the point of not existing.*

A point only alluded to in this chapter, which is worth highlighting in this introduction, is the extent to which elaborate psychoanalytic theories of the sort Britton developed to explain Miss A.'s intolerance of interpretations can oftentimes prove hard to put to good clinical use when the analyst tries to do just that. This isn't to say these theories aren't of considerable use to the analyst; it is only to note that there are times when what these theories reveal to the analyst cannot then be revealed to the analysand as such, though the understanding gleaned from the interpretation may go some way toward helping the analyst withstand and contain rigorous clinical conditions. It is worth noting that what most people readily remember and quote from Britton's paper (e.g., Aron, 1995; Astor, 1998; Caper, 1997; Schoenhals, 1995) – his satisfying, understandable, and believable *symbolic* understanding of what the patient's words "stop that fucking thinking" meant – was far beyond Miss A.'s capacity to grasp. Given what Britton went on to say, it can't even be said for sure that the patient's words had meant to her what they had meant to Britton. Britton knew better than to try and convey to the patient his understanding about what "fucking thinking" meant, having concluded that the only way he could proceed was to *keep his thoughts* to himself "whilst communicating to her *my understanding of her point of view*" (p. 89). So, as comprehensive and sophisticated as Britton's theory proved to be, he could find no way to introduce his theory into the treatment and, accordingly, had to settle with making the most of a difficult situation, thus illustrating an all-too-common phenomenon whereby elaborate conceptualizations about unfolding clinical events may not lend themselves to being effectively fashioned into an effective interpretation that furthers the analysand's understanding of herself.

Chapter 6 addresses a clinical approach to the treatment of patients who, like those described in the preceding chapter, find interpretations hard to handle. Rather than suffering from intense separation anxiety, these patients exhibit the tendency to think concretely. Concrete thinkers have impaired ability to think symbolically and self-reflectively about themselves and about the nature of their thinking. These patients lack the capacity to shift their attention into "meta" mode – into a position from whence they might observe their thinking (engage in metacognition) and think about their thinking. Being able to do so requires an individual have enough ego strength to be able to split his ego sufficiently to then be able to momentarily step outside himself and join the analyst in the exercise of mutually considering their own interactions as well as the separable behaviors of each. Theories that have been offered in the past to account for concrete thinking include defenses against symbolization (against forming symbols, linking symbols, and/or understanding symbols) and failures to properly differentiate fantasy from reality, self from other, signifier and that which is signified. To this list of candidates responsible for concrete thinking this chapter proposes a third candidate: the lack of a sufficient "theory of mind" – an inability to fully and more or less consistently appreciate the representational nature of the mind, which can arguably be thought to lie at the heart of concrete thinking. Theory of mind is a branch of academic cognitive psychology that's assumed the mantle as the leading perspective on cognitive development – a distinction that had previously been held by Jean Piaget and his followers for several decades. Theory of mind research outlines the developmental stages that culminate in one's ability to understand and appreciate the representational basis of the mind – that minds represent rather than reproduce external reality. The chapter concludes by stipulating the sorts of technical modifications needed to treat patients whose thinking tends to be more concrete. Modifications include a shift in emphasis – downplaying interpretations in general, and transference interpretations in particular, while inviting patients to focus more on the general workings of their mind – to rely more heavily on *metacognition*.

The third section of the book contains three chapters, each addressing technique from the vantage point of different psychoanalytic perspectives – the interpersonal (Chapter 7), the self psychological (Chapter 8), and that of the British Middle School (Chapter 9). It is unfortunate that some analysts who hail from certain schools of thought tend to keep to their own. While this is obviously an overstatement, it nevertheless captures a phenomenon that happens often enough. Analysts oftentimes publish articles in journals that chiefly cater to like-minded analysts, thus limiting the amount of cross-fertilization that might otherwise have taken place and would have enriched the field if only certain analysts would transcend parochial tendencies by availing themselves of the broader literature. Richards and Richards (2015) noted this phenomenon after discovering the contributions of Benjamin Wolstein – a man whose work they were late in reading; a man who they recognized as being "way ahead of his time" (p. 242). These authors attribute their not having read Wolstein earlier to the fact that Wolstein publishes exclusively in *Contemporary Psychoanalysis* – an interpersonal journal. "We are trying to convey a sense of what has been lost to the psychoanalytic community as a whole," lament the authors, "by these decades of estrangement [between schools of thought]" (pp. 233–235).

Richards (2015) traces the problem back to the exclusionary politics of A.A. Brill who fought to restrict psychoanalytic training to those with medical degrees during the early days at the New York Psychoanalytic Institute, which – Richards argues – had "enduring institutional effects" (p. 27). But certain present-day conditions must certainly perpetuate the problem. Maybe analysts limit the breadth of their reading because there is far too much to read. Maybe some steer clear of journals they anticipate contain papers that are out of keeping with how they themselves think and practice. This tendency is aggravated, I believe, by the tendency of certain writers to rely heavily on the terminology most closely associated with a given school of thought, which has the unfortunate effect of triggering a knee-jerk reaction in readers who find the language off-putting and who are then apt to set the paper down rather than forge ahead. For example, to this day I am amazed to have heard Robert Stolorow declare, in no uncertain terms, that there is no such thing as projective identification. Though the phenomenon described by that term is called by other names by other schools, there is widespread belief that such things do in fact happen, as we will see in the first of these three chapters, which focuses on the thinking and clinical approaches of those from the interpersonal school. It is opposition to such parochialism that leads me to this section of the book.

Chapter 7 compares the understanding and technical management of countertransference enactments from a few different psychoanalytic perspectives, with special emphasis on how analysts from the interpersonal school have come to think about and treat such enactments, which differs considerably from how more classically oriented analysts approach the subject.

Chapter 8 addresses an aspect of self psychological theory that has to do with the relationship of analyst-induced empathic failures and "transmuting internationalizations" (Kohut, 1971), which are thought to come about after a series of such failures have successfully been worked through. This chapter, previously published as a paper in the mid-1990s, represents my understanding at the time of the role empathic failures played in self psychological theory. Whether the position I'd taken back then holds up now is for the self-psychology-savvy reader to judge. Back then, I had the impression that self psychologists had overlooked certain complexities in their thinking about empathy and empathic failures, and I wrote this paper in reaction to what I saw as an over-emphasis on the importance of empathic failures, which represented yet another pendulum swing in theory creation. In this chapter, I argue that as vital as empathy is, to the extent it may provide the necessary selfobject ingredient that had been pathogenically missing during a patient's formative years, some patients are not keen on the analyst's display of empathy. Beside the question of whether empathy is universally welcomed is the complex question of which aspect of the patient's experience takes preference when the analyst endeavors to offer his empathy. Attempting to empathize simultaneously with different aspects of the patient can prove to be an impossible task. How do we as analysts decide which of the patient's current experiences deserves foremost attention? Do we empathize with patients who need us to be emotionally drawn in to the point of enactment, or with patients who need the reassurance that we have not been injured by their behavior? Do we empathize with patients as they are, or with who we believe they are on the way to becoming (Loewald, 1960)? Do we empathize with patients who are grandiose (and feel *so* different as to be unfathomable to others), or with patients who yearn to be fathomed but fear becoming ordinary as a result (Kohut, 1971; Tuch, 1993)?

Chapter 9 addresses technique from the vantage point of the British Middle School highlighting the work of W.R.D. Fairbairn, Donald Winnicott, and John Bowlby and addressing commonalities in how these theorists viewed the effect of environment on the developing individual and how those theories translate into particular types of treatment approaches outlined in this chapter.

The fourth section of this book – which focuses chiefly on pedagogy – contains three chapters, the first two of which address teaching from different angles. Chapter 10 focuses on the teaching of psychodynamic psychotherapy to students enrolled in psychotherapy training programs at our nation's psychoanalytic institutes and Chapter 11 examines styles of supervising case work. The final chapter educates our psychoanalytic candidates and our psychotherapy students, who often feel besieged by the charges leveled by our most vocal and harshest critics, who claim, in the face of evidence to the contrary, that psychoanalysis lacks scientific backing.

Chapter 10 addresses both the needs of those wishing to expand their clinical skills by learning more about how to conduct psychodynamic psychotherapy as well as the needs of analysts wishing to teach these students. This chapter serves as a primer for students new to the field and it also provides an outline of topics and a list of suggested readings for instructors who want to educate students about the methods of psychoanalytic psychotherapy.

Chapter 11 addresses the varying styles used by analysts in the course of supervising cases. The chapter presents a somewhat controversial thesis: the supervisor is better situated than the supervisee to be able to make out the dynamics of the case and to ascertain the nature of what is going on between the supervisee and his patient; on the other hand, the supervisor is poorly positioned to know how to make the best use of this knowledge in the actual treatment setting. Such ideas can substantially affect how supervisors go about conducting supervision.

While this book chiefly addresses controversies about psychoanalytic technique, we cannot ignore controversy within society at large about whether psychoanalysis is a viable, worthwhile, and effective form of treatment, which is the main topic of the last chapter of this book. Historically, psychoanalysis has been dogged by questions about whether it is scientifically based, and in the spring of 2015, that challenge suddenly intensified with the publication of claims made by two noteworthy experts: one was leveled by Jeffrey Lieberman, Chairman of Columbia University's Department of Psychiatry, who charged psychoanalysis with being "dogmatic and anti-scientific" (Lieberman, 2015, p. 69); and the other was made by Edward Shorter, Professor of Medical History at the University of Toronto's Department of Psychiatry, who likened psychoanalysis to "witchcraft" and called upon psychiatric training programs to "abolish psychoanalysis from the psychotherapy training of residents," positing that psychoanalytic instruction was "like making a course in astrology requisite for the training of astronomers" (Shorter, 2015). The publication of these opinions served as impetus for the writing of Chapter 12, which reviews in some depth the studies and meta-studies that scientifically establish not just the efficacy of the practice of psychoanalysis but, furthermore, scientifically validate several of the field's core assumptions about repression, the unconscious, the existence of unconscious motivation, and the like. This chapter also contains a review and rebuttal of the theories of Adolf Grünbaum (1976, 1977, 1981, 1984, 1993, 2006), a widely respected philosopher of science who has dedicated enormous amounts of time and energy to "proving" that psychoanalysis fails to meet criteria that would earn it the right to be truly considered "scientific." The chapter ends with an examination of the concept of "scientism" – the tendency to believe that questions about all matters can simply be settled by applying the scientific method, which leaves us to wonder about the extent and limits of the domain about which science itself, and psychoanalysis in particular, can claim authority.

The subtitle of the final chapter, "Truth comes in many colors," pays homage to Roy Shafer (1996), who wrote: "There is plenty of truth. It is just that truth comes in different versions. It always has" (p. 251). This book aims to address the nuances of treatment from many different perspectives. Hopefully, it will contribute to the ongoing debates about technique, which should help further our field by improving our collective understanding of how one goes about conducting psychoanalytic treatments. There are a wide array of opinions about how one conducts psychoanalysis, and these differences issue, in part, from different background theories held by different schools of thought. These theories, in turn, direct the analyst's attention to different sorts of clinical phenomena that he will then use to arrive at an understanding of who the patient is and what he is about. I find it hard to declare a winner in the race to prove one theory superior to all others. Efforts to do so are made to seem all the more ridiculous when one realizes that the theory a given analyst picks as his own is largely a function of who he is as a person, so arguing that an analyst "ought" to do this or that at a given point with a given patient makes little sense if one isn't personally inclined to work in the fashion being prescribed by the critic who's spelling out his view of how psychoanalysis should be conducted.

Whether or not such a thing as common ground exists, I do not believe we need be discouraged by seemingly irreconcilable differences between our most revered theoreticians and clinicians. Grotstein was keen on being psychoanalytically multilingual, and while some argue that switching back and forth between differing theories when treating a given patient might prove counterproductive and confusing for the patient, there are others who continue to believe that one is better off having several viewpoints to pick from one's quiver than sticking with one theory come hell or high water.

Notes

1 For those doubting my claim, evidence will be provided in Chapter 3.
2 The analyst continues to satisfy the criterion, outlined by Bion, requiring that they enter each session without memory or desire – which does not mean that background theory does not play an active role in implicitly directing the analyst's attention.

Section I

The duties of analyst and analysand

Chapter 1

Daring to let go

The therapeutic benefits of free association

Over the course of the last several decades, several competing, core psychoanalytic theories have cropped up that aim to explain how individuals become psychologically and emotionally impaired and – by extension – to propose how damaged minds can psychoanalytically be repaired. In opposition to such pluralism, Leo Rangell (1997) called upon psychoanalysts to recognize that only one theory – a "unitary theory" – could account for the efficacy of psychotherapy, echoing Fenichel (1945), who insisted "psychoanalysts are of the opinion that only psychoanalytic science understands what is going on in neuroses, and that there is but one theory to give a scientific explanation of the effectiveness of *all* psychotherapies" (p. 554). Accepting *theoretical* pluralism as a given, Wallerstein (1988, 1992) chose instead to find "common ground" not in theory but, rather, in practice – in the commonalities of how analysts conduct analysis. In support of his position, Wallerstein references the widely held observation that "adherents of whatever theoretical position within psychoanalysis all seem to do reasonably comparable clinical work and bring about reasonably comparable clinical change in the (comparable enough) patients" (p. 555), leaving us to define psychoanalysis not in the way in which Rangell chose – through theory – but rather in how psychoanalysis takes place on a daily basis in consulting rooms throughout the world.

If Wallerstein is correct in his estimation, then we are left wondering which methods, techniques, therapeutic approaches, or clinical beliefs psychoanalysts share in common. First and foremost would be an acceptance of the idea that individuals fall ill to the extent that aspects of their psyches or, alternately, aspects of their selves have – in whatever way – become lost to the individual, either by way of a horizontal split effected by repression or a vertical split brought about by dissociation. In either case, the individual is poorer for having lost a piece of him- or herself, making the retrieval of lost parts an essential mission of psychoanalysis. Whether one effects change by rendering the unconscious conscious or by helping a patient retrieve and "own" dissociated aspects of the self that – for a time – had been recognized as belonging to another (via projection or attribution), the self is made whole by re-establishing lost "continuities" (Kris 1996). I would submit that this goal lies at the core of psychoanalytic practice,[1] with other matters (addressing transference, recognizing resistances, utilizing countertransference, etc.) subsidiary to this chief aim. Whether one realizes this goal by identifying and addressing transferences of whatever sort – selfobject transferences, "dead mother" transferences, enactment-emerging transferences, etc. – matters little in the scheme of things, just so long as the central task of making the patient whole (or, more precisely, "more whole") is approximately achieved.

Aside from the task of helping patients retrieve lost, dissociated, or repressed parts of themselves, one would be hard-pressed to name a technique or clinical method that is universally employed by analysts of varying theoretic persuasions. A reliance on the fundamental rule comes closest to hitting the mark, given the widespread utilization of this particular technique.[2] Aron (1990), writing from a relational perspective – which routinely challenges classical techniques – insisted that "free association, as a method, can be useful to psychoanalysts of all theoretical orientations" (p. 439), and while he described many of his like-minded analysts as having "minimized or abandoned the free association method" (p. 439),[3] this seems only to have been the case when it came to the treatment of the most troubled patients.

While psychoanalysis has evolved in remarkable ways over the last century, free association (the "fundamental rule" or "basic rule") remains a cornerstone – arguably *the* cornerstone – of psychoanalytic practice. This isn't to say that free association is understood or used in quite the same way as it had been back then; in fact, our understanding of this essential technique continues to evolve, and this chapter addresses our thinking about the subject in the 21st century and explores the question of whether free association, which propels the psychoanalytic process and provides the analyst access to a patient's unconscious, might additionally be therapeutic in and of itself.

Kris (1996) referred to free association as "the principal method of psychoanalysis" (p. 3) – the chief technique by which the analyst brings to light *discontinuities* in the patient's associations, toward the ultimate goal of helping patients "regain lost connections" (p. 5). Identifying discontinuities involves, first and foremost, the process of observation – *not interpretation.* Noting discontinuities is the central task of "close process monitoring" (Gray 1973, 1982, 1994; Busch 1995) – which begins with an emphasis on observation. The patient seems headed in a particular direction, for example, then hesitates or – even more dramatically – abruptly changes course, even to the point of truncating a word he was midstream in articulating – leaving it half mentioned.[4] Breaks in continuity are a suggestive sign of resistance in action – the product of a defense designed to save the patient from having to experience what he unconsciously fears will prove too much to bear. After noting breaks in the patient's associations, the analyst calls the patient's attention to the "data" constituted by these breaches, inviting him to engage in a self-reflective ("meta") process. "Instead of seeing resistances as a barrier to free association," notes Busch (1994), "[Gray and Kris] see free association as a method by which resistances can become the centerpiece of the analytic process" (p. 370).

Essential aspects of the free associative method

It was Freud's (1913) recommendation that analysts make the fundamental rule as clear as possible to patients at the outset of treatment, suggesting that the analyst say something to the analysand along the following lines:

> One more thing before you start. What you tell me must differ in one respect from an ordinary conversation...You will be tempted to say to yourself that this or that is irrelevant here, or quite unimportant, or nonsensical, so that there is no need to say it. You must never give in to these criticisms, but must say it in spite of them – indeed, you must say it precisely *because* you feel an aversion to doing so...So say whatever goes through your mind...Finally, never forget that you have promised to be absolutely honest, and never leave anything out because, for some reason or other, it is unpleasant to tell it. (pp. 134–135)

There are four important aspects of Freud's recommendation worth noting. Freud makes clear just how *out of the ordinary* such communication will seem to the patient – how much it contradicts everything the patient had been taught when he was young about what *not* to do. Hence, Freud's recommendation, at its core, is subversive insofar as it requires that the patient work against the implicit (though typically non-consciously operating) rules for censoring any mention of certain sorts of thoughts and feelings – those the patient assumes might be judged as offensive, unwelcomed, trouble-making, and/or "inappropriate" for a host of reasons: because it is embarrassing, shows the patient in a bad light, is rude, says what everyone knows but no one wishes to hear said, is nonsensical (lacking a "connecting thread"), is self-centered, and so on. Freud also addressed the *temptation to dismiss (hold back) thoughts* that come to mind based on certain "criticism and objections" because they are believed to be: off topic ("wander too far from the point"; Freud, 1913, p. 131), irrelevant to the matter at hand (mere "side-issues"; p. 134), or too "unpleasant to tell" (p. 135).

Though Freud identified the fundamental rule as the *sole* directive the patient is given, patients sometimes believe they can "make out" other unspoken wishes and desires of the analyst (e.g., think like me, don't talk back or challenge what I say, suppress your competitive or aggressive impulses toward me, tell me how great I am, etc.). Admittedly, there are instances (far more than most analysts might care to admit) when patients correctly ascertain just such unconscious wishes in the analyst, but Freud is declaring free association to be the one thing (aside from attending sessions and paying) the patient *must do* for the analysis to work – the one thing that's being asked of them. And while his instruction may seem a simple one to follow, nothing could be further from the truth; therein lies the rub.

A final matter has to do with Freud's noting the *passive quality of free association* by analogizing it to sitting on a train, watching and reporting as the scenery *passes by* (Freud, 1913). This last aspect of free association – its passive quality – differentiates an active mode of cognition, whereby one works hard to dredge up fruitful topics worth discussing in analysis, from the more passive modes of cognition, whereby psychic material is *permitted* to spontaneously "come to mind" (on its own accord). It is worth noting that the German phrase Freud used to describe free association is "*freie Einfalle*" – which alternately translates as "to come into mind," "to cross one's mind," "to chime in" (as if musically), or "to break in upon" (also, in a different context: to invade a country, to raid a village), with the added modifier "*freie*" – specifying these things happen on their own accord. The term underscores the passive nature of free association – what "occurs" to the patient in the way of "chance thoughts," "spontaneous thoughts," or "unwilled thoughts" (Mahony, 1979). Free association involves surrendering to a process ("letting go" of the tendency to actively select which topics will be mentioned), which helps one "tune in" to what otherwise might seem like incidental "background noise" meant to be filtered out because it's considered insignificant or distracting. The fundamental rule calls for a shift in attitude that ideally leads the patient to *attend* to such background thoughts, honoring them not only as worthy of consideration, but as potentially mutative. Traditionally, the value of attending to the patient's associations involved what those associations implicitly revealed in the way of hidden psychic content. In this chapter, an added value is being proposed – that of the patient learning how to attend to, and see value in, a different way in which he can use his mind relative to the chief mode of cognition he tends to use throughout the day when engaged in goal-directed thinking.

Before proceeding, it's worth acknowledging that the active/passive distinction being drawn throughout this chapter is not as absolute as it might seem. In fact, situations often involve an admixture of both elements. Regarding free association, Hoffman (2006) mounts the following argument:

> Rather than simply "happening," like the weather, or even, perhaps, a dream, the patient's thoughts might emerge as a function of the patient's actively thinking them. Thinking can be a voluntary "action" no less than moving one's arm or one's leg. At a minimum, there is a subtle interplay in the patient's experience between active agency in thinking and passive receptivity to emerging "associations." [What if] the patient feels he or she has several things coming to mind simultaneously, several things that he or she could speak of, so that only by choosing will it be possible to speak at all?...If the injunction against active choosing is strong

> enough, patients will – in effect – be encouraged to deny the sense in which they have felt themselves to be participating as agents in the process. (pp. 44–45)

While Hoffman's thoughts lead one to realize that the distinction between active and passive modes of cognition is not as clear cut as one might think, there nevertheless is value in continuing to talk about a form of thinking that seems to be, in the scheme of things, *more or less* passive in nature relative to other types of thinking.

Shifting between active and passive modes of cognition

One advantage of becoming more adept at freely associating is a heightening of the individual's capacity to flexibly shift back and forth between alternate modes of cognition – active and passive – which, arguably, is a sign of mental health. Accordingly, there is intrinsic therapeutic value in helping patients exercise their ability to shift between alternate modes of cognition – from the more active "doing" mode (making happen) to the more passive "being" mode (letting happen) – adapting to the present situation by utilizing the mode of cognition best suited to the task. Rosegrant (2005) notes:

> It is generally understood that free association is therapeutically helpful because it is a route toward exploration and understanding of unconscious resistances, drives, and object relations...the free-associative state, together with regulation of the interplay between the free-associative state and the more usual state of consciousness, is also therapeutically helpful. (p. 737)

Free association is a distinct mode of cognition that differs from the way we generally tend to use our minds during the lion's share of our waking day. We get things accomplished mostly by using our goal-oriented cognitive skills that involve taking measure of the situation at hand, consciously deliberating about alternate courses of action, choosing and implementing a plan, assessing whether the plan is on track toward realizing a goal, and so on. Such competencies are a measure of one's ego strength (what has widely come to be known as "executive functioning"), and they depend on one's facility in marshaling one's mind, focusing one's attention on the task at hand, and engaging in stepwise linear thinking with an eye toward a chosen end point.

We work intentionally to "bring about" a desired outcome – we "make it happen" and are roundly rewarded not only by achieving the desired goal, but also by a heightened sense of agency – feeling ourselves proudly capable. Analysands oftentimes mistakenly believe, at the outset of treatment, that they must use this same active, goal-oriented approach if they hope to get the most out of treatment. Patients who have become well acquainted with, and highly reliant upon, this active mode of cognition – which has proven singularly helpful in most other areas of life – may find it hard to believe the analyst actually expects them to abandon this routine, highly reliable mode of cognition and adopt an entirely different way of thinking to solve the sorts of problems that brought them to treatment. Paradoxically, an over-reliance on this linear-type thinking may lie at the heart of what the analysand seeks to have treated.

The fundamental rule requires the patient to surrender to a more passive mode of experiencing and attending to internal psychic content – letting things "occur" to him without actively picking the topics to be discussed – those he believes constitute the most potentially fruitful subject matter to discuss. Since "choosing" is an essential component of goal-oriented thinking, it may not occur to the patient that a selection process aimed at determining what constitutes mention-worthy material can easily be co-opted by a defensive agenda that unconsciously strives to steer clear of paths one unconsciously senses could become most upsetting if travelled. Only by trying to *not* try – surrendering oneself to the task of uncensored candor, unwavering honesty, and spontaneity – can a patient hope to participate in an analysis that stands a chance of making a substantial difference in his life. The fact that most patients, at best, can merely muster an approximation of free association doesn't undercut free association as a worthwhile instruction and worthy aspiration. Difficulties encountered along the way yield critical data about resistances that trip up the patient as he attempts to do what he's been asked to do. Those who discount the value of freely associating because such an assignment is unachievable miss the point, to the extent they fail to recognize that the inability to freely associate becomes the treatment's chief focus, which can be milked to good effect.

It is worthwhile considering at greater length these two alternate modes of cognition or states of consciousness – actively *making* happen and passively *permitting* to happen. It's instructive to liken free association to certain bodily functions – namely, those of breathing and defecating. Just as one can control an otherwise automatically operating process like breathing by holding one's breath or hyperventilating, one can control one's thoughts by either focusing one's attention on a select mental task or permitting one's automatically operating thoughts – which often go unrecognized – to take center stage. Such spontaneously operating, background thoughts are like stars that are always in the sky, which cannot be seen in the glare of day. Defecating is another bodily function that has bearing on free association. "Holding in" and "letting go" represent, respectively, the active and passive elements of bowel control. While the child may consider himself responsible for the creation of the fecal bolus – believing he's labored it into existence – this is not at all the case. In actuality, the passing of feces comes about by *relaxing* the anal sphincter, permitting the involuntary musculature of the colon to "do its thing" ("letting happen") – *for which the child then takes credit*. An adult who has trouble "letting go" – relinquishing control – will likely find it exceedingly hard to let his mind "do its own thing" and may experience himself *working hard to make things happen* when he could just *let things happen* – permit processes to run their natural course.

Some readers will undoubtedly object to my having drawn a clear distinction between the dual modes of active and passive. Certainly, some would say, this can't possibly represent reality insofar as situations are likely to contain admixtures of both, as Hoffman (2006) argued when he registered his complaint against seeing free association as free of conscious choice and intention – which he amply demonstrates is never the case. Nevertheless, Hoffman fails to acknowledge that it may well be enough of the case to the extent it does seem to approximate a condition that lies *toward* the extreme end, if not *on* the extreme end, of the active/passive spectrum. Throughout this chapter, I will be drawing a link between active and "doing," as well as passive and "being." This too will likely cause some to object, arguing that such a dichotomy is in my mind only and is not in line with how things "really" are in the world. To this I would answer accordingly: if one imagines such matters as existing within the transitional space, where distinctions between reality and illusion are not insisted upon, then one begins to see how something could simultaneously *have and yet not have* features worth describing as "passive" or "being" relative to the alternatives of "active" and "doing." Such a distinction is "sort of" valid and, accordingly, valid enough in a fuzzy logic sort of way – logic that acknowledges that such a thing as "degrees of truth" exist as a legitimate concept, that "realities cannot always be recognized [in digital fashion] by yes (1) and no (2), such as in mathematics…[but rather] there exists ambiguities everywhere in daily life. Reality is a sea of ambiguity" (Mukaidono, 2001, p. 2).

Shifting from an emphasis on active and passive modes to the related modes of doing and being alerts us to ways in which patients may think about the therapeutic process, at least at the outset of treatment. Patients alternately may think in terms of being helped to change (a facilitated process) versus being changed (through intervention from an outside agent). Furthermore, patients sometimes enter treatment believing that there is something missing within – not because it has been repressed or dissociated and projected, but because they see their upbringing as having been deficient to the extent they'd not been given something they needed when they were young (a lesson, a skill, "tools," secret knowledge, insight, etc.) and now feel personally deficient on this account. Such patients may seek to be provided with this missing ingredient (e.g., by being taught or otherwise provided with some essential instrumentality, which the patient sees as curative), which is a very different idea about how therapy works in comparison to a model of therapeutic action that conceptualizes a patient's difficulties issuing from an internal lack that has resulted from a patient having become alienated from an aspect of themselves. Without enough of a sense of who one is, patients may feel clueless about how they themselves ought to approach a variety of life situations – clueless and compass-less, and feeling a need for the concrete guidance of a counselor who can step in and provide the ego functions the patient feels they are lacking.[5]

Difficulties following the fundamental rule

Patients who tend to stay strictly focused on this active mode of cognition ("doing" rather than "being") often find it difficult to permit their mind to think on its own (to "just be"). Instead of freely associating, such patients may, for example, bring outlines to treatment of what they plan to talk about (spelled out "agendas"), justifying the practice by explaining they want to "make the most" of their time in treatment. While such reasoning makes abundant sense, from the standpoint of the analysis it makes no sense whatsoever and is a sure way of preventing the requisite analytic process from developing.

Certain patients have great difficulty believing in and following the fundamental rule. Some can't quite believe what is being asked of them, figuring that if they don't *try* to think of something to say, nothing whatsoever will come to mind. A commonly encountered fear early during certain analyses involves a patient's expectation that they will quickly run out of things to say, at which point – they fear – their core inadequacy will come to light, becoming undeniable. One such patient mentioned early in his analysis that he left each session glad he'd come, seeing how productive the session had been, but this didn't change the fact that he'd approach each subsequent session with the same awful dread that "today's the day" that he'd run out of things to say and, accordingly, would be revealed to be the utterly vapid person he'd always known himself to be – though he'd hoped the analysis would prove otherwise. Some patients are uncomfortable with the task of free association because they experience it as requiring them to *surrender* to the process. Some patients equate surrendering willful control to submitting to the will or demands of the analyst, triggering intense transference resistances against the task of free association. For example, Donnet (2009) notes:

> Freud cites as an example the case of a man who became mute when the fundamental rule was imparted, owing to the displacement onto the analyst of a conflict with parental authority. It can be seen, then, that the rule, which is supposed, *a priori*, to further the investigation of an intra-psychic conflict, loses its status as a tool and becomes its unconscious factor on the analytic stage. (p. 134)

Other patients are terrified of being caught off guard (unprepared), to the extent they first learn what they are thinking at the precise moment the analyst learns what they are thinking, which they find utterly unacceptable since they feel they must first think their thoughts to themselves before then divulging them to the analyst, lest they blurt out something they are unprepared for him to hear. There are many other reasons why patients struggle with the fundamental rule, *not all of which have direct bearing on the task of keeping specific types of repressed material hidden from sight*. Difficulty free associating can also develop when the patient feels pressured to come prepared each session with enough "juicy" material to keep the analyst preoccupied, if not fascinated or, at least, entertained. Such patients see the danger of daring to speak out loud – to say what's on the top of their head – because it risks being discovered to be shamefully inadequate, to have no "self" to speak of, to be exposed as repellant, and so on and so forth.

Some patients, upon hearing the analyst's recommendation that they say *whatever comes to mind*, find it hard to believe that the analyst literally means what he says. Some patients seek to figure out what it is that the analyst wants to hear, figuring that pleasing him will heighten his desire and willingness to be helpful, or reasoning that they haven't any experience of being analyzed so they haven't a clue about what topics would be most productive to mention. Some come to believe that they won't be able to progress in the analysis until they are finally able to freely associate, which every analyst knows is *not at all* the case. The recommendation that the analysand freely associate is intended to establish something he is to *aim for*, not something he's literally expected to be able to do right off the bat and, going forward, on a regular basis. A gross though instructive simplification of psychoanalysis could be offered in a condensed fashion: recommend the patient free associate; see the extent to which he can't; work to discover what is getting in his way; help the patient see what is limiting his ability to freely associate; see how he becomes much better able to free associate (assuming one's correctly identified the "blocks"); then, when he seems to be much more freely associating, discharge him from treatment having accomplished one's end goal.

Difficulties accessing and utilizing alternate modes of thinking

Certain sorts of patients are particularly challenged by the task of freely associating – in particular, patients whose thinking tends to be obsessional in nature. Such individuals typically find it hard to relinquish control when the situation calls for *inaction* rather than action. When such individuals lie down on the couch and attempt to free associate, they typically find it hard to relinquish the tendency to actively think up what they want to say rather than permitting thoughts to come to mind on their own accord. Patients whose thinking tends to be obsessional have a notoriously difficult time freely associating (Fenichel, 1945). These patients have a particularly rigid and restrictive style of thinking (Reich, 1949), and their cognitive style keeps them from being able to use their minds in the most autonomous and adaptive fashion

(Shapiro, 1965, 1981). Such patients have a limited ability to easily shift back and forth between the twin cognitive modes of activity and passivity: *actively* focusing attention on the task at hand, willfully authoring, exerting control, and "making happen," versus *passively* "letting happen" and recognizing and appreciating that one's mind has a mind of its own that can be accessed if one patiently waits and listens. It stands to reason that patients who develop considerable facility at shifting between alternate modes of cognition should, as a result, be more adaptive – marking an essential benefit provided by the patient's increasing capacity to freely associate. This is one way in which freely associating may prove therapeutically beneficial in and of itself.

Wilhelm Reich (1949) noted that the less "hardened" one's character armor, the better able one is to respond to situations in a fluid and adaptive fashion, marking the difference between healthy character structure and neurotic character structure. Reich emphasized the extent to which these rigid and inflexible individuals, who are highly productive and proficient implementers, cannot function as creative visionaries capable of "pioneering" by coming up with new ideas that could lead to a paradigmatic shift. Building on Reich's observations, Shapiro (1965, 1981) elaborated on the idea that a highly rigid character structure can greatly limit an individual's autonomy and capacity to adapt. Shapiro notes that life conditions sometimes require one to be able to access an entirely different set of cognitive tools in contrast with the specific mode of cognition most closely associated with an individual's given character type or style. For example, individuals with obsessive–compulsive character types, notes Shapiro, have trouble shifting their mode of cognition from a single-minded, detail-oriented focus on the task at hand to a more diffuse, impressionistic consideration of such "data" as hunches, reverie, "vibes," affects, intuition, and so on. Shapiro (1965) notes:

> The obsessive–compulsive cannot allow such wants, wishes, hunches, etc. to be the initiator or the first stage of willful directedness and effort... Thus, for these people, impulse or wishes is only a temptation which can corrupt their determination [and] interrupt their work...They are, therefore, *cut off from the sources that normally give willful effort its direction.* (p. 37, italics added)

Rosegrant (2005) asserts:

> Free association is in and of itself therapeutic because it facilitates the patient's learning to integrate and to shift flexibly among states of relatively objective self-awareness and reality adherence, and states of relatively subjective self-awareness and disregard of reality. By becoming more aware of this therapeutic value of free association, we will be more likely to let free association continue when it is to the patient's benefit... the *interplay between free association and intervention* also facilitates the

> patient's learning to integrate and shift flexibly among states. (p. 765, italics added)

Shifting flexibly between alternate states of consciousness, notes Rosegrant, is facilitated by the analyst's interventions, which have the effect of interrupting the free associative process. Rosegrant references Lewin's (1954, 1955) notion that the freely associating patient is as if sleeping or dreaming; certain of the analyst's interventions that "awaken" the patient (e.g., interpretations regarding repressed content), while others soothe the patient – the former pulling the patient in the direction of heightened *objective* self-awareness and rationality, the latter encouraging *subjective* self-awareness and disregard for reality. Rosegrant notes:

> I have the impression that our technical literature is biased toward the importance of "awakening" interventions, emphasizing what we do or say that has an immediate effect on the patient – demonstrating our impact. Greater appreciation for the complementarity of the free-associative and more usual states of consciousness can lead to greater appreciation of technique that is "soothing," as well as of how we help the patient integrate these states. (pp. 751–752)

Difficulties finding a mind of one's own

Beside patients who exhibit difficulties shifting back and forth between alternate modes of cognition are other patients who have difficulty free associating because they literally don't believe that they have a mind of their own that can be relied upon to generate material on its own accord and not merely in reaction to the thoughts and actions of others. A related problem is the difficulty shifting back and forth between a focus on the mind of another (causing one to lose oneself in others' minds to the extent they feel incapable of distinguishing self from other) and a focus on what it is they themselves have in mind.

While obsessives tend to have trouble shifting gears, adopting a mode of cognition that is neither familiar nor comfortable, patients who exhibit certain features in common with "as if" personalities (Deutsch, 1942) also struggle with the instruction to speak openly, candidly, and spontaneously – not because they have trouble shifting between modes of cognition, but because they've lived their lives adapting to their environment in a chameleon-type fashion in order to fit in and be accepted by others. Such an individual may dread ever meeting one group of friends when out with another group of friends because the person he's known to be by one group is nothing like the person he's known to be by the other group. Such "as if" patients exhibit "a highly plastic readiness to pick up signals from the outer world and to mold oneself and one's behavior accordingly" (p. 304). These patients manifest a high degree of adaptability combined with an insufficient sense of authenticity. They present themselves to others in alternating and contrived versions of themselves – in line with Winnicott's (1960) notion of a "false self." Speaking from a sociologic perspective, David Reisman (1950) describes much the same in his explanation of what he terms the "outer-directed" (versus inner-directed) individual – one who is a complaint conformist striving to be like others and to be accepted by them. Such individuals lack a stable sense of self and suffer from feelings of loneliness and anxiety over a fear of non-acceptance issuing from his not being enough like others.

Patients who dare not know their mind as separate and independent of the analyst's mind can benefit greatly from being required to free associate, even though they may at times protest that such an expectation is beyond their ability. Such patients resemble the "as if" personality or patients who have a well-developed false self and have lost track of what they truly think or feel "deep down." Such was the case with Albert Z., a brilliant though somewhat schizoid graduate student in his late twenties who had been in five-days-a-week, on-the-couch analysis for over three years when the following sessions occurred. Albert wasn't sure it made sense to talk in terms of "being himself"; he wasn't at all sure who he'd be being if he were to try and "be himself." In a previous treatment, the patient was flummoxed when the therapist asked him a simple question about the sorts of things he liked to do, which threw the patient because he could not imagine knowing how to answer the question given his lack of knowledge about himself. Lacking a sense of self, Albert took his cues from others, mimicking how they acted and mouthing their beliefs as his own. For Albert, being in the moment – which is what free associating required of him – was utterly unthinkable, to the extent he saw moments as being pre-determined and not spontaneously emergent. Being in the moment required that Albert know who he was, what it was he wanted, how he felt, what he thought – all of which was simply beyond his capacity.

In the first of two successive sessions, Albert begins by asking me point blank what I thought his analysis was supposed to be achieving, covertly telegraphing his opinion that the analysis had accomplished nothing and was, in fact, a colossal waste of time. Albert offered his opinion that his analysis was supposed to determine "whether there is a 'me'" separate and apart from his well-developed ability to slip inside of others and steal away with their way of being (his chameleon-like tendencies). We had discussed how strongly Albert felt he needed to be relieved of the expectation and pressure to "be himself" – whatever that meant. He spoke of how he lived in the minds of others – imagining how they saw him, which was his way of knowing himself by reflection – not on a first-hand basis, but on a second-hand basis.

Seeming to switch topics, Albert then spoke about his habit of working hard in class to *appear to be listening* (to portray listening) for the professor's benefit, which got in the way of his ability to merely listen – which he would tell himself was too risky of a thing to do. This seemed to mirror his efforts to appear to free associate rather than actually risking doing so, as well as his difficulty listening to me – which he was only able to do intermittently. To truly listen to the professor, the patient now realized, required he momentarily shift his attention on to his own thoughts – separate and apart from the professor's thoughts – as they emerged in reaction to what the professor had been saying. To his surprise, Albert found himself doing just that in class the day before – which he found a true revelation, though it frightened him a bit, given it ran counter to his self-defined assignment of making sure the professor saw him as seeming to be focused on the professor's every word. It was this single-minded attention to the needs of others, in combination with his aversion to thinking his own thoughts, which often left Albert clueless about what it was he had in mind. I suspected that Albert's single-minded attention to my needs made it hard for him to freely associate.

As the session progressed, the patient asked me another question that, once again, put me on the spot. Now he wanted to know why I wanted to treat him: "What's in it for you?" he asked. He offered his opinion that I wanted to take things from him and make them mine – things that I was lacking that he had, which I envied him for, and couldn't stand to be without. It came to my mind that Albert had me confused with himself; we had been working together on his envy of others as well as his conflict over having abilities and attributes he dared imagine others might envy – leading him to work hard to hide these positive attributes lest he would feel he was injuring others by virtue of what he had or being more than they could ever be. Attributing to me the wish to rob him of things that I envied about him seemed to reflect the patient's confusion about who's who – his inability to imagine that my motives and feelings differed from his own and that I had a mind of my own that organizes relationships in a distinctly different fashion.

The next session, Albert once again talked about the impossibility of being in the moment – in particular, of thinking out loud without first thinking to himself what it was he wanted to say. If he were to speak spontaneously, he added, it would put him at tremendous risk of "getting the shit beat out of me," as had happened whenever someone in his family dared go out on a limb by declaring what they liked, what they wanted, how they thought, and so on and so forth. Albert then launched into a story about having been to dinner with his family the weekend before. His sister had ordered wine, tasted the wine, and declared that it was "okay." This did not sit well with the mother, who got it in her head, after drinking the wine, that the daughter wasn't speaking honestly. For the next five minutes, mother and daughter went round and round trying to establish what it was the other was "truly" feeling. The entire event sounded like a farce; neither party seemed willing to take a stand without knowing how the other felt about the matter. The dance was much like what the patient manifested in his own inability to know his mind as distinct from the mind of others. The patient explained that had his sister taken a stand (saying the wine was fine), and others had disagreed, she would then "be nailed to the cross" for having committed the family to accept and consume the wine.

Albert elaborated that speaking the truth as one knows it (being true to one's subjectivity) is destructive to others and will likely cause others to hate you. "That's why saying what comes to mind is dangerous; having a mind of your own gets you into *big* trouble! It will be a disaster, no question." I offered a response that I later realized was long-winded. Albert struggled to say what he was thinking and feeling, and eventually got around to telling me to shut up, though not in so many words. I told him that I thought he wanted me to shut up so that he could have a chance to speak – that he felt I'd gone on and on, which prevented him from being able to get a word in edgewise. In response, Albert pointed out that this is precisely why speaking spontaneously and honestly is dangerous – that it can lead him to say the most awful things to me. Albert then admitted that he had been waiting for the better part of the analysis for me to come right out and tell him what I thought of him – which he was sure would not be positive and would likely prove insulting. He imagined my doing so, then imagined, in response, stomping out and, maybe, never coming back, given what I'd said about him. But I had robbed him of a chance to have that very experience, he half complained, because I never seemed to get around to sharing my opinions of him.

Albert went on to outline the problem of speaking his mind: he can be insulting and abrasive, and he is quite sure, regardless of what I say, that I felt plenty peeved at him for him having told me to shut up and, furthermore, for him having criticized me earlier in the session for not having helped him in the least – which he didn't blame me for, seeing that I was a nice enough guy who was, nevertheless, clinically ineffectual – which, he pointed out, was not my fault. Now he felt like an absolute heel – he felt guilty for having let me have it – for saying such mean things. This was followed by expressions of anger and protest: it was just awful that a man his age would have to be laying on an analyst's couch, revealing his every thought, exposed as being a weak, pathetic, inadequate baby. I pointed out that, on the one hand, he was hoping I could tolerate the things he had said to me about me – hoping that I could take it in my stride without feeling awful about myself, without hating him, and without feeling a need to retaliate. If he were going to let himself go and think out loud, I noted, then doing so would require some assurance from me that I could handle what he had to say to me about me. But therein lies the rub: I pointed out that feeling assured that I possessed the psychological wherewithal to withstand the onslaught meant that I had developed an ability to do just that – which is something he might well have envied me for, to the extent he felt that I was demonstrating an ability he had yet to develop. Albert agreed with how I'd fashioned the matter, and went on to say that he now felt that I had such a gut-level grasp of his condition that I was likely to be so "bummed out" by my being in touch with his situation that I would find it hard to function for the rest of the day – an expression of a wish and a fear.

On the surface, thinking as much caused the patient to seek my reassurance that this was not so, though I suspect he also wished that I would be so "in the thick of it" with him that he then would not feel so alone with his condition. I told him that I could put myself in his shoes without losing myself in his shoes. Albert got up off the couch, seemed much relieved, and thanked me for having said as much.

What we see operating at this juncture is what Fonagy et al. (2002) refer to as "marked mirroring" – the caregiver's style of mirroring that helps the child distinguish his mind/experience from that of the caregiver to the extent the caregiver makes it clear that he knows what the child is experiencing, even though the caregiver himself is not having the same experience and, accordingly, isn't being as deeply affected as the child. This helps the child know "who's who" – thus helping facilitate his sense of separateness as a distinct entity unto himself (able to differentiate subjectivity from objectivity – otherness).

The task of freely associating presents challenges and advantages for such patients. Not having the ability to know with any degree of certainty who the analyst is or who the analyst wants the patient to be or what he wants him to do (aside from the instruction that he is to free associate) leaves such patients in a cold sweat – robbed of the data they typically rely upon to comfortably be who the analyst is (via identification) or to be what they imagine the analyst is wanting them or needing them to be. This isn't to suggest such patients aren't extraordinarily adept at ascertaining what is on the analyst's mind; it is only to acknowledge the pressure they experience, and the difficulties they encounter when confronted with a novel circumstance – one that requires they free associate without the help of the typical clues about who the other is looking for them to be. Being required to freely associate in the presence of a relatively neutral and non-self-disclosing analyst (to whatever extent that is possible) is, in a way, just what such a patient needs to begin the journey of finding himself hidden amongst the rubble of his attempts to adapt to others in a chameleon-type fashion.

Other reasons that patients struggle to free associate

Patients who heavily employ narcissistic defenses also feel challenged by the task of free association. The potential shame and feeling of inferiority that can result when shown the limits of how much one truly knows oneself can lead narcissistic patients to be less than forthcoming and to report associations in ways designed to be less revealing of their psyches. One often notes how such a patient monitors his free associations "in order to develop his own 'analytic' understanding of what evolves in the session" (Kernberg, 2015, p. 629). The free association of such narcissistic patients is often characterized by "imitation spontaneity that makes it difficult for the analyst to perceive what, if anything, is emotionally relevant" (p. 628). Rather than allowing themselves to surrender to the process of freely associating, such patients work to control the process as they work to protect themselves from experiencing the unexpected emotional impact that could be triggered by what the analyst has to offer.

Patients who operate on the borderline level of psychic functioning typically find free association more than they can psychically bear. Free association requires the patient to have the capacity to split their mind between experiencing and self-observing (self-reflecting) functions (Sterba, 1934) – which borderline patients find a particularly challenging task. Frieda Fromm-Reichmann (1950) declared the use of free association to be contraindicated with borderline patients, as she believed that it leads to disintegrated thinking, an idea echoed over a half-century later by Donett (2009). Modell (1984) suggested that analysts cannot make use of the associations of such primitive patients, and Kernberg et al. (2008) described how the primitive conflicts of such patients "manifest themselves in dissociated behavior rather than in the content of free association" (p. 607). Green (2000) described a patient who spoke in a broken and muddled fashion "as if he was trying to avoid an outcome toward which he would have been pulled irresistibly had he let himself go" (p. 431). The interpretations Green offered his patients never gained traction – they never ignited a process culminating in a flurry of patient associations that served as meaningful and elaborating commentary about what Green had surmised. This led Green to identify a type of free association characterized by "the phobic avoidance of spontaneous thought" (p. 435) that works in anticipation of, and attempts to fend off, a "cascade of traumas echoing each other" (p. 434), whereby traumas that had been kept separate within the patient's mind risk coming together in crescendo fashion, which the patient fears would be the death of them – leading to utter madness.

The link between free association and play

The inherent value of developing a greater capacity to freely associate is illustrated when one considers how free association is linked with play. Rosegrant (2005) asserts that "normal play is a forerunner of ego qualities that are a part of free association, and pathological play is a forerunner of difficulty in free associating" (p. 474), which builds upon Winnicott's (1968) claim that "playing facilitates growth and therefore health...playing can be a form of communication in psychotherapy; and lastly, psychoanalysis has been developed as a highly specialized form of playing in the service of communication with oneself and others" (p. 41). Writing about Donald Winnicott's life, Abram (2008) notes:

> It is only through playing that the individual can *ad infinitum* discover a sense of self...The capacity to play is synonymous with creative living and constitutes the matrix of self-experience throughout life. Transposed to the analytic relationship, playing is the ultimate achievement of

> psychoanalysis, because only through playing can the self be continually discovered and thus strengthened. Clinically, this could be seen to extend Freud's technique of free association and the continuous discovery of the unconscious. (p. 1208)

Writing about the therapeutic effects of the free-associative state of consciousness, Rosegrant (2005) notes:

> Psychoanalytic free association shares important qualities with the state of consciousness a child enters during play. Because a child's naturalistic play can be "therapeutic," and a child's play during psychoanalysis can be directly therapeutic even without interpretation, the commonalities between the free associative state and the state of mind of a child engaged in play illuminate the *therapeutic effects of free association*. An assumption of continuity in development supports the idea that *the play-like qualities of adult free association may be therapeutic even without interpretation*. (pp. 746–747, italics added)

Three targeted goals of free association

At the time Freud happened upon the free associative method, he was still chiefly focused on the therapeutic task of *uncovering repressed content*. Free association was at first believed to clear the way to catching sight of "the repressed" – as if adherence to the fundamental rule would inevitably ensure that subtle hints about unconscious content would gradually come into view. Hansell (2008) writes:

> The technique of free association was originally developed as a procedure designed to *evade* the influence of the "censor" because self-censoring interfered with the verbalization of unconscious derivatives. Freud thought he had figured out how to outfox the censor with the free-associative process; that is, by insisting that patients report every thought, analysts could bypass the censor and get access to the unconscious... [More recently] the censor...had to be *analyzed* and permanently altered for lasting change to occur. Fortuitously, free association turned out to be just as good a technique for *analyzing* the censor (and the myriad defensive operations at its disposal) as for *evading* the censor. One simply shifted one's interest from a primary focus on the *content* of free associations to a primary focus on the associative *process*, so that the nature and purpose of defensive disruptions in associations could be analyzed. (p. 1184)

Busch (1994) argues likewise – noting how, at first, free association was introduced as a way of *overcoming resistance*, rather than analyzing and understanding it. Busch describes how many analysts, such as Greenson (1967), "persist in seeing their purpose as 'getting out' the strangulated affect or unconscious fantasy in spite of seemingly sophisticated views of the resistances" (p. 367). Some analysts persist in seeing the primary value of free association as its function as "a fundamental tool of data gathering for analyst and patient" (Hoffer & Youngren, 2004, p. 1989), utilized to help the analyst arrive at, fashion, and offer interpretations that make the unconscious conscious – highlighting insight as the chief tool of therapeutic action (Arlow & Brenner, 1990).

Paul Gray (1982, 1994) concluded that a "developmental lag" existed within psychoanalysis, to the extent many analysts continued to focus on the task of interpreting repressed content, rather than attending to disruptions of the free associative process, which hinted at the operation of resistances. Gray considered this a development lag because analysts who were single-mindedly focused on directly accessing "the repressed" had not kept abreast of changes in Freud's thinking about technique that dated back to 1914, when Freud wrote:

> When hypnosis had been given up, the task became one of discovering from the patient's free associations what he failed to remember. *The resistance was to be circumvented by the work of interpretation* and by making its results known to the patient...Finally, there was evolved the consistent technique used today, in which the analyst...contents himself with studying whatever is present for the time being on the surface of the patient's mind, and he employs the art of interpretation mainly *for the purpose of recognizing the resistances* which appear there, and making *them* conscious to the patient. (p. 147, italics added)

Rather than work to harvest the patient's free associations in a concerted effort to make the unconscious conscious, Kris (1996) saw the goal of the free association method "as the enhancement of the patient's free associations and not as the production of insight" (p. 3), which isn't to say that Kris ruled out insight as a laudable though *distal goal* of the process; rather, he identified the *analyst's immediate concern* as helping the patient more freely associate in order to regain lost connections by identifying and repairing "discontinuities" (p. 15) in the patient's associations with the aim of "the promotion of continuity" (p. 14). Kris saw the chief aim as increasing the patient's freedom to think without undue restriction or resistance,[6] with a heightened ability to freely associate representing a metric of therapeutic progress and improved mental health. Kris notes that "the activity of free association can be satisfying, even when the substance of the communication is most unhappy" (p. 51).

We now arrive at the point of asking whether the patient's gradually developing capacity to freely associate, in and of itself, might prove to be therapeutic. Catalina Bronstein (2004) opines that "Free association is not an end in itself. It is the tool, the procedure we use...to gain access to an understanding of the patient's inner world. It is directed toward an acquisition of insight" (p. 479). Not all would agree, and some may even wonder whether the notion that free association is not an end unto itself is necessarily true. Kris (1996), for one, thought that a patient's developing capacity to freely associate was one indication of analytic improvement. But is free association, in and of itself, therapeutic? In fact, free association is the *necessary but insufficient* condition for accomplishing what might be considered the goal of free association: to repair discontinuities, to help the patient be in better touch with a larger portion of his mind – to know about and be better able to tolerate certain of his memories, desires, beliefs, impulses, and the like. For free association to prove therapeutic requires the patient associate in the presence of a facilitating other – the analyst, whose ways of responding enhance the free associative process. Hoffman (2006) notes that the way in which the analyst conducts himself contributes to the creation of an environment in which:

> ...the patient feels safe enough so that what has been alien and forbidden can be allowed into consciousness, even if in disguised form, and can be communicated, and accepted [allowing] aspects of the patient's self that have been shut out in one way or another are seen as finding their way into the flow of the patient's thoughts. (p. 47)

Leavy (2005) describes the therapeutic effect of the analyst's capacity to dependably and attentively listen and respond to a patient's free associations, accurately and consistently mirroring the patient's associations, as "analogous to the ability of parents to share intuitively in the child's beginning readiness to be recognized as a self" (p. 119). Leavy notes:

> The curative effect of the process lies in the effective demonstration to the sufferer of hitherto inaccessible mental content, affect-laden, and therefore experienced as a discovery, or recovery of valuable property of the self. The "I" then speaks from a new base, *although the sources of conflict have not necessarily been revealed.* (p. 109, italics added)

Leavy is quick to note that this process requires that the patient's free associations be shared with another: "the recovery of what has been felt to be lost, or just absent, takes place in the special presence of another" (p. 121). In his review of Steven Leavy's book, Mark Levey (2006) writes:

> By free associating the patient begins to live his aliveness, and the self is changed...Free association in the presence of the analyst changes the self, the I. Traditionally this was seen as the result of greater access to internal content. Leavy sees it as a result of reconnection with signifiers and the process itself as enlivening. What the patient says is *from* the self as well

> as *about* it. Analysis reinstitutes the parental function of recognizing the self. Free association is an encounter with the patient's self, whether the analyst responds by empathizing or by analyzing defenses. (p. 1431)

Rosegrant (2005) adds his voice to those who contend that free association, in and of itself, can prove therapeutic, writing:

> Experiencing the free-associative state of consciousness can be, in and of itself, therapeutic for patients. Our usual psychoanalytic rationale for free association, that it provides material needed for insight, is correct but is not the whole story, and I think it is important that we supplement this rationale with respect for the value of the free-associative state even when it is not interpreted. (p. 763)

Final thoughts

In summary, we see how proper handling of the free associative process has two essential benefits. The first has to do with an essential goal of analysis – one that arguably is held in common by the clear majority of analysts – to heal discontinuities, to retrieve lost parts of the self, to reverse dissociations, return projections, and – yes – in the end, to help retrieve aspects of what has been repressed – though not solely, or even chiefly – through the psychoanalyst's direct interpretation of unconscious content. In this chapter, we are also noting what might either be considered an ancillary benefit of a patient's developing capacity to free associate or, in some cases, the essential benefit: to train the patient's mind to be able to more gracefully and effortlessly shift between the two competing modes of thinking (modes of consciousness) – active and passive, doing and being – and to be confronted with a need to come to know one's own mind as separate and apart from the minds of others. It's conceivable that these later goals make free association potentially therapeutic in and of itself without the added value of providing access to the patient's unconscious, which then positions the analyst to say something meaningful and intelligible about the patient's inner life.

Kris (1996) stated unequivocally that "psychoanalysis has demonstrated that the components of psychopathology invariably include significant limitations in freedom of association…[and] the psychoanalytic treatment method offers a substantial approach to the resolution of psychopathology by focusing upon limitations and disorders of free association" (p. 4). Given Kris's position, it seems reasonable to assume that helping a patient become better able to more freely associate can widen the patient's cognitive repertoire, not only permitting him greater access to passive modes of cognition, but also heightening his ability to be cognitively flexible enough to shift back and forth between alternate modes of cognition in response to changing conditions that require different sorts of cognitive skills.

Notes

1 With the exception of psychoanalytic theories that suggest you cannot lose what you never had – theories based in developmental arrest and deficit psychopathology based on a failure of provision.

2 A few select analysts have been reported not to rely on the free associative method to elicit material that then becomes the focus of analytic attention. For example, Clara Thompson reportedly abandoned the use of free association largely because she found patients weren't able to freely associate and instead "just natted on" (Levenson, 2001, p. 380), and Frieda Fromm-Reichmann (1950) described free association as "unnecessarily time consuming" (p. 72).

3 Aron makes this claim without providing sufficient support. Instead, he makes note of notable relational analysts who value the free associative method.

4 Though the analyst is often able to piece together what that word had likely been.

5 Feeling alienated from aspects of oneself is not the only way in which patients become ill. Beside the presence of an absence are conditions where – for example – success is prohibited or inhibitions are strong for a host of different reasons.

6 Kris drew a critical distinction between reluctance to share (a conscious process) and resistance (unconscious motivations to keep content hidden).

Chapter 2

The analyst's activity and his search for evidence

Theory-determined salience and selective perception

In the first chapter, we addressed an essential aspect of the patient's activity – his efforts to freely associate – which provides the analyst a glimpse into the operation of the patient's unconscious and offers the patient a chance to practice using his mind in a relatively novel fashion. In this chapter, we turn our attention to the analyst's activity – specifically, two sorts of activities: his search for evidence (which helps determine how the analyst interacts with the patients) as well as the specific way in which he goes about interacting with the patient (how he employs his interpretation of the patient to help determine how he interacts with his patient: when, how, and whether he verbally communicates to the patient who he sees the patient as being). The offering of interpretations is one sort of activity; so too is the particular way in which the analyst comes to believe he would best conduct himself when interacting with the patient.

Specifying how one goes about conducting an analysis – his search for evidence and his chosen style of interacting with a given patient – is something most analysts are loath to do – in part, because it runs counter to the open-minded stance that analysts adopt when analyzing patients, but also because spelling out the rules that analysts ought to follow is not at all in keeping with the depth, complexity, and creativity of psychoanalytic thinking, nor is it in keeping with psychoanalytic thinking in general and psychoanalytic practice in particular. In his introduction to Freud's paper on technique, Strachey (1958) noted that Freud considered psychoanalysis "too complex and variable to make any hard and fast rules possible," further insisting that "a proper mastery of the subject could only be acquired from clinical experience and not from books" (p. 87).

Following in Freud's footsteps, analysts who have written about technique by and large avoid offering edicts and instead write about how *not* to conduct treatment: don't enter sessions with memory or desire (Bion, 1967a); don't focus too much on any given bit of data (maintain "the same 'evenly-suspended attention' (as I have called it) in the face of all that one hears"; Freud, 1912, p. 111); don't "side" with any one psychic agency over another (remain "equidistant" from the patient's id/ego/superego; Freud, 1936).

Sigmund Freud (1912) refused to speak definitively about technique, offering "recommendations" rather than "rules" and admitting that his own particular clinical approach was uniquely suited to his personality, acknowledging, "I do not venture to deny that a physician quite differently constituted might find himself driven to adopt a different attitude to his patients and to the task before him" (p. 111). Even the initial call for analysts to conduct themselves in a restrained fashion (in accordance with the principles of abstinence, anonymity, and neutrality) represented a sort of *subtraction*, the removal of elements of the analyst's personhood in place of what was then feared would prove to be a *potentially distracting and distorting presence* – evidence of the analyst's subjectivity. It took decades before a segment of analysts came to the realization that legitimate data ("evidence") came not just from the process of subtraction ("blank screen") that was thought to beget projection, but from the impingement of the analyst's being brought about by his making explicit his subjective responses to the patient in order to help patients grapple, in turn, with the effect the patient has on others.

While psychoanalysts have tended to shy away from speaking authoritatively about how one goes about conducting analysis, there is one tool no analyst can do without – an indispensable tool that primes the analyst's mind to attend to certain sorts of data over other sorts (Friedman, 1988). While Bion (1967a, p. 163) advised analysts to approach each hour "without memory or desire," he did not include "*without theory*." Quite the contrary! Bion knew such a thing was neither desirable nor possible, though he – like others – recognized it was best that theory operate *in the background*, implicitly helping the analyst sift through the vast amount of patient-related and analyst-related data coming through a variety of channels in order to decide which data to attend to and which to ignore. Theory helps us separate the wheat from the chaff, leading us to enter sessions with "prepared minds" (Schafer, 1996, p. 239) and to organize data in accordance with preconceived expectations (Edelman, 1987). But what is wheat and what is chaff differs depending on which theory an analyst is chiefly employing. Without theory, analysts wouldn't have a clue about the sorts of clinical data they should prioritize as they search for evidence that will go on to become the basis of their understanding of the patient. Clinical phenomena that one analyst sees as clear-cut "evidence," for example, of the patient's selfobject hunger may mean next to nothing to another analyst who's attending to different sorts of clinical data, which he will rely upon to create and support different sorts of conclusions about the patient.

Theories function like polarizing filters that "let in" only a certain select segment of the data – that which is noted because it's deemed salient (relevant) to one's theory.[1] The way in which theory affects perception is a matter of "selective attention." The invisible gorilla experiment (Chabris & Simons, 2010) illustrates the principle to a tee: one watches a video clip in which two teams of men wearing different-colored jerseys pass a basketball back and forth. If the observer pays close attention and follows the instruction to count the number of times those with white shirts pass the ball, most viewers fail to notice a man in a gorilla suit ambling across the screen in "clear view." This eye-opening experiment drives home the fact that we can fail to see things that are right before our very eyes.[2] Once the analyst is implicitly primed to be on the lookout for certain kinds of data, he may not realize the extent to which selective attention necessarily implies selective *inattention* to a wide range of other data that is implicitly judged to be irrelevant – "beside the point." One fails to take note of certain data; furthermore, one even fails to take note *that one is failing to take note* – meaning that one doesn't know what one doesn't know.

Analysts subscribe to a *general psychology theory* about human nature and human behavior that helps them recognize certain sorts of patterns – alerting them, for example, to instances when a slip of the tongue or an interrupted association indicates something meaningful is happening (something that amounts to "psychologically significant data"). Analysts also generate, in the course of analyzing patients, *patient-specific theories* that aim to explain the psychological bases of a particular patient's symptomatology. These patient-specific theories also serve to direct the analyst's attention to behavioral manifestations of the patient's psychology as they emerge in session (e.g., signs pointing to the operation of compromise formations that develop in response to defenses against the threatened emergence of unbearable unconscious content). Aside from the analyst's general psychological theories and his patient-specific theories is a third set of theories – the analyst's *clinical theory* about what interventions, stances, approaches, interpretations, and so forth may help bring about psychic change. Clinical theory not only directs the analyst's activity, it also helps determine how the analyst goes about listening to the patient.[3] For example, an analyst who subscribes to modern ego psychology – one who sees value in sharing his observations about notable breaches in the patient's associations – will be apt to "closely monitor" shifts in the patient's associations (Busch, 1995; Gray, 1994), alerting him to the fact that something is "up" that deserves attention (e.g., the patient suddenly switches topics, suggesting he'd unconsciously concluded that he had better not continue to travel down his associative path lest he end up becoming psychically overwhelmed with unbearable affect). Alternately, analysts who place stock in their countertransference reactions as *primary evidence* will be on the lookout for subtle and not so subtle instances when they have become drawn into an enactment. Some analysts use their subjective reactions to patients in another way – drawing the patient's attention to how the patient makes them feel so that the patient has a better sense of the effect he has on others (Ehrenberg, 1992, 1996). Still other analysts primarily attend to their own experience of reverie, believing that the content of such private-seeming mental activity isn't nearly as private nor as personal as one might think – but rather is "an aspect of a jointly (but asymmetrically) created unconscious intersubjective construction" (Ogden, 1997, p. 569). Analysts who alternately prioritize the analysis of the *patient's subjectivity* as it is revealed in the patient's transference reactions will be especially attentive to clinical material that suggests how the patient has constructed the analyst in his mind's eye. Some analysts utilize a number of such lenses to consider clinical material, while others tend to specialize, leaning in the direction of listening in certain ways and not in other ways. Some consider all such approaches valid, while others are vocally insistent on their own particular brand of listening, believing that they themselves listen better to patients than do analysts who listen in ways they argue overly prejudice the analyst's conclusions (e.g., Schwaber, 1992).

Types of evidence: the selected fact versus the overvalued idea

The analyst's explicit or implicit search for, and efforts to make sense of, the gleaned data ("clinical evidence") eventuates in the analyst reaching certain sorts of conclusions about the patient – realizations about the patient's underlying organizing principles, ways of thinking, styles of relating, fantasies, and the like. This, in turn, helps clarify aspects of the patient's psychology made apparent by noting certain commonalities (pattern recognition) in his behavior. Once recognized, these patterns will help predict and explain why the patient acts or reacts as he does. Recognizing such patterns doesn't always come easy – though, once noted, they may leave one wondering in retrospect why it had taken so long to catch on to the existence of what now seem like obvious patterns. It needs to be noted that I am not implying that a search for patterns constitutes the entirety of the analyst's focus or the sole means by which he effects change, though pattern recognition is a powerful tool. Pattern recognition comes about as a result of either the analyst's focused, willful search for evidence or his intuition-based epiphany that suddenly makes itself known without any willful effort on the analyst's part. To refer to what goes on in the analyst's mind as a "search" is a bit misleading to the extent it makes the process sound far too conscious and intentional. As noted earlier, theory works best if it is allowed to function in the background implicitly. To the extent theory is allowed to play, or – more disconcerting – is actively enlisted to play too much of an explicit, deliberating role (e.g., when the analyst's anxiety causes him to actively take charge of the process rather than allowing it to operate on a more automatic level), there is a distinct danger that linkages will be forced into being rather than coming into view on their own accord. This parallels what was said in the first chapter relative to free association and the relationship between active (doing) and passive (letting happen) modes of cognition. Having *the patience* to wait for a pattern to reveal itself, along with *the faith* that it will reveal itself, is necessary in order for one to be able to conduct an analysis.

What factors may interfere with the analyst's ability to initially recognize such patterns? Patients are ambivalent about helping the analyst in his effort to know the patient; the patient comes for help and hopes to change and not change all at the same time. While they may covertly be providing indirect evidence that helps the analyst catch the patient's drift, patients are oftentimes simultaneously presenting distracting explanations meant to account for their behavior. The patient may successfully engage in negation that unconsciously strives to convince the analyst "this isn't what you think it is." In response, the analyst may not feel sure enough to press the matter, and may have to wait until further confirmatory evidence surfaces before he feels enough of a conviction that the pattern he thinks he is seeing is a distinct possibility in spite of the patient's initial insistence that it isn't so.

Before a greater level of clarity about the patient is reached, the analyst may have to bide his time, endure the experience of not knowing, and wait patiently until something more is revealed that offers him something upon which to build a case. This process cannot be rushed and must be allowed to run its course, with the analyst accepting that the process is beyond his control – is something to which he must surrender if he hopes to be shown the light. Bion (1977) describes the need for the analyst to have "faith" – to trust that a clarifying perspective will eventually emerge so long as he waits patiently and keeps an open mind in order to recognize the emergence of "internal evidence" within him that brings a clarifying perspective into view. Naturally, having to wait patiently and surrender control can be quite unnerving for the analyst, who may be chomping at the bit to intervene in a therapeutic fashion. Feeling pressured to come up with something meaningful to say can develop for a host of reasons – some issuing from the analyst and others from the patient himself. The patient's impatience, his continuing symptomatology, and his expectation that the analyst should provide something tangible in the way of interpretations, answers, and the like exerts pressure on the analyst, pushing him toward the action end of the letting happen/making happen spectrum outlined in the previous chapter. Tolerating states of unknowing, sometimes for extended periods of time, can be hard for analysts to bear, even though such demands are inherent in the task of conducting an analysis. Britton and Steiner (1994) note:

> ...as we listen to our patients in analysis and try to understand the meaning of what is going on, it is common to find a bewildering variety of impressions competing for our attention. The resultant uncertainty and confusion is often difficult to bear, and pressure to reduce the uncertainty may influence both patient and analyst to search for a means of integrating or limiting the impressions in order to create a meaningful whole. Sometimes the situation is altered by the emergence of an observation linking disparate facts. (p. 1069)

To whatever extent the analyst feels pressured to "come up with the goods," he may act prematurely, talking himself into believing he has seen something worth mentioning, failing to recognize that his "intuition" has failed him to the extent he has created something that, frankly, does not really exist or, if it does exist, doesn't tell enough of the story (i.e., is an "inexact interpretation"; Glover, 1931) to justify the mutual celebration that may follow a seemingly pattern-clarifying interpretation.

What's been said thus far about pattern recognition is set in motion by what Bion (1963) referred to as "the selected fact" – something in the material that catches the analyst's eye, which suddenly connects (relates) what had appeared to be, up until this point, disparate phenomena. Suddenly, a selected fact is *illuminated and, in turn, proves illuminating* to the extent its effect extends beyond the light shed on the situation presently at hand. Bion defined the selected fact as "that by which *coherence and meaning* is given to facts already known but whose relatedness has not hitherto been seen" (p. 19, italics added).

Bion based his idea of the selected fact on the thinking of Jules-Henri Poincaré, philosopher of mathematics, quoting him as follows:

> If a new result is to have any value, it must unite elements long since known, but till then scattered and seemingly foreign to each other, and suddenly introduce order where the appearance of disorder reigned. Then it enables us to see at a glance each of these elements in the place it occupies in the whole. Not only is the new fact valuable on its own account, but it alone *gives value to the old facts it unites*. (p. 72, italics added)

Applying this concept to psychoanalysis, Bion (1963) described the analyst's spontaneous discovery of meaning as he recognizes the connection (the existence of a relationship) between what previously had seemed disparate phenomena. These connections aren't created in the moment of discovery – though it may appear so; rather, as Grotstein and Franey (2008) note:

> The selected fact – the collective fact – exists holographically in each association and its link with the previous and succeeding association... It is inherent and implicit in the link between the associations, how two belong to one. It's there all along until you get to the point where you can recognize it. (p. 102)

The experience of "coming upon" a selected fact, Bion notes, is emotionally satisfying to the extent the selected fact serves as a nucleus for a crystalizing process – a process that provides "answers" as confusion, chaos, and instability (meaninglessness) give way to order, clarity, and stability as meaning becomes apparent. In a panel discussion, Likierman noted:

> Life surrounds us with a multiplicity of fragments out of which we need to make sense. At a certain point, the fragments will be united in a certain

> way, illuminating a wholeness that makes sense. But there might be different ways of uniting fragments and each comprises a different angle of truth. Bion exemplified this with the idea of a young child's being exposed to, say, three fragments: the sound "daddy" uttered by his mother, the presence of a particular man, and the child's own very strong emotional reaction whenever this particular man arrives. A presence of elements that are continually conjoined in this way eventually leads to a particular idea, in this case, of a father. Such ideas are a way in which we choose to notice a pattern and represent it. (Britton et al., 2006, pp. 269–270)

As clinically useful as the selected fact may be, there is danger that the selected fact may lead to premature closure around a particular idea (e.g., resulting in a theory-based, "saturated" interpretation) that is then accepted as explaining all that needs to be explained about the situation at hand – which, Bion (1967b) notes, can hardly be the case. A more optimal pathway leads from not knowing, to suddenly realizing something of note, to then realizing that realization fails to tell the whole story – it doesn't provide all the answers as one hoped it might – which, in turn, results in a sense of deflation as analyst and analysand go back to the drawing board to discover what more might be discovered, having discovered that the previous discovery – while valid – is not sufficient to put the entire matter to rest. In this regard, Bion speaks of how "discovery has exposed further vistas of unsolved problems – 'thoughts' in search of a thinker" (p. 166). Sandler (2006) alerts us to the fact that the selected fact "has a potentially illusory character; that is to say, it continues to be non-intrinsic to the fact observed but resides in the observer's mind (Bion, 1962, p. 75). The *experience of discovery* is more important than the eventual discovery-in-itself" (p. 184). Gonzalez (2013) writes:

> The gestalt and coherence that arrives with the selected fact cannot be fixed; it too must give way to further disintegration in order to allow other, novel formations. Thing or no-thing, either is a terminus in danger of reification. What is necessary for growth is the rhythm of movement between the two…more tolerance for the nothingness that makes this movement possible. (p. 442)

Britton and Steiner (1994) describe the similarities and notable differences between "the selected fact" and what they refer to as "the overvalued idea." Both have in common a sense of conviction that the links that were discovered between what previously had seemed like disparate phenomena are real in nature; however, in the case of the overvalued idea, this proves to be a "false insight" (p. 1070). The "overvalued idea" appears to provide answers and to integrate data far more than it actually does. Such overvalued ideas typically arise when either the patient or analyst (or both[4]) cannot contain their intolerance of uncertainty and, accordingly, feel pressured to come up with an idea/

interpretation that one hopes will put the chaos of not knowing to rest. "In such circumstances," they note, "interpretation may become a means of seeking security rather than of inquiry, and its consistency more highly valued than its truth"[5] (p. 1077). Premature closure around pseudo-understanding is an ever-present danger in every analysis (Gabbard, 2007). Sometimes, a "clarifying" interpretation – one that seems to pull together loose ends – has the unintended effect of blocking further exploration because the rendered interpretation is highly saturated (Bion, 1962) – meaning that it creates the illusion that there is nothing left to explain. Naturally, no analyst intends for an interpretation to shut down ongoing inquiry, given the analytic habit of saying "no" to any seemingly final destination that puts everything to rest (Friedman, 1997).

No analyst is immune to generating and offering an overvalued idea in place of a bona fide analytic insight. Britton and Steiner (1994) write:

> We believe that it is usually not possible to distinguish between these two sources of integration [selected fact versus overvalued idea] at the time of formulating an interpretation, since either process may lead to a conviction of meaning. The distinction can only be made through an evaluation of the value of the interpretation as it is responded to by the patient in the course of the session and as it is repeated over the months and years of the analysis. In our view, the distinction between a creative use of the *selected fact* and a delusional one which supports an *overvalued idea* may be small at the moment of its formulation, but becomes crucial in the events which follow the verbalisation of an interpretation. (p. 1070)

These authors further note:

> ...an awareness of the possibility that an insight may be an *overvalued idea* helps to alert the analyst to the need to sustain doubt and to examine subsequent clinical material to evaluate his understanding...It seems to us likely that both the achievement of a sense of conviction and the testing of this conviction as an hypothesis are part of the process of interpretation, and that evaluation and formulation cannot be usefully separated. (p. 1070)

Britton and Steiner (1994) make clear how similar the processes leading to a selected fact or an overvalued idea can be – so similar, in fact, that they believe it is not possible to know at the time which is which. In each case, the notion seems to arise on its own accord through the operation of intuition. It is only by an examination of how things pan out after the fact – once the interpretation is offered and attention is then paid to the subsequently unfolding process set in motion by the interpretation – that one can differentiate between the two. Here, the problem isn't one of forcing one's thinking too far in the direction of "activity/doing" on the "active–doing/passive–letting happen" scale; rather, the problem is one of shutting down continued inquiry and investigation after the overvalued idea is reached because – after all – the job is done, and the resulting parade celebration of a job well done continues to make its way down the street to the cheering of the crowd.

We are now left to consider the following question: how does the analyst who has lapsed into relying upon an overvalued idea work his way clear to seeing things anew – setting aside what he'd thought he'd seen, and had celebrated seeing – in order to approach the question from a different angle, freed of the prejudice created by the elaboration of what had seemed, at the time, like a perfectly good solution to a rather sticky problem? Sixty odd years before Britton and Steiner (1994) introduced the notion of an overvalued idea, Glover (1931) wrote about how the analyst's offering of an "inexact interpretation" is more problematic than many had thought, given the fact that it provides a pseudo-solution to the patient's core problem, permitting him – if you will – to cop to a lesser charge rather than continue to search for the root causes of his anxiety-driven symptomatology. Glover notes: "There is a type of inexact interpretation which, depending on an optimum degree of psychic remoteness from the true source of anxiety, may bring about improvement in the symptomatic sense at the cost of refractoriness to deeper analysis" (p. 400). Glover offers as an example of the sorts of inexact interpretations spontaneously offered by patients that "are often extremely accurate in reference to *some* aspect of their phantasy activity, more particularly when the interpretation is truly intuitive, i.e. is not stimulated by intellectual understanding or previous analytic experience" (p. 400). If the analyst accepts the interpretation at face value as essentially solving the riddle, the patient in turn is greatly relieved and immediately feels a diminution in his level of anxiety. Glover concludes by noting: "The moral is of course that, unless one is sure of one's ground, it is better to remain silent" (p. 400) – to which we might add: better said than done, given Britton and Steiner's elaboration of the problem that makes clear how clueless the analyst is in the moment about whether his inexact interpretation/overvalued idea is, in fact, dubious.

More will be said about the subject of "breaking set" in Chapter 6, though it is apropos that we touch on the subject at this juncture. "Breaking set" (Koller, 1992) refers to an individual's ability to dismiss conclusions he had reached on the basis of pattern-recognition thinking in order to rethink the situation – to revisit the matter having set aside the blinding, prejudicial effect of having seemed to have arrived at a "perfectly good" answer to the posed riddle – what lays at the root of the patient's difficulties? To accomplish this goal, one must circumvent a default reliance on routine associative learning (McGaughey, 2008) in order to approach the novel situation anew. Breaking set is a metacognitive skill that distinguishes individuals referred to as "gifted" from those who merely test exceedingly well on IQ tests (Chmiliar, 1997; McGaughey, 2008; Veenman, 2008), which primarily measure an individual's ability to recognize patterns in order to solve problems (Dover & Shore, 1991; McGaughey, 2008). "Giftedness" implies higher degrees of cognitive flexibility, the ability to set aside a tried and true piece of learning that had, up until this instance, proven remarkably reliable, in order to appreciate the emergence of a new, exceptional pattern.

Regina Pally (2007), one of our field's resident neuroscientists, describes the process in this fashion:

> To function adaptively, the brain needs to determine whether what was predicted occurred or not. While the monitoring of errors operates primarily non-consciously, when what was expected does not occur consciousness is automatically engaged to assess the situation and make corrections where necessary…*It is only consciousness that allows for voluntary control and choice, and thereby frees us from non-conscious operating repetition.* (p. 865, italics added)

Pally's thinking explains, from a different vantage point, what Britton and Steiner (1994) refer to when they talk in terms of the need for the analyst to pay rapt attention to the effect his interpretation has going forward – how the patient adapts the analyst's thinking to his own – and whether the interpretation opens up or closes down the associative pathways, leading to greater clarity – to a truly selected fact.

The analyst's activity

Having introduced one of the two themes of this chapter – the analyst's theory-based search for evidence, the results of which form the basis of his understanding (his patient-specific theories) about a given patient – we now turn to the second topic of this chapter that has to do with the analyst's activity: the way in which he intervenes in treatment either by sharing his interpretations or by permitting his interpretations to shape his non-interpretive ways of relating to the patient.

The line of thinking pursued in the first chapter about the value of surrendering to a passive mode of cognition in order to be able to freely associate has thus far in the present chapter been applied to the process by which the analyst, with the aid of a theory-primed mind, generates his patient-specific theories by waiting patiently for patterns/linkages to reveal themselves to him rather than actively forcing the data into a theory in an effort to speed up the process or settle the anxiety generated by not yet knowing. If the process by which a selected fact comes to be known becomes encumbered by too much activity on the analyst's part – too much doing, if you will – the process will be interrupted from naturally coming to fruition by generating an interpretation (based on a selected fact) that stands the best chance of being "on the money" relative to the question of what ails the patient at his core. As we move from a consideration of the generation of patient-specific theories (interpretations) to what the analyst does with these theories, we return to the matter of passive acceptance versus active contrivance with respect to the analyst's activity – what he "chooses" to do with the interpretations he has reached about the patient he is treating.

For the better part of the 20th century, analysts wrote as if they chiefly envisioned clinical interventions to be the result of conscious deliberation that carefully weighs the pros and cons of considered options. Instances when something would just "blurt out" of the analyst's mouth were considered a matter of much concern and were chiefly seen as a manifestation of the analyst's uncontained countertransference reactions. However, over the last couple of decades, more and more analysts have unabashedly admitted to instances when they'd acted unwittingly in session. These analysts are unapologetic about engaging in such countertransference enactments (Jacobs, 1986), which they see as not only unavoidable, but also as *potentially valuable* to the clinical process *if handled properly*. The point of prefacing a discussion about the analyst's activity (his clinical intervention) is to acknowledge that the analyst's activity isn't always a matter of choice and sometimes is very much unintended, though it is still generally believed to be best if deliberation and choice are the rule rather than the exception (Tuch, 2015).

Theories of therapeutic action

The beneficial and mutative effect of making the patient's unconscious conscious – of educating the patient about how his mind works and introducing him to psychic content about which he'd largely been unaware – has historically been seen as the chief mutative factor that explains how and why psychoanalysis works ("therapeutic action"). Over the course of time, other mutative factors were recognized and introduced, beginning with Strachey's (1934) description of the way in which a patient's harsh superego may be softened through identification with the analyst's more accepting attitude. Martha Stark (1999) summarizes what she sees as the three main modes of therapeutic action: "enhancing of knowledge" (insight), "provision of experience" (e.g., providing growth-promoting experiences the patient had missed out on during childhood), and "engagement in relationship" (establishment of a "new relationship" that differs from the original childhood experience) (p. xv). Naturally, these modes overlap and don't exist in any pure form, though one can observe certain analysts emphasizing one mutative factor over others in their clinical theory.

Today, many analysts see the *process* by which the patient acquires self-knowledge, not just the resulting self-knowledge, as an essential aspect of the therapeutic process, as illustrated in Ogden's (2016) observation:

> Psychoanalysis as a therapeutic process centers much of its energy on helping the patient *experience, and give voice to,* a truth that has been

> disturbing him for much of his life, a truth that he has been *unable to think or feel* because it has been too much to bear. Language plays a pivotal role in bringing to life the emotional truth of previously unbearable experience in the analytic session. (p. 411, italics added)

Fink (2014) also emphasizes the mutative effect of articulation when he notes how a Lacanian approach to analysis "is not about providing meaning but, rather, about *putting the unspeakable into words*" (p. 7), illustrated in Lacan's (2001) words: "What is at stake is not, in fact, a move to consciousness but, rather, to speech…and that speech must be heard by someone" (pp. 139–140). The *process by which the patient acquires self-knowledge* may prove more mutative than the resulting insight itself, in which case it might boldly be claimed that insight (the "thing") is of lesser importance compared to the task of exercising the muscle of reflective thinking (and strengthen it in the process), making the development of a much-improved capacity for reflective thinking a more essential mutative factor in psychoanalysis (Sugarman, 2006; Tuch, 2007). Accordingly, more may be gained *in the journey* (*gaining* insight as a process, a verb) than in arriving at a *final destination* (*derived* insight as an entity, a noun). It may further be postulated that the supposed "moment of insight" (the "Aha!" experience) is rarely a moment in the way it's oftentimes portrayed to be, as there is typically a greater lag time between "Ah…" and "ha!" than most tend to acknowledge, again underscoring insight acquisition as a process taking place over time rather than a mere moment in time.[6] Ogden (2016) notes:

> The truth of the individual's experience that is nascent in the moment cannot be passively "taken in" in a moment of epiphany; unconscious psychological work must be done. What is true to that moment must be created psychically – "dreamt up" – as patient and analyst together engage in the conscious and unconscious experience of being changed by the truth of the moment, a truth that is always on the move, accruing verbally symbolic meanings as it goes. (pp. 413–414)

While insight has generally been considered a cornerstone of psychoanalytic treatment and an important explanation of why and how therapy works, many believe this mutative factor has been overemphasized, particularly if such knowledge turns out to be something the patient intellectually accepts rather than affectively experiences (is "experience-distant"). To ensure that a gut-level experience drives a patient's acceptance of a given insight requires the analyst to carefully choose when to optimally intervene to lessen the chance that interpretation will function as either indoctrination or intellectualization.

An analyst may sometimes recognize evidence suggesting that a patient has failed to internalize (make his own) interpretations the patient carried away from his former analysis and now parrots without much conviction as a sort of talisman, having failed to translate those ideas into the patient's own words, carrying them around like a foreign body. If an analyst hopes to accomplish more with a patient than leaving him spouting the analyst's favored notions, it will often be required for him to help fashion an experience that convinces the patient from the inside out. In order to accomplish that goal, it often helps if the analyst allows the intensity of the transference to heighten to the point that it becomes a lived experience against which the patient may then mount a resistance, making psychoanalysis a laboratory experiment rather than an at-the-blackboard didactic lecture.

Observing versus interpreting: drawing the patient's attention on selected subject matter

Modern ego psychologists (Busch, 1995; Gray, 1994; Kris, 1996) find reason to intervene in treatment whenever the otherwise smooth operation of free association becomes noticeably disrupted, signaling and demonstrating a problematic or troubled area in the patient's psyche. "Close process monitoring" (Busch, 1995; Gray, 1994) reveals instances when the patient implicitly or explicitly senses that he is coming dangerously close to topics/affects that are likely to produce extreme discomfort. At such moments, one sees the patient's associations suddenly truncate or veer off – the patient fails to complete a word or sentence midstream, changes the subject abruptly, loses track of the point he was about to make, falls silent, or the like. Such breaks in the associative flow are seen as indicative of the sudden emergence of resistance triggered by impending discomfort, which the patient quickly dispenses with by, for example, suddenly shifting topics. The patient takes care to *not* note the defense he's employing, since noting one's use of a defense is the beginning of undoing it – of rendering the repressed material conscious. It's at this precise juncture that analysts working in the modern ego psychological tradition help the patient take note of the fact he'd been trying to not notice something – which is evidence that something fishy is going on that warrants the analytic couple's attention[7] (Busch, 1994).

How the analyst draws the patient's attention to matters that the patient clearly wishes to avoid is a critical aspect of psychoanalytic technique and depends upon a given analyst's clinical theory. Some analysts are prone to make "deep" interpretations that confront the patient with the most buried aspects of his psyche (addressing the maximum point of anxiety[8]), while others believe it best to employ a more gradual approach – one they believe will be less likely to intensify the patient's level of resistance (Gray, 1986). Freud (1940) was decidedly against interpreting at too deep a level, noting if an analyst overwhelms the patient with an interpretation that the patient isn't prepared to hear, "our information would either produce no effect or it would arouse a violent outbreak of resistance which would make the further progress of our work more difficult or might even threaten to stop it altogether"

(p. 178). Modern ego psychologists speak of "working at the surface" (Busch, 1995, 1999; Gray, 1982, 1994) – drawing the patient's attention to psychologically meaningful behaviors that the patient can recognize as indicative of the fact that there is more going on than meets the eye. Fenichel (1945) sketches the outline of such an approach by suggesting technique (his clinical theory) involves: "The demonstration to the patient that he *is* defending himself, *how* he defends himself, *why* he does it, and *what the defense is directed against*" (p. 570, italics added).

Working at the surface differs dramatically from what Busch (1997) refers to as the "semiotic method" used by certain analysts:

> In this method the patient's associations are viewed primarily as *conveyors of buried content* in an area the analyst expects will be signified. In plain talk, the analyst is expecting the patient's conflicts to be expressed in a particular form, and the patient's thoughts are *scanned for the expected sign*. (p. 414, italics added)

Naturally, these analysts are stimulated to intervene whenever they catch wind of just such a sign, triggering the analyst to share with the patient what the analyst had uncovered by providing an interpretation that aims to create insight in the patient about unconscious *content* – with an emphasis on content over demonstrations of the way in which the patient's mind works – which is the primary focus of modern ego psychologists.[9]

Problems with interpreting

An interpretation is a theoretical explanation fashioned by the analyst that links two clauses with the word *because* and is offered to the patient in the hope of helping him recognize and understand something about the hidden contents of his mind and/or about the workings of his mind. An example that addresses hidden content is as follows: "You didn't want to say X, because you feared if you did I (the analyst) might feel Y, the end result of which you feared might cause me to feel/think/do Z" (e.g., "You didn't want to express your criticism of me because you feared I would feel hurt and I would withdraw from you, leaving you bereft; furthermore, you anticipate such abandonment because you'd experienced the same when you were young, vulnerable, and terrified by being left all alone by your mother").[10] An interpretation aimed at helping a patient better understand the workings of his mind might, for example, highlight the patient's characteristic use of particular types of defenses, styles of relating, overall narcissistic sensitivity, and so on.

Thus far, we've addressed *interpretive* interventions triggered by the appearance of resistance that manifests either in: (1) disruptions in the patient's free associations; (2) the appearance of symbolic derivatives of repressed material (in accordance with the "semiotic method"); or (3) a characteristic style of relating ("character defenses"). Whichever the case, the therapeutic focus is on making the unconscious conscious. *Interpretive interventions* may not be limited to addressing the resistance and may also be triggered by other sorts of clinical phenomena that are not necessarily, or predominately, defensive in nature. Aside from interpretations, the analyst's activity may also involve interventions that are *non-interpretive* in nature, which isn't to suggest that the analyst hasn't formed an implicit or explicit opinion/interpretation about the patient that guides the way in which he's chosen to interact with the patient. It only means that the interpretation per se isn't articulated to the patient as such, but instead *prereflectively* informs the analyst's approach to the patient, without ever becoming explicitly conscious (Josephs, 1992). The fact that some – possibly much – of the analyst's activity relies upon implicit theories about which the analyst is dimly aware – at best – led Josephs (1992) to wisely observe that the field of psychoanalysis needs "a theory of the analyst's preconscious and volitional execution of a rational strategy of nonverbal interventions tailored to the unique needs of a particular patient" (p. 50) – what is being referred to herein as the analyst's "patient-specific theory." While such non-interpretive interventions may go unarticulated, this doesn't mean the patient doesn't nevertheless nonverbally sense what it is the analyst has concluded about him, though he might be hard pressed to be able to offer hard evidence that supports his belief that the analyst thinks or feels a given way about him.

Not all patients are able to work interpretively (Britton, 1989, 2004; Slochower, 1996; Tuch, 2007). What differentiates patients who understand the analyst's intention – and accordingly can tolerate and be helped by the analyst's interpretations – from those who cannot may partly have to do with whether a given patient's issues are conflict-based or deficiency-based. When it comes to the later, Killingmo (1989) suggests the task of therapy isn't *searching for concealed meaning*, as it is with patients who primarily are conflicted, but rather *establishing meaning* by finding meaning in experiences that the patient felt to have been meaningless – confirming both the reality as well as the reasonableness of the patient's past or present experiences (e.g., "you had good reason to feel insecure when I don't answer you. It is just like what you were feeling when mother didn't answer you when you were a little girl and you desperately needed to know what she really thought of you"; Killingmo, 1989, p. 74). The analyst's task, notes Killingmo:

> ...is to confirm the patient's need for – and right to – being confirmed. That is, he gives his empathic understanding of how it must be not to have received the wished-for recognition when it was most needed and rightly to be expected, thereby justifying that the patient feels as he does. (p. 76)

From time to time, every analyst has encountered patients who cannot tolerate the experience of being interpreted. Slochower (1996) advocates against offering interpretations of any sort to these patients until they develop the capacity to better tolerate the analyst's "otherness," made clear by the extent that the analyst's interpretations differ from what the patient has in mind. Slochower recommends the analyst adopt a "holding" stance with such patients – one that screens out or "brackets" the analyst's subjectivity to insulate the patient from having to confront their separateness.[11]

Another problem with the act of interpreting has to do with the fact that patients have their own explanations about why they do the things they do and feel the things they feel, which the analyst's interpretation need not necessarily be seen as invalidating even as it illustrates another way in which the data in question can be seen – a way that ideally takes into consideration a greater share of the observable data. Problems develop, however, if the patient feels that his own interpretation about a matter has been upstaged, even negated, by the analyst's interpretation. Problems may also develop if the patient feels he needs to accept and agree with an interpretation offered by the analyst in order to satisfy the analyst's narcissism. Alternately, a patient may feel a need to fight against considering the offered interpretation because he'd grown up with parents who'd refused to let the patient have a mind of his own. In other words, the analyst's interpretation can covertly represent to the patient a critical judgment about the quality of his own theory, a testament to the narcissism of the analyst who wants the patient to say it's so, a repetition of parent-like behaviors.

The issue of how patients interpret the act of being interpreted led Betty Joseph (1985) and her followers (Feldman, 2004) to concern themselves with how the patient *responds* to the offered interpretation – what he feels he's expected to do with it, what he does do with it, and what conflicts are aroused by recognizing that he and the analyst are of two minds (that they are less alike than the patient wishes to believe). Until enough is known about what the patient "makes" of the experience of *being interpreted* (and of being interpreted in a particular way), the actual content of the interpretation may be beside the point. Feldman (2004) notes, "One of the fundamental aims which Joseph articulates is to enable the patient increasingly to hear our interpretations as interpretations, as the communication of understanding [and]...not primarily experienced as concrete manifestations of earlier object relationships" (p. 26).

Interpretations of a very different sort

An often-heard complaint lodged against psychoanalysis by patients and critics alike is the observation that insight doesn't always translate (or, more emphatically, rarely if ever translates) into behavioral change, particularly when insight supports a rationalization, is intellectualizing, or otherwise fails to leave a deep emotional impression on the patient (is "experience-distant"). In his review of Betty Joseph's selected papers (Spillius & Feldman,

1989), Roy Schafer (1991) notes that "Joseph discourages casual reliance on the effectiveness of the formulated insight that she calls 'understanding'; that reliance, she believes, tends to block rather than facilitate emotional experience...Joseph puts her trust in immediate emotional experience in the analytic here-and-now" (p. 170). To mitigate against the possibility of conveying sterile knowledge – stimulating insight that brings about no psychic change (Fink, 2014) – followers of Jacques Lacan tend to offer enigmatic interpretations ("oracular speech"; Fink, 2007, p. 87; Lacan, 1971), which allude to something that seems real enough to the extent it inexplicably rings a bell, yet stops far short of spelling it out. An important point seems to have been illuminated in a way one can't quite put one's finger on (it seems tangible but not tangible enough), which makes the interpretation not so real as to be readily brought into sharp focus (it isn't exactly identifiable so it cannot be co-opted by being assimilated into the patient's standard ways of thinking). Such opaque interpretations are *evocative* in the same way that good art often can be – drawing from each viewer something that is uniquely his own. Fink (1997) notes: "Rather than spoon-feeding meaning to the analysand, regardless of how brilliant and insightful that meaning may be, the analyst must arouse the analysand's curiosity and kick-start his or her associative processes" (p. 45). Such an approach would prove to be more Socratic than instructive in nature. Alternately, if the analyst elects to play the role (or is seen by the patient as trying to play the role) of *le sujet suppose savoir* ("The one who is supposed to know;" Lacan, 1975), the patient is at risk of being reciprocally relegated to the position of "the one who doesn't know," which clearly sends the wrong message to patients.

Lacanians go a step further when they speak about the danger of making understanding the goal of analysis. Unlike analysts who emphasize the ego-strengthening effect of making the unconscious conscious, Fink (2014) notes:

> An emphasis by the analyst on *meaning and understanding* often leads the analysand to become very adept at finding psychological explanations of her behavior but does little to nothing to foster change in the analysand... Part of the analyst's job is to *take meaning apart*, to undermine understanding by showing that far from explaining everything, it is always partial, not total, and leaves many things out. (p. 7, italics added)

Furthermore, it can function as a grand rationalization that seems to say much when, in fact, it captures but a miniscule portion of what there is to be grasped.

Implications

The analyst's search for *clinical evidence* is largely, implicitly directed by three factors: the analyst's general psychological theory, his patient-specific theory about the particular dynamics of the patient he is treating, and his clinical theory about how patients can be helped to get better in the course of treatment. Together, these three theories prepare the analyst's mind and, in turn, inform the analyst's activity, whether his interventions are of an interpretative or non-interpretative nature. Relevant clinical evidence abounds in the form of the patient's use of defenses, disruptions in his attempts to freely associate, his particular style of relating to the analyst, noteworthy expressions of affect or the glaring lack thereof under conditions expected to produce affect, and so on. Relevant evidence about the patient may also emerge more exclusively *within the analyst himself* in the form of his countertransference reactions, reverie, or other sorts of psychic states that become stimulated through the analyst's interactions with the patient that, in turn, prove translatable as commentary about the patient's dynamics. Aside from evidence manifesting more strictly from within the patient or within the analyst are other forms of evidence that are more intersubjective in nature, reflecting a back-and-forth, chicken-or-egg process that culminates in a transference–countertransference configuration that makes it hard to pin the sole – or even chief – responsibility on either party. How the analytic couples get on – what each contributes to help co-construct the therapeutic relationship – differs from a strict focus on what the patient brings to treatment in the way of transference-readiness (or, for that matter, what the analyst brings to the table in terms of his own transference-readiness), though such readiness always plays somewhat of a role in helping shape the relationship that develops. Analysts who work in the intersubjective or interpersonal tradition are particularly attuned to noting data ("evidence") emanating from the way in which analyst and patient reciprocally influence and impact one another (e.g., Ehrenberg, 1992). As can be seen, all sorts of data can be deemed clinically relevant, theoretically illuminating of a given patient's dynamics, and ultimately determining of therapeutic action – whether the conclusions the analyst reaches about a patient are or are not directly shared with the patient in the form of articulated interpretations.

Not only do analysts differ with regard to what they see as relevant clinical evidence upon which to base their conclusions about a given patient, analysts also differ markedly with regard to their clinical theory – what they consider to constitute *therapeutic action* that accounts for therapy-induced psychic change. Some analysts place great emphasis on making the transference explicit to patients, while others seem to believe that sufficient psychic change can be brought about just so long as the analyst is sufficiently empathic and lends himself to the task of "provision" – functioning as the developmentally facilitating self-object the patient had needed during his formative years.[12] Not all who subscribe to relationally based theories agree with this proposition. For example, Ehrenberg (1992) asserts:

> What defines an analytic relationship is that our impact, whether the result of deliberate interventions or the result of inadvertent aspects of

> our participation, *must be explicitly clarified*...The hallmark of an analytic relationship is that it is essential that there be no covert manipulation and that the patient be cognizant of whatever critical transactions have occurred as well as their impact. (p. 540, italics added)

The analyst's *patient-specific theory* ideally is determined by evidence the analyst notes in session. A theory is a hypothesis that awaits further verification (further evidence) that either supports or refutes that theory. Many a psychoanalytic war has been waged by analysts who've lost track of the fact that our theories are just that – theories, and nothing more, and any analyst who thinks otherwise – who insists his theory (or, more to the point, his group's collectively embraced theory) is superior to those used by other analysts – will be hard pressed to prove his assertion with "objective clinical data" that supposedly hasn't already been contaminated by his subjectivity or by the selectivity of the particular theory he espouses.

While some analysts accuse other analysts of the wholesale imposition of their theories on to patients, I suspect this charge reflects the fact that different psychoanalytic theories deem different sets of clinical evidence salient. What analysts tend to attend to is not naively noted; rather, it is determined, at least in part, by that analyst's favored psychoanalytic theory. Accordingly, theory plays an important role in helping determine the sorts of data certain analysts notice that other analysts tend *not* to notice. As a result, theoretically differing analysts reach different sorts of conclusions about patient dynamics based on somewhat different sets of data.

The *analyst's interventions* are determined by a host of different factors and assume a variety of different forms. *Theory-based (intended) interventions* don't define the universe of possible interventions, given the fact that analysts sometimes unwittingly intervene in unintended ways, as happens in the case of enactments. Intended interventions employed by psychoanalysts who differ in their theoretical orientation tend to address somewhat different constellations of psychic phenomena and interpret at different levels (surface versus depth). Intended interventions needn't be limited to interpretations per se – they may also involve the way in which the analyst goes about relating to the patient, in which case his patient-specific theory helps him decide whether and how he'll go about sharing his observations and/or interpretations with the patient.

A number of concerns have been expressed about the *analyst's use of interpretations* (Tuch, 2001), including: (1) proscriptions against utilizing interpretations with patients who are intolerant of the act of being interpreted; (2) the danger of misleading patients into accepting the analyst's interpretations without their giving due consideration to whether the interpretation truly fits – the result of the patient's gullibility and/or concern about the potential peril of injuring the analyst's narcissism by not embracing his ideas as fact; (3) the danger of introducing "saturated" interpretations that the patient comes to believe represents the final word on a given matter, rendering further exploration pointless; and (4) the danger of conveying experience-distant interpretations that don't resonate with the patient on an emotional level.

The analyst's activity differs with respect to *what the analyst hopes to achieve* through his interventions. The analyst may *make raw observations* (lacking any hint of what the analyst believes the observation might indicate[13]), which are meant to draw the patient's attention to behaviors and/or associations that the analyst believes to be indicative of unconscious aspects of the patient's mind. The patient, in turn, is then expected to make sense of the observation, with the analyst serving as facilitator/midwife in line with the Socratic method. The analyst may go a step further by offering *digested observations* (interpretations) for the patient's consideration, which ideally the patient is on the verge of making himself (Busch, 1996; Freud, 1940), in which case the analyst's interpretation serves to crystallize an insight that had been on the tip of the patient's tongue, if only pre-consciously. Another style of intervening involves throwing a metaphoric curveball into the patient's way of organizing his world by utilizing "oracular speech" that presents the patient with enigmas that lack sufficient form to be easily incorporated *in toto* into the patient's psyche, yet are sensed to contain some truth that the patient is then expected to discover on his own.

The analyst's activity – the choice of when and how to intervene – is guided by a consideration of tact and timing that is based on the analyst's assessment of what a given patient can and cannot tolerate. Beside a search for evidence and activity geared toward heightening the patient's self-knowledge are other sorts of activities the analyst engages in to help establish and maintain the therapeutic relationship, facilitated by his empathic understanding of what the patient needs and what the patient can tolerate. Empathy manifests not only in the words the analyst chooses, but in his actions as well – how he goes about relating to the patient.

A final comment is needed in anticipation of concern that some readers may have that my stance represents a form of radical relativism that asserts that one psychoanalytic theory and approach to treatment is as good as the next – a position some may believe undermines the scientific basis of our field. To those who harbor such concerns, I would note the following – it may be far more important to help disabuse patients of the rigid notions they hold about themselves, about others, about their relationships with others, and about human nature in general than it is to provide them with a *specific alternate viewpoint* – one that should "work better" than the notion they currently hold dear. Alternate perspectives/interpretations then become not ideas for the patient to agree with and incorporate; rather, they can be thought to chiefly demonstrate another way (one amongst many) that the presenting data can be explained. Whatever analysts do to increase the flexibility of a patient's thinking – opening their minds to alternate ways of thinking – should have a beneficial effect to the degree such efforts effect psychic change.

Notes

1 Ideally, one attends both to evidence that either supports or refutes one's theory, though some may be inclined to overlook data that contradicts the theory one has adopted to understand the patient.
2 Granted, this experiment is hyperbolic insofar as the experiment doesn't precisely replicate the conditions of an analysis. Still, the issue of selective perception and inattention are powerfully illustrated with this example, which applies to some degree to every analyst's perceptual activity.
3 Admittedly, this subdivision of theories is somewhat arbitrary to the extent these three types of theories – general psychological theory, patient-specific theory, and clinical theory – aren't wholly distinguishable, and the first two are sometimes seen as identical, which I think runs the risk of operating like the proverbial Procrustean bed into which an analyst might try to fit each and every patient – though suggesting there are such analysts might be little more than a straw-man argument.
4 The drive for premature closure around a supposed "answer" may be co-constructed, to whatever extent, as the analyst responds to the patient's desperate need to know.
5 A concern also taken up in Glover's (1931) paper on "inexact interpretations."
6 This isn't to suggest that insight never comes in a burst, only that it is rarer than had been thought.
7 As helpful as this clinical approach may be, it is hard to imagine an entire treatment that focuses exclusively on attending solely to breaches in the patient's flow of associations.
8 This had been a habit of Kleinians in the past, though most modern Kleinians are now disinclined to practice in this fashion.
9 Some may disagree with this dichotomization, which nevertheless strikes me as relatively true, if not absolutely true.
10 Still more: "But you are no longer as vulnerable as you'd once been, so we'd anticipate you're now better able to handle such matters that had previously been ones you avoided at all cost. And it's the current cost of these defenses that now drives you to seek treatment."
11 Some analysts see this as an impossible task to the extent the analyst's subjectivity is irreducible and must accordingly intrude into the treatment, even if the analyst tries to subtract its manifestations (Renik, 1993).
12 Many relational-based analysts do not place stock in provision alone as a chief mutative agent; rather, they emphasize making explicit the analyst's empathy-based understanding of what the patient felt he'd missed out on during childhood, without believing the analyst can turn back the clock and fully provide for those early needs, because that train has already left.
13 To the extent such a thing is possible.

Chapter 3

The analyst's way of being

Method as a function of the analyst's personality

The psychoanalyst's way of being – his personality, temperament, characteristic style of relating to others, unresolved transferences, and the like – helps determine his response to, and his clinical interventions with, a given patient. In turn, how he intervenes in treatment can significantly contribute to the way in which the patient's transference manifests. This chapter aims to explore these two subjects: the theoretic range of possible ways in which different analysts might respond to a given patient as a function of their way of being, and how these varied responses help determine the way in which the transference ultimately gets expressed. This chapter also questions current trends in certain quarters to overvalue countertransference enactments per se – arguably distinguishable from more contained and considered transference reactions – as the preeminent clinical tool without which psychoanalytically facilitated psychic change is less likely to occur.

It is helpful having terms that single out a phenomenon by which the analyst's way of being contributes to the creation of the patient's *manifest transference*, which is distinct from what the patient brings to the treatment – his *core transference*. The core transference refers to a range of ways a given patient's transference *could* manifest; the manifest transference refers to the *particular* way – one among many – transference ultimately ends up manifesting. Unlike the manifest transference, which is more or less co-constructed in the process of analysis, the patient's core transference issues are neither of the analyst's making nor a product of the intersubjective field. According to such thinking, transference is both *essential and invariant at its core* while, at the same time, it is *context-specific and variable in its surface presentation*. The terms *core transference* and *manifest transference* are being introduced to drive home the point that a given patient's manifest transference may differ as a function of how the analyst relates to the patient.

The analyst's way of being helps determine his or her countertransference reactions in general (e.g., the "hook" upon which a projection may be hung). It furthermore inclines or disinclines the analyst to engage either in chronic or acute countertransference enactments. The degree to which a given enactment is, on the one hand, more or less equally co-constructed with each party contributing substantially to its creation or, on the other hand, determined more heavily by either one of the two party's separable subjectivity varies considerably. As one slides along a continuum from equal contribution on each party's part to a heavier emphasis on either the analyst's or the analysand's contribution, one moves from an emphasis on a two-person psychology to that of a one-person psychology. Though some countertransference enactments appear to develop as a result of the patient's conscious or unconscious efforts to engage with and impact the analyst – for example, attempting to draw the analyst into acting out an assigned role – believing this invariably to be the case, as some seem to do, disallows for each party's *separable subjectivities* in accordance with a one-person psychological perspective that is reflected in Benjamin's (1995) brand of intersubjectivity, which leaves room for "the other who is truly perceived as outside, distinct from our own mental field of operation" (p. 29). Countertransference reactions that lead to such enactments aren't always the result of the patient's efforts to *provoke* the analyst into assuming a role coincident with the patient's expectations or needs and may primarily be the manifestation of the analyst's unresolved issues that have been *evoked* in him by the patient's transference behavior.

Aside from the analyst's way of being, another topic explored in this chapter has to do with current trends in our thinking about *countertransference enactments*. In particular, we'll explore current trends that appear to overemphasize the clinical value of countertransference enactments – seeing them as clinically indispensable to the extent successful analysis invariably hinges on their development and clinical resolution (Boesky, 1990; Chessick, 1999; Renik, 1993). Some analysts seem to celebrate countertransference enactments as *the* quintessential psychoanalytic intervention – reflected in the way in which some have interpreted Boesky's (1990) often-quoted declaration[1] – which has gone on to become a sort of rallying cry for those who insist on the desirability, even necessity, of enactments[2]: "If the analyst does not get emotionally involved sooner or later in a manner that he had not intended, the analysis *will not proceed* to a successful conclusion" (p. 573, italics added). Hirsch (1998) reiterates how most read Boesky's proclamation:

> He [Boesky] is not simply speaking of emotional involvement with the patient in the form of caring about the patient or becoming aware of countertransference feelings...He is saying that the analyst's countertransference, in the form of enactment, *must* become an actualization of the transference resistance in order for the analysis to be truly and profoundly effective. (p. 87)

I believe the current trend that overemphasizes the centrality and indispensability of countertransference enactments has carried us too far afield into territory that strikes some as absurd – for example, by declaring countertransference enactments not only to be extraordinarily helpful, but the very essence of the entire psychoanalytic enterprise (Renik, 1996).

Ted Jacobs' vignette

The first clinical material to be considered is a published vignette (Jacobs, 1993), one of the many that Jacobs presents to illustrate his thesis – how his own personal dynamics sensitize him to react in a particular fashion to how patients go about relating to him:

> It is 7:55 a.m. on a Monday. I am in the new office to which I have moved over the weekend, waiting for Mr. V. to arrive. He is 38, single, an attorney, slim, handsome and polished…He often speaks of himself as a kind of impostor, someone who gives the impression of being far more knowledgeable in his field than he actually is. He is terrified of being exposed for his inadequacies. There is, however, something menacing about Mr. V…Today as I wait for Mr. V. I am more tense than usual. I anticipate his criticism of my new office and I am apprehensive about this. Mr. V. attaches a great deal of importance to appearances and when displeased by surroundings that he regards as unattractive, he can be caustic. I realize, in fact, that I am rather self-conscious about the appearance of my new place and I am angry with myself for not having anticipated the problem and invested in some new furnishings…Mr. V. rings the bell. [I open the door]. He goes to the couch, unbuttons his jacket, and stretches out on it…[After] Mr. V has completed his silent survey of my office [he comments]: "You are nothing if not consistent," he says. "It's amazing. Your Sears decorator has done it again. She has duplicated the old place right down to the last shabby detail." He pauses and then goes on. "Wasn't it some philosopher who said that consistency is the hobgoblin of little minds?" A flash thought occurs to me, accompanied by a momentary feeling of triumph. Mr. V. has it wrong. The actual quote – I think it was from Emerson – is "a foolish consistency is the hobgoblin of little minds." It is on the tip of my tongue to say this but I know that in correcting my analysand I would merely be showing off and acting defensively. I refrain. (p. 9)

One might consider Jacob's restraint to be the proper and appropriate response to what could be considered Mr. V.'s baiting behavior. Rather than act out his countertransference irritation by retaliating, Jacobs "*chose*" self-restraint, which could be explained as both an act of discretion – his wish to avoid embarrassing the analysand by calling attention to his error – as well as the maintenance of the proper analytic stance: contain your countertransference reaction, reflect on its meaning, and use the resulting insight to further the treatment by fashioning an intervention based on this newly acquired insight. So far so good, until one considers what Jacobs discloses about what he believes had likely driven his "choice," making it seem a whole lot less "chosen" than it first appeared:

> My transference to Mr. V. has drawn much from my relationship to my father and other male authorities. Made anxious by the prospect of a clash with them, I avoided conflict. To ensure peace I let them be the winners...and sought to conceal my feelings of rivalry and competition. This, I think, is what has been happening with Mr. V....I realize, however, that my aggressive feelings have begun to slip out around the edges in the form of the kind of thoughts I have just had. (pp. 8–9)

Suddenly, what had appeared to be a well-thought-out instance of self-restraint for the good of the treatment and the protection of the analysand's narcissism begins to look more like action motivated chiefly by Jacobs' struggle with his own competitiveness, leading us to wonder whether a less conflicted analyst might be relatively more inclined to enact his retaliatory impulses.[3]

It seems likely that Mr. V. sensed – consciously or unconsciously – Jacobs' disinclination to strike back, which could well have given the patient license to speak up just as he had – no holds barred! Alternately, had Mr. V. been in treatment with an analyst who was apt to push back when taken to task, the development of the manifest transference might have looked somewhat different. Had this been the case, Mr. V.'s core aggression might have been expressed in a less direct fashion – for example, through passive-aggressive channels – just so long as – *and this is essential* – Mr. V. was reasonably comfortable with, and could abide by, such *alternate* expressions of his aggression without feeling he'd been strong-armed into that position by the analyst. Such situations are unconsciously negotiated in the process of analysis on a regular basis. Alternately, if Mr. V. felt he was being forced to back down by the analyst's overly aggressive response, he might have felt he was being relegated to the position of "the one done to" (Benjamin, 2004), which could have led him to resist the role assignment. Another possibility has the analytic couple locking horns with neither party backing down, resulting either in the rupture of the therapeutic alliance or in a highly charged thrust in the therapeutic process that might prove productive to the extent the analytic couple struggles to work their way past the emerging power struggle. As can be seen, there are a number of different ways in which the situation could have played out *as a function* of the analyst's way of being.

Important implications of Jacobs' vignette

There are certain things worth noting about Jacobs' analysis of this clinical moment. To begin with, Jacobs had more than one countertransference reaction. His most immediate (core) reaction was an impulse to retaliate, to strike back by shaming the patient for having misquoted Emerson. This we might consider *countertransference proper*. In response to this initial reaction, Jacobs had a second *meta-reaction* – a reaction to his reaction. Jacobs was not one to experience retaliatory aggression without becoming deeply unsettled by such feelings, and it was this second countertransference reaction – his meta-reaction – that had been instrumental in determining whether his initial impulse to retaliate had a chance of becoming openly expressed. Just as patients have a core and a manifest transference, the same can be said of analysts, who have corresponding core and manifest countertransference reactions. In this particular case, Jacobs' core countertransference reaction, which most likely served as commentary about what was going on in his patient's mind, had been eclipsed by his meta-countertransference, which played a determining role in what became manifest.[4]

Jacobs does not consider the *content* of his meta-reaction to have been determined by the patient's behavior. He does not see it as having resulted from being assigned a role to play by the patient (Sandler, 1976a), nor does he believe it to be a response to the patient's transference expectations. He also fails to see his reaction as a manifestation of projective identification. While Jacobs admits he was triggered by the patient's provocative critique, how Jacobs *ends up* responding to Jacobs' way of thinking was *of Jacobs' own making* – a function of his one-person psychology. Jacobs takes responsibility for *what it is in him that is his*, rather than imagining he'd been "made" by the patient to react in this particular fashion. Accordingly, he does not believe his meta-reaction serves as commentary about what was going on in his patient's mind. And while Jacobs' behavior undoubtedly ends up contributing to the intersubjective field – the two-person psychology – it did not directly originate from that field, seeing that Jacobs considers his reaction as a manifestation of his *separable subjectivity*. Current trends that over-emphasize the two-person psychological perspective contribute to our forgetting we each bring our own psychologies – our separable subjectivities – to the consulting room independent of the analytic third that's constituted once the process gets underway. Diamond (2014) refers to these trends as a "rational turn," which some see as tantamount to a radical paradigmatic shift (Fabozzi, 2012; Pine, 2011).

What I am proposing by emphasizing the analyst's separable subjectivity is a focus on how the analyst feels about what's become stirred up in him (a *meta*-feeling) – whether he finds such psychic states, on an affective continuum, irresistible, highly pleasurable, a bit taxing though reasonably tolerable, emotionally inconsequential, disquieting, hard to live with, or completely unbearable. Trouble is likely to result on either end of the spectrum – when countertransference reactions are intensely positive or negative. How the analyst ends up interacting with an analysand is partly determined by where the analyst's meta-reactions lie on this continuum – how personally desirable, tolerable/manageable or intolerable his stirred-up internal state is tending to be. In turn, the shape that the analysand's transference assumes (how it manifests) is partly a function of whether the analyst's internal responses to the patient's emerging transference is *in concert with, or in opposition to* – is "conjunctive" or "disjunctive"[5] relative to the patient's way of being – what his behavior seems to be requiring of the analyst in terms of particular kinds of involvements and responses.

It is important to note that chronic countertransference enactments (Cassorla, 2012) may result when the analyst experiences intensely positive countertransference reactions in response to, for example, a particular role or attribution he's being assigned by the analysand – one that is welcomed by the analyst to the extent it is consistent with how he likes to or is inclined to think of himself. Acute enactments, on the other hand, are more likely to develop when the analyst experiences countertransference reactions that are so deeply disturbing as to result in a sudden and dramatic attempt to protest and/or break free of the assignment, attribution, or projection. Chronic enactments tend in general to be less dramatic and oftentimes, though not invariably, stem from positive countertransference reactions that, for whatever reason, are allowed to go unexamined. Sandler's (1976a) handing his patient tissues each time she cried comes to mind in this regard. It wasn't until Sandler *stopped* enacting such behavior that he and the analysand were able to make sense of what the two had together been enacting. An example of a chronic enactment stemming from intensely negative countertransference reaction is provided by Vida (2001), who describes how an analysand's tyrannical scorn, experienced by the analyst as "disruptions of terrifying magnitude" (p. 29), proved so intimidating that the analyst ultimately "said less and less and eventually became unable to free associate or even to think during her session" (p. 30).

The analyst's way of being

There are two essential points that have been made thus far about the analyst's way of being: the range of ways in which various analysts differentially respond to a given patient's way of being is *a function of the analyst's particular way of being*; and how a given analyst responds to a particular patient contributes to how the patient's transference takes shape. Analysts vary in their personal proclivity to "get into it" with patients by "taking the bait" – subtly slipping into a chronic enactment or more dramatically launching into a more active type of embroilment. Depending on the analyst's way of being, he may feel – along a continuum – resistant to, comfortable with, or desirous of opportunities to act on the impulse to explicitly vent his or her countertransference reactions. Analysts who are characterologically disinclined to engage in acute enactments may feel aghast at the prospect and may accordingly dedicate themselves to do whatever they can do to stave off certain calamity. Whether such anxiety prohibits such reluctant analysts from becoming sufficiently engaged with the patient is a question to be taken up at the end of the chapter. Analysts also vary with regard to how prone they are to feel as if they are "being made" by the patient to react in a given way. Some analysts feel as if the patient is "pushing their buttons," drawing them in, stimulating their emotions, limiting their range of options, and so on. Some feel they're being assigned a role that is personally repugnant – enough to "set them packing," metaphorically if not literally – a "disjunctive" experience that puts the patient's needs and those of the analyst at cross-purposes.

The analyst's *way of being* can also play a determining role in the sorts of *clinical interventions* he makes. Along these lines, Freud's own *way of being* figured heavily in his thoughts about how one goes about conducting an analysis, admitting his recommendations were "the only one[s] suited to my individuality," adding "a physician quite differently constituted might find himself driven to adopt a different attitude to his patients and to the task before him" (1912, p. 111). What a psychoanalyst sees as salient in the clinical material – be it a subtle shift in the analysand's associations, a slip of the tongue, the symbolic aspects of a dream, where his own reverie leads him, his countertransference reactions, the nature of the intersubjective field, and the like – might seem to be a function of that analyst's theoretical bent until one considers the possibility that an analyst gravitates to one theory over another not strictly, or even chiefly, because of the strength of the convincing arguments set forth in support of that theory so much as the analyst's personal psychology (Faimberg, 1992; Jacobs, 1986), a position some find unnerving to the extent they feel it undermines the scientific basis of psychoanalysis.

The varying dimensions of transference

The essence of transference was historically considered to be *perceptual* in nature: past experiences help determine how one presently sees, interprets, and/or experiences the actions and attitudes of others. The analysand scans the data emanating from the analyst, highlighting and overemphasizing the salient behaviors *most consistent* with what he anticipates finding. Psychoanalysts long ago came to the realization transference extended beyond a *readiness to perceive* and often manifests in the analysand's turning to the analyst to satisfy, or contain, certain of the analysand's wishes, needs, desires, or affect states. Accordingly, transference is not limited to perceiving the analyst as being like someone from one's past (the "old object"); it can also involve looking to the analyst to fill the shoes of a once *wished-for* parent (the "new object").

A two-person psychological perspective broadens our understanding of transference beyond the confines of the analysand's *perception* of the analyst or his *efforts to seek gratification* from the analyst. Here, I am thinking in terms of roles assigned by the patient to the analyst and the complementary roles assumed, in turn, by the patient.[6] For example, the analysand may assume the role originally played by the transference figure, resulting in his treating the analyst much as he'd been treated by the original object as a child ("identification with the aggressor"). This is but one of the varied ways roles are assigned and assumed. This two-person perspective draws our attention to how the analysand unconsciously *works to induce* the analyst to adopt a particular role, combined with how the analyst behaves in response as the two co-construct the resulting transference–countertransference configuration. The one-person psychological perspective, by contrast, focuses on each party's separable subjectivity – what it is they bring to the table in the way of personal, context-independent proclivities and resistances to react or resist in a particular fashion. Recognizing that neither the one- nor the two-person perspective can claim exclusivity, notes Benjamin (1995), requires we struggle with the tensions produced by having to keep both perspectives in mind, even though doing so can only be achievable sequentially if not simultaneously.

What's been laid out thus far is not new; it is generally understood and accepted, though some disagree with the extent to which the person of the analyst can affect the expression of the transference (Etchegoyen, 1991; Kernberg, 1993). What I wish to now add to the equation is the analyst's *unique affective response* to the experience of becoming stirred up in response to what is taking place in the consulting room – ranging from feeling that what he's feeling is desirable, on one end of the spectrum, to feeling it to be utterly intolerable, on the other end. Problems can develop on either end of the spectrum. How the analyst feels about what he's being "required" to experience by virtue of his involvement in the treatment – if not specifically required *by the patient* – has much to do with his own way of being. Following this reasoning, the analyst may end up realizing (or frustrating) the analysand's transference expectations by virtue of his willingness (or resistance) to behave in ways that roughly replicate those of an actual, or wished for, figure from the analysand's past. In this way, the analyst's behavior helps validate (or negate) the analysand's construction of the analyst as the process moves from perception into "actualization" (Chused, 1991; McLaughlin, 1991; Poland, 1992; Sandler, 1976b). In comparable fashion, the analyst may also gratify or frustrate the patient's efforts to draw him into an enactment, get him to accept a role assignment, or induce him to receive and contain his projections.

Progression in our understanding of countertransference

The evolution in our thinking about countertransference can be thought to have taken place in three successive stages. The first stage occurred halfway through the last century with the publication of papers by Heimann (1950) and Racker (1957) that together helped redefine countertransference as an essential clinical tool rather than a bothersome impediment to the work. Heimann (1950) argued:

> ...the emotions roused in [the analyst] are much nearer to the heart of the matter than his reasoning, or, to put it in other words, his unconscious

perception of the analysand's unconscious is more acute and *in advance* of his conscious conception of the situation. (pp. 82, italics added)

After stating as much, Heimann went a step further by declaring the analyst's countertransference to be "*the patient's creation*, it is a part of the patient's personality" (p. 83, italics added), moving into theoretical territory many consider problematic to the extent such thinking fails to consider the analyst's separable subjectivity – the "hook" (Gabbard, 1995; Stanicke & Killingmo, 2013; Westen & Gabbard, 2002) within the analyst upon which the analysand's projection could be hung.

Racker's (1957) contribution to our understanding of countertransference chiefly involves his introduction of two contrasting terms – *complementary* and *concordant* – for differentiating two types of countertransference reactions.[7] *Complementary reactions* are defined as those involving the analyst being seen by the analysand as being like the original object, leading to the analyst feeling and/or reacting in kind *in accordance with this perception-interpretation*, potentially stimulating him to adopt the corresponding counter-role that "plays against" the role assumed by the patient. By contrast, *concordant reactions* are characterized by the analyst "identifying" with the analysand's situation, resulting in an empathic response to the analysand's experience.

We've now arrived at one of the chief goals of this chapter – a proposed refinement of Racker's definition of complementarity based on the analyst's level of comfort or discomfort with what's become stirred up in him as he goes about treating the patient. With role responsiveness (Sandler, 1976a) as the model, to the extent the analyst's and the analysand's assigned and assumed roles more or less *comfortably complement* one another (are affectively acceptable to both parties), one would call the complementary relationship *conjunctive*. By contrast, *disjunctive* relationships are those in which the roles assigned prove personally repugnant to one or both parties (Faimberg, 1992), being unacceptable in that they feel alien to one's general way of being (Benjamin, 2004). Under such conditions, the situation may feel non-negotiable, thus jeopardizing the ongoing viability of the analysis. Mermelstein (2000) notes "complementarity becomes problematic when the perceptions and organizing schema of both participants are diametrically opposed, reciprocally threatening the other's functioning, and cannot be easily reconciled" (p. 726).

If the analyst doesn't welcome what's become stirred up in him as he interacts with the patient, he may work to counter its effect. For example, if the analyst detests the role into which he feels he's being implicitly drawn, he may bristle and resist the role assignment, not realizing he's doing as much until after the fact. To the extent the analyst begins to experience, while interacting with an analysand, highly unpleasurable internal stirrings (affects, memories, thoughts), the resulting countertransference reaction is disjunctive and may result in the analyst strongly rejecting the role he feels he's being assigned, traits or characteristics the patient attributes to him that he finds repugnant, and/or the projections he feels he's being asked to receive and contain. For example, feeling controlled by the pressures brought to bear for him to adopt a personally repugnant role assignment could result in the analyst's conscious or, more likely, unconscious efforts to turn the tables to show the analysand "who's boss" – taking charge of the interaction and imposing an agenda of his own that dictates how he and the analysand are to be relating to one another, preempting the analysand who, the analyst feels, was trying to do likewise – a battle over who is to be "the doer" and who's to end up "the one done to" (Benjamin, 2004).

The second stage in the evolution of our thinking about countertransference, which furthered our thinking about the analysand's impact on the analyst, occurred in the mid-1970s to 1980s. Sandler (1976a) noted how he'd sometimes *find himself* (that's the operative phrase) unwittingly acting in ways with certain analysands that were uncharacteristic of him for reasons that escaped him. Jacobs (1986) went a step further by exploring how particular factors in his own background led him to engage with the analysand in "an enactment." Of import is the fact that Jacobs did not believe his analysands were motivated by a wish *to cause* him to think or feel what it was Jacobs ended up thinking or feeling, placing him on the same page with Sandler (1976a), who did not see role responsiveness as a function of the analysand's efforts to foist a role upon the analyst but, instead, saw it as "a function of the analyst's receptivity, not of the analysand's unconscious intention, and should not be regarded as projective identification, as something that the analysand wants to 'put into' the analyst" (Sandler, 1993, p. 1105). Again, we see both these authors insisting on their separable subjectivities, rather than conceptualizing themselves as if psychologically yoked to the patient's efforts to "make them" feel certain things, do certain things, have certain memories, and so on.

Since Jacobs introduced the term in the mid-1980s, the concept of enactments has increasingly been referenced and utilized in order to understand clinical material. As noted by Bohleber et al. (2013) in their sweeping overview of the subject, "the term 'enactment' is here to stay" (p. 509). This does not mean, however, that all agree about what the term means or what light it might shed on the patient's psyche. Bohleber et al. (2013) offer a serviceable definition of the phenomenon:

> Enactment involves a collapse in the analytic dialogue in which the analyst is drawn into an interaction where he unwittingly acts, thereby actualizing unconscious wishes of both himself and the patient. This collapse implies disturbance of the symbolic function; something emerges that at the moment of enactment is not accessible by language. What follows this moment will determine whether the enactment will have therapeutic value, that is, whether the symbolic function will be restored and integrative work can or cannot happen. (p. 517)

Enactment is thought to involve a loss of analytic capacity on the analyst's part, in reaction to instances when the patient's verbalizations are "meant *to do something or bring something about* rather than communicating something" (Busch, 2009, p. 55, italics added).

A final stage in the evolution of our thinking about countertransference, evidenced in Aron's (1996) concept of "mutuality," pictures analyst and analysand reciprocally influencing one another in a circular, back-and-forth, chicken-or-egg fashion, making it nearly impossible to make out whose behavior set the wheels in motion in the first place. Many favor this model not only because it emphasizes mutual influence, but also because it makes room for the possibility that roles might be assigned by the analyst to the analysand just as they are assigned by the analysand to the analyst.

Clinical illustrations

Let's begin by considering two clinical examples where the transference needs of the patient proved deeply unsettling for the analyst and, accordingly, were disjunctive relative to the patient's needs. In the first abstracted example, the patient's transference involves seeing the analyst as someone incapable of understanding what the analysand is going through (see Joseph, 1985). In this particular case, what the patient was expecting and/or needing from the analyst was that he play the part, or "wear the attribution" (Lichtenberg, Lachmann, & Fosshage, 1992, 1996) of "the one who will never understand," playing against the patient's role of "the one who will never be understood." Feeling trapped within the assigned role of "the one who can't understand" – at a loss as to how to extricate himself from having to live out that role – would likely prove unsettling for any analyst, though *more so* for analysts who pride themselves on their ability to help their analysands feel understood – underscoring the role that the analyst's separable subjectivity plays in leading him to react to the patient in ways that may influence how the transference ends up manifesting. Interpreting to the patient his expectation/need to have an analyst who *does not and cannot understand* is a kind of understanding in and of itself and accordingly may be likewise disallowed by the analysand who wants nothing to do with the analyst's efforts to prove he does, in fact, understand – motivated, in part, by his need to feel it is so. Under such conditions, it might be in the best interest of the treatment to accept, at least for the time being, the role of "the one who can't understand," which the analyst will only be able to do to the extent this role is on the *conjunctive end* of the conjunctive–disjunctive spectrum. Doing so, paradoxically, might be the sole way in which one might actually demonstrate understanding.

Other analysts have provided examples of how they'd come to experience aversive states in the process of treating particular kinds of patients. Steiner (2000) presents two cases in which the patients themselves "created states of discord [disjunctions] that left me confused and uncertain and sometimes led me to try to provide meaning that would make sense of the confusion and *reduce my anxiety*" (p. 246, italics added). Note the use of language – it was the patients who created Steiner's internal state – placing responsibility for what had gotten stirred up in him squarely on the patient's shoulders. Also note Steiner's admission that his enactment was in the service of making himself more comfortable – moving him closer from the disjunctive to the conjunctive end of the spectrum. McLaughlin (1991) describes a similar countertransference reaction in which his patient's behaviors:

> ...left me repeatedly in states of futility and bewilderment, doubting my capacities to see anything clearly about her or to articulate effectively. I took myself to task for my ineptitude and felt helpless and angry...her behaviors effectively pressured me to experience these affects *as my own* with an intensity I found unusually painful. (p. 604, italics added)

In both these clinical instances, the ways in which these patients related to the analyst is conceptualized by these authors in terms of projective identification, where something is done to one by another, where the pressure from the patient creates in the analyst a narcissistic imbalance (Ellman, 2010) sufficient to cause him to act in accordance with the pressures the patient is bringing to bear to promote action rather than containment by adopting a particular role, actualizing a particular transference expectation (Sandler, 1976b), or engaging in a particular type of enactment.

The second example of disjunctive intersubjectivity is that of Mr. R., a retired, married man about twenty years my senior who was referred to me after a lengthy treatment with another clinician had "petered out." He presented with depression and intermittent suicidal impulses, complaining that "no one gives a shit about me, including myself." Though he'd received considerable professional recognition in his field, this did little to bolster his self-esteem. While he felt quite needy of praise from others, his neediness typically met with impatience from others who felt imposed upon by the patient's incessant demands they provide an audience for him to impress with his most recent, praiseworthy project.

The patient's father sent mixed messages – he cherished his son yet denigrated him as incapable of achieving much in life, leaving the patient to feel he could not rely on himself and accordingly needed others "over" him to tell him what to do. By contrast, the patient presented his mother as a ghostly figure – someone who was in the background and was relatively inconsequential in his early development.

For several months, the patient's behavior stimulated something in me that led me to play the role of the mirroring parent who'd "ooh and aah" over his display of a recent invention or his considerable knowledge about a wide variety of topics. Then, several months into the treatment, the patient began a session by noting that the fichus tree in my office was shedding leaves, using this observation as an opportunity to instruct me about how best to care for the plant. He told me that I should turn it so the unexposed side could get more light, and he suggested a watering schedule that was best suited for the plant. I understood these to be metaphoric references to his feeling I'd been inattentive to him, but before that could be addressed, something intervened that got us on an entirely different track.

As the patient went about educating me about indoor gardening, I found myself growing irritated. I wasn't aware of the fact at first until I suddenly stated after the patient completed his "lecture": "You know, I've had that plant for over twenty years!" The moment those words left my tongue, I had a sinking feeling, aghast at what I'd just said. It was a simple statement, but its meaning was not lost on the patient. The following session, we had a chance to return to the event when the patient noted upon entering the room that I'd tended to the tree, which I had in fact neglected. Admitting to having heeded his advice was driven by my guilt and a wish to somehow "make up" for having responded to him in the fashion I had – another enactment.

I came to realize my feelings about having the patient educate me about plants could be expressed in this fashion: "Who do you think you are, coming in here and treating me as if I am some sort of naive imbecile who doesn't know the first thing about plants? Let me tell you something, buddy. I have had this plant for twenty years. Did you hear that? *Twenty years!* Doesn't that say *something* about my abilities as a gardener? Do you think you could keep a plant alive for twenty years? *Huh, pops?*" Naturally, none of this was ever said to the patient, though my irritation provided us an opportunity to analyze what had been going on in the room unbeknownst to either of us.

The patient had a father, not unlike my own, who could be discounting of his son's abilities. This led to an interesting situation, for neither the patient nor I was anxious to play the part of the imbecilic child. At the point he chose to "educate" me or, alternately, to show off how much he knew about yet another in a string of topics, I experienced the patient as treating me as his father had treated him and as my father had treated me. I was determined to have no part of this, and spoke up to "set the record straight." If I was being assigned the role of imbecilic child to play against the patient's role of all-knowing father, I wasn't buying. Something had to give!

But was this, in fact, what the patient intended for me to feel? All I knew at this juncture was that I had ceased to play the role of the father who marveled at his son's achievements and wealth of knowledge. The idea that the patient had unconsciously intended to treat me as his father had treated him was a distinct possibility. But it seemed just as possible that his unconscious wish was for me to continue to play the role of admiring father rather than experiencing his "lesson" as I had – as an effort to make me feel like an imbecile, just as his father had made him feel. Whichever the case, my own separable subjectivity had something to say about the matter, intruding in the way it had for reasons that were, at that moment, more driven by my own personal issues than by my continued availability to respond in kind to what it was the patient was trying to say or accomplish with me at that moment in time. While, on one level, the patient's intention may well have chiefly been aimed at my continuing to admire him for being knowledgeable, he ended up getting more than he'd bargained for. Had I not had the type of father I had, I might have been better positioned to continue to play the role of admirer that could serve as someone who could mirror back to the patient a view of himself as wonderfully capable and extraordinarily knowledgeable. But another aspect of my subjectivity emerged. As a result, I ceased to be in conjunctive harmony with the patient. What I wanted was off this train! In contrast with the case of Ted Jacobs and Mr. V., in which the core countertransference impulse to retaliate seemed to serve as commentary about what was going on in the patient's psyche, in this particular instance my core countertransference reaction seems to have been more of his own making.

Let's consider another of Jacobs' (1986) clinical vignettes – this time one that illustrates conjunctive rather than disjunctive complementarity, which resulted in a more insidious, chronic enactment. Jacobs found his patient, Mr. K., *so* captivating that his mind never wandered once as it typically would from time to time with other analysands. Jacobs found this curious, ultimately leading him to realize the autobiographical basis of this "enactment." As it turns out, Mr. K.'s propensity to be "a captivating orator" ostensibly "transported" Jacobs back to a time he'd been sitting at the dinner table listening in awe as his father held forth on any number of topics as young Ted sat transfixed. "It was his show," writes Jacobs, "and if I spoke at all it was simply to ask for more details – the equivalent of my interventions years later with my analysand…[whose] transference wish [was] for me to play the role of appreciative audience" (p. 295).

Jacobs's revelation raises an interesting question that highlights the central thesis of the chapter. While certain aspects of his experience with Mr. K. may have felt disjunctive to Jacobs, on balance, the prevailing sense of his experience was chiefly conjunctive. We might wonder how Mr. K.'s co-constructed transference might have manifested had he been in treatment with a different sort of analyst – one, for example, who felt he was being asked to play a role he found personally offensive (an example of disjunctive complementarity). It seems easy to imagine such an analyst experiencing, for example, competitive strivings to prove that he, too, had much worth hearing, interrupting the patient's tendencies to "hold forth" in order to get a word in edgewise.

Discussion

What has been proposed in this chapter is a further subdivision of Racker's (1957) complementary type of countertransference reaction into conjunctive and disjunctive subtypes based on the degree to which the analyst's internal state, in response to how the patient is behaving, is – along a continuum from highly pleasurable, to tolerable/manageable, to utterly intolerable. Conjunctive reactions are those the analyst can more or less bear and may even take pleasure in experiencing. Conjunctive reactions that are highly pleasurable may give rise to subtle, chronic enactments. Disjunctive reactions, on the other hand, can prove quite aversive and may trigger active efforts on the analyst's part to fight off such feelings. Whether the analyst's countertransference reaction, on balance, leans more heavily in one direction or the other plays a determining role in: (1) his openness to accept the analysand's "role assignment"; (2) his comfort living with, rather than immediately challenging, the analysand's transference-based beliefs about who the patient believes the analyst to be ("wearing the attribution"); (3) his personal predisposition and availability to engage with the patient in an enactment; and (4) his willingness and ability to receive and contain the patient's projections. Whether the analyst is comfortable, open, and available to participate with the analysand in these varied ways – in our proposed terminology, whether his countertransference reactions are more conjunctive than disjunctive – can have tremendous clinical consequences.

A final point I wish to make has to do with the question of whether the pendulum has swung too far in the direction of over-privileging countertransference enactments as the quintessential mutative therapeutic maneuver bar none. This brings us full circle to the vignette presented at the beginning of this chapter: Jacobs' treatment of Mr. V. – the patient who was acerbically critical of Jacobs' new office. In a paper I'd submitted for publication to a leading psychoanalytic journal, I cited Jacobs' case and wrote that I regarded Jacobs' reticence to react when provoked to be a sign of good psychoanalytic technique.[8] To my surprise, two of the three reviewers begged to differ – expressing the opinion that Jacobs had, in fact, robbed the analysand of a potentially mutative experience by failing to allow himself to become more reactively engaged with the analysand. This struck me as odd and led me to consider how far the pendulum had swung from one extreme to the other – from the condemnation of countertransference as a serious impediment to the treatment to a celebration of the countertransference enactment as *the* preeminent mutative event. The opinions of these reviewers, in conjunction with those expressed by various authors (Boesky, 1990; Heimann, 1950; Renik, 1993, 1996; Whitaker & Malone 1953), illustrate how the overvaluing of enactments has gone so far as to lead some to fault analysts who are *characterologically disinclined* to succumb to the urge to act, as was the case with Jacobs in his treatment of Mr. V.,[9] seeing such a "resistance" to enact as tantamount to a refusal to engage the patient. I consider this to be a most unfortunate development. The reviewers who'd insisted it would have been better had Jacobs "hauled off" and "let the analysand have it" in the name of enactment for the sake of the treatment were *ignoring the simple fact that this is not who Jacobs is* – an aspect of his way of being, his separable subjectivity, as seen from a one-person psychological perspective, which fails to take into consideration the analyst's irreducible subjectivity, which can neither be eliminated nor denied (Renik, 1993). Such matters are the sort that caused Diamond (2014) to counsel "caution in today's more exaggerated weighing of here-and-now transference interpretations, with its focus on *process* often replacing rather than supplementing the significance of unconscious content" (p. 544).

One's attitude about a given analyst's inclination or disinclination to become "embroiled" in an acute enactment varies depending on one's stance about such matters. Analysts vary to the extent they are susceptible to "regressions to less evolved perceptiveness in consequence of the stirring in him of old and only partially mastered conflicts" (McLaughlin, 1991, p. 600). Some seem more inclined to slip into acute enactments, others less so – though all are susceptible to lapsing unwittingly into chronic enactments. Whether one judges analysts who are more inclined to jump into the fray and actively enact as reckless – as *insufficiently cautious* – or, alternately, as having sufficient faith in their ability to regain their analytic footing whenever they momentarily lose their capacity to contain and reflect, makes a great deal of difference in one's attitude about such practices. The same can be said looking from the opposite direction – faulting analysts who are less inclined to engage in acute enactments as being overly intellectualizing and hence emotionally unavailable to their patients.

"The question of how to understand and use the meaning of the analyst's inner experience remains controversial," notes Diamond (2014, p. 541). One consideration is the fact that there is something romantic in the notion of intersubjectivity as it seems to be seen by some – which is very much at odds with Benjamin's (1995) perspective on the matter that underscores the analyst's separable subjectivity. The notion that we are connected to one another to such a remarkable degree that whatever happens in one person makes *direct reference to* (is commentary on) what is going on in the other's mind may be overstating the case. For example, Ogden (1997) writes:

> …as personal and private as our reveries feel to us, it is misleading to view them as "our" personal creations, since reverie is at the same time an aspect of a jointly (but asymmetrically) created unconscious intersubjective construction that I have termed "the intersubjective analytic third." (p. 569)

Seeing one's psychic wanderings as *inevitably* tied to what is going on in the patient denies the analyst's separable subjectivity and may be used in the service of relieving one's guilt that one's been "asleep at the wheel" when one ought to have been carefully attending to material that *can be shown* to be relevant to the patient, rather than tending to one's separable subjectivity. It is both appealing and reassuring to think that whatever becomes stirred up in the analyst's psyche must serve as commentary about the patient's state of mind, since such thinking helps lessen the sense of isolation and aloneness that is part and parcel of the human condition. But envisioning the analyst's reveries, affect states, evoked memories, and countertransference reactions as *invariably syncing* with what is emanating from the patient – and providing commentary about it – seems to me to be akin to the ideal, highly attuned mother–infant state of symbiotic union (Tower. 1956).[10] Some of the analyst's countertransference reactions are undeniably "about" the patient's current psychic condition; some are not. Leaving room for both possibilities is essential to the success of the psychoanalytic process.

Notes

1 Quoted in print twenty-nine times to date (the Psychoanalytic Electronic Press), and frequently often heard during paper presentations at analytic meetings.
2 A careful reading of Boesky's paper indicates this quote is taken out of context, seeing that Boesky doesn't mean to imply that an enactment, in and of itself, could be considered mutative. Rather, it is essential to recognize the analyst's inevitable, inadvertent contribution to the patient's resistance, which sooner or later must be faced if treatment is to progress toward a successful conclusion.
3 I am not implying that all who are comfortable with their aggression will necessarily act on those impulses, only that being more comfortable with one's aggression moves one *in that direction*, if not over the line.
4 Not to imply Mr. V. would not have been able to sense a stifled impulse to retaliate – only to note that a directly expressed and a stifled reaction will contribute differently to helping mold the patient's manifest transference.
5 Following a distinction drawn by Atwood and Stolorow (1984).
6 And vice versa (Ellman, 2010; McLaughlin, 1991) – seeing that role assignment does not issue strictly from the side of the patient.
7 It is worth noting that sharp distinctions necessitated for the purpose of illustration leave one with the impression that such thinking reflects reality when, in fact, such dichotomies are only drawn for the sake of the discussion and, in fact, are misrepresentations of reality, which does not in the final analysis permit such simplification. This issue arises time and again in our literature. It deserves notice, though it is inevitably insurmountable.
8 Granted, I had at that moment overlooked his personal reasons for having acted as he had.
9 In fact, Jacobs' inactivity, under the circumstances, could equally be considered an enactment of another sort.
10 While I have no doubt whatsoever that Ogden is capable of using reverie in the most productive fashion, I for one have not been able to use my own reverie in this way, and in my discussions with others, I have found that most have a comparable difficulty employing reverie in the way Ogden does.

Chapter 4

Questioning the analyst's use of authority

For better and for worse

Over the course of the last quarter century, many psychoanalysts have questioned whether the benefits associated with their use of authority in the clinical setting outweigh the attendant risks. Concerns abound regarding the analyst's *general* use of authority – taking advantage of the power tilt that results when patients regress – in order to influence the mind of the analysand and encourage change. Concerns also center on the analyst's *claim* to be authoritatively knowledgeable about the workings of patients' minds by virtue of (1) an ability to be objective and (2) knowledge of the unconscious workings of the mind, acquired through personal experience, clinical experience, and professional training. Such a claim underlies the analyst's presentation of interpretations as authoritative.

Arguably, the psychoanalytic process is fueled by the power tilt between patient and analyst, which is the result of techniques – gratifying attentiveness mixed with a modicum of abstinence – that foster regression. This regression contributes in turn to the creation of a relationship that replicates crucial aspects of the patient's relationship with his or her parents during childhood. The analyst's genuine concern and encouragement stimulate the patient's love for the analyst. During the course of psychoanalysis, the analyst's encouragement (subtly transmitted as "I know you can do it!") takes on new meaning and comes to matter a great deal to the patient. The analyst's palpable concern (referred to by some as the analyst's "love") serves to heighten the analyst's influence over the patient. Under such conditions, maintaining the analyst's love becomes an important factor in psychoanalysis – so important, in fact, that it offers opportunities for the analyst to take unfair advantage of the patient.

Though some might consider change under such conditions a transference cure – yet another manifestation of the analyst's use (or abuse) of authority – others are not so quick to dismiss such influence as mere manipulation. Freud (1916) wrote of how the analyst "makes use of one of the components of love" (p. 312) to help patients come to terms with the reality principle. "Love is the great educator," he wrote, "and it is by the love of those nearest to him that the incomplete human being is induced to respect the decrees of necessity and to spare himself the punishment that follows any infringement of them" (p. 312).

Beyond this worry that the analyst will take unfair advantage of the power tilt to influence patients, exception is taken by some to the analytic practice of presenting interpretations as authoritative. The fear is that they might be heard as an assertion of what is "really" going on in the patient's mind and that this might cause patients to feel that their own understanding has been dismissed and replaced by the superior understanding of the analyst. Perceiving the analyst's interpretations in this light can be the result of a patient's having had parents who perpetually promoted their views as more reality-based than those of their child. But it could also stem from the analyst's narcissistic or philosophical need to have interpretations validated by the patient, which could occasion a resort to authoritarian maneuvers to ensure that the analyst's view prevails (Poland, 1984). It is this prospect that has some analysts worried.

Yet another source of concern regarding the analyst's claim to be authoritatively knowledgeable about the patient's mind is the implication that the analyst knows the patient's mind better than the patient does (Gill, 1979; Kohut, 1984; Schwaber, 1983). Renik (1993) has questioned whether this is possible given the analyst's "irreducible subjectivity," which, he argues, irreparably contaminates the analyst's efforts to be objective about patients. Others (e.g., Mayer, 1996) have gone so far as to declare the impossibility of ever arriving at any conclusion regarding the patient that would justify being called "objective," given the postmodern philosophical position that truth is indeterminable.

Such concerns have led some analysts to wonder whether the analyst's use of authority has proven so problematic as to justify a shift in analytic technique away from encouraging regression and offering interpretations. By creating a more egalitarian treatment environment, emphasizing the authority of the patient's subjective experience (Schwaber, 1996), privileging the patient's interpretations over those of the analyst (Roughton, 1994), and being more self-disclosing in the analysis (Renik, 1995; Shane, Shane, & Gales 1997), these analysts hope to circumvent the problems associated with the use of authority. Henry Friedman (2000) has argued that by optimally providing for the patient's needs, one can avoid regression and so eliminate the depth of desire that can only result in the patient becoming hopelessly frustrated. Such thinking suggests that patients need not be punished for infringing on the "decrees of necessity," as Freud had suggested, because such boundaries cease to be erected in analyses conducted by analysts who take care to minimize frustration.

There has also been a shift away from articulating one's interpretations about the workings of the patient's mind and toward the more subjective tasks of emotional attunement and immersion in the intersubjective field (e.g., Stolorow, Brandchaft, & Atwood 1987). Some express concern that the interpretive process may too often reflect theoretically based preconceptions about what the analyst can expect to find. This concern has led some analysts (e.g., Schwaber, 1992a, 1992b) to urge their colleagues to resist the inclination to organize material along familiar, preconceived lines. Concern has been expressed also about the use of "experience-distant" interpretations that lack emotional immediacy and relevance to patients' lives. The interpretive process has also been criticized as flawed due to its being hopelessly contaminated by the analyst's irreducible subjectivity (Renik, 1993). For analysts sharing such concerns, the task of making the unconscious conscious has given way to a different agenda, one that places the analyst's subjectivity squarely in the center of the treatment.

I believe that the current tendency to shrink from a reliance on one's authority, whether through attempts to lessen the power tilt or by downplaying the role of interpretation, does not adequately address the concerns that have been raised. To begin with, it seems unlikely, given the clear difference in needs brought to the consulting room by patient and analyst, that one could ever establish an even playing field. Further, while some analysts may think it preferable to downplay their authority, this does not stop patients from continuing to view the analyst as someone who knows better. As for attempts to leave one's theoretical baggage at the consulting room door, as well intentioned as such efforts might seem, it is impossible for analysts to set aside their theoretical preconceptions to see things strictly from the patient's perspective. Just as the analyst's subjectivity is inherently irreducible, so too is the analyst's tendency to organize data along certain predetermined lines. To think otherwise is to deny the innate operations of the human mind.

Discounting the analyst's authoritative knowledge about the patient threatens to rob the analyst of the leverage needed to facilitate change. When analysts come to regard their understandings of patients' lives and minds as lacking authority and, as a result, shy away from offering their interpretations to patients, they are on the verge of abdicating their responsibility to provide a different perspective for their patients' consideration (Raphling, 1992). Rather than bending over backward to avoid being experienced as imposing our constructs on patients, we are better off admitting that we rely on our authority when we use covert measures designed to ensure that patients are made ready to consider alternative ways of understanding themselves. In this I agree with Hoffman (1996). Rather than apologize for the ways in which analysts use their authority to manipulate patients, we should admit that we use our authority in just this way.

Problematic aspects of regression and the power tilt

In certain ways, the relationship between analyst and patient replicates that of parent and child, thus furthering the analyst's role as an authority. The analyst's single-minded attentiveness gratifies the patient in ways reminiscent of very early childhood experiences, or, if the patient did not experience such attentiveness during childhood, it reawakens unconscious childhood wishes for that gratification. The regression set in motion by the analyst's attentiveness is furthered by a degree of abstinence that stimulates frustrations similar to those the patient endured in childhood.

Though some take issue with the techniques of abstinence and neutrality, on the grounds that they result in a level of regression that is iatrogenically disorganizing rather than clinically productive (Renik, 1998b), it is my belief that every analysis inevitably runs up against a boundary that sets the analytic relationship apart from what it could otherwise be, were it permitted to run its course based on the intimacy, tenderness, and caring that characterize most analytic relationships.

How does this regressive process develop? Hoffman (1996) notes that Freud (1916) understood analysts were "in the position of a particular kind of authority, an intimate, loving authority that has continuity with the kind of authority that parents have in the lives of their children" (p. 1160). Lawrence Friedman (1997) contends that psychoanalytic technique is "seductive" (p. 26) insofar as it "court[s] a personal, affective intimacy" with patients (p. 25). This seduction derives its power from "an arrangement whereby the patient is led to expect love [because of]...the analyst's special interest, his constant, exclusive selfless attentiveness" (p. 26). But instead of love, the analyst provides something different in its place. The analyst's authority is made apparent when he or she uncovers what the patient wants (limitless love) yet delivers what, in the analyst's estimation, is in the patient's better interest, an empathic understanding of the patient's internal condition.

The resulting regression affects both the operations of the ego – formal regression – and the patient's object relations. Cognitive (formal) regression facilitates analysis by rendering the patient receptive to interpretations other than those to which he or she has been wedded. There are times, however, when this regressive process gets out of hand and can lead the patient back to a time of great impressionability, of doubt regarding one's perceptions and constructions, and of uncritical acceptance of the views of adults, who "obviously know best." This cognitive regression is reinforced by regression in the patient's object relations, which results in the re-emergence of childhood needs, wishes, and drives, and leads typically both to an idealization of the analyst as omniscient and to a wish to do whatever it takes to win the analyst's love.

Regression endangers the patient's ability to judge ideas independently of the patient's emotional attachment to the person offering them. The more regressed the patient, the greater the tendency to incorporate indiscriminately the analyst's ideas in place of the patient's own. Being open to the consideration of a viewpoint alternative to one's own can prove pivotal to a patient's growth. But if the alternative viewpoint is accepted on faith, rather than on its merits – if the patient blindly accepts the analyst's ideas out of fear or idealization, to satisfy the analyst's narcissism by submissively accepting them in the hope of winning the analyst's love – the patient and the analysis are in trouble.[1] Such are the real dangers of psychoanalytically induced cognitive regression. And these dangers are not limited to analyses conducted by analysts who need the personal validation of having their ideas confirmed by patients. Even well-meaning analysts who remain vigilant to such dangers may fall prey to the covert needs of some patients to have their minds made up for them. It is these very concerns that have led some analysts to modify their technique in the hope of avoiding these consequences.

Problematic aspects of interpretation

The main instrument of influence for many analysts is their interpretation of the patient's inner life: the patient's wishes and fears, conflicts and compromises, and ways of organizing understandings of interpersonal interactions in accordance with certain predetermined expectations as to how a relationship will unfold. The process of offering interpretations to patients has been criticized on the grounds that the resulting interpretation may be: (1) nothing more than the analyst's preconceived notion of what he or she expected to find; (2) overintellectualized, theoretically based, and therefore experience-distant; and (3) too contaminated by the analyst's subjectivity to be a truly objective construction of the patient's situation.

Preconceived notions: the Procrustean bed argument

Learning through experience leads to the creation of personal theories that direct the human mind to scan the environment for signs that suggest recognizable patterns, ones the individual has previously encountered. This is as much the basis of transference as it is the root of the analyst's tendency to meet clinical material with a prepared mind (Schafer, 1996). The human mind is geared to organize perceived data in accordance with these preconceived expectations (Edelman, 1987). Though many analysts try hard to keep their minds open to potential encounters with completely novel dynamics, it is almost always the case that clinical material becomes assimilated (in the Piagetian sense) into the analyst's preconceived ideas, determined by a set of theories, of what he or she expects to find. As hard as some analysts try to create a theory-free treatment environment, such efforts are doomed to failure.

I believe it is the exception when psychoanalysts accommodate (again, in the Piagetian sense) to the patient's novel material by perceiving it as novel and by developing a completely new theory to account for it. Even a theory that addresses a patient's expectation that he or she will feel misperceived as a result of the analyst's inability to shake off the habit of relying on theory-based expectations is neither theory-free nor novel. Sometimes the most an analyst can do in response to a patient's complaint that the analyst seems to be trying to fit the patient into the analyst's theoretical Procrustean bed is to admit guilt and recommit to the task of neutrality by keeping this in mind (for an example, see Renik, 1998b). Surprisingly, this willingness to genuinely accept the patient's objections and concede the point is often sufficiently novel to satisfy the patient and yield real change. This is so even though the analyst may never be able to completely rectify the tendency to assimilate material into his theories rather than accommodate to the material by changing his beliefs. It can be argued, however, that analysis has a more potent effect when the analyst is open to being taught something by the patient, so that the mutative process becomes truly mutual. It can further be argued that the mutual effect each party has on the other may ultimately make it easier for the patient to tolerate the unrectifiable inequalities inherent to the psychoanalytic situation.

Experience-distant interpretations

Among the most frequently criticized types of interpretation are those deemed too intellectual to reach down and arouse a visceral reaction in the patient, and too theoretically based and experience-distant to make much affective sense to the patient. It is necessary to digress by reviewing the history of psychoanalytic treatment in order to understand how interpretations have evolved to the point where they are at risk of being too intellectualized and experience-distant. Freud's initial model of therapeutic action – abreaction – was anything but intellectualized, over-theoretical, or experience-distant. Accessing strangulated affects by retrieving repressed reminiscences produced dramatic results. And though some patients still hope to experience just such an effect at the outset of treatment, psychoanalysis as conducted today typically does not resemble this version of therapy.

Freud gradually shifted his therapeutic focus away from the abreaction that accompanies retrieval of repressed reminiscences and turned his attention to the reconstruction of the patient's childhood experience:

> The path that starts out from the analyst's constructions ought to end in the patient's recollection; but it does not always lead so far. Quite often we do not succeed in bringing the patient to recollect what has been repressed. Instead of that, if the analysis is carried out correctly, we produce in him an *assured conviction* of the truth of the construction which achieves the same therapeutic result as a recaptured memory. (Freud, 1937, pp. 265–266, italics added)

Thinking in terms of "assured conviction" shifts the psychoanalytic endeavor into the realm of convincing the patient on the basis of what Schafer (1996) calls the best-grounded assertions "that lead the co-participants to durable, rational, and useful agreement on evidential matters" (p. 236). Thinking in these terms clearly leads us back to the issue of the analyst's use of authority – in particular, the authority to interpret. The type of analysis Schafer is describing is a far cry from that characterizing the earliest stages of psychoanalysis. If taken to an extreme, the earlier approach can lead to a straw-man caricature such as the one Wheelis (1973) provides:

> When in therapy a life story is examined in such a way that what the patient knows and feels, what he remembers and can reason from, is systematically discounted, while significant causality is located only in those unconscious forces postulated by the therapist...in all this one is rewriting the past, is taking a story which must have contained elements of freedom and responsibility and retelling it in terms only of causes lying outside awareness and hence beyond control, so teaching the patient to see himself as the passive product of inscrutable forces. (p. 113)

If what Wheelis describes in any way resembles what actually happens during an analysis, it is not surprising that many analysts have taken steps to ensure that the analyses they conduct are relevant, psychologically meaningful, and emotionally immediate by grounding the experience in the here-and-now affective interchange between analyst and patient. The result that is sought is represented by Coburn (2001), who writes of the need to help patients develop a "sense of the real – not to be confused with a belief or a faith in what is real, *but the lived experience of something being real*" (p. 2, italics added).

The authority to know the patient's mind: the objectivity debate

The concept of psychoanalytic objectivity has been hotly debated of late. Renik (1993) argues that psychoanalytic interpretations, given the irreducible limitation of the analyst's blinding subjectivity, cannot possibly capture anything "objective" about the patient's mental life. Renik (1995) challenges us to consider the following question: "When the analyst looks inside, how is it that the analyst sees a re-creation of the patient's infantile life, rather than the analyst's own experiences?" (p. 470).

Adherents of intersubjectivity theory, two-person psychology, and self psychology are among those most inclined to challenge the analyst's claim to enjoy "privileged access" to knowledge about a patient's mind. Stolorow (1988) takes issue with what he regards as the pervasive, unchallenged psychoanalytic assumption that such a thing as "objective reality" exists, and that the analyst is in a better position than the patient to know this objective reality, in that the analyst is better able to be neutral toward what is encountered in the patient. As Renik (1993) notes, "the fact that we still use the term *interpretation* would seem to indicate the extent to which we retain a conception of analytic technique as potentially objective, rather than inherently subjective" (p. 559). Citing the analyst's irreducible and insurmountable subjectivity,

Renik takes issue with calling an analyst's interventions "interpretations" since, in his opinion, no analyst ever transcends personal psychology, "*even for an instant*," in order to remain "objectively focused on a patient's inner reality" (p. 560).

The postmodern emphasis on the indeterminate nature of truth is the underpinning of the positions taken by Renik and Stolorow, as well as those taken by several other writers, notably Schafer (1996) and Hoffman (1983, 1992, 1994). The postmodern view is in keeping with the philosophical positions taken by Descartes and Kant (for an excellent discussion, see Cavell, 1988). Beginning with the realization that he held beliefs that ultimately proved erroneous, Descartes went on to reason that all he could claim to know with authority was his own subjectivity. The corollary to this thesis was that only God can know anything worthy of being considered "objective." In a similar vein, Kant concluded that knowledge is inherently relative, the product of a particular conceptual scheme that gives form to raw perceptual data. According to such thinking, Cavell (1988) writes, "the 'truth' of a proposition is merely its consistency within a system of beliefs which is possibly incompatible with other systems; and no system is measurably closer than any other to external reality" (p. 864).

The postmodern perspective grew out of a philosophical reaction to "positivism" or "essentialism," which takes the position that there is "a knowable reality, an ascertainable truth that…we can arrive at provided that we apply objective methods carefully and for long enough to eliminate uncertainties" (Schafer, 1996, p. 250). Some believe that postmodernism, if taken to an extreme, leads to "radical relativism" (Friedman, 1999), a "nihilistic denial of the possibility that an analyst can acquire any 'objective' information and knowledge regarding the patient's unconscious motivation and psychic past" (Kernberg, 1996, p. 139). Elliott and Spezzano (1996) argue against those who take postmodern thinking to its illogical extreme; they write reassuringly that "in the clinical situation a postmodern attitude does nothing so radical as to force the abandonment of the quest for truth about the patient's unconscious psychology. It does, however, question and make problematic any rigidly modernist pursuit of this truth" (p. 71). Schafer (1996) echoes these sentiments from his narrativist prospective: "This point of view does not deny truth. There is plenty of truth. It is just that truth comes in different versions. It always has" (p. 251).

Cavell (1988) offers us a way around the current debate between positivists and postmoderns. Raphling (1997) describes Cavell's position as follows:

> The psychoanalytic process confronts each party with the immediacy of the other's version of reality. The superordinate goal of analysis – to know one's own mind – can be achieved only in relation to the mind of another, since 'only a person who is or has been in communication with at least one other creature can know his or her own mind' [Cavell 1988, p. 877].

> Thus, self-knowledge obtained in isolation is limited by the absence of a frame of reference…The analyst's consistent verbal interpretations of, and continuing affective and nonverbal responses to, patients' experience and beliefs present an emotionally and cognitively relevant counterpoint that heightens patients' awareness and provides them with a sustained and emotionally intense contrast to their own sense of reality and inner experience. (pp. 245–246)

In a similar vein, Britton (1998) and Gabbard (1997) see the word *objective* as having two meanings: one associated with the assertion that one's "take" on reality is superior to all other competing constructions, the other implying that one individual observes another from a perspective that is different from the one from which that second individual views him- or herself. This is not to say that an observer's "objectifying" perspective is not influenced by that observer's subjectivity; it is to assert only that, of necessity, how things appear when one is inside one's own skin is bound to differ from how things seem to an outside observer. Any doubt about this matter can be put to rest by remembering how different we sound to ourselves when we speak and when we hear a tape recording of our voice. Even Renik, who had earlier proclaimed the impossibility of analysts ever being objective because of their "irreducible subjectivity," backpedaled on this position when he realized he was dangerously close to disclaiming the scientific basis of psychoanalysis. He then claimed that objectivity was possible if by that term one meant the analyst's acceptance of subjectivity as an insurmountable factor in interpretation (Renik, 1998a).

Other concerns about the analyst's use of authority

In addition to the concerns thus far expressed regarding the analyst's use of authority, there are two sociological factors that contribute to a movement away from the analyst's functioning in an authoritative fashion. Patients today are no longer lining up at our doors clamoring to be analyzed, as they did half a century ago, during what has come to be known as the golden age of psychoanalysis. No doubt the authoritarian stance was better tolerated when analysis was the rage and one felt lucky to have gotten through the analyst's door. Today, however, it's a buyer's market, and prospective patients can pick and choose among the glut of therapists. This surely contributes to the current shift away from analysts tending to be authoritarian.

Another factor contributing to the tendency to question the analyst's interpretive authority is the more general cultural shift, over the last half-century, in our collective conceptions and attitudes regarding authority. As a culture, we are no longer sufficiently idealizing of our leaders to elevate them to a position of unquestioned authority. Gone are the days when we could take comfort in accepting and trusting in what our leaders said. As a field, psychoanalysis grants undue authority to no current psychoanalytic thinker, no matter how clear and compelling that thinker's vision might seem. The time is not yet right for the appearance of another group of leaders like Freud and his immediate disciples. Freud, the man, was brilliant. He had incredible insights and a gift for communicating them to others. But for all his remarkable abilities, Freud, the man, could never have become Freud, the phenomenon, had he not lived when he did. There was something about the late 19th century that facilitated his playing successfully the role of the authoritarian. The social dynamics of that era contributed to his ability to inspire those ripe to become disciples, just as it provided leverage to muster the type of consensus needed to initiate a world movement. No analyst today could pull off such a feat. We have become a skeptical society, and this skepticism leads us to question what we, and what others, have a right to claim to know.

Attempts to circumvent the analyst's use of authority

Given all that has been said about the dangers inherent in the analyst's use of authority, it is understandable that some analysts have developed approaches they believe will lessen the role of their authority with patients.

Lessening regression

As analysts have become increasingly concerned about the potential abuses inherent in their use of authority, some have questioned any adherence to technical measures designed to heighten regression (Friedman, 2000). In particular, they doubt the utility and necessity of abstaining from gratifying many of the patient's wishes, and they argue that neutrality and anonymity serve only to unduly heighten the analyst's authority, making it more likely that the analyst's ideas will be accepted blindly rather than on merit (Renik, 1995). These analysts question the wisdom of fashioning treatment so that patients re-experience the non-gratifying aspects of childhood in an analysis – the very factors, they argue, that caused the patient to become sick in the first place.

As hard as some analysts try to circumvent assuming the role of authority with patients, the structure of the analytic relationship limits the degree to which this is possible. While technical modifications may minimize the power imbalance that renders the analyst's use of authority potentially problematic, this imbalance will remain a factor in all analyses, I believe, so long as one party is paying the other, one party is seeking help from the other that differs substantially from what the paid party wants or needs from the party seeking assistance, and the situation will not slip into one of mutual analysis. Further, efforts to minimize the patient's frustrations are limited by the extent that the analyst becomes ultimately reluctant to say yes at each and every juncture. Aside from relationships in which one is willing to accept the condition of mutual surrender, there is always a point beyond which one remains unwilling to go.

By being honest about the realities of the analytic relationship, and by tenderly confronting the patient about the limits of the relationship when the need to do so eventually arises, the analyst helps the patient come to terms with the inevitable limits and boundaries of the parent–child relationship. Whether one sees this as the central, mutative task of analysis, or rather as something the analytic pair must attend to as an unfortunate byproduct of the confusing intimacy they share, it becomes an unavoidable task during analysis. While some analysts disagree with Kohut and believe that no amount of frustration can be considered optimal during an analysis, and that negative transference is avoidable so long as one provides optimally for patients, it is hard to imagine an analysis that can successfully avoid an ultimate confrontation with frustration, with the "decrees of necessity" invoked by Freud. It might be argued that were patients not regressed to the extent they sometimes are by techniques emphasizing abstinence and neutrality, the intensity of their needs, and therefore their frustrations, would be markedly lower (Friedman, 2000). But I am not convinced that the level to which the patient regresses is entirely under the analyst's control, though the analyst's conduct can doubtless contribute to the patient's tendency to regress.

Privileging the patient's perspective

Some analysts have become reluctant to share their views with patients, out of fear that doing so might be experienced as an authoritative criticism of the patient's construction. While some might wish to think of interpretation as mere information, it inevitably carries a great deal more along with it. Raphling (1995) writes:

> It is difficult for the patient not to experience an interpretation as advocating something, and difficult for the analyst to frame an interpretation that is not, in fact, advocating something. The interpretations that analysts make cannot be as neutral as they would wish because of the pervasiveness of implicit agendas that are in the framework of the interpretive process. (p. 105)

He notes further that the analyst's interpretations are at risk of communicating "that there is something undesirable about [the patient's] defenses and that change is being advocated" (p. 105). Thus, interpretations may be experienced as either a criticism or an insult.

To avoid discounting their patients' constructions, some analysts have adopted an attitude that instead discounts their own interpretations while privileging those of the patient (Roughton, 1994). "After all," such analysts reason, "the subject matter up for discussion is the *patient's* subjectivity, about which the patient is the presumed authority" (see, e.g., Schwaber, 1997). When taken to an extreme, this attitude has led some analysts to adopt the role of *le sujet sait rein* – the one who knows nothing (nothing, that is, beyond the limits of one's subjectivity) – to steer clear of playing the part of what Lacan (1975) refers to as *le sujet suppose savior* (the one who is supposed to know). Take for instance this passage from Kohut (1984):

> If there is one lesson that I have learned during my life as an analyst, it is the lesson that what my patients tell me is likely to be true – that many times when I believed that I was right and my patients were wrong, it turned out, though often only after a prolonged search, that my rightness was superficial whereas *their* rightness was profound. (pp. 93–94)

While we expect analysts to take care not to conflate their subjective truth with objectivity, analysts who privilege patients' constructions do not seem to expect the same of their patients. Instead, these analysts accept the patient's subjective reality as if it were objective. This is partly the result of the way patients sometimes react when reminded by the analyst that their experiences are just how things *seemed* to them. Some patients experience such a reminder as the analyst's way of implying that their memories are distortions or misperceptions. To avoid being cast in this light, some analysts permit the patient's constructions to go unchallenged.

Evidence of the tendency to accept the patient's constructions as if they are objective fact can be seen in the language of case reports. The patient's childhood experience, including the experience with caregivers, is often reported as objective fact (e.g., "his mother would..." or "his father was..."), without the use of qualifiers (e.g., "he *experienced* his mother as being..."; "he *interpreted* his father's actions as meaning that he..."; "it *seemed* to him as if..."; "he had a *fantasy* that he himself was..."). While it could be argued that such qualifiers are unnecessary since, by convention, they are implied by the writer and understood by the reader, one cannot let such an assertion go unchallenged. Unqualified descriptions that take the patient's report at face value signify the writer's acceptance of the patient's experience as objective fact.

Feigned perspectivelessness

Radical relativism – justified as a reaction to the indefensible position of essentialism – has brought some analysts to the position of discounting the value of offering patients another point of view to consider; to do so, they believe, runs the risk of implying that the analyst's interpretation represents "objective truth" – or, at the very least, a better "truth" than the patient's subjectively misguided "truth." I believe such feigned perspectivelessness is an abdication of the analyst's duty to offer patients something new to think about. The very fact of living, to a certain extent, outside the patient's closed system places the analyst in a position to present something meaningfully different from the patient's traditional constructions or assumptions – which, I would add, have proven not to serve the patient well.

Authority and influence

It is my belief that psychoanalysis often involves interacting with patients in ways designed to get them to question their most cherished beliefs. If this is done properly, the vertigo that results from losing one's bearings will prove tolerable. The style with which one interprets will play an important role in ensuring that the interpretive process is respectful of the patient's viewpoint. Such efforts help patients maintain their autonomy and dignity while opening their minds to alternative points of view.

Readying the Patient's Mind for a Consideration of Alternative Constructions

Many analysts continue to see their task as facilitating their patients' awareness of the unconscious factors that determine the ways they react, the conclusions they reach, and the choices they make. For these analysts, *challenging* patients' constructions – how they account for those reactions, conclusions, and choices – can be considered central to the task of psychoanalysis. This is so because the success of an analysis often hinges on the analyst's ability to stimulate open-mindedness in the patient, and getting a patient to be open-minded often depends on the analyst's ability to get that patient to doubt the constructs on which he or she has come to rely.

Instilling doubt is often the first step toward getting patients to realize that there are reasons beyond the veridical picturing of reality that account for their construction of reality. My main thesis is that psychoanalytic technique is designed to create enough doubt in the absolute explanatory power of patients' constructs to open their minds to the possibility that there may be other ways in which the data of their lives can be organized and understood – some of which may provide relief or free them to become more satisfied with their lives. But challenging patients' time-honored belief systems can be considered an adversarial thing to do – one prone to produce all kinds of problems. As Raphling (1997) notes:

> A pervasive and formidable obstacle to insight and learning for a patient is the extent and tenacity of investment in her or his own world-view and self experience. It is a narcissistic defense that protects the patient from challenges to a familiar and stable sense of existence in the world. (p. 244)

One method psychoanalysts have for inducing cognitive (formal) regression – which may render the patient's mind more pliable – is to adopt a particular attitude toward the patient's beliefs, one that challenges the patient by posing the question: are you sure about that? Often, this seemingly innocent query operates as a subtle manipulation intended to undermine the patient's certainty about a belief. Some parents employ this tactic as a way of circumventing a power struggle with their children by appearing to be doing nothing more than ensuring that the child is not acting merely on impulse. The manipulation, whether by parents or analysts, lies in the fact that the answer to this question must almost always be no, since there is little one can ever truly be certain about. By posing the question, the parent or analyst causes the more thoughtful child or patient to step back and reconsider.

When an analyst challenges a patient's interpretations by asking him or her to explore the reasons things seem as they do, the analyst is treading on dangerous ground: "Why?" – like the question "Are you sure?" – can be heard either as a question or as a statement. Both questions can function either as a genuine inquiry or as a covert manipulation. The analyst's question, "Why do you think I possess the same sort of attributes (e.g., attitudes, feelings, and intentions toward you) as had your father?" can be heard by patients as either a simple query or as a statement meant to shame: "Why in God's name would you distort my actions and attitudes into those resembling your father's?" The ambiguity of the question "Why?" permits patients to hear the analyst asking the latter question, just as it permits some analysts to be implying the latter without it becoming obvious they are doing so. This ambiguity can make an apparently innocent question seem like a subtly manipulative attempt to shame the patient into abandoning a belief.

Styles of interpreting

How, then, might analysts deal with their responsibility to provide alternative perspectives and yet avoid the attendant risk of acting as an authority on the patient's mind, thereby violating what the patient regards as his or her sovereignty in this area? How, for instance, might an analyst interpret so as to lessen the chance that the patient will be uncritically accepting of the analyst's interpretations? While it may not always be possible to avoid such a reaction, the way in which one delivers an interpretation must have something to do with how the patient handles interpretations and the process of being interpreted.

There are many styles of imparting interpretations. Fine and Fine (1990) have demonstrated how analysts of different theoretical persuasions tend to deliver interpretations either with conviction and certainty or with a degree of tentativeness, as evidenced by their use of the words *perhaps* or *possibly*. They found that analysts who themselves tended to err in the direction of certainty considered the interpretations of analysts who tended to hedge as "vague, nebulous, nondirective" (p. 1032). Analysts of the first sort might argue that an interpretation delivered with an air of uncertainty can be misunderstood by the patient as conveying a lack of confidence in what is said. These analysts may also regard such circumspection as a disingenuous ploy used to circumvent the patient's defensiveness. This attitude, of course, may well represent the inability of analysts who are sure of their interpretations to imagine analysts who are not. In contrast, Fine and Fine discovered that analysts who tended to pose their interpretations as questions rather than as statements faulted analysts who make definitive interpretations for acting as if they have "privileged access" to the patient's mind. The latter practice, it was argued, can undermine patients' belief in their own experience, and can therefore be regarded as an abuse of authority. An open-minded consideration of the analyst's ideas does not require that patients concede that those ideas are necessarily better than their own. The ongoing debate over whose interpretation is better, the analyst's or the patient's, misses the point. While there may be times when the explanatory power of an analyst's interpretation proves superior to the patient's (insofar as it better accounts for the data – the patient's behavior), there are other times when the analyst's interpretations serve only to demonstrate how the data allow for alternate interpretations. Whether the analyst's interpretation ultimately proves to be a better explanation than the patient's may not be as important as the effect that interpretation has on the patient's conviction that his or her point of view is the only one possible given the "facts." By offering alternative perspectives to those long held by their patients, analysts open their patients' minds to the possibility that the data of their lives might be organized in other ways. The chances of a patient embracing this possibility increase to the degree that the analyst does not appear unduly wedded to the idea that there is but one correct way to view the material.

Nor is it always so clear whose interpretation a construction is in the first place. The model of therapeutic action that pictures psychological change beginning with the analyst's interpretation, followed by a "light" going off in the patient's mind (the "Aha!" experience), which then leads to the retrieval of previously repressed memories confirming the analyst's contentions, is a rarely achieved ideal. Interpretations are more likely to be the product of the mutual influence exerted on one another by analyst and patient than the product of the analyst's mind in isolation. This idea is well captured by Modell (1991): "The most effective interpretations," he writes, "are those made when we do not know whose construction it is, ours or the patient's" (p. 234).

Discussion

Through the use of authority, reinforced by the effects of regression, the analyst gains considerable power with which to influence the patient's psychological development during the course of analysis. As we have seen, questions regarding the analyst's use of authority are based on a host of different concerns. Analysts are seen, at best, as incapable of avoiding the problems that sometimes develop as a result of the regressive techniques they employ. A more sinister view of the process suggests that some analysts abuse their authority to reinforce their theoretical beliefs or remain in control of the interpersonal situation. In either case, regression is seen as a threat to the patient's ability to operate autonomously and to exercise judgment with regard to the analyst's offerings. Interpretations are also considered suspect, particularly when they are viewed as theoretical preconceptions, as experience-distant, or as contaminated by the analyst's subjectivity. For these reasons, the use of authority in the analytic process is thought by some to be manipulative and interpretation to be aggressive, particularly when it robs patients of their bearings by casting doubt on their orienting constructions of life and their understanding of the nature of relationships.

The aggression involved in the analyst's exercise of authority – in confronting patients with interpretations that conflict with those on which the patient has come to rely – accounts for the problem some analysts have with the analyst's use of authority. Take, for example, Renik's (1993) description of the aggression he employs to drive his ideas home to patients:

> Sometimes the best way to facilitate a patient's self-exploration can be for an analyst to present his or her own, different interpretation of reality for the patient's consideration – even to present it as persuasively as possible, in order to be sure that the patient has taken full account of it. (p. 567)

One can find even self psychologists who think likewise. Consider Bacal (1995): "Analysts of all theoretical persuasions encounter instances in which the *invalidation* of the patient's experience will be experienced as more therapeutic than its empathic tracking or validation...Sometimes a confrontation is more effective than an empathic echo or empathically elaborated interpretation" (p. 358).

Those inclined to minimize the analyst's rightful role as an authority do so, according to Levy and Inderbitzin (1997), because they view the use of the analyst's authority as dangerous, even destructive, and anticipate that it will stimulate counteraggression in the patient. According to Raphling (1992),

> Aggression called forth by the interpretive act is problematic for analysts and is...largely responsible for the persistent trends in psychoanalysis that have aimed at reducing the importance of interpretation for analytic technique...Although analysts may accept the aggressive aspect of interpretation intellectually, the act is frequently experienced by them as assaultive; this can generate anxiety in analysts and an exaggerated expectation of patient vulnerability. (pp. 352–353)

Continuing where Raphling leaves off, Kernberg (1996) notes:

> …an analyst's excessive concern with the effects of authority on the patient – with the patient's 'vulnerability' to any viewpoint different from the patient's own – may bring about a masochistic submission to the patient's pathology and a loss of the psychoanalytic perspective, rather than the analytic resolution of the origins of this vulnerability as a defense. By the same token, the patient's conscious and unconscious efforts to seduce the analyst into accepting the patient's conscious view about him/herself may bring about temporary improvements in the patient's condition as part of the supportive effects of such a collusion, but it will inhibit the psychoanalytic work in the long run. (pp. 147–148)

In the final analysis – even with all its limitations and pitfalls – psychoanalytic interpretation remains a respectable, profitable, defensible, and indispensable tool. The debate over the rightful role of interpretation in psychoanalysis ultimately boils down to matters of tact and style – when, whether, and how one interprets. I would argue that analysts still have something authoritative to say about their patient's motives and adaptations to life. Analysts are fooling themselves if they think otherwise. By shying away from offering alternate perspectives for patients to consider, analysts shortchange their patients. Failing to provide patients another point of view to consider, one that stands a chance of opening the patient's mind to alternate constructions of reality that might just prove personally liberating, is an abdication of the analyst's responsibility to patients.

Note

1 Of course, the proffered viewpoint could stimulate just the opposite reaction: competitiveness, defiance, or a wish to defeat the analyst.

Section II

Treating certain sorts of patients

Chapter 5

Thinking with, and about, patients too scared to think

Can non-interpretive maneuvers stimulate reflective thought?

A patient's tolerance of the analyst's efforts to think (to reflect on and interpret) depends in large part on whether the patient can tolerate moments when the analyst disengages from being fully emotionally present so that he can reflect upon the material from a more removed perspective. Whether the patient understands what the analyst is attempting to accomplish when he does so depends on the patient's capacity for higher-order thinking (e.g., symbolic and reflective thinking).[1] Patients capable of such thinking tend to be more tolerant of the analyst's efforts to think, more likely to view the analyst's intentions as benign – as meant to be helpful – and better able to engage with the analyst in the task of self-reflection. By contrast, patients incapable of higher-order thinking (those who think more concretely) are often less tolerant of instances when the analyst momentarily transcends his immersion in a here-and-now emotional engagement with the patient long enough to reflect upon the material. For such a patient, the realization that the analyst has been *thinking about* him, rather than just *being with* him, can leave him feeling that the analyst is no longer as present as he once had been. This realization often triggers intense separation anxiety that may result in the patient's: (1) intolerance of the analyst's efforts to think; (2) suspiciousness of the analyst's motives for interpreting; and (3) inability to join the analyst in the task of self-reflection.

Patients who lack the capacity for higher-order thinking manifest what Josephs (1989) refers to as a "concrete attitude." For these patients, "the concrete is more immediate, compelling, and real than the symbolic [and] the abstract may seem no more than just empty words" (p. 493). These patients look to the analyst "not as much for interpretation of the facts but for consensual validation of the accuracy of the account" (p. 478). With such patients, the analyst's task is a bit more complicated than merely deciphering the unconscious wishes that arise in minds that are no different *structurally* from the mind of the analyst. These patients exhibit a deficit in their ability to symbolize and haven't a clue what the analyst is referring to when he uses metaphors to make his point.

While psychopathology has traditionally been viewed as a product of unconscious conflicts and unrecognized mental contents (wishes, drives, fantasies, etc.) that need to be rendered conscious in order for psychic change to occur, more recently some authors have taken to viewing psychopathology as the product of an individual's failing to develop, or losing the capacity for, symbolic thought (higher-order thinking), seeing psychic change as resulting from the patient's gaining or regaining a capacity for symbolic thinking and reflective thought (Busch, 1995; Friedman, 2002; Herzog, 2001; Sugarman, 2006). Sugarman (2006) argues that interesting a patient in the general workings of his mind – helping him view himself as a thinking self by regarding him as such – helps facilitate the development of higher-order thinking (including a capacity for reflective thought or insightfulness), and is more important therapeutically than the acquisition of specific insights into one's unconscious conflicts or unrecognized mental contents. "All psychological functions," he notes, "seem to work better and to facilitate greater self-regulation when they work in symbolic ways" (p. 971). He also states:

> ...a variety of benefits accrue from patients gaining insightfulness at an abstract–symbolic level of functioning...self-boundaries are strengthened...empathy improves...interpersonal interactions are more easily understood and navigated...relationships feel safer...reality testing is facilitated...separation-individuation is promoted...primary and secondary thinking is enhanced...[and] affect regulation is improved. (p. 981)

In this chapter, I present and explore three related topics. The first is the way patients less adept at symboling sometimes react when the analyst's primary mental preoccupation shifts from being with the patient (fully affectively present "in the moment") to reflecting upon the material (noticing, thinking about, and interpreting). When the analyst shifts from an "experiencing" to an "observing/reflecting" mode of psychic functioning (Busch, 1995; Gray, 1986; Greenson, 1967; Sterba, 1934), he expects the patient will follow suit by adopting an observing stance of his own (Greenson, 1967; Sterba, 1934). But not all patients are capable of this psychic feat. When a more concrete-thinking patient is confronted with the evidence (i.e., reverie) or results (i.e., interpretations) of the analyst's reflective thinking, he may feel distanced in the process, which threatens him with the realization of his essential separateness triggering intense feelings of anxiety.

The second issue concerns the ways in which concrete patients tend to experience and react to interpretations. The fruits of the analyst's reflective thinking, which become crystallized in the form of interpretations that provide alternate constructions to the ones held by the patient, underscore the ways in which patient and analyst are unalike. This confrontation with the analyst's otherness furthers the patient's realization of his separateness, often producing levels of anxiety beyond what he is developmentally ready to face.

If this weren't reason enough for such patients to be hostile toward the process of interpretation, their misunderstanding of the analyst's motives for offering interpretations intensifies their suspiciousness of the interpretive process. Rather than viewing interpretation as the analyst's way of expanding the patient's self-understanding, these patients may instead view such efforts as defensive and self-serving, as a manifestation of the analyst's inability to accept what the patient knows to be true. In this light, an interpretation comes to be seen as an attempt to refute or "explain away" who the analyst *has become* for the patient. But the concept "has become" is nonsensical to these patients, who leave no room between perception and reality for an intervening perceptual process that does more than just represent reality as is. This tendency to view the analyst as desperately attempting to maintain the superiority of his view over competing views reflects the attribution/projection of the patient's own intolerance of alternate perspectives. Under such conditions, the patient may become hostile toward the analyst's efforts to think, potentially leading him to attempt to disrupt the analyst's capacity to think (Bion, 1959).

My third focus is to raise questions about how an analyst might work psychoanalytically with patients who are intolerant of reflective thought and suspicious and hostile toward the process of interpretation. How might an analyst work around the limitations posed by a patient's intolerance of the analyst's otherness? If a patient becomes overwhelmingly anxious in response to the analyst's interpretations, must the analyst abandon the practice of interpreting in favor of some other maneuvers? Can these non-interpretive maneuvers stimulate the development of higher-order thinking and reflective thought? If so, by what means? The model I am proposing, based on theory of mind research, links reflective thought with one's ability to comfortably entertain multiple, competing constructions/representations of the same phenomenon – to keep an open mind and resist tendencies to premature closure. According to this theory, a patient can be helped to appreciate and tolerate multiple perspectives and multiple views of himself and his objects to the extent he participates in an analytic experience with an analyst who demonstrates a capacity to accept and tolerate, rather than prematurely "interpreting away," the varied ways in which the patient represents the analyst. Witnessing the analyst's capacity to genuinely absorb and consider how he is being viewed by the patient, without being destroyed by, or lost within, that characterization (i.e., surviving projective identification), provides the patient an experience with which to identify, thus helping establish a capacity for reflective thought.

While identification with the analyst's capacity to entertain and tolerate multiple perspectives may contribute to a process that ultimately leads to the patient's development of a capacity for reflective thought, identification in and of itself is not likely to be sufficient to bring about such psychic change. The analyst needs to work to interest the patient in the *broad* workings of the patient's mind, rather than rely on traditional interpretations that elucidate unconscious content. He needs to persistently draw the patient's attention to behavioral and psychological phenomena indicative of underlying psychic processes, particularly when the patient has deemed such phenomena meaningless or, alternately, fully explained by the patient's beliefs about the phenomena. While insinuating doubt about the adequacy of a patient's explanations threatens to leave the patient feeling as if his very sanity is being questioned, getting a patient to question the adequacy of certain of his beliefs to account for his behavior or reactions is often the first step in the process of opening a patient's mind to the task of self-reflection.

The development of higher-order cognitive capacities

In order to understand how individuals develop a capacity for higher-order thinking, it is necessary to review theory of mind research. Theory of mind refers to the practice of making inferences about one's own and others' mental states (beliefs, desires, intentions) and, on the basis of those inferences, offering explanations and predictions about one's own behavior and the behaviors of others (Dennett, 1978; Leslie, 1988; Premack & Woodruff, 1978; Wellman, 1988). Theory of mind explains and predicts human actions in terms of what we believe to be so, what we desire to have happen, and what we think we intend to accomplish.

The ability to think psychologically about our own minds and the minds of others is predicated on the ability to make "second-order" mental representations of one's own and others' mental contents (beliefs, desires, intentions). Second-order representations are representations of representations (e.g., thoughts about thoughts, thoughts about beliefs), which indicate an individual's awareness that minds actively create representations (mentally process perceptions via interpretation, inferential thinking, conjecture, etc.). An awareness of one's own, as well as others', mental representations leads to such recursive statements as: "I believe you knew that I was thinking that..." (Flavell, 1988). Such thinking reflects the interaction of minds concerned with the other's mental states and, as such, is the basis of the ability to function socially (Forguson & Gopnik, 1988; Perner, 1988). By contrast, first-order representations are those that represent the world in a literal way (Leslie, 1988). Young children who don't appreciate the meaning-making nature of the mind are said to possess a "copy" (e.g., photographic) model of the mind (Chandler, 1988). They believe that the mind faithfully reproduces the external world without any intervening interpretive process.

As children begin to think in terms of second-order representations, they can be said to be on the verge of appreciating the "constructivistic" nature of the mind – the fact that the mind's way of representing the world involves a great deal more than merely picturing reality as is. Once one appreciates the constructivistic nature of thinking, one understands that "we have beliefs about the world that may or may not be true" and "our actions are a function not of the way the world is but of the way we think it is and want it to be" (Forguson & Gopnik, 1988, p. 228). A constructivistic model of the mind leads to the realization that there are multiple perspectives that one could adopt regarding any given situation.

A constructivistic model of the mind is not something that develops in a sudden quantum leap; rather, it emerges in progressive stages over the course of several years, usually culminating sometime, though not invariably, during adolescence in a sophisticated postmodern appreciation of epistemological relativism when:

> ...young persons begin to understand that divergent views are not always or even primarily the consequence of correctable ignorance or personal bias, but come about instead as a function of all beliefs being inescapably relative to the framework of the entire knowledge constitutive enterprise. (Chandler, 1988, p. 407)

This level of cognitive sophistication has been referred to as the "Rashomon phenomenon," a reference to the 1950 Kurosawa movie *Rashomon*, where four characters witness the same events yet come up with radically different interpretations about what happened.

A capacity for reflective thought: case in point

A capacity for reflective thought requires an appreciation of the constructivistic nature of the mind, which entails a realization that there are a seemingly endless number of competing perspectives that could explain any given situation. The ability to employ higher-order thinking (to think abstractly and metaphorically) combined with an ability to regress in the service of the ego keeps the mind open to alternate interpretations and helps counter the tendency to either think concretely about the matter or employ reality as a defense, both of which might be seen as precluding the need for any further understanding or discussion. Accepting that there will always be other, yet-to-be-discovered interpretations besides those one has already discovered helps prevent tendencies toward premature closure.

Reflective thought requires that one notice a configuration of phenomena (e.g., patterns, slips of the tongue, behavioral repertoires) as constituting, in and of itself, a significant phenomenon worthy of further investigation – even though one has yet to pinpoint its significance. So *noticing* and *resisting premature closure* about what the noticed phenomena mean (open-mindedness) are prerequisites to reflective thought. Once phenomena have been selected for consideration, the mind must think about the material in a particular way. If the patient is capable of self-reflection but has failed to apply such thinking to phenomena the analyst deems significant, the analyst may draw the patient's attention to what, in the analyst's estimation, constitutes evidence of a psychodynamic process. In this way, the analyst helps the patient recategorize as significant phenomena that the patient had tended to overlook or downplay. Suggesting, for example, that uncharacteristically leaving one's wallet at home likely reflects an unconscious conflict worth knowing more about invites the patient to reconsider behavior he had, up to that point, dismissed as meaningless. Once the analyst has the patient's attention, he may insinuate doubt about what the patient accepts as a perfectly adequate explanation (including the inclination to not give the situation a second thought), thus opening the patient's mind to a consideration of alternate perspectives (Tuch, 2001).

Reflective thought is similar to the concept of "psychological-mindedness." Many view a patient's psychological-mindedness as predictive of a positive psychotherapeutic outcome (Appelbaum, 1973; Coltart, 1988; Farber, 1985; Piper et al., 1985). Appelbaum (1973) defines psychological-mindedness as "a person's ability to see relationships among thoughts, feelings, and actions, with the goal of learning the meanings and causes of his experiences and behavior" (p. 36). McCallum and Piper (1997) define it as "the ability to identify dynamic (intrapsychic) components and to relate them to a person's difficulties...[a receptivity] to the hypothesis that current difficulties are linked to unconscious conflicts" (p. 28). Farber (1985) defines it as "the disposition to reflect upon the meaning and motivations of behavior, thoughts and feelings of oneself and others" (p. 170).

Of the theories offered to account for the development of reflective thought, those proposed by Sterba (1934), Britton (1989), Gergely and Watson (1996), Bion (1962), and Aron (2000) are among the most widely cited. While he never refers to it as such, Sterba (1934) offers the first psychoanalytic account of how the psychoanalytic process induces reflective thought. Sterba references Freud (1933), who writes about how "the ego can take itself as object" as the result of a "split" within the ego between one part that observes and another that is the object of observation. Sterba proposes that such a split is the "fate of the ego in analytic treatment," and he suggests this split is brought about by the analyst's offering of explanations "uncolored by affect" (p. 120) that establishes within the patient a "*new point of view of intellectual contemplation*" (p. 121, italics in original). Through identification with the analyst's capacity for reflective thought, the patient is expected to approach the material from this new vantage point.

Might Sterba's clinical theory also account for the development of reflective thought in childhood? In fact, experimental research has demonstrated a positive correlation between a mother's capacity for reflective thought and the child's developing capacity to mentalize (Fonagy, 1991) and reflect (for a complete review of the research, see Bateman & Fonagy, 2004, Chapter 3). Mothers who engage in reflective thought, who think of their children in mentalistic terms (theory of mind), and who see things through their children's eyes produce children who are securely attached, and being securely attached greatly facilitates a child's capacity to mentalize and reflect (Bateman & Fonagy, 2004).

By contrast, Britton (1989) locates the origins of this observational/reflective mode of functioning in the "triangular space" formed by the infant's recognition of the link joining the parents together – a link that excludes the infant, forcing him into the position of witness rather than participant. From this experience, Britton reasons, the child learns that, between three relating individuals, one either becomes the observer of the linked pair or the observed member of that pair. Britton posits this as the basis of an individual's capacity for self-reflection: "This [developmental step] provides us with a capacity for seeing ourselves in interaction with others and for entertaining another point of view whilst retaining our own, for reflecting on ourselves whilst being ourselves" (p. 87).

Gergely and Watson (1996) have identified a developmental process they believe accounts for the ability to form secondary representations of internal states, thus leading to a capacity for emotional self-awareness. These authors refer to a "biofeedback training procedure," whereby:

> ...the repetitive presentation of an external reflection of the infant's affect-expressive displays [by the mothering figure] serves a vital "teaching" function that results in gradual sensitization to the relevant internal state cues as well as to the identification of the correct set of internal stimuli that correspond to the distinctive emotion category that the baby is in. As a result of this process the infant will eventually come to develop an awareness of the distinctive internal cues that are indicative of categorical emotion-states and will become able to detect and *represent* his/her particular dispositional emotion-states. (p. 1190, italics added)

Though these authors do not tie this process to reflective thought, it stands to reason that the capacity to psychically represent internal states is the necessary precondition for an individual's ability to step back and reflect upon these states since this representation offers an intervening mental process between the direct experience and the individual's thoughts about that experience.

This theory sounds remarkably like that proposed by Bion (1962) thirty years earlier, which envisions the process of projective identification as a healthy developmental stage responsible for the integration of experience and the development of the capacity to think. According to this theory, the infant first experiences life in a raw, sensory fashion ("sense impressions" referred to as β-elements) and, literally, has no idea what to "make" of the experience. In order for the infant to begin to understand this experience, it must first be contained, processed, and re-presented to the child in a modified form (as α-elements, such as thoughts) by the caregiver, who functions as the "container" for the infant's experience. Only then can the infant begin to *think about* the experience since it is no longer experienced in so direct and raw a fashion.

Until the infant learns how to think for himself, he will continue to need the object to think for him (to convert β-elements into α-elements) in order to supplement the functioning of the infant's own ego.

The infant experiences intense anxiety upon realizing that he cannot psychically manage on his own – that he is incapable of providing for his most basic needs. Lacking a way to mentally represent the circumstances that will satisfy his mounting drives/needs – short of imaging (hallucinating) the breast into seeming existence, which forestalls frustration for only so long – the infant cannot tolerate much frustration and depends on the caregiver to help him develop a facilitating thought ("oh, *this* is what I've been needing all along!") that will then help him tolerate periods of non-gratification of the need, representing, as it does, the object's functional absence even in the object's physical presence.

Bion's theory functions both as a developmental theory and as a clinical theory that suggests a treatment approach best suited to facilitating the development of higher-order thinking such as reflective thought. Bion's theory emphasizes: (1) the *role* of the analyst in opening the patient's mind to a *consideration* of the analyst's thoughts and thought processes (the first sign of reflective thought); and (2) the developmental importance of acquiring a capacity to tolerate an awareness of the analyst's separate existence, which, by necessity, simultaneously brings the patient face to face with an awareness of his own separate existence. Bion's theory favors early and active intervention. Bion envisions the process as one in which the analyst actively interacts with the patient in ways that require he takes the analyst's thoughts and thought processes into consideration (thus hastening the patient's ultimate acceptance of the analyst's separate existence).

Differentiating self from other establishes the existence of two distinct mental representations, which contributes to the establishment of the ability to distinguish between the experiential modes of "being fully in the moment" and "observing from a distance." Being at a distance from the immediacy of the experience offers the child an opportunity to think about it, via identification with the second-hand viewpoint of the observer, in a way he previously was unable to do when he was mindlessly immersed in the first-hand experience. This differentiation within the ego is facilitated by the working through of separation anxiety (Quinodoz, 1993, 1996), a heightening of the individual's frustration tolerance, and a heightening tendency to remain in the depressive, rather than in the paranoid–schizoid position.

Recently, Aron (2000) has introduced the term *self-reflexivity*, which he distinguishes from the type of *self-reflection* – ("a cognitive process in which one thinks about oneself with some distance, as if from the outside" p. 668) that Sterba (1934) had in mind when he noted a differentiation in the ego between experiencing and observing parts. By contrast, Aron (2000) regards self-reflexivity as more than an intellectual observational function, viewing it as an intellectual, emotional, experiential, and affective process. He describes self-reflexivity as "the capacity to hold in mind both the subjective and objective aspects of both self and object" (p. 668), "the capacity to move smoothly between subjective and objective perspectives on the self" (p. 673), and "the capacity to maintain the dynamic tension between experiencing oneself as a subject and as an object" (p. 673). He quotes Bach (1985, 1994), who attributes severe psychopathology to a patient's difficulties in moving back and forth between subjective awareness and objective self-awareness and his difficulties integrating these two perspectives into his representational world. Lacking the ability to move smoothly between these two perspectives results in an individual's "inability to tolerate ambiguity and paradox; to deal with metaphor (which is inherently ambiguous and may simultaneously express contradictory points of view); or maintain multiple points of view, especially about the self" (p. 673). Aron feels self-reflexivity can only arise within a relational matrix – the product of a mind reflected in the mind of another – and never arises intrapsychically independent of other minds.

Separation anxiety, reflective thought, and prohibitions against the analyst's efforts to think

For patients who think more concretely and who are incapable of reflective thought, the invitation to set aside a familiar and orienting belief in order to consider a new view threatens to leave the patient feeling psychically unanchored and adrift. Under such conditions, interpretations aren't primarily resisted because they represent unconscious material; rather, they are resisted because they threaten the precarious balance of the individual's belief system. Furthermore, if the analyst's interpretations run counter to how the patient is accustomed to viewing matters, the concrete patient may experience intense anxiety as he becomes aware that he and the analyst are not of like mind with regard to their understanding of things, which tends to heighten the patient's awareness of the analyst's separate existence. Having not yet adequately individuated, these patients continue to rely on the analyst's ego to supplement the functioning of their own ego. Since they cannot function autonomously, realizing the object's separate existence generates intense anxiety. The analyst cannot hope to facilitate reflective thinking in such patients until he attends to the patient's separation anxiety, the working through of which plays a critical role in readying the patient to think reflectively (Quinodoz, 1993, 1996).

In order to develop a capacity for reflective thought, one must become sufficiently individuated from one's objects, which depends largely on the acceptance of one's own, and the object's, separate existences. But in order to arrive at this point, one must first resolve the following (depressive position) dilemma: is it better to risk becoming a differentiated, independent entity – capable of thinking one's own thoughts, clear about who's who, yet admittedly powerless over the much-needed object and aware that one's object-based needs might go unmet – or remain hopelessly compromised, an undifferentiated nonentity whose entire existence seems to depend upon the object without whom one feels terrifyingly alone, incapable of functioning or even surviving on one's own, yet, at the same time, "safe" within the illusion one has omnipotent control over the needed object?

How does a patient resolve such a dilemma? Having the object survive one's own murderous impulses without retaliating (Winnicott, 1969) and being provided the words and concepts needed to be able to think about, not just live, one's experiences (Bion, 1959, 1962) represent two of the environment's contributions to the working through of this dilemma. But there are other feats the patient himself must accomplish, chief among which is the working through of anxieties associated with the realization of one's autonomous existence.

Separation anxiety proper

Clinically, separation anxiety typically appears in response to the discontinuities of treatment imposed by the weekend breaks and holidays apart. But a more basic type of separation anxiety is experienced by patients who cannot tolerate being made aware of the analyst's separate existence even when they are in the analyst's presence. For instance, when the analyst shifts from an *experiencing* to an *observing* mode in order to gain a perspective on "the situation," he ceases to be in the room with the patient in quite the same way. No longer will he be experienced by the patient as intersubjectively immersed with the patient in a first-hand experience. The effect this has on patients who cannot tolerate the analyst's otherness can be quite dramatic, as will be illustrated in the case material that follows.

Patients who suffer from this level of separation anxiety may not welcome times when the analyst is absorbed in reverie, communing with himself, or reflecting on the process in order to better understand the patient's situation. Learning that the analyst was *thinking about*, rather than just *being with*, the patient can feel like a rejection – a sign that the analyst cannot tolerate the full force of the patient's being. It may also be experienced as an abandonment – a betrayal of the imagined promise that the analyst would remain qualitatively with the patient in the same way at all times. The *product* of the analyst's reflective activity – delivered as an interpretation – is the most obvious sign that the analyst has been doing more than just "being with" the patient, and some patients react more to the act of being interpreted (thought about analytically) than to the manifest content of the interpretation. For these patients, "being interpreted" may mean being objectified – made into an object of observation – which can be off-putting.

The interpretation itself may be experienced as the analyst speaking a language that goes over the patient's head insofar as it involves a level of symbolic thought that lies beyond the patient's cognitive wherewithal to understand. Interpretations can also stimulate a patient's envy since the interpretation causes the patient to realize that the analyst possesses cognitive capacities the patient lacks, that the analyst can creatively synthesize material in ways the patient cannot. Interpretations can force the patient into an unwelcomed confrontation with the analyst's otherness, thus heightening the patient's awareness of just how *unalike* the two are. Aspects of the analyst's otherness inevitably dump cold water on the warmth of intersubjective immersion, thus threatening to disrupt the patient's illusion of oneness – making him aware that he had been mistaken in thinking that he and the analyst were of one mind about all matters.

Clinical vignette I

Britton (1989) presents a case that illustrates the difficulties an analyst may encounter whenever he tries to psychically disengage from being fully present in order to gain a perspective on what was going on in the room. In this paper, Britton presents the case of Miss A., a woman who could not tolerate times when Britton would try to think about her, leaving him to realize:

> What I felt I needed desperately was a place in my mind that I could step into sideways from which I could look at things. If I tried to force myself into such a position by asserting a description of her in analytic terms, she would become violent. (p. 88)

Once Miss A. had calmed down, she was able to put her experience into words, demanding that the analyst "Stop that fucking thinking" (p. 88).

Based on his theory, referenced earlier, that reflective thinking is the product of the infant's experience of *witnessing*, rather than participating in, the oedipal dyad, Britton reasons that his efforts to consult his "analytic self" left the patient feeling as though she'd been forced into witnessing an act of "internal intercourse" between different aspects of Britton's ego, which Britton reasoned was analogous to parental intercourse. This illustrates how patients may feel intensely jealous and painfully excluded to the point of non-existence when the analyst engages in the practice of self-reflection, causing the patient to fragment and/or become enraged in response to the analyst's activities.

What people most readily remember and quote (e.g., Aron, 1995; Astor, 1998; Caper, 1997; Schoenhals, 1995) from Britton's paper is his understanding of what "fucking thinking" meant – his satisfying, understandable, and believable *symbolic* understanding of the patient's words. What typically goes unnoticed, however, is the fact that Britton's conceptualization went far beyond what Miss A. was capable of grasping. Given what Britton goes on to say, it cannot even be said for sure that the patient's words had meant the same thing to her as they had to Britton. Britton tells us that these moments of "communing with myself about her" led the patient to feel that "*I was eliminating my experience of her in my mind*" (pp. 88–89, italics added). Hence, the patient was left feeling excluded *to the point of not existing*. Ultimately, Britton concluded that the only way he could proceed was to keep his thoughts to himself "whilst communicating to her *my understanding of her point of view*" (p. 89).

Clinical vignette 2

Mr. A., a young, gay attorney, came to see me complaining of his inability to form relationships with others. He complained of feeling anxious and depressed. At the age of 4, his mother had placed him and his three younger siblings in separate foster homes because she could no longer afford to care for them as a result of divorce. Two years later, her financial situation changed and she was able to reunite the family.

I saw the patient three times weekly. Use of the couch was contraindicated for reasons that will shortly become clear. The patient and I couldn't have been less alike with regard to race, social background, religion, and sexual orientation. These differences formed an important basis for our relationship – causing the patient to alternate between envying me for who he thought I was and what he thought I had, devaluing me for being the dorky, slimy Jew-boy who he intermittently saw me as being, and lamenting the gap between us which he felt could not be bridged.

Mr. A.'s behavior toward me was unlike anything I had ever experienced. He would impulsively act out his feelings in whichever way he saw fit. For instance, he would physically trespass into my personal space and thought nothing of touching me whenever, *and wherever*, he wanted. I had no privileges in this regard. My attempts to help him understand this behavior were treated by him as an annoyance – as just something I *had* to do because I was, after all, an analyst. And he forgave me these distractions on that account. Slowly, it dawned on me how radically different our views were about what therapy entailed. The patient did not seem to be coming for the type of help I imagined providing – psychological change through a heightened awareness of unconscious processes and content stimulated by the interpretations I would offer.

Sometimes, when I offered an interpretation, Mr. A. responded in a dismissive manner that gave me no sense that he had even considered what I had said. At other times, he became enraged by my inconsideration for bothering him with my ideas when he had more important, pressing matters to discuss. When I invited him to share his thoughts, feelings, or reactions about a particular matter, he would ignore my query, acting as though I'd said nothing. He was unabashed in his insistence that I think for him – that I tell him what he was thinking and why – rather than having to think about his own thoughts and share them with me, and he reacted with suspicious hostility when I encouraged him to tell me what was going on in his head because having to tell me what he was thinking meant I didn't already know, and thinking that was intolerable.

It seemed that Mr. A. could not allow either of us to momentarily separate from the other in order to "huddle" alone with our thoughts in a moment of self-reflection. To think to myself in his presence was seen by the patient as a betrayal of my promised presence, and it left him feeling as though he momentarily ceased to exist in my mind. For him to think in my presence was, for him, unthinkable. The very act of thinking – on my part or his – seemed to represent a kind of intolerable separation.

When Mr. A. used a particular word, he then expected me to parrot it back. If I used a slightly different word or term, he charged me with not listening. In fact, my inability to remember the patient's precise words indicated that I had *processed* what he had told me and was now, through this slight variation of words, reflecting back an internal process of my own. This introduced into the room my otherness, proof that I was experiencing the patient in my own way, translating his words into my own, which left him feeling separate and alone.

Mr. A. would rail against every conceivable boundary. He had strong reactions to the beginning and end of every session, as well as to anything that demarcated my separate life, be it evidence of my separate subjectivity, my private thoughts, or my life away from him. Limits were a particular problem. The time-limited nature of our sessions was something he particularly couldn't stand, and any sign that I had been looking in the clock's direction produced rage and charges that I did not love him and couldn't wait to be rid of him. He often turned my clocks around so that I wouldn't know when the session was drawing to an end.

Sessions typically began in the waiting room. On the way in, Mr. A. would rub up against me the way a cat would its owner, pressing up against me long enough to leave a scent of his cologne, ensuring that I'd become similarly scented – a sort of olfactory forget-me-not that would linger for hours. It was as if the patient had marked his territory, and it left me wondering how my wife would react to my coming home doused in an unfamiliar scent of another's body. Once in the room, Mr. A. took the liberty of sitting anywhere he chose, including at my desk, where he would rifle through my papers. He enjoyed my obvious annoyance, which left me feeling outraged and on edge, unable to consistently maintain an ability to think analytically.

Any evidence of my separateness produced intolerable anxiety. At the end of a session, Mr. A. would first deny that the time was up. "How could it already be over?" he would whine in dismay, with a pained expression on his face. Then he would physically cling to me as a child might to his mother's leg. I would have to peel him off me in order to get him to leave. He would then plead with me, asking, "Why do we have to stop?"

Whenever I would announce I'd be away from my practice for a time, Mr. A. would demand I tell him how I'd make it up to him, as if making it up could somehow undo the separation and reassure him that I still loved him. Again, there seemed to be no way to get the patient to explore what his demand meant. He would threaten to "go to war" when he felt abandoned. He took my leavings as indisputable evidence that I didn't love him, and he was unwilling and/or unable to consider this feeling worthy of analysis. Things weren't much better when *he* initiated the separation. He would return demanding that I declare how *I* had missed *him*. When I pointed out that he seemed incapable of speaking about his own feelings of having missed me, the most he would settle for was a statement that we had "missed each other." The words *we* and *us* were demanded in place of first-person pronouns. The idea that we might not be exactly of like mind was intolerable, causing more feelings of aloneness, disintegration, and rage.

But it wasn't just these actual separations that were difficult for the patient. When I ceased to be in my usual state with him (i.e., vigilant, on edge, even a bit fearful, focused on content), Mr. A. would begin to feel intolerably alone. At times, when I slipped into a more relaxed mode – one that might permit a moment of reverie – the patient became alarmed and would act in ways he would later admit were designed to recapture my "full attention." If he found me to be anything less than sharply focused on his every word, the patient would treat me as a drill sergeant would a private who had been caught at something less than "full attention." Evenly suspended attention (Freud, 1912) was strictly out of the question.

When I shifted my physical position or engaged in some gesture such as scratching an itch, Mr. A. demanded an explanation for the behavior, resulting in a level of self-consciousness on my part that was incompatible with reflective thought. When I asked him about the effect my change in posture or actions had on him, he refused to explore how this change in my behavior made him feel or why it concerned him. Rather, he insisted that I tell him what my changed posture said about my feelings about him. It was as if he suspected these changes in my posture came *from within me* and were *solely about me*, and he tried hard to deny this awareness by making these changes always *about* him, which they only occasionally were. Considering the idea that such changes were a manifestation of something within me that had *nothing to do with him* was an absolutely intolerable idea!

Discussion: intolerance of the analyst's otherness

The case of Mr. A. dramatically illustrates how the patient and I were forbidden by the patient from engaging in any activity that heightened his awareness of our differences. Anything I did that threatened to crack the illusion of our oneness produced a violent reaction on his part. He suffered from intense levels of separation anxiety, and reflective thought was bilaterally prohibited. Under no circumstance could he sustain what Winnicott (1958) refers to as the capacity to be alone in the presence of another, and he worked hard to restrict my ability to be alone in his presence long enough to think.

When the analyst offers his *understanding* of the patient, it draws the patient's attention to a more cognitive, distant, less direct, and immediate way of being known, subtly emphasizing the existence of an intervening process by which one comes to know another. Acknowledging this intervening process objectifies the act of perceiving, which may be experienced by the patient as a disruption of the intersubjective experience of *being with* the analyst.

Psychic reality is representational and not at all synonymous with the thing itself. A metaphoric lens exists between that which is signified and its signifier. The awareness of this metaphoric lens – this thing between us and the world – heightens our sense of separation and aloneness, in the same way that remaining cognizant of the *act* of seeing disrupts the transparency of vision to the extent that one's attention is drawn to the intervening physiological processes and apparatuses upon which sight depends, thus diluting the immediacy of the experience.

Paradoxically, words can be the thing that stands between one's primary experience of the world and secondary ways of knowing. The most direct, primary way of knowing is, by definition, nonverbal. As much as we gain from the acquisition of language, which helps capture and communicate our primary experiences, we simultaneously lose a direct connection with "the force and wholeness of the original experience" (Stern, 1985, p. 177). So verbal understanding and communication, upon which psychoanalysis depends, has this inherent limitation.

Recognizing that one's experience of another necessarily involves an intervening interpretive process – that our minds stand between us and a direct experience of the world – brings one face to face with our essential separateness. For Mr. A. to recognize that who he thought I was and why he thought I did what I did was, in part, a product of his own ways of organizing relationships is not a thought he found thinkable. He steadfastly insisted that who he knew me to be was unquestionably true, and he was hostile toward the suggestion that this wasn't necessarily so. In this way, Mr. A. functioned like a child who has yet to realize that such a thing as a false belief exists. Before the age of four, children cannot accept the concept of a "false belief" because it threatens to undermine their tenuous hold on reality (Premack & Woodruff, 1978). Struggling to understand the world, the young child cannot afford to question what he "knows" to be true. Realizing that one's beliefs could be false is the first in a series of cognitive achievements that ultimately culminates in a sophisticated theory of mind – in the development of higher-order thinking. At the outset, Mr. A. could not tolerate recognizing his essential aloneness, so it became impossible for him to imagine that his interpretations of me were just that – products of a mind that separates the world from the world perceived.

Clinical development of reflective capacity

For the longest time, it seemed as if my treatment of Mr. A. offered us no way out. Interpretations proved consequential, which I slowly realized had little to do with their content and had more to do with the fact that the patient found the process of being interpreted neither acceptable nor helpful. I got to the point of feeling that tolerating the treatment was about all that I could muster and all I had to offer. While my intermittent ability to think analytically helped me withstand and emotionally survive the treatment, developing ways to tolerate a patient cannot pass as an adequate explanation of therapeutic action. Something more has to have happened in this patient's treatment to account for the substantial changes he has, in fact, undergone over time. He has moved from a strict reliance on action, is no longer wholehearted in his expressed rages, can better tolerate separations, and has ceased to invade every nook and cranny of my office and psyche. He can better tolerate having his curiosity frustrated, now makes requests rather than demands, and no longer possesses a sense of entitlement. In addition, he is beginning to consider what I have to say without reflexively dismissing it.

If the capacity for self-reflective functioning is a necessary prerequisite to undergoing psychoanalytic treatment, this patient was ill-suited for psychoanalysis and would be viewed by most analysts as unanalyzable. But there are those who believe psychoanalysis can actually help patients develop a capacity for self-reflexivity, making self-reflexivity a goal rather than a prerequisite for psychoanalysis. Aron (2000) suggests that "at the end of an analysis it is not insight or other knowledge of psychic content that would best demonstrate the patient's growth or the success of the treatment, but rather it is the capacity for self-reflexivity" (p. 677), and he sees analysis as "the only treatment that operates directly to improve the capacity for self-reflexivity" (p. 674).

If my work with Mr. A. is to be considered psychoanalytic in nature, then it succeeds to the extent it can help him develop self-reflective functioning. What about our work together has helped Mr. A. begin to establish self-reflective functioning? It was not the knowledge I attempted to impart that made a difference. I had plenty of knowledge that might have proven useful to the patient, but he was having none of it. He did not, or could not, conceive of my helping him in that way, and my insisting on that form of help only made matters worse. I suspect that interpretations only tended to make him anxious to the extent they highlighted our differences, putting him in touch with a feeling of aloneness. Mr. A. envisioned a different sort of help, one that involved my ability to withstand aspects of his being that he knew would challenge my very being – ideas he knew I'd find distasteful at best, and might prove hard – if not impossible – for me to tolerate.

The following situation is prototypic of many that occurred during the analysis and illustrates how my insistence on interpreting only tended to worsen matters.[2] For the longest time, Mr. A. persisted in telling me how dorky I was. I ultimately came to understand and accept that the patient truly felt this way about me and wasn't just saying it for effect. But this is not what I initially thought. Being characterized in this way was very painful, which fueled my need to focus on the sadistic motives behind his expressed view.[3] It seemed to me that Mr. A. felt driven to express this opinion in response to times he was feeling deeply hurt by me. But suggesting that he was now feeling the need to hurt me in retaliation for my having just hurt him caused him to feel that I could not tolerate learning the "truth" about the "me" – or more precisely, one of the many "mes" – he carried around in his head.

The patient saw my insistence on interpreting his sadistic motives as evidence of my inability and/or unwillingness to take in and consider one of the ways he truly viewed me. The patient was right, in part. For quite some time I did regard his characterization of me as groundless and unworthy of consideration – a feigned opinion adopted just to hurt me, I imagined. Dismissing what he had to say about me made it hard for the patient to hear what I had to say about him. He could neither consider my interpretation of his retaliatory wish to hurt me back, nor accept an empathic expression of my realization that I had hurt him independent of any interpretation of his wish to retaliate, because he interpreted both of these offerings as self-serving – a defensive maneuver meant to save my own hide at his cost. The patient characteristically used such maneuvers, so he naturally assumed the same of me. But, if I were more concerned with protecting my narcissism and willing to dismiss his expressed views of me to that end, then I could not help him. What I considered valid and useful information – the fact that I recognized how I had hurt him, and that he needed to do something to me to rectify matters – were not experienced by the patient as empathic and, instead, felt like a further rejection of him. Not until I realized how deeply disturbed I was by Mr. A.'s view of me as dorky, and considered the evidence that permitted such an opinion – that there were, in fact, aspects of my behavior that justified such an opinion – could I relax my need to explain away the patient's views of me by getting him to focus on the reason he felt the need to share such personally unpalatable views of me at that time. Understanding the basis of his view of me as dorky, and not coming unglued in having to see myself through his eyes, propelled the analysis forward, demonstrating for the patient how one might survive the consideration of another's views no matter how threatening they may seem at first.

Aron (2000) notes that by permitting himself to become a *subject* within the analytic process, the analyst allows the patient "to observe some of the relations among the analyst's multiple selves" (p. 677). He goes on to note how a triangular space is thus created within the analytic dyad by the analyst "inviting the patient to observe the analyst's relation to him- or herself as both subject and object" (p. 677). In this way:

> ...the patient learns to establish a more complex self relation by playing out an exchange of roles with the analyst, who is not locked into any single view of this exchange because he or she has a more complex and multiple relationship with him- or herself. (p. 680)

This results in an "internalization of a multiplicity of perspectives" (pp. 680–681), which lessens the patient's tendencies to adhere to a single aspect of the self.

Summary

Psychoanalysts are driven to make contact with a particular aspect of the patient – that part capable of joining the analyst outside the in-the-moment frame in order to think together about what has transpired between them. Analysts hunger to know the patient in this particular way, and if the patient shares this same appetite, the couple stands a good chance of connecting in a deep and meaningful way. If, however, the patient neither understands nor tolerates the analyst's wish to engage in this sort of activity because of intense separation anxiety and/or or his paranoid inclinations, and, instead, wishes to be known in a more experience-near fashion, frustration is likely to arise and problems are likely to develop.

Not all patients share an ability to reflect upon the material created in the session, and those who lack a capacity for higher-order thinking present a particular challenge to psychoanalysts since they often cannot tolerate instances when the analyst disengages momentarily in order to think about what has transpired in the room. For patients who have yet to establish a sense of themselves as separate entities, the separation anxiety that develops when the analyst "goes away" in this fashion proves more than the patient can bear, giving rise to the patient's intolerance of the analyst's efforts to think.

Patients who struggle with the analyst's otherness, who cannot engage in reflective thought nor tolerate times when the analyst is so engaged, challenge the analyst's capacity to continue to reflect upon the material from a vantage point that transcends the analytic couple's moment-to-moment existence. In the end, the analyst needs to meet the patient where he finds him, adapting his approach accordingly. But this comes with its regrets – even anger, disappointment, and a refusal to accept the situation as it is.

Part of psychoanalysis involves a consideration of both how the patient internally represents the analyst and why he chooses to share this representation at a particular point in time. Offering interpretations that are technically correct insofar as they accurately capture and communicate the whys and wherefores of a patient's shared representations of self and other may, in another sense of the term, be technically incorrect insofar as these explanations prove to be, for this phase of treatment, beside the point, or – worse – counterproductive. Patients who have yet to develop a sophisticated theory of mind and, as a result, lack a capacity for reflective thought may not be able to work with certain sorts of interpretations. Suggesting, for example, that the patient is expressing sadistic impulses when he shares an unflattering representation of the analyst may be dismissed by the patient as the analyst's desperate attempt to explain away unacceptable ideas – a projection of the patient's own tendencies to do likewise.

If the most developmentally pertinent, and most clinically relevant, motive behind a patient's need to express a particular representation of the analyst is to test the analyst's capacity to entertain, tolerate, and live with a representation counter to the ones included in the analyst's self-representations, therapeutic success may hinge on the analyst's ability to demonstrate the workings of his own theory of mind that affords him an appreciation of the relativity of perspectives and, as a result, a capacity to accept the patient's representation non-defensively. If a particular representation is repugnant, and disruptive to the analyst's sense of him- or herself, he or she may rush to interpret the patient's motives for sharing this representation as a way of asserting it isn't so. If, instead, the analyst resists the urge to explain away this representation and "wears" the attribution long enough to demonstrate to the patient his or her capacity to survive being viewed in this way, real headway can be made toward helping the patient develop a capacity to tolerate multiple perspectives within himself, which, in turn, may stimulate a capacity for reflective thought. Whether one views such work as preparatory for subsequent psychoanalytic treatment or, alternately, as the earliest stages of a genuine psychoanalytic process, it seems a necessary approach in the treatment of patients lacking a capacity for reflective thought.

Notes

1 For the purposes of this chapter, I offer the following four cognitive capacities as constituting higher-order thinking: (1) to think on higher symbolic planes (e.g., to think metaphorically); (2) to engage in reflective thought (facilitated by a shift from being "in the moment" to a more observational stance); (3) to employ a "theory of mind" approach when considering the patient's situation (to infer the patient's mental states and use these inferred states to explain and predict the patient's behavior; and (4) to grasp the constructivistic nature of the mind – to understand that the patient interprets reality rather than faithfully recording it. Though they are being presented in this chapter as if they are distinct, these four cognitive capacities overlap and are interrelated to such a degree that they depend upon, and phenomenologically blend into, one another.

2 This example is but one of many I could provide. For instance, the patient was also inclined to express the most noxious opinions about Jews, knowing me to be one. He talked about how concerned Jews were about money, and he insisted that the word *slimy* was reserved just for Jews. While I suspect he actually envied aspects of my being Jewish, pointing this out prematurely would also have been experienced by him as defensiveness on my part.

3 There are a number of other functions also served by the patient holding, and expressing, this view of me. It was a provocation. It was also a way to lessen his envy of me by viewing me as less than ideal. Our racial differences were encapsulated in this offensive view that stereotypically captured an aspect of my whiteness. But it was also a disappointment to the extent it rendered me less than ideal, and it angered him that I could not live up to what he sometimes needed me to be. Finally, it was a test to see whether I could bear the thought of myself as a dork – to see whether I could accept the validity of this representation and find myself within it, no matter how painful doing so might be.

Chapter 6

Thinking outside the box

A metacognitive perspective on the treatment of concrete thinking

As with patients described in the last chapter who lack the capacity to be self-reflective, the ability to appreciate symbolic meaning, and the tolerance of signs of the analyst's otherness, patients who think concretely likewise challenge the analyst's ability to analyze. Psychoanalysis was founded on the identification and working through of symptoms that were considered manifestations of intrapsychic conflict. Psychoanalysts thirst to make contact with, and interact with patients on these more symbolic levels. It is what most analysts find intellectually fascinating, personally satisfying, and therapeutically efficacious. Concrete thinking is a massive boulder blocking the analyst's path towards this goal.

Concrete thinking is an extraordinarily difficult condition to treat. It produces symptoms in its own right and greatly complicates the treatment of a host of other conditions it is associated with: somaticization, alexithymia, eating disorders, perversions, and addictions, to name a few. This chapter describes the clinical manifestations of concrete thinking, compares the various theories offered to account for such thinking, and outlines the technical modifications needed to make the psychoanalytic treatment of concrete patients more efficacious.

Before describing the manifestations of concrete thinking, it is important to make clear how variable such thinking can be. Patients who are prone to think concretely do not do so reliably and consistently. Depending on the subject matter being considered, these patients vary to the extent their thinking proves concrete. A capacity for symbolic thought – the opposite of concrete thinking – is not an all-or-nothing matter. Even the most symbolic thinkers among us – psychoanalysts included – are nevertheless susceptible, under certain conditions, to lose this capacity momentarily, and patients prone to think concretely can, at times, demonstrate an ability to think symbolically in situations where they don't feel psychically threatened. So when we speak of "the concrete thinker" it should be understood that this does not refer so much to an actual individual as it does to an individual caught in a moment in time who is contextually exhibiting a tendency to think concretely. Of course, like all matters that exist along a continuum, a capacity for symbolic thinking is relatively consistent in some yet rather spotty, at best, in others – in those we somewhat misleadingly refer to as "concrete thinkers."

A concrete perspective toward psychic life manifests in a host of different ways. The concrete thinker tends to be literal-minded. He prefers to stick as closely as possible to the narrow meanings denoted by words, fearing he will become hopelessly lost in the hinterlands of connotation and abstraction. Concrete thinking also entails the reification of experience that turns the intangible and less tangible into the utterly tangible. Words are no longer vehicles of understanding so much as they are implements of action. A wife's motives for mentioning to her husband the impact his actions had on her is now framed by him in concrete terms not as a wish to be understood, but as an attempt to control – for instance, through the induction of guilt, without any ability to imagine other possibilities. In a similar fashion, an analyst's interpretations are seen by the patient as an attempt to *do something* to the patient above and beyond explaining and conveying meaning. The concrete thinker maddeningly assigns thing-like qualities to even the least material aspects of life so that he can then manage them in ways he knows best. Though he is clueless about the effect this has on his experience of life, concrete thinking drains experience of the vital juices that saturate the tissue of experience with meaning. What is lost in the process is lost on the concrete thinker. He doesn't know what he is missing, though he comes to the analyst feeling that things are, in ways he hasn't words to describe, not quite right.

Typically, concrete thinking leaves little if any room for the concept of interpretation – the idea that a mind operates like a lens positioned between the stimuli perceived and the perception rendered that contributes its own unique "take" on what is being seen. The concrete thinker cannot loosen his vice-like grip on the hard-and-fast perception of concrete reality long enough to think imaginatively, since doing so threatens to undermine the comforting knowledge of things as they are. It is the vertigo and disorientation created by considering things from a totally new, symbolic perspective, not the content itself, that is more apt to account for the concrete thinker's inability to give due consideration to alternate interpretations of the facts as represented by the analyst's interpretation.

Underlying the limitations of concrete thinking is an individual's inability to engage in metacognition – to think about why he thinks and how he thinks about what he thinks. Metacognition is needed to keep an open mind and maintain healthy doubt about the veracity of each and every one of one's beliefs and formed conclusions. Metacognition reminds us that perception is relative, easily corrupted by one's preconceived beliefs and core desires – what one expects to see and/or hopes to see. And it is metacognition that opens our minds to a reconsideration of beliefs given the offering of another's alternate perspective.

It isn't so much that concrete thinkers are utterly incapable of appreciating the abstract-symbolic aspects of, for instance, a painting or a poem. Some concrete thinkers are more than able to use symbols – to let one thing stand for another (unlike the concreteness of schizophrenics who are unable to think metaphorically), to grasp the larger truth, the broader truism exemplified by the specific example used in a proverb or parable (e.g., "a stitch in time saves nine" is not just about tailoring). It is when the concrete patient is asked not to just think his own thoughts, but to *think about* those thoughts – which are acts of metacognition – that he runs into trouble: when the hidden meanings he is asked to consider aren't those symbolically imbedded within a piece of art, but that which might potentially be revealed in a serious consideration of his own thought processes. As a rule, the more anxiety-provoking the topic under consideration, the less likely it is that an individual will retain an ability to think symbolically about it, particularly when the level of anxiety is primitive in nature.

A failure to engage in metacognition is an important and largely overlooked aspect of concrete thinking. Segal (1957) describes a psychotic man who refused to play the violin in public because doing so would be tantamount to masturbating in public. Clearly, this patient knows how to symbolize, *though he has lost track of the fact that this is precisely what he is doing*. It isn't the lack of an ability to symbolize that makes an individual's thinking concrete; it is the *failure to recognize the nature of one's thinking*.

Metacognition

Metacognition (Flavell, 1979) refers to a broad set of cognitive functions, chiefly *metacognitive activities* ("thinking about one's thinking") and the resulting *metacognitive knowledge* – thoughts about one's thoughts, thoughts about the process by which one goes about thinking, and the conclusions reached about the nature of one's own thinking having given due consideration to one's thought processes. Metacognition additionally includes mechanisms for determining which cognitive strategy might prove most efficacious in understanding a given situation and assisting in assessing one's progress in reaching one's intended goal.

There are a host of comparable-seeming psychoanalytic concepts – theory of mind, mentalization, reflective functioning/self-reflective thinking, psychological mindedness, and mindfulness – which aren't truly equivalent to metacognition in that each is relatively limited in scope and, hence, subordinate to the overarching concept of metacognition. Metacognition subsumes, but extends far beyond, *theory of mind*, which postulates the way in which the human mind explains one's own actions and reaction as well as those of others. Possessing a theory of mind is necessary to understand that minds do not faithfully reproduce the external world as is and, cannot help but distort, to whatever extent, the essence of what is perceived due to misjudgment, misunderstanding, misinterpretation, expectation, and errors in perceptions caused, for example, by wishful thinking or an over-reliance on outdated theories that have, unbeknownst to the patient, outlived their usefulness. Theory of mind further stipulates that one must first know something about one's own, or another's beliefs, desires, and intentions, before one can reasonably surmise the meaning of one's own behavior or the behavior of others.

Theory of mind is a highly specific form of metacognitive knowledge that captures certain truths about the nature and functioning of the human mind *in general*. Other forms of metacognitive knowledge specify *unique* truths about the way a given individual's mind works relative to the minds of others, which is necessary not only to fathom one's own motives and mental tendencies (strengths, weaknesses, proclivities), but also to be able to distinguish one's own psychology from that of others – a skill that permits one to genuinely see things from another's perspective, to transcend the tendency to attribute, or project, one's own psychology into others.

Another overlapping term, that of *mentalization/reflective function*,[1] is defined by Fonagy (2008) as a process involving the largely preconscious mental activity of imagining what others might be thinking and feeling in an effort to interpret the underlying intentions of their actions as a function of that individual's mental states (e.g., beliefs, desires, etc.). While Fonagy's definition of mentalization seems nearly equivalent to that of theory of mind, he is quick to differentiate the two by noting that theory of mind "fails to encapsulate the relational and affect regulative aspects of interpretive behavior in mental state terms" (p. 3). Like theory of mind, mentalization is likewise a subset of metacognition given that this latter term considers a much broader field of mental phenomena. The same can be said of other related terms – *self-reflective thought* (limited to one's own unique psychology), *insight* (which does not specify the method by which that insight was acquired), and *psychological mindedness* ("the ability to identify dynamic [intrapsychic] components and to relate them to a person's difficulties"; McCallum & Piper, 1997, p. 1) – each of which proves equally narrow in comparison to metacognition.

Mindfulness (Epstein, 1990, 1995; Linehan, 1993; Siegel, 2007) refers to the state of mind of being fully in the moment, attending in a single-minded and open-minded fashion to the flow of one's inner thoughts and feelings. Mindfulness requires that one: (1) resist any inclination to become focused on mental content of whatever sort (e.g., thought, feeling, memory, emotion); (2) unquestioningly accept "what is" without labeling, judging, or categorizing it; and (3) resist temptations to suppress unpleasant realities or alter them to be more to one's liking. Mindfulness is an entirely different state of mind from that required to reach an understanding about the nature of one's thinking (metacognition) or the meaning of what one is experiencing. If one were pressed to draw a link between mindfulness and metacognition, it would be that the former prepares for the latter (Teasdale et al., 2002).

"Breaking set": the metacognitive basis of therapeutic action?

Consider the following riddle: a father and son have a car accident and are both badly hurt. They are both taken to separate hospitals. When the boy is taken in for an operation, the surgeon says, "I cannot do the surgery because this is my son." How is this possible? The structure of the riddle manipulates the listener into thinking the problem to be solved is: how can a man be in two places at the same time? Solving the riddle requires one to think "out of the box" by breaking an ingrained inclination to think surgeon = man. In this case, the surgeon is the boy's mother, which is the now "obvious" solution to the riddle.[2]

Cognitive psychologists use the term *breaking set* to refer to the process by which an individual transcends the application of previously developed pattern-recognition schemas so as to be able to gain an alternate perspective on novel situations that are exceptions to the expected pattern (Koller, 1992). This task is particularly difficult, if not impossible, for the concrete thinker. While pattern recognition makes the world infinitely easier to understand, there are instances when this cognitive achievement seriously impedes one's understanding of the situation at hand. In order to avoid becoming blinded by one's focused search for the expected pattern, one must first circumvent a default reliance on routine associative learning (McGaughey, 2008) in order to approach the novel situation anew. Breaking set is a metacognitive skill that distinguishes individuals referred to as "gifted" from those who merely test exceedingly well on I.Q. tests (Chmiliar, 1997; McGaughey, 2008; Veenman, 2008), which primarily measure an individual's ability to recognize patterns in order to solve problems (Dover & Shore, 1991; McGaughey, 2008). "Giftedness" implies higher degrees of cognitive flexibility, the ability to set aside a tried and true piece of learning that had, up until this instance, proven remarkably reliable, in order to appreciate the emergence of a new, exceptional pattern.

It can be argued that psychoanalysts clinically "teach metacognition" by example insofar as they adopt an attitude that is decidedly not wedded to the concrete reality that seems to define the literal aspects of the patient's presented material. In this regard, psychoanalysts simulate the type of metacognitive thinking naturally employed by gifted individuals. By thinking outside the box, the analyst demonstrates his ability to hear the patient's communications in an entirely novel fashion. The content is treated as if it were a meta-message for some other, deeper underlying truth that is trying to make itself known, unbeknownst to the patient who initially accepts his material concretely. Jorgensen (2004) writes about how the development of metacognitive ability is one of the goals of analytic therapy, "to step beyond the immediate reality of our own experience, and to grasp the distinction between that immediate experience and the underlying mental states that give rise to it" (p. 529).

The roots of concrete thinking: symbolization, differentiation, and metacognition

This chapter offers a metacognitive perspective on concrete thinking – one that views concrete thinking as a developmental arrest – in contrast to the approach taken by writers who either focus on the concrete patient's difficulties in symbolizing and/or his failure to differentiate. Difficulties in symbolizing are seen as the product of defenses against: (1) the formation of symbols (Klein, 1930); (2) the capacity to link symbols, to be able to advance preconception to conception (the concept of attacks on linking; Bion, 1959); or (3) the capacity to fathom the meaning of already formed symbols (Freud, 1900). Difficulties in differentiating can manifest as a failure to distinguish fantasy from reality, self-representations from object representations (Bass, 1997; Jacobson, 1957; Rosenfeld, 1952; Searles, 1962), or a signifier from that being signified. As we shall see shortly, symbolization and differentiation are integrally linked.

Freud (1900) posited the origins of symbolic thinking in the infant's psychic struggle to cope with states of unsatisfied need. Freud proposed the solution of hallucinatory wish fulfillment as a symbolic substitution for what the child desires but cannot presently have, as if a revival of the memory of satisfaction is tantamount to satisfaction itself, which has the infant believing in this psychic reality as if it were a tangible piece of reality (fantasy/hallucination of feeding at the breast = actual experience of feeding at the breast, an example of symbolic equation; Klein, 1930; Segal, 1957). This device only works as long as the child continues to think concretely (continues to conflate fantasy with reality) and keeps himself unaware of the "as if" proposition contained in the preceding sentence. This defense relies on the infant's use of disavowal – a defense that keeps the infant unaware of the undeniable, but easily overlooked, reality of the absent breast. Disavowal involves the creation of a vertical split in the ego that allows one to simultaneously know and not know some intolerable truth, which is relegated to the preconscious. This contrasts with repression, which involves the creation of a horizontal split that locks things safely away in the unconscious. As we shall see, disavowal plays a critical role in support of concrete thinking.

Symbol formation is the result of one thing being used to stand for, or substitute for, another on the basis of some inherent similarity between the two, whatever that might be. Susan Isaacs (1943) describes a twenty-month-old girl who'd become terrified of her mother's shoe that had a sole that had become partly detached. As the mother walked, the sole would flap repeatedly, making it look like a mouth that was opening and shutting. The girl literally equated the shoe with a mouth, overlooking dissimilarities between the two, and became quite sure the shoe would eat her up. She hadn't the ability to think "it is *as if* my mother's shoe is the same as a mouth." Symbolic equation is based on a failure to differentiate between "looks like" and "is identical to," and patients who operate on the level of symbolic equation often find it hard to differentiate between the symbol and that which it is meant to symbolize. Symbolization and differentiation are related in this fashion.

Depending on the degree of their concreteness, concrete patients demonstrate varying difficulties in differentiating fantasy from reality. On the psychotic end of the spectrum, the concrete thinker lacks an ability to test reality – to differentiate psychic from material reality – in contrast to the non-psychotic concrete thinker, who can test reality yet chooses not to, granting himself license to "keep his treasured beliefs untested" (Grossman, 1996, p. 512). While he knows better, he acts as if he has effectively eliminated any awareness of a disagreeable aspect of reality (akin to a negative hallucination), a product of the mechanism of disavowal that is reinforced by the creation of a fetishistic object (akin to a positive hallucination) meant to symbolically substitute a more agreeable reality in place of the disavowed reality (Basch, 1974). In the case of a frank perversion – itself a manifestation of concrete thinking – the anxiety aroused by the perception of a vagina (disagreeable because it reinforces the fantasy of castration) is momentarily set to rest by the perception of a penis-equivalent, the fetish itself. This symbolic substitution (fetish = penis) works only so long as the individual keeps himself unaware of just what he is doing – convincing himself, through the use of symbolic equation, that the fetish is as good as the real thing. This failure of differentiation is a cute trick that the non-concrete individual is too metacognitively aware to be able to pull off. For this mental sleight of hand to work, the concrete thinker must resist, at all cost, any attempt at metacognition, since metacognition, by definition, involves looking at the big picture – becoming aware of how and why one thinks as one does. Metacognition risks bringing down the house of cards created by the symbolic equations that perverse thinking erects, and this is something the individual can ill afford, thus explaining the threat posed by metacognitive thinking.

A specific way in which concrete patients exhibit difficulties in differentiating fantasy from reality is their failure to differentiate self from other. The intense anxiety that, for some, accompanies the recognition that one is separate from the much-needed object can contribute to the blurring of boundaries between self and other, which both results from, and contributes to, the persistence of concrete thinking. As long as the other functions as an auxiliary ego for the infant/child, recognizing one's separateness from that object is likely to produce intolerable levels of anxiety, experienced as tantamount to the loss of a much-needed part of oneself. Until such a time as the overwhelming anxiety caused by recognition of one's essential separateness lessens, "symbolic equation is used to deny the separateness between the subject and the object" (Segal, 1978, p. 316).

Concrete thinking as developmental arrest: theory of mind

This chapter outlines a metacognitive approach to the understanding of concrete thinking, which is based on the proposition that concrete thinking can be a developmental disorder – the result of a developmental fixation that leaves the individual functioning with a less sophisticated theory of mind, much like that of a latency-age child. When we speak of an individual possessing a theory of mind (Perner, 1991; Premack & Woodruff, 1978; Wellman, 2002), we mean he has a theory that essentially grasps what a mind is and how a mind works – how it psychically represents internal and external reality. Before the age of four, children lack a theory of mind insofar as they think of the mind as camera-like in its ability to faithfully capture and reproduce reality as is, oblivious to the existence of a perceiving organ – a figurative lens capable of introducing distortions of its own – interposed between stimuli and perception. Accordingly, young children find it inconceivable that the mind might arrive at a belief that is factually false. The realization and acceptance of the existence of false beliefs is the first stage in the acquisition of a theory of mind. Further development takes place in incremental steps over the course of childhood, evolving from more rudimentary theories of mind to increasingly sophisticated theories, optimally culminating at the outset of adolescence in a highly sophisticated model of the mind manifesting as an ability to appreciate the extent to which the mind interprets or constructs what it sees. It is important to keep in mind that a theory of mind is not something one has or lacks. Individuals differ from one another, and even differ themselves from one moment to the next with regard to how sophisticated their current theory of mind is presently being.

Before the age of four, children cannot grasp what for them is the mind-blowing fact that the mind can't always be trusted to faithfully represent reality. After the age of four, children begin to appreciate that people are sometimes mistaken about what they think is so. Having come to accept that beliefs can be false, they nevertheless hold to the idea that false beliefs are simply the result of one having been insufficiently informed – poorly positioned vis-à-vis the observed stimuli. They further believe, with enough conviction to lead them to think of it as "knowing," that all one need do to determine which among the competing perspectives correctly captures reality is to be in possession of enough of the facts. Confusing "believing" with "knowing" in this way is evidence of the absence of metacognition. Through latency, children maintain a rudimentary theory of mind that is limited by the child's failure to realize that "truth" is sometimes indeterminable – an idea that threatens that child's faith in his mind's reliability. Young children are too busy with the task of making sense of the world to be able to step back and examine the nature of their thinking. It is the lack of this particular ability – the ability to think metacognitively – that may persist into adulthood, thus contributing to the maintenance of concrete thinking.

The latency-age child can accept the fact that they'd been wrong once. What they aren't yet ready to accept is the possibility that they may be wrong again...and again...and again. And while the latency-age child has begun to appreciate that the world can be interpreted in many different ways, he or she still believes that only one of these many interpretations has any real legs to stand on. Latency-age children write off all other competing theories as misguided, the product of simple and correctable illusions that can, in principal, be set right.

An insufficiently developed theory of mind plays an important, though overlooked role, in concrete thinking. An incomplete theory of mind is both the product and result of one's inability to engage in metacognition regarding the nature of one's own thought processes. Concrete thinking can be thought to be rooted either in a persistence (fixation) of more rudimentary theories of mind or in a regression back to these modes of thinking.

Environmental factors contributing to the persistence of concrete thinking into adulthood

While the timetable outlined above might give the impression that the development of theory of mind comes "online" in a predetermined fashion regardless of environmental factors, this is not the case. Parents who have well-developed theories of mind and use language that emphasizes mental states in their communications with their offspring accelerate the ability of their children to master the false belief tasks (Brown et al., 1986; Meins et al., 1998). In particular, the quality of a child's attachment pattern as measured on the Adult Attachment Interview (AAI) is a significant factor in his or her performance on theory of mind tasks during childhood and the development of metacognitive ability in adulthood. Parents who demonstrate a capacity to think metacognitively raise children who tend to be more securely attached (Fonagy et al., 1991; Moss et al., 1995); children who have insecure attachment patterns perform poorly on theory of mind tasks (see Fonagy & Target, 1998, for a review of the literature), and adults who rate as "insecurely attached" on the AAI demonstrate poor metacognitive monitoring as measured in their attachment narratives (Main, 1991). Psychosocial stressors can also help undermine an individual's theory of mind mechanisms and, through this, his capacity for metacognition (Fonagy & Target, 1998).

Theory of mind research permits us to see concrete thinking in action during childhood, making it easier to recognize the persistence of such thinking when it's encountered in adulthood. We are still left to wonder, however, why some adult patients don't develop more sophisticated theories of mind and/ or fail to evolve past the point of using symbolic equation. Environmental factors may contribute to this fixation, the persistence of which, some might argue, serves the function of defense, which makes it difficult to separate developmentally based cognitive disturbances from those primarily serving as a defense.

Fonagy (1991) describes the treatment of an extraordinarily difficult male patient, Mr. S., who challenged many of Fonagy's notions about psychoanalytic treatment. Though he never identifies the patient's concrete thinking as such, Fonagy's description of the manifestations of the patient's behavior surely warrants thinking of the patient in these terms: the patient's associations lacked depth and evocativeness and were so monotonous and repetitive that they nearly put the analyst to sleep; the patient would reify his words, making them into things. Fonagy holds environmental factors primarily accountable for this patient's failure to acquire a theory of mind (to be able to "mentalize," as he calls it). After paying lip service to the notion that Mr. S. may well have projected his sadism into his parents, causing them to appear cruel in their intentions toward their son, Fonagy goes on to posit:

> To the extent that the establishment of a theory of mind is predicated upon the contemplation of the mental state of one's primary object, it is imperative that the generally prevailing disposition of the primary object towards the self is sufficiently thoughtful and benign. Faced with profoundly cruel and mentally vacuous parenting, Mr. S. had no opportunity fully to acquire a theory of mind...The parents' abuse undermines the child's theory of mind, so that it is no longer safe for the child for example to think about wishing if this implies the contemplation of the all too real wishes of the parent to harm the child...Individuals whose primary objects are unloving and cruel may find the contemplation of the contents of the mind of the objects unbearable. The abandonment of their capacity for secondary representation thus becomes an adaptive, if extreme, measure. (p. 108)

While Melanie Klein saw symbol formation developing out of a need to cope with anxiety, she realized that if anxiety became too great – if a child's sadistic impulses toward the mother were so intense as to produce fantasies of retaliation accompanied by intolerable levels of persecutory anxiety – the child would then cease to use symbols altogether (Klein, 1930). This was the conclusion Klein reached in her treatment of an autistic four-year-old named Dick, who was oppositional and hostile toward his mother. Mentioned, but underemphasized, in the clinical report is the nature of Dick's environment: a cold mother incapable of breastfeeding to the point her son nearly starved to death, and a father and wet nurse who provided no tenderness whatsoever. "Though he had every care," writes Klein, "no real love was lavished on him" (p. 28). Though Segal reinforced Klein's ideas in her 1957 paper by concluding that projective identification per se leads to concretization, she amended this theory 21 years later utilizing Bion's (1957) container-and-contained model, which postulates that concrete thinking is the result of a failure of the object to effectively contain, detoxify, and return in a metabolizable form the infant's hostile projections. A proper container facilitates the infant's achievement of the depressive position by providing the experience of containment and, with it, a good object for internalization – which both facilitates, and is facilitated by, the process of symbolic representation.

Treatment considerations: the futility of transference interpretations in the treatment of concrete patients

Patients who tend to think concretely are oftentimes made floridly, even psychotically, anxious when confronted/affronted with transference interpretations. For such patients, transference interpretations are contraindicated. Other types of interpretations may also prove intolerable. Having one's most cherished and seemingly reliable theories or perspectives called into question can be so psychically destabilizing and anxiety-provoking for the concrete patient as to threaten the analysis altogether. Like the latency-age child who believes that every problem has but one solution, concrete patients confronted with a view that differs from their own will assume that only one of the two competing views can possibly be correct. In this regard, the concrete patient has yet to enter the postmodern world. If the analyst seems invested in his particular viewpoint regarding a given matter, it may seem to the patient as if the analyst subscribes to his own view *to the exclusion* of the patient's view. Feeling his knowledge is being negated can lead to the patient becoming defensive and to him perceiving the analyst as overly eager to be proven right. The way in which the analyst delivers his interpretation (e.g., doing so with an air of certainty) may further reinforce the patient's fear that he and the analyst are about to lock horns over the question of whom of the two is correct. Since the concrete patient thinks in terms of right and wrong, true or false, all or nothing, he finds it hard to imagine that the analyst doesn't do likewise. Coming to the realization that the analyst actually thinks in terms of "both x and y," rather than "either x or y," is one step in the direction of developing a more sophisticated theory of mind, facilitated by the patient's engaging in a bit of metacognition that leads to the realization of how differing minds may work. This, in turn, contributes to the patient's capacity to differentiate his own psychology from that of the analyst. This description encapsulates a process often encountered in the treatment of concrete patients. Grasping the nature of how one thinks in distinction to how others think is an essentially metacognitive lesson. In the course of an analysis, this metacognitive realization often develops in relation to an alternate way of thinking demonstrated by the analyst in his work with the patient.

The concrete patient develops a sense of certainty about what he thinks (he calls it "knows") to be true. Concrete thinkers are remarkably closed-minded.

They feel no need to test reality because they regard their beliefs are indisputable. This often manifests clinically in a patient's assertion that he knows this or that to be true of the analyst, even though he cannot back up his claim – nor does he feel it necessary to back his claim – with some objective piece of evidence beyond mere intuition. If challenged about how he "knows" such a thing to be true, the patient is likely to become defensive.

Bass (1997) presents just such a clinical situation in which a patient insists the analyst accept her view of him as indisputable. A female patient, who is in the habit of keeping certain thoughts to herself out of fear her analyst will be critical of her, is late for an early morning session. She begins by saying that she "knows the analyst is mad at her for being late." She and the analyst had recently been talking about her conflict over her aggressive feelings, which primes the analyst to interpret her belief that he is mad at her as a matter of projection – her projecting her anger at him into him, causing her to then assume, dare we say "misperceive," that he, not she, is the one who is angry – a clear failure to differentiate self from other. Bass picks up on the fact that the patient's communication contains not one but two important pieces of information: the first, her assertion that she "knows" something, and the second, the content of what she claims to know – her fantasy. Because analysts are hounds for symbolic meaning, her analyst seizes on the second part of her communication, the *content* of her fantasy, entirely ignoring her assertion that this is something she knows. When the analyst attempts to interpret the content of what he considers her fantasy, which she calls her knowledge, his efforts backfire. The two are drawn into a power struggle about whom of the two is right. What the analyst is missing is the patient's desperate *need to know* (the known devil is worse than the unknown devil), her *need to unquestioningly know* (terrified of the alternative of not knowing), and her *plea to be permitted to continue to know* that which she claims to know. Bass notes that a subsequent reorientation of the analytic couple's focus on why the patient needs to know and insists on knowing, rather than on the content of what she knows, permits therapeutic progress to resume, even though this attempt to get her to think metacognitively leaves her feeling terribly unsettled: "I don't like this," she comments. "It feels like trees flying in the air" (p. 667). In similar fashion, Mr. A. felt absolutely certain about the conclusions he reached regarding his analyst. Tuch (2007) notes:

> ...for Mr. A. to recognize that who he thought I was and why he thought I did what I did was, in part, a product of his own ways of organizing relationships is not a thought he found thinkable. He steadfastly insisted that who he knew me to be was unquestionably true and he was hostile toward the suggestion that it wasn't necessarily so. In this way, Mr. A. functioned like a child who has yet to realize that such a thing as a false belief exists. (p. 104)

In effect, without saying so in so many words, Bass proposes that the most effective approach to the treatment of concrete patients is metacognitive in nature: the analyst invites the patient to consider why the patient needs to think what he thinks – an approach that differs markedly from one that translates the symbolic content of a patient's fantasies. Renik (1992) describes patients who turn the analyst's concrete presence and interpretations into fetishistic objects that, for the patient, indisputably represent the actual satisfaction of the patient's wishes, even while the analyst is trying to interpret as much through his words. The only way around the dilemma, reasons Renik, is to adopt a process-oriented clinical stance aimed to addressing the *kind of thinking* the patient is engaging in, which is essentially a metacognitive approach to treatment. Along these same lines, Josephs (1989) writes that when analysts:

> ...interpret the concrete attitude in terms of its defensive and symbolic meanings, [they] misconstrue a developmental necessity as a resistance. The maintenance of the concrete attitude may be crucial in preserving a sense of reality, and to question the validity of the concrete attitude is to threaten the patient's insecurely established sense of reality. (p. 494)

This brings us around, full circle, to theory of mind research that demonstrates how young children are too busy making sense of the world and too much in need of believing the products of their minds to entertain a different (metacognitive) perspective.

Lecours (2007) suggests a psychoanalytically informed approach to patients prone to thinking nonsymbolically, which he refers to as "supportive" – not to be confused with the defense-promoting, repression-heightening variety of treatment that typically comes to mind when this term is mentioned. Lecours envisions this supportive approach as primarily aimed at lessening the patient's intense, fragmenting persecutory anxiety, which he believes can ultimately result in the slow transformation of nonsymbolic content into "more containable, symbolically manageable or meaningful forms" (p. 908). Lecours' approach suggests that patients can and do develop capacities for symbolic thinking so long as the analyst manages the situation so as not to heighten the patient's primitive anxieties to mind-boggling levels by forcing the patient to have to contend with the symbolic aspects of the transference by directly interpreting the transference. The supportive approach Lecours recommends is:

> ...aimed at helping the patient catch a glimpse of the illusory nature of her transference...[by creating] a (symbolic) space between the reality of our relationship and her experience of this reality...to prise the conviction of reality out of the transference experience. (p. 906)

Lecours operationalizes this supportive approach in reference to a brief clinical vignette he presents:

> Rather than trying to reveal the unconscious meaning of [this patient's] feelings toward me, I was attempting to gain some emotional distance from their actual quality or, in other words, I was striving to help her "symbolize her experience of the transference." In the session presented above, I strove to exist in reality as an object different than the one pervasively activated by her transference. (p. 906)

Lecours believes his approach strives to simultaneously lessen the patient's persecutory anxiety, the projection of which leads to a belief in the analyst's irrefutable malevolence, and to interact with the patient in ways that might prove sufficiently benevolent to contribute to the creation of a much-needed good internal object.

Where Lecours and I differ is that he fails to take up the question of when and whether patients may be receptive to thinking more symbolically; not prospectively, but in the here-and-now. The proper handling of such patients involves picking and choosing the subjects about which these patients are, in fact, more capable of metacognitive (symbolic) thinking. The transference is clearly an area that is often too hot for these patients to handle, so transference interpretations are generally off limits. This is not to say, however, that nonsymbolic patients are never capable of thinking symbolically about others, or even about themselves, so long as the topic is far enough away from transference to keep their anxiety to a manageable level.

The compelling feature of concrete thinking: effects on the analyst

It is not just the patient's lack of receptiveness to, or the typical ineffectiveness of, the analyst's interpretations that characterizes the transferences of concrete patients. Such patients may express outright hostility toward the analyst's attempts to even think analytically, mocking his introduction of a more experience-distant, reflective stance that momentarily distances the analytic couple from feeling immersed in the in-the-moment, here-and-now experience (Tuch, 2007). Such a maneuver on the analyst's part threatens the concrete patient with the realization of the analyst's otherness, the fact that he and the patient aren't always of like mind, which challenges the concrete patient's wish to think of the two as one. This hostility toward interpretation echoes society's general antagonism toward the unconscious and toward anyone "foolish enough" to delve below the surface of concrete experience in search of God knows what. Freud is credited with having said "sometimes a cigar is just a cigar" – a literal-minded statement if there ever was one.

A thorough review of his writings finds no such reference, though some claim he might have said as much during a lecture he delivered at Clark University in 1909 (Elms, 2001). The perpetuation of this myth illustrates a level of overt hostility that society in general, and concrete thinkers in particular, harbor toward those who find symbolism underlying all human experience. In the consulting room, hostility toward the symbol-minded analyst often results in the patient's effort to shame the analyst, to make him feel ridiculous for having adopted such an analytic stance – all of which is unconsciously intended to throw the analyst off the patient's scent.

No matter how well developed the analyst's capacity for symbolic thought, every analyst retains a propensity to lapse into concrete thinking – it's their cognitive heritage – and this propensity leaves the analyst vulnerable to regressing, given the "right" circumstances. Sometimes regression is the result of a patient effectively shaming the analyst about the oddity of the analyst's failure to see and accept things as they are. The commonsensical nature and compelling logic of the patient's use of "reality as a defense" is also seductive and undermining of the analyst's capacity to see past the allure of simplicity. Reality can be used, for example, to justify and explain away each and every instance a patient has shown up late for a session, ultimately leaving the analyst to throw his hands up in despair having tired of trying to swim upstream against the current. Sometimes it gets to a point where it just doesn't seem worth the fight.

Shaming the analyst for adopting an analytic stance and the utilization of reality as a defense are but two of the many ways in which a patient may effectively attack and disrupt the analyst's ability to think – an ability that depends on the maintenance of a "third space" (Britton, 1989) in which the analyst is beyond the reach of the potentially mind-seductive effects of the patient's projections and provocations that oftentimes draw the analyst unthinkingly into an enactment (Aron & Benjamin, 1999). No matter how well analyzed an analyst has been, he still remains vulnerable to the loss of his capacity to think, leading Bion (2011) to suggest that analysts sometimes have to make "the best of a bad job" (p. 321).

What often proves maddening about concrete patients is the way in which their thinking challenges the analyst's ability to retain his commitment and ability to think symbolically. A dedication to do so is oftentimes not enough, and every analyst – at one time or another – has succumbed to the draw of concrete thinking. Concrete thinking is compelling insofar as it pushes toward immediate actualization in comparison with symbolic thinking that lessens the intensity of anxiety, thus permitting a degree of delay before one's curiosity must be satisfied. Lecours (2007) observes:

> ...the concreteness of nonsymbolized contents is embodied in action-based modes of expression that have a high interpersonal pull...when

actualized in relationships, these emotional contents tend to attract an equally concrete mode of responding by the other, facilitating a countertransferential responsiveness when that other is an analyst. (p. 901)

Concluding remarks

The clinical challenges posed by concrete patients are many and varied. These patients prove to be less than ideal candidates for psychoanalysis or analytically informed psychotherapy because they are typically unreceptive to the most potent tool that the analyst has to offer – transference interpretations. These patients have little, if any, interest in the analyst's interpretations and may even decompensate when asked to consider an alternate perspective from their own. Such patients don't completely understand what the analyst is up to when he tries to interpret. They are looking for concrete solutions – hardly the analyst's stock and trade. These patients may regard the analyst's interpretive activity as self-serving, seeing it, for example, as meant to result in the analyst's intellectual triumph over the misguided patient, his need to educate heathens, a sort of psychoanalytic "white man's burden." Or, worse, he may regard the analyst's interpretations as if he were sadistically toying with the patient's mind by casting doubt on what he knows to be true.

If these problems aren't already enough of an impediment to treatment, concrete patients can be a drag to treat. As a rule, concrete patients provide analysts no royal road to the unconscious, given their propensity to rarely, if ever, present dreams. In fact, they provide little road whatsoever along which the analyst might make his way to an understanding of the patient's unconscious. They report their fantasies as concrete, reality-based fears for which they seek the analyst's reassurance rather than his understanding (Josephs, 1989). Their language fails to evoke imagery, ignite the analyst's imagination, or stimulate his reverie or curiosity. Their language is stultifying and their detailed and repetitious speech tends to be soporific. Being with such patients can be deadening. For these patients, Joseph (1989) observes "the analyst as audience to the report is looked to not as much for interpretation of the facts but for consensual validation of the accuracy of the account" (p. 478). To make matters worse, concrete thinkers tend to enact their issues to a much greater degree than patients who think symbolically – patients who can tolerate delayed gratification and who can sit, for a time, with an uncomfortable affect without moving into action. Concrete enactments have a way of drawing the other in, leading the analyst to engage in some concrete thinking of his own. While enactments can occur in every analysis, they are more commonplace, and more formidable, in the treatment of concrete patients.

Theories offered to account for concrete thinking include defenses against symbolization (against forming symbols, linking symbols, and/or understanding symbols) and failures to properly differentiate fantasy from reality, self from other, signifier and that which is signified. Symbolization and differentiation are, in fact, intertwined at the level of symbolic equation, where the signifier and the signified are treated as if they are one and the same (not differentiated). A concrete patient who fails to draw a distinction between signifier and that which is signified will fail to appreciate the irony and humor of Magritte's thought-provoking painting "The Treachery of Images" (1928–9), which contains a painting of a pipe and the inscription "*Ceci n'est pas une pipe*" ("This is not a pipe").

This chapter proposes an additional theory – the persistence of a rudimentary theory of mind – that manifests in the kind of concrete thinking evident in childhood. This developmental arrest can result from environmental factors that inhibit one's inclination and/or capacity to consider what is on another's mind given experiences with caregivers who harbored intense hostility toward the child or who were markedly careless regarding the child's well-being – whose thoughts about the child were more than the child could bear (Funagy, 1991). Concrete thinking can also result when intense levels of anxiety are aroused by the analyst challenging the routine and comforting explanations about all psychic matters that concrete patients cling to for dear life.

If concrete thinking is predicated on symbolic equations, it is further reinforced by the careful avoidance of metacognitive thinking. Were the concrete thinker to consider why he thinks what he thinks, were he to attend not just to his thoughts but to his thought processes, he would soon recognize his reliance on disavowal – a psychic mechanism that permits one to simultaneously know and not know a bit of unacceptable reality – which permits him to continue to believe that the signifier and signified are identical. This is particularly well illustrated in perversions, where the fetishistic object is seen as no different from the missing penis, or in the case of hallucinatory wish fulfillment, where the perception of the breast is thought to be every bit as satisfying as the breast itself. Metacognitive thinking is inconsistent with concrete thinking, since the former tends to undo the latter. Once an individual recognizes his use of disavowal, that mechanism can no longer work, in the same way that sleight of hand no longer does the trick of mystifying the observer once he understands how the trick is accomplished.

Metacognition is a complex set of cognitive activities that results in metacognitive knowledge about the way one's *own* mind works (self-reflective functioning) and the way in which *everyone's* mind works (theory of mind, mentalization). In the case of concrete patients, working to understand how their mind works may prove more palatable to such patients than their having to contend with content interpretations, particularly when focused on the transference. Sugarman (2006) argues that interesting a patient in the general workings of his mind – helping him view himself as a thinking self by regarding him as such – helps facilitate the development of higher-order (metacognitive) thinking, which – in Sugarman's estimation – often proves more therapeutically helpful than the acquisition of specific insights into one's unconscious conflicts or unrecognized mental contents. Aron (2000) contends that "at the end of an analysis it is not insight or other knowledge of psychic content that would best demonstrate the patient's growth or the success of the treatment, but rather it is the capacity for self-reflexivity" (p. 677), and he sees analysis as "the only treatment that operates directly to improve the capacity for self-reflexivity" (p. 674).

From a clinical standpoint, it's been suggested that therapeutic change may come about through a strengthening of metacognitive functioning (Eagle, 2003) and that improvement in metacognitive functioning may be one way of measuring therapeutic change (Lichtenberg, 1999). Metacognitive functioning is posited as having "protective value" insofar as it may lower the risk of certain kinds of maladaptive patterns (Fonagy et al., 1995; Main, 1991), and a deficit in metacognitive functioning is said to "account for self-regulation deficits such as problems of affect regulation, frustration tolerance, impulsiveness, and self-esteem problems, as well as social deficits, such as poor peer relationships, poor communication skills, and aggressive or violent behavior" (Fonagy & Target, 1998, p. 104).

Metacognitive research has additionally provided a model, known as "breaking set," that could amply explain the underlying mental mechanisms that permit one to proceed from the illumination of enacted transference assumptions to the deconstruction of those assumptions (breaking set), which then paves the way for a new piece of learning (the "new relationship"), which the old pattern-recognizing systems had made impossible to imagine or perceive. Psychoanalysts would be well served studying the fascinating conclusions being reached in this emerging area of cognitive development.

Once an analyst has tasted what it's like to work with patients on a symbolic level, working with patients who are less able to work symbolically can, quite frankly, be a letdown. Particularly disappointing is the fact that the analyst's interpretations fall on deaf ears. Most psychoanalysts had a different type of patient in mind when they entered the field. The fact that we find concrete patients gracing our doorsteps means we must find ways to reach these patients as well. Wishing them to be more like the often-preferred symbol-proficient patient, and treating them as such, is an exercise in futility. The technical modifications needed to treat these patients needn't be so radical, since they mainly involve a shift in emphasis – downplaying interpretations in general, and transference interpretations in particular, while inviting patients to focus more on the general workings of their mind – to rely more heavily on metacognition. In addition, it is important that the analyst pays rapt attention to the management of the patient's level of anxiety, which one must do with every patient, but which often proves clinically pivotal when one undertakes the treatment of concrete patients who are prone to decompensating or fragmenting when their anxiety is intensified by clinical maneuvers better tolerated by the more symbol-minded patient.

Notes

1 These two are used almost interchangeably by those writing in the field (e.g., Shaughnessy et al., 2008).

2 Or is it? Satisfaction about having solved the riddle, combined with the mindset that riddles have one and only one solution, interferes with the realization that there are other boxes – ones less likely to come to mind – that could also solve the riddle, solutions like: (1) the surgeon is the boy's biological (versus adopted) father; or (2) the one reporting the facts of the riddle is either mistaken or lying (an almost inconceivable, but still viable, possibility).

Section III

Psychoanalytic schools of thought

Chapter 7

The interpersonalist's handling of enactments

The effect of comparative theories on technique

Since Jacobs (1986) introduced the term "countertransference enactment" roughly thirty years ago, the role of enactments in psychoanalytic practice has come to be widely regarded as pivotal, culminating in Gabbard's (1995) declaration that enactments had become the new "common ground" of psychoanalytic practice. A growing appreciation of the clinical value of enactments was seen as drawing together analysts with different theoretical perspectives who all seemed to agree that enactments are inevitable, commonplace, oftentimes unavoidable, and potentially beneficial if handled properly. Where analysts differ is on three counts: whether enactments might be less innocuous than some make them out to seem; whether enactments chiefly emanate from the patient or can also be set in motion by the analyst's actions; and how enactments can best be harvested to reap the maximum therapeutic benefit. This chapter addresses these differences on the way toward illustrating how an understanding about and the management of countertransference enactments differ as a function of varying psychoanalytic theories. As we shall see, the difference lies in whether one sees enactments, on the one hand, as an actualization of the transference (a sign of intrapsychic conflict, repression, and projective identification) or, on the other hand, as a manifestation of dissociation whereby aspects of one's experience are perceived as existing in the person of the analyst.

While the analytic management of enactments represents, in the minds of many, a major breakthrough in psychoanalytic technique, some analysts express concern about the tendency to glorify enactments as the new royal road to the unconscious. These analysts see enactments not as an indispensable, but as a troublesome and regrettable, occurrence. Steiner (2006), for example, is of the opinion that "enactments are harmful to the patient and the analytic process" (p. 315), elaborating:

> It is difficult to reconcile the idea that enactments can give helpful information about the patient and his relationships with the recognition that, in the process, boundaries may be violated and to a greater or lesser extent both the patient and the analytic work can be damaged. (p. 315)

While many disagree with Steiner's view on the matter, which Levenson (2006) sees as "demonizing" enactments, some agree with Steiner's assessment that enactments represent a failure on the analyst's part to "contain" what the patient is needing her to contain, which led Ivey (2008) to caution us about "making a virtue of enactments" (p. 26). Given the rush to embrace enactments as "transformative" (Varga, 2006), as critical to the working-through process (Bass, 2003), and as a therapeutically powerful process "that links current and past experience with a vividness of affect and intersubjective relatedness that imparts enormous conviction (Chused, 1991, p. 634), I would counsel caution against the potential dangers of becoming swept up in a trend that likely represents a hyperbolic, pendulum-like swing to an alternate extreme in reaction to the faults of our fathers who, admittedly, had failed to take sufficient note of, and had failed to develop effective ways of addressing enactments, as had been noted in Chapter 3 of this book.

Denis Carpy (1989), a Kleinian analyst, identifies both a valuable aspect as well as a potential danger of enactments. On the one hand, enactments can afford a patient a sense of having had a powerful impact on the analyst; on the other hand, believing one had so impacted the analyst as to cause her to lose her capacity to analyze, throwing her completely off kilter, is likely to produce a mixture of triumph, anxiety, guilt, and dread in the patient. Carpy writes about how enactments provide an opportunity that "allows the patient to see that the analyst is being affected by what is projected, is struggling to tolerate it, and, if the analysis is to be effective, is managing sufficiently to maintain his analytic stance without grossly acting out" (p. 292). This thinking is in line with Chused's (1996) thoughts on the matter:

> ...when [the analyst] is expected to be prohibiting, threatening, rejecting, provoked, seductive or seducible, and [she] is not, when [her] actions do not fulfill transference expectations, whether [her] behavior pleases or disappoints, it will inform the patient about himself. And that is what analysis is all about. (p. 1070)

As we consider interpersonalist theories about enactments further along in this chapter, we shall see an exception to Chused's overly global statement of "this is what analysis is all about," seeing that interpersonalists view enactments as the result of a patient's tendency to relate to disowned parts of the self as if they are experienced as existing within the analyst's mind. Given this perspective, the clinical management of enactments differs markedly from how more classically oriented analysts work to the extent interpersonal analysts do not consider the task of making the transference explicitly mutative.

Two-way street versus the "doer/done to" dynamic

Beyond the question of whether enactments are generally beneficial or seriously problematic is the matter of whether enactments are recognized as truly being a two-way process that can just as easily be set in motion by the analyst as by the patient. All analysts seem to appreciate that enactments are co-constructed – that each party contributes his or her fair share by reacting in her own particular way to what has been elicited in them by the other. Enactments are a back-and-forth process in which analyst and analysand influence one another in a chicken-or-egg fashion that often makes it hard to determine who fired the first shot – whose behavior got the ball rolling in the first place. While many analysts appear to recognize that enactments can chiefly be analyst-initiated just as they can chiefly be patient-initiated,[1] definitions offered to describe the enactment process tend to emphasize the patient's contribution while making little to no mention of instances when an enactment seems to stem from the way in which the analyst relates to the patient, interprets the patient, conducts the analysis, and so on and so forth.

After extensively reviewing the literature on the subject, Ivey (2008) sums up what he sees as the general consensus about enactments in the following manner: an enactment is recognized to have occurred "when the patient unconsciously recruits the analyst's subjective predisposition to feel and respond in certain ways by behaving in a manner intended to elicit an emotional reaction from the analyst that confirms a transference fantasy" (p. 20). Note the one-way directionality. Ivey goes on to observe how "this definition emphasizes what the patient, under the sway of his or her transference, *does to the analyst*...[and] while the analyst's unconscious emotional responsiveness is crucial to the enactment, this is *activated and driven by the patient's transference*" (p. 21, italics added). This one-way view of enactment, notes Ivey, leaves aside instances when the process is chiefly of the analyst's making (Levine & Friedman, 2000) – a view shared by many in the relational school that see enactments as fully "co-constructed" by virtue of the analyst's cooperation and, at times, initiation.

The doer/done perspective of enactments

One sure way to remain lost in the maze of an enactment is to see the situation from a one-person perspective that envisions one party as "the doer" and the other as "the one done to" (Benjamin, 2004). One can observe this perspective in play in an everyday sort of way when one hears the formulaic expression "you made me [do, or say, or feel, or act] x." Enactments occur both inside and outside the consulting room, and certain patients are more prone than others to becoming caught up in enactments on a regular basis. Such instances of enactment can be analyzed fruitfully just so long as the analyst steers clear of accepting the patient's self-portrayal as the "one done to," which sometimes proves difficult to the extent the patient has become entrenched in believing that he had, *in fact*, been forced against his will into an enactment, or "made" to have to assume a particular role. Thinking as much constitutes a major hurdle in the task of climbing one's way out of an enactment. Benjamin (2004) notes how, in the consulting room, enactments typically involve both analyst and analysand believing that they had been "made" to feel or think or do something on the behest of the other. Therein lies the rub!

Benjamin (2004) identifies the "doer/done to" perspective that is often adopted by both parties who've become so embroiled in an enactment as to lose track of where their subjectivity ends and that of the other begins, violating Benjamin's (1988, 1992) brand of intersubjectivity, which is defined in terms of *mutual recognition* – one's ability to recognize the subjectivity of the other as distinct from one's own. From Benjamin's (2004) perspective, enactment involves "the impossibility of acknowledging the other's reality without abandoning one's own" (p. 30). If, for example, the analyst takes to heart how she's being viewed by the patient, as typically happens in the midst of an enactment, the patient's malignant view of the analyst can seriously threaten the analyst's ability to maintain an alternate and preferred self-image. Naturally, the same can be said of the effect of the analyst's view of the patient on the patient. "When the patient's reality is that 'You are toxic and have made me ill, mad, and unable to function,'" notes Benjamin (2004), "the analyst will typically find it nearly impossible to take that in without losing her own reality" (p. 30). Benjamin sums up the situation in this fashion:

> Where this kind of malignant complementarity takes hold, the ping-pong of projective identification – the exchange of blame – is often too rapid to halt or even to observe. The analyst cannot function empathically, because attunement to the patient now feels like submission to extortion, and it is partly through this involuntary response on the analyst's part to the patient's dissociated self-experience that trauma is reenacted. Neither patient nor analyst can have a grip on reality at this point. (pp. 30–31)

It can be instructive to examine the enactments of everyday life, illustrated in the following example. A powerful executive in his mid-fifties is anticipating the arrival of his parents – now in their eighties – who are coming to town for the week. The patient finds it hard to endure his domineering father's style of relating to him – a mixture of domination and a rigid, classically defined paternalistic attitude – the kind of father who likes calling his son "son." The patient wonders, this time around, how long he'll be able to civilly tolerate his father before becoming utterly unglued, as he's apt to do. He talks in terms of his father "making" him feel particular ways, which leaves the patient's participation – his way of responding to his dad – completely out of the picture. This makes it appear as if the patient hasn't a hand in the matter, which can't possibly be the case, given his own tendencies to make what he makes of the father's way of being. Working to help the patient regain his capacity to experience his subjectivity as his own requires he be helped to extricate himself from feeling as if he's the one "done to" so that he then can begin to take responsibility for recognizing and maintaining, against the powerful gale winds of enactment, his subjectivity as distinct from his father's, which requires he begin to appreciate what it is he "does" with how his father relates to him.

In the session following the one during which my patient had reported dread over his father's upcoming visit, the patient is reporting a phone conversation he's just had with his son. In response to the patient's seemingly solicitous invitation for the son to share how things have been going, the son mentions, "I am having a hard time getting out of my own way." My patient can't make heads or tails of the comment, and while he's previously been inclined under such circumstances to accuse his son of obfuscating, the patient is now better able to steer clear of attributing that particular motive to the son's oblique communication. Had he said to the son, "You are just trying to confuse me" (phrased as if he were doing nothing more than making an observation), doing so would have been a sure sign of an enactment in action to the extent it "nails" the son with a saturated interpretation that is likely to result in the son's efforts to either debate the matter in order to get away from being forced to accept an interpretation that didn't fit or, more likely (given the son's past behavior), to withdraw, resigned to his fate that "Dad will never understand me." Note that I am not claiming to know whether the son was, in fact, being oblique in an effort to purposefully confuse the father; that remained a possibility. But knowing a bit about the son, it seemed more likely that the son's actions were in the service of saving his own psychic hide by hiding from himself. At any rate, my patient was on the path of learning that he'd be better off sharing his own state of confusion about what his son had meant, and his own wish that the two might find ways to better understand one another, otherwise father and son were at risk of falling into yet another enactment as had been their habit. Benjamin (2004) sums up the situation in this fashion:

> The recovery of subjectivity requires the recognition of our own participation…Once we have deeply accepted our own contribution – and its inevitability – the fact of two-way participation becomes a vivid experience, something we can understand and use to feel less helpless and more effective…The experience of surviving breakdown into complementarity, or twoness, and subsequently of communicating and restoring dialogue – each person surviving for the other – is crucial to therapeutic action. (p. 11)

When the analyst successfully extricates herself from an enactment and comes to realize something about herself and the patient that she wishes to convey, she may feel inclined (if more classically oriented) to fashion this understanding into an interpretation. Working one's way free of the blinding effect of an enactment and regaining one's capacity to be self-reflective in the process may be followed by the analyst acting on her wish to share with the patient her newly acquired realizations about the enactment, offered in the form of an interpretation. There are times, however, when this only serves to dig a deeper hole *if the patient isn't yet ready to also make the shift*. If this be the case, the patient may incorporate the interpretation itself, or the analyst's motives for interpreting, into a furtherance of the enactment (Chused, 1991).

The analyst's contribution: refusing to "wear the attribution"

While enactments often involve the analyst adopting and playing out a role in reaction to and in concert with the patient's transference expectations (Sandler, 1976; Jacobs, 1986), a different sort of enactment comes about when the analyst steadfastly *refuses* to do just that – when the analyst fails to "wear the attribution" (Lichtenberg, Lachmann, & Fosshage, 1992, 1996) – arguably failing in his responsibility to contain, if but for a time, psychic material emanating from the patient.

Steiner (2006) notes how containment involves the analyst's capacity to "make space for the patient in his mind" (p. 317), which "relies on the capacity of the analyst to receive projections, respond to them emotionally and, yet, tolerate the tension without too much recourse to action" (p. 316). One wonders about the possibility that an enactment might arguably be a way of containing the patient, rather than it representing a failure to contain, as Steiner suggests. This would occur, for instance, if the analyst unconsciously collaborates with the patient in creating an enactment that might, for a time, suit the patient's need. A middle ground pictures the analyst side-stepping the attribution altogether ("without too much recourse to action," which some analysts consider a near impossibility) – neither accepting nor refuting it – but this leaves aside the extent to which the tenor and/or direction of the analyst's interpretations may nonetheless challenge the patient's transference beliefs, subtly indicating the analyst's disagreement with the attribution *by virtue of the fact* she chooses to address the content of the attribution (what the patient "makes" of the analyst), rather than primarily working to understand what the admittedly transference-tinged attribution says about how the patient is presently *experiencing* the analyst. With certain sorts of patient, it may seem wisest to momentarily set aside a focused exploration of the transference roots of the attribution (how the patient has sized up the analyst and why he has sized him up in this particular fashion) until the patient is ready to allow the analyst to take up and address *that dimension* of the phenomenon of transference. After all, transference includes, but is not limited to, how the patient perceives the analyst, which remains a worthwhile issue to *eventually* explore at some point before the analysis is completed. In the meantime, with some patients, it proves best to handle the transference experience *as an experience*, rather than chiefly addressing its content – what the patient has come to believe about the analyst.

The analyst's incapacity to contain what's emanating from the patient can manifest in the analyst's palpable, if subtle, objection to the role she's been assigned to play – either the way in which she is *being seen* in the moment by the patient, or how she is covertly *being asked to act*. When the analyst refuses to *play along* – rejecting the role assignment because she finds it personally repugnant, out of line with how she likes to see herself, or not in keeping with how she typically likes to behave – an enactment is likely in the offing. The analyst, in effect, initiates a campaign designed to say it isn't so – to refute the patient's transference claims – which typically does not play well to the extent the analyst's refusal to play along not only thwarts the patient's wish and/or expectation, but also runs counter to the patient's sense of reality – her belief of who the analyst is. The analyst may, for example, challenge the patient's perception by simply asking why the patient might be inclined to see the analyst thusly, which is predicated on a covert assumption that the patient's attribution is off-base and, accordingly, in need of being analyzed. Such a refusal to wear the attribution challenges the analysand to make sense of the analyst's denial – to try to ascertain her motives – which may lead the patient, who remains steadfast in her assertion about the analyst, to draw the conclusion that the analyst is out of touch with the reality of who she is or how it is she's been acting. This was spelled out in Chapter 5, where I noted:

> If the most developmentally pertinent, and most clinically relevant, motive behind a patient's need to express a particular representation of the analyst is to test the analyst's capacity to entertain, tolerate, and live with a representation counter to the ones included in the analyst's self-representations, therapeutic success may hinge on the analyst's ability to demonstrate the workings of his own theory of mind that affords him an appreciation of the relativity of perspectives and, as a result, a capacity to accept the patient's representation non-defensively. If a particular representation is repugnant, and disruptive to the analyst's sense of him- or herself, he or she may rush to interpret the patient's motives for sharing this representation as a way of asserting it isn't so. If, instead, the analyst resists the urge to explain away this representation and "wears" the attribution long enough to demonstrate to the patient his or her capacity to survive being viewed in this way, real headway can be made toward helping the patient develop a capacity to tolerate multiple perspectives within himself, which, in turn, may stimulate a capacity for reflective thought.

The assertion that enactment is the inverse of containment, advanced by Steiner, is challenged by illustrations of how an analyst's attempts to avoid an enactment by refusing a role assignment might bring about an enactment of a different sort, illustrating how hard it can sometimes be to escape the gravitational pull of enactment.

What sorts of attributions/roles assigned by the patient to the analyst might an analyst find personally unacceptable? By and large, analysts pride themselves on their capacity to understand their patients on a profound level. As a result, analysts typically struggle with the patient's claim that they either do not understand the patient or, alternately, are failing to provide the requisite healing experience in line with what the patient seeks and believes will be mutative. To the extent an analyst is enamored with the idea that she is providing her patient with the requisite growth-promoting relationship by serving as a "new object" (Loewald, 1960) – providing the patient with that "special something" that had been missing during their formative years – that analyst will be troubled when the patient fails to see that good food is being provided by a good object. The patient may complain that he feels misunderstood or otherwise feels the analyst's offerings of concern, attention, and the like are insufficient, bogus, "hard to buy," and so on and so forth. Under such conditions, recognizing the situation for what it is and interpreting to the patient that his expectation/need to have an analyst who, for example, *does not and cannot understand*, is a kind of understanding in and of itself. Such an interpretation may be disallowed by the analysand who wants nothing to do with the analyst's efforts to prove she does, in fact, understand (that is, understands that the patient experiences her as not understanding) – which may merely reveal the analyst's motive to prove, in a roundabout fashion, that the patient's claim doesn't hold water when all is said and done. With such a patient, it is likely in the best interest of the treatment for the analyst to accept, at least for the time being, the role of "the one who can't understand," however hard that might be. Doing so, paradoxically, might be the only way in which the analyst might demonstrate understanding. Accordingly, the analyst may need to keep such thoughts to herself for a time, allowing this realization to do nothing more than help her endure the experience – help her wear the attribution. Chused (1996) elaborates upon this theme when she notes:

> When an analyst tries to be the nurturant, available object he believes the patient (whatever his age) "needs" to complete development or compensate for past deficits…it may also destroy the opportunity analysis offers to develop a new capacity for object relationships. To achieve such a capacity, an individual needs to learn *how he makes all objects into old objects*; that is, through the informative experience provided by abstinence, a patient needs to learn about transference. (p. 1057, italics added)

Let's consider an example that illustrates this point. A patient who has been in analysis for several years announces he wants to end treatment so that he can "get on with his life." The analyst-in-training, who I was supervising, takes a big gulp and proceeds to argue in earnest why he should continue. The following day, the analysand describes the analyst's efforts as "desperate," to which she responds by admitting that while she'd put considerable energy into getting the analysand to recognize that much more could be accomplished by continuing the analysis, she herself would not characterize her efforts as "desperate." So here we have a compound clinical situation involving, first, the analyst becoming drawn into an enactment that has her strongly advocating for the continuation of the analysis rather than analyzing why the patient was announcing a wish to end the treatment at this juncture, and, second, the analysand's claim that her efforts smelled of desperation.

Taking issue with the analysand's characterization of her as desperate falls into the category of the analyst "failing to wear the attribution." The analyst's "no" could alternately be seen as an instance of "negation" (Freud, 1925) or as representing her having been made intolerably uncomfortable by the mere fact of *being seen* as desperate – that her "no" could alternately mean "I can't stand being seen in that light," just as it could mean "I've been caught in the act of being desperate and can't face the fact." In this instance, the analysand gravitated to understanding the analyst's negation as the latter, not the former, furthering the enactment's agenda of disavowing his own need and experiencing the state of being in need (of continued treatment) as if it were solely attributable to the analyst. It appeared that the patient had a need to view his analyst in this light – to experience her as the one who desperately wanted him to remain in treatment against his own self-portrayal as being unambivalent about his wish to terminate. The analyst "took the bait," resulting in her prematurely outlining the indications for continued treatment. In this fashion, the patient succeeded at exteriorizing an internal conflict by making it appear as if it were a conflict between him and his analyst. At the same time, he succeeded at wresting from the analyst a covert admission of her investment in him and the treatment.

Other sorts of analyst-initiated enactments

Besides refusing to wear the attribution, analysts may also initiate enactments in a host of other ways: by how they interpret, by what they chose to interpret, by the way in which they relate to the patient, by the nakedness of certain of their motives and/or desires vis-à-vis the treatment or the patient. What an interpretation seems to spell out – what it denotes – can differ markedly from what it connotes. What gets conveyed – versus what one had intended for it to convey, and believes it did convey – often depends on more than the specific meaning of the words used to demonstrate the analyst's understanding of the patient. How the interpretation is phrased (e.g., word choice) along with accompanying meta-messages (e.g., tone of voice, nonverbal communications of various sorts) can telegraph contradictory messages, with the more implicit (meta-)message oftentimes proving to be the more salient of the two from the patient's perspective. Writing from a Kleinian perspective, Steiner (2006) outlines the various ways in which an analyst may initiate an enactment by what he says to the patient:

> Words, and the way in which they are spoken, do more than communicate information, and many patients experience words as things which impinge concretely on them, exciting them or wounding them as actual seductions and attacks would do...Seduction can be done with words, cruelty inflicted with the tongue and moral condemnation with the tone of voice. (p. 316)

Building upon Joseph's (2003) concept of "*interpretive enactments*," Steiner (2006) explains how enactments may inadvertently and unconsciously masquerade as interpretations that convey how the analyst feels about the patient – whether positive or negative – which Steiner believes can negatively impact the patient's capacity to develop his own thinking and judgment. Instances when the analyst is chief initiator of an enactment may be set in motion when the analyst "finds it difficult to tolerate the constraints of the analytic setting...especially if pressure from the patient coincides with an area of his own frustration that he may be tempted to compromise the setting, in a collusive enactment" (p. 318). Beyond how the analyst feels about a patient are her underlying intentions that account for why she's offering a given interpretation at a given point in time, which needn't always be in the best interest of the treatment. When more personal motives are seen operating, an enactment is often in the offing.

Writing from an interpersonal perspective, Levenson (1972) writes about how the content of the analyst's interpretation may reflect underlying attitudes that become incorporated in her style of interpreting, conveyed in the way the interpretation is delivered – whether it be "stern, kindly, sympathetic, no-nonsense, whatever" – often proves most relevant to the patient to the extent that attitude "integrates with the patient's world" (p. 184). Those familiar with Joseph's (1985) concept of the "total transference" will hear an echo in Levenson's words. Most classically oriented analysts appreciate that the totality of what gets conveyed through an articulated interpretation is not limited to its verbal content, underscoring the limits of thinking in terms of an interpretation benefitting a patient strictly through the conveyance of the analyst's verbally articulated understanding of the patient, which aims to heighten the patient's insight into herself.

Catching wind of the analyst's covert motives can also contribute to the initiation of an enactment, whether the analyst's implicit wish is for the patient to psychically evolve in a particular fashion over time or for the analysis to take shape in a particular way. Furthermore, analysts may contribute to enactments to the extent they exhibit "therapeutic zeal": "If the analyst is frustrated with the lack of, or speed of, therapeutic progress", notes Steiner (2006), "he may be tempted to pressure the patient and he may express his disappointment and guilt by subtle implications that the patient is to blame for his failure to improve" (p. 319). Naturally, there are other ways that therapeutic zeal may also bring about an analyst-initiated enactment, particularly when the patient senses that the analyst is personally invested in the analysis, arriving at a particular outcome for reasons that may not solely, or even largely, have to do with the patient.

The analyst's inherent susceptibility: the "hook"

Before analysts got into the habit of speaking in terms of enactment, Sandler (1976) wrote a surprisingly short paper, given its considerable significance, in which he noted how some of his patients seemed to be assigning him a role to play that was complementary to the one the patient unconsciously planned to play. In one such enactment,[2] Sandler found himself uncharacteristically handing a patient tissues every time she cried, wondering to himself why he was doing what he was doing, given that this was not at all in his nature. Unlike Jacobs (1986, 1991, 1993), who wrote about the personal factors that predisposed him to become drawn into enactments of various sorts, Sandler admitted he hadn't a clue why he was acting as he was, so he simply ceased to act as he had, resulting in the emergence of new material that drove the treatment forward.

Sandler's (1976) original paper and Jacobs' (1986) subsequent paper raise interesting questions about what it is about the analyst that makes her susceptible to assuming a particular role assignment. Assuming for a moment that enactments are products of projective identification (Feldman, 1997; Joseph, 1989; Spillius, 1992) – which is not universally accepted – leaves us to wonder what the patient tugs on in the analyst that facilitates the development of a projective identification process. Addressing this question, Gabbard and Westen (2003) posit the requirement of a pre-existing "hook" (p. 477) that lies dormant in the analyst, upon which the patient's projection can be "hung." This perspective suggests that the patient must locate and act upon something in the analyst for the projection to "take" – something that belongs to the analyst, something in her that is hers. Accordingly, factors favoring the analyst's engagement in an enactment have much to do with a given analyst's inherent proclivities. Following this reasoning, it would seem – for example – that an analyst who is particularly prone to experience narcissistic injury will be more inclined than other analysts to assume the assigned role of the injured party/parent vis-à-vis the patient. This illustrates Faimberg's (1992) point that "the patient cannot create the analyst's response but only the *conditions* for the analyst to respond with his *own psychical functioning*" (p. 543).

Harvesting enactments

An enactment is of no therapeutic value in and of itself unless it is processed in ways that make the most of its occurrence (Chused, 1991). How analysts go about working with enactments, once the enactment is realized as such, varies from analyst to analyst, depending largely on the nature of her particular school of thought. In this section, we will compare two general ways of working with enactments: one in accordance with a more classic psychoanalytic approach that sees enactments as an actualization of the transference, emphasizing intrapsychic conflict and the process of projective identification; and the other illustrating how interpersonalists describe working with such phenomena, based on the theory that an enactment results when dissociative processes render aspects of the patient's experience unrecognizable to the patient as belonging to her, resulting in the patient recognizing these "not me" parts (Bromberg, 1998, 2003, 2011) as existing in the analyst.

Bohleber et al. (2013) offer a serviceable definition of the phenomenon of enactment:

> Enactment involves a collapse in the analytic dialogue in which the analyst is drawn into an interaction where he unwittingly acts, thereby actualizing unconscious wishes of both himself and the patient. This collapse implies disturbance of the symbolic function; something emerges that at the moment of enactment is not accessible by language. What follows this moment will determine whether the enactment will have therapeutic value, that is, whether the symbolic function will be restored and integrative work can or cannot happen. (p. 517)

This definition makes clear the extent to which an essential task of analysis[3] is breached with the occurrence of an enactment – that the effort to help give voice to the patient's internal experience momentarily gives way as the experience is acted out with both parties' cooperation. Though some celebrate the advent of the age of enactment, the development of an enactment calls for a bit more sobriety and a tendency to be circumspect about the matter. As valuable as enactments may end up being, one necessarily must regret its occurrence out of respect for what remains, in the minds of many, the chief goal of the treatment – to heighten understanding by providing words to help articulate experiences – relying upon the development or restoration of symbolic function as a bridge to access repressed, projected, or dissociated aspects of inner experience. Yes, enactments can be clinically helpful, but dangers remain about which we all must remain vigilant. And, no, providing words to help patients articulate their experiences is not tantamount to an interpretation per se.

Information gleaned from an enactment

The classically oriented analyst generally focuses on the *informational content* of an enactment – in particular, how it provides insight into the patient's transference reactions, insight that the analyst will then offer the patient, thus rendering the unconscious conscious. The classically oriented analyst harvests the fruits of enactment, making wine of her expanded understanding of transference that results as she comes to the realization that an enactment had been taking place and what the enactment revealed about how the transference had been actualized in the process. During the enactment, the analyst's participation provided the patient "proof" that her transference beliefs were not merely perceptual distortions but, rather, were accurate to the extent the analyst had been caught acting like the original transference object had acted. Chused (1991) notes:

> ...during an enactment, the patient has a conviction about the accuracy of his perceptions *and* behaves so as to induce behavior in the analyst which supports his conviction. Even if an analyst is neither angry nor critical, a patient's accusations can still induce guilt, defense, and retaliatory impulses. This is one aspect of the evocative power of enactments. (p. 617)

If the analyst's behavior falls in line with the patient's transference expectations, it might be harder for the patient to see *the extent to which* she contributes to the enactment – that the transference realization is largely (though certainly not wholly) of her making. No therapeutic gain results from engaging in an enactment unless and until the analyst, whose presence of mind is typically clouded when she is caught up in an enactment (Chused, 1991), disengages sufficiently from the experience to be in a position to explore its unconscious determinants (Chused, 1991, 1996, 2003). The therapeutic value of an enactment strictly derives from the opportunity it affords to – first – help the analyst appreciate something about the patient she had heretofore not appreciated – then – to make strides in understanding the psychological implications of what had been happening so that – ultimately – the analyst can enlighten the patient about an aspect of the patient's psychology that had heretofore been inaccessible to the patient. This is often easier said than done. To begin with, getting a patient to accept and appreciate that an enactment had, in fact, taken place can prove clinically challenging. Chused (1991) makes this abundantly clear when she writes about how the analyst:

> ...wants to share his understanding of the enactment and its determinants with the patient. However, to a patient enmeshed in transference, the very act of intervening can become a vehicle for an enactment. Interpretations, heard as meaning that the analyst understands something which the patient does not, are denied. If the analyst tries harder to clarify the experience, he is heard as defensive or irritated, and his words become evidence of his authoritarian stance. (p. 635)

Enactments: the interpersonal perspective

While countertransference enactments are classically conceptualized as resulting from the patient acting in ways designed to stimulate the analyst to *actualize the transference* (Chused, 1991), analysts writing from the interpersonal school see the process in terms of a dissociated part of the patient becoming recognized by the patient as belonging to the analyst, where it remains until the patient develops the capacity (is helped by the analyst to develop the capacity) to recognize aspects of the self she'd labeled "not me" that are, in fact, genuine aspects of her own being.

To appreciate the interpersonal approach to the management of enactments requires we briefly describe how interpersonal analysts typically regard the model of a one-way conveyance of knowledge from analyst to analysand expressed through the vehicle of the analyst's interpretation. Interpersonal psychoanalysts such as Donnel Stern and Phillip Bromberg don't place stock in the process of acquiring knowledge (via transference interpretations) as the essential, mutative task of psychoanalysis. Stern (2009) sees the central task of analysis with certain patients as helping them retrieve previously split-off, dissociated parts of the self that the patient had seen as existing within the analyst. In this model, the successful clinical culmination of an enactment is measured by the extent to which "not me" parts of the patient are returned to/retrieved by the patient, thereafter being experienced as belonging to the patient and not to the analyst. Bromberg (1998) believes that the analyst's offering of his understanding in the form of an articulated interpretation (explaining) isn't nearly as powerful clinically as is the analyst *surviving the enactment* well, arriving at a point where he can successfully extricate himself from it, thus permitting him to re-emerge as a subjective entity *separate and apart* from who the enactment had – for a time – made him seem to be. In the final analysis, this development ultimately requires the patient contend with *his construction of the analyst*, which had – for a time – become animated in the process of the enactment. But it is not through an initial realization by the patient of his transference wishes and expectations that this comes about.

The process I am describing sounds much like how I had handled Mr. A. (described in Chapter 5) – the patient who was too scared to think, thus requiring I not challenge his view of me (which he considered "reality") until such a time as he was ready to see the transference for what it was. Until he was ready to see me as distinct from who the transference made me out to seem, interpretations were strictly forbidden, given that the patient wasn't yet ready for me to step out of a transitional space where his view of me and the reality of me would be understood as not being one and the same, hence, would have to be questioned and explored for the sake of the treatment. Until he could tolerate confronting my otherness, my subjectivity would need to remain cloaked, much as Slochower (1996) describes regarding the need to maintain a holding process when treating certain types of patients where:

> ...clinical movement is effected not as a result of an active analysis (or interpretation) of dynamic process or of mutual enactments, but because of the analyst's capacity to create emotional space that more or less protects the patient from the impact of the analyst's "otherness." (p. 2)

Analysts who subscribe to different theoretical orientations, notably interpersonal psychoanalysts and Lacanian psychoanalysts, see the role of interpretation (information and the utility of conveying knowledge) in a very different light, one that is not at all in keeping with Freud's original dictum that the goal of analysis was to make the unconscious conscious – or, more to the point, that the analyst was to be the *chief agent* rendering the unconscious conscious. This isn't to suggest that other analytic schools of thought believe that the analyst plays no role whatsoever in a patient developing the capacity to *see* what he previously could not *see*, to *experience* what he previously could not *experience*; it is only to elaborate on other possible mechanisms that might account for the patient retrieving lost aspects of himself that are not predicated solely on insights provided to the patient by the analyst. What I have in mind is the way the analyst conducts herself, which helps facilitate a developing process that ultimately results in the patient's ability to recover lost parts of herself, with insight coming retrospectively – at the end of the process – rather than it being the chief initiator of the process. Allowing for this possibility doesn't negate the task of making the unconscious conscious, which remains in the eyes of many analysts one of the chief goals of treatment, but it changes when knowledge comes about in the scheme of things relative to therapeutically facilitated psychic change. Whether insight begets change or is the result of changes that have been taking place is the question.

Consider how Lacanian psychoanalysts think about the matter of therapeutic action. Fink (2014) observes that a Lacanian approach to analysis "is not about providing meaning but, rather, about *putting the unspeakable into words*" (p. 7), illustrated in Lacan's (2001) words: "What is at stake is not, in fact, a move to consciousness but, rather, to speech…and that speech must be heard by someone" (pp. 139–140). Fink opines:

> …meaning serves the purpose of *rationalization*, which keeps the unconscious at bay. An emphasis by the analyst on meaning and understanding often leads the analysand to become very adept at finding psychological explanations for her behavior but does little or nothing to foster change in the analysand…Part of the analyst's job is to take meaning apart, to undermine understanding by showing that far from explaining everything, it is always partial, not total, and leaves many things out. (p. 7)

If expanding self-knowledge is seen as an important goal of treatment, interpersonalists are less inclined to see a heightening of a patient's self-awareness as strictly coming about from information flowing in a one-way fashion from analyst to patient. If enactments result in the retrieval of dissociated parts, making the patient more whole – which is how some interpersonalists envision the beneficial outcome of an enactment – this process is not seen as taking place through the analyst imparting information via interpretation. Instead, it is seen as coming about in a much more roundabout, experiential fashion, one that is facilitated by the analyst providing a safe, facilitating environment that encourages the patient to "own" previously dissociated parts of himself that could not previously have been included in his sense of what is me (versus not me). Interpersonalists see this happening chiefly after the analyst comes to his senses, extricates herself from the enactment, sees the analysand's subjectivity in a new light, and relates to the analysand through this new perception of the analyst (Stern, 2017).

If knowledge be the goal – the facilitator of change – it is only through an enlivened, experiential process that the acquisition of said knowledge is seen as making a difference – the process by which knowledge comes to light – not the mere conveyance of knowledge per se. If I understand the matter correctly, this – in a nutshell – is the interpersonal perspective on enactments, though the details are more complex than this simple schema makes it out to seem. And, it may even be the case that insight is the result of, rather than the force behind, the resolution of an enactment.

One gets the impression from a reading of the literature that the expansion of what one knows about oneself is what gets primarily emphasized by the more classical analysts, whereas the expansion of what one can experience is what is primarily emphasized by the interpersonalists. Naturally, expanded knowledge can trigger, or be triggered by, an expansion of one's capacity to experience, and vice versa. Furthermore, it may be the case that only on the extreme ends of the classical–interpersonal spectrum might an analyst seem solely interested in either knowledge or experience. And, after all, it is on the far end of the spectrum where the often-mocked, theoretical straw-men reside.

The dissociative model of enactment

Interpersonal analysts do not conceptualize enactments as *the products of conflict* (split-off, unconscious psychic content that is *potentially accessible* save for the fact that intrapsychic conflict produces forces capable of keeping the repressed repressed); rather, they see enactments as *the products of dissociation* (Bromberg, 1998; Stern, 1997, 2003, 2004), which renders certain psychic content unthinkable – beyond access to the extent such psychic content is unformulated (has not been symbolized; Stern, 1997) and is, accordingly, unknowable in the usual sense of the term. Stern suggests "that a significant part of the pain of human relatedness occurs because conflicts that might be actualized within us are not" (p. 229).

Dissociation involves "the experience we never have" (Stern, 2004, p. 222). Dissociated experiences can lead one to recognize one's own dissociated parts as they are *seen to exist in another*, which Stern (2004) refers to as "the interpersonalization of dissociation: the conflict that cannot be experienced within one mind is experienced across two minds" (p. 213). Pressure is brought to bear on the analyst to act accordingly – to act in ways that support the illusion that dissociated aspects of oneself exist in the other. Stern argues that enactment is never the *result* of intrapsychic conflict; rather, it is the *absence* of internal conflict that represents one defining feature of an enactment, resulting in a depletion of the self given the externalization of internal conflict. In this model, the working through of an enactment results in the growing capacity to tolerate *intrapsychic* conflict. This is thought to come about through a process that helps formulate previously unformulated, dissociated aspects of one's experience. An expansion of one's sense of self, and with it a heightened sense of freedom, is in the offing – the result of a patient's heightened capacity to psychically tolerate and contain a greater portion of his lived experience, which heretofore had to be disowned and experienced as belonging to another.

Extracting oneself from an enactment

There is a broad acceptance of one defining feature of enactments – their "lost in a maze-like quality" that robs the analyst of her capacity to step back and reflect, to see the forest from the trees. In order to find a way out, the analyst must gain a bird's eye view of the situation, which requires a signal – the gut-level sense that something is amiss. Only then will the analyst be in a position to come to her senses and break the spell in order to regain her ability to think about the situation from a position that is less saturated by one's own subjectivity and by the subjectivity of the other.

While analysts generally appreciate that an enactment involves an altered state of mind, they differ in terms of how they conceptualize the nature of that state of mind. Interpersonalists envision this as issuing from a dissociated part of the analyst's mind that resonates with the patient's dissociated state of mind. Other analysts alternately envision the analyst as having been held hostage through the process of projective identification, as having regressed to a less differentiated state where confusion between self and other reigns – with the lost capacity to self-reflect being the notable casualty. Enactments could even be likened to a mutual repetition compulsion that has both parties unwittingly acting out a piece of their past, oblivious to the fact they are doing just that. As can be seen, there are many alternate ways to account for enactments.

Of critical interest is the matter of how the analyst regains a sense of equilibrium (comes to her senses) after having succumbed to living for a time within the confines of an enactment that had felt imposed, as if it had robbed the analyst of her sense of freedom as well as her capacity to be self-reflective (i.e., to think analytically). Not until the analyst regains sufficient presence of mind will she be in a position to make good clinical use of the enactment. Stern (2004) suggests this involves the analyst catching on to the fact that she'd been engaged in an enactment, being alerted to the fact by her experiencing strange affects – "emotional snags and affective chafings" (p. 209) – signaling to the analyst that more is going on than she had imagined.

Only when the analyst has regained her capacity to maintain multiple perspectives (regaining her rightful role as participant-observer) will she then be on the road to being able to help the patient *formulate unformulated experience* so that the patient can then psychically tolerate and personally contain "not me" parts that had previously been experienced as residing solely in the analyst. Stern (2017) sees the resolution of an enactment taking place *not* through an articulable (intellectual) understanding of the situation but, rather, through an alteration, on either party's part, in the way in which they view the other. This development ends the couple's tendency to continue to engage in the enactment, freeing them of the mutual tendency to continue to see one another in a highly limiting light – freeing them to discover disowned parts of themselves, which necessarily results in their relating to one another in a new fashion. Put in other terms, an enactment yields to the widening scope of a patient's potential responses and capacities to connect at different levels with others as a result of alterations in the patient's view of others and his relationship with others. Stern (2017) makes clear that this is not a matter of analyst or analysand purposely attempting to see things in a different light; rather, it is something that "just happens" without intention or conscious, willful effort. A change in perception begets changes in the way in which each relates to the other, which, in turn, heightens the ability of both parties to experience their separable subjectivity (see Chapter 3 of this volume), which changes how they respond to, and interact with, one another. Again, insight may follow, but insight is not envisioned as the driving force behind these changes.

In this chapter, we have seen how analysts working from different theoretical perspectives consider and manage countertransference enactments in somewhat different ways, approaching the situation with different understandings about what drives the enactment – its underlying mechanisms. Analysts who see enactments as actualizations of the transference are inclined to work through the enactment by making the transference more consciously explicit so that the patient can find words by which the situation of the enactment can be symbolized. One may see meaning-making (interpretation) as the chief way in which the fruits of enactment will be harvested. Alternately, one may see enactments as resulting in a patient's newly developed capacity to put his experiences into words – experiences he had previously only known to act out, only known by acting them out. A more classical psychoanalytic approach might favor meaning-making, while a Lacanian approach favors helping patients find words for experiences that previously could not be represented or symbolized thusly.[4,5] By contrast, interpersonalists work with enactments by allowing disowned, "not me" parts of the patient – which the patient had yet to be able to experience as her own – to reside in the analyst for a time. According to interpersonal theory, for an analyst to be in a position to help the patient work through an enactment requires she regain enough of a sense of herself after she'd been lost within the enactment to the extent dissociated parts of herself resonated with dissociated parts of the patient. Once the analyst comes to her senses, she is in the position to be able to see herself and the patient in a new light – one that will result in her interacting with the patient in ways that help reconfigure the patient's sense of himself to now include previously vanquished "not me" parts that had, for a time, been beyond the patient's ability to self-contain.

A final remark seems in order. It seems likely that all analysts, regardless of their theoretical persuasion, are at least intermittently cognizant of the fact that interpretations can, and often do, convey information beyond what is verbalized in the form of the analyst's understanding – her surmise about the patient. I would submit, however, that this level of awareness about the nature of interpretations is variable and oftentimes not constant, waxing and waning throughout the analyst's day. Contrasting a classical approach to enactments, which emphasizes the conveyance of content-rich interpretations, with the interpersonal approach, which de-emphasizes interpretations per se in favor of other mutative maneuvers, may amount to a straw-man argument predicated on the notion that classical analysts are unaware of the fact that there is more to transference than meets the eye. Naturally, this is not completely the case, nor is it not the case at all – it is *both*, in a fuzzy logic sort of way. Put in other terms, picturing the classical analyst as single-mindedly focused on the conveyance of articulated information (the interpretation of the enactment) is partly true to the extent that all analysts will, from time to time, lose track of the broader data conveyed through by an interpretation in the moment they are focused on the function of interpretation in the narrowest sense – as the conveyer of verbally formattable and verbally formatted information. Sometimes an analyst remembers it's more complicated than that; sometimes she forgets as much. Such oscillations are inevitable, but they must not leave us believing that the classically oriented analyst is blind to the likelihood that, at any given moment, she may inadvertently be conveying much more than she presently is aware of conveying.

Notes

1 It must be acknowledged that it is somewhat arbitrary to draw a distinction separating patient-initiated from analyst-initiated enactments, as this artificially separates what surely more accurately would be described as a chicken-or-egg process. Noting as much, there nevertheless is heuristic value in drawing this distinction for argument's sake.
2 Sandler didn't use that term at the time.
3 According to certain analysts and not to others.
4 This section of the paper developed out of a collaboration with Susan L. Orbach with whom I had worked on a contribution to *Precarious Predicaments: working with clinical conundrums in psychotherapy and psychoanalysis* (Tuch and Kuttnaver in Press)
5 This isn't to say that classically oriented analysts don't also offer interpretations to help patients find words for their experiences; it is only to suggest that the function of interpretations is seen more in terms of revealing defenses and, ultimately, defended-against mental content.

Chapter 8

Beyond empathy

A wrinkle in self psychology theory

Self psychology is founded on the idea that healthy narcissistic development depends upon the availability of objects who prize and admire the child ("mirroring") and who can be idealized (and then gradually de-idealized) by the child. Objects that provide for these bipolar needs are termed *selfobjects*. Caregivers who function as selfobjects help regulate the child's narcissistic equilibrium from without while the child gradually develops an ever-increasing ability to self-regulate.

Kohut (1971, 1977) believed that a child's ability to regulate his or her own sense of self results from the proper handling of instances when the caregiver fails to satisfy the child's selfobject needs. The caregiver's demonstrated appreciation of the child's response to that caregiver's intermittent failures to function as an adequate selfobject substantially moderates the intensity of the child's disappointment. Tolerable disappointments of these selfobject needs ("optimal" or "micro" frustrations) lead to a process termed *transmuting internalization*, which then leads to an ever-increasing ability to tolerate narcissistic insults. Intolerable disappointments lead to traumatization and to a continued over-reliance on external selfobjects for self-regulation.

Self psychology places a special importance on the role of empathy in the development of healthy narcissism. Empathy operates in three very specific ways. First, empathy provides the understanding that enables caregivers to best provide for the child's selfobject needs. Second, empathy informs the caregiver about how best to interact with the child to help re-establish the child's narcissistic equilibrium after the child has been narcissistically injured by the caregiver's failure to provide adequately for the child's selfobject needs. Finally, empathy facilitates comprehension of the child's affective state so that caregivers can put into words or otherwise demonstrate their appreciation of "where the child is at."

When a caregiver fails to satisfy the child's need to idealize or to be mirrored, we call these *selfobject failures* (Stolorow, Brandchaft, & Atwood, 1987, p. 17). When that person fails to understand how and why a child feels a certain way, we call these *empathic failures*. While empathic failures may contribute to selfobject failures, it is essential that the two terms not be considered synonymous. A failure to differentiate the two has led to murky thinking, especially with regard to the concept of optimal frustration.

Not all empathic failures entail a selfobject failure. This is true because the need to feel understood or empathized with is not one of the bipolar needs that originally defined a selfobject. Sometimes the need for empathy has been elevated to the status of a basic need, on a par with the needs of the bipolar self, to idealize and to be mirrored. Some feel that if analysis could be conducted free of empathic failures (an admittedly impossible task), analysands would undergo sufficient change just by having their needs for emotional attunement met, and the venture could be regarded as truly psychoanalytic.

Kohut's (1971) original description of transmuting internalization involved the optimal therapeutic aftermath of an analyst having failed to adequately satisfy a patient's selfobject needs. By demonstrating the analyst's understanding of how and why his or her actions affected the patient as they had, the analyst helps the patient re-establish narcissistic equilibrium. In this way, empathy prevents a selfobject failure from becoming so traumatic that it irretrievably damages the analytic relationship. "Optimal frustrations" of the patient's selfobject needs are made optimal by their falling within a given patient's ability to tolerate them, followed by the demonstration of the analyst's empathic attitude toward the patient's experience of having been let down.

Bacal (1985) and others have written in support of shifting emphasis from optimal frustration to optimal responsiveness. He writes:

> It is possible that the gratification of being understood by one's selfobject is of central importance in the curative process. Our responses must satisfy (a better word, perhaps, than gratify) the frustrated need for understanding of a particular patient or they will not be helpful. (p. 207)

Bacal questions whether optimal frustration is, in fact, as critical to an analytic cure as Kohut thought. He further writes: "The patient brings to the analyst his frustration at not being understood so that any additional frustration caused by the analyst's lack of understanding cannot be regarded as optimal" (p. 210). However, Kohut's concept of optimal frustration never involved frustrating the patient's need to be understood! Quite the contrary, part of what made optimal frustration optimal was the analyst's continued ability to understand why his or her actions had affected the patient as they had.

Given the extent of the current confusion in this area, the time seems ripe to review what constitutes an empathic failure and to explore how such failures relate to selfobject failures. To this end, I will critically examine two assertions found in the literature: first, that empathic failures which arise during treatment are primarily due to the *analyst's* failure to be properly attuned to the patient; and second, that empathy is a life-sustaining "psychological nutriment" (Kohut, 1978, p. 705) which, by definition, is something that is yearned for, even needed, and accordingly unlikely to be experienced as unwanted, intrusive, or distancing. Such thinking disregards what patients may contribute to their own failure to be understood. Resistance to empathy is seldom considered. Finally, I will demonstrate how an analyst's consistent empathic responsiveness may prove insufficient to produce lasting psychological change.

Defining terms

Although empathy has emerged as a critical concept within self psychology, there is, in fact, no consensus regarding its meaning. Some equate the term *empathy* with affect resonance. Greenson (1960) spoke of empathy as "the experiencing of another's feelings" in order to "emotionally know" (p. 418) what another person is going through, while *A Glossary of Psychoanalytic Terms and Concepts* (Moore & Fine, 1968) defines empathy as a "mode of perceiving by vicariously experiencing (in a limited way) the psychological state of another person" (p. 67). However, many take issue with defining empathy as the firsthand experiencing of another's feelings. Schafer (1959) argues that becoming "angry, anxious, or guilty when another is angry is thus not empathic...though it may be a preliminary or signal stage of empathy" (p. 349), while Stern (1985) argues that empathy is more than affect resonance because empathy requires "the abstraction of empathic knowledge from the experience of emotional resonance" (p. 145). In a similar vein, Shapiro (1974) describes how empathy "permits *comprehension* of another's predicament rather than simple *recognition*" (p. 22).

Taking such objections into consideration leads to an expansion of the definition of empathy to include the mental processing of the raw data of affect resonance, which then leads to the comprehension of why others feel as they do. But this definition fails to consider the fact that affect resonance is *not* the only raw data upon which empathy is based. In fact, one of Kohut's (1971) earliest definitions of empathy – "a mode of cognition which is specifically attuned to the perception of complex psychological configurations" (p. 300) – makes no reference to affect whatsoever. Basch (1983) states that empathy "includes, but is not limited to, an affective experience" (p. 110).

This brings us to my proposed definition of empathy: "empathy describes the methods by which one comes to know how and why others feel as they do." This definition includes both the method and its goal (empathically derived understanding). The methods by which empathy is achieved are purposely left unspecified. Sometimes the empathic process begins as an affective response to the patient. Sometimes empathy comes to the analyst's mind in the form of a seemingly personal and idiosyncratic fantasy which is ultimately understood as "a commentary on the patient's experience" (Beres & Arlow, 1974, p. 39). Even theory can inform empathy. The fact that knowledge of developmental research or psychoanalytic theory can guide empathy is something

Kohut (1984a) said "cannot be affirmed too emphatically" (p. 84). He spoke of how self psychological theory can alert an analyst to "perceive configurations that would otherwise have escaped his notice" (p. 84).

It is irrelevant whether empathy begins as an affective response, a fantasy, an insight, or a theory. Ultimately, empathy may involve all these realms. The definition I have proposed emphasizes the cognitive aspect of empathy. Some may complain that "knowing" seems too limiting a process to account adequately for a phenomenon as complex as empathy. However, I believe that empathy's usefulness as a psychoanalytic tool is determined by the extent to which it leads to insight. This insight need not be shared with the patient via interpretation. It may do nothing more than direct the analyst's interactions with the patient. This definition stops short of the broader definition of empathy as "understanding how and why another person's mind works." This latter definition considers more than just affects and includes defenses, mental structures, and a host of other mental mechanisms. To refer to all of that as empathy would so broaden the term as to render it meaningless.

The definition of empathy proposed above underscores the fact that empathy involves knowing not just how but *why* others feel as they do. It accordingly requires that one understand enough about the individual's situation (the context in which the affects arise) to *comprehend* how such feelings fit into that person's life and make sense, given that individual's personality and past. While this definition fails to account for instances in which one feels an immediate sense of empathy toward a stranger – someone whose life we think we know nothing about – such instances of empathy are most likely based on how we expect the "average expectable" person to react under similar circumstances. Such "generic" empathy may come close enough as long as the stranger approximates the average expectable model.

It is noteworthy that what has been left out of the definition is the concept of empathy as a mode of relating to others. One often hears of how an analyst had been "empathic" with a patient when what is meant is that the analyst used his or her understanding of how and why the patient feels, in a way that demonstrates compassion (sensitivity or tenderness) toward that patient's feelings. The term *empathic failure* is sometimes erroneously equated with interventions that either lack compassion or are intentionally hurtful. But empathically derived knowledge can also serve "inimical ends," as Kohut (1978, p. 706) pointed out. For example, effective sadism relies heavily on an empathic understanding of one's victim.

Others have also used the term empathy to describe something that an individual needs from others to thrive emotionally (Grotstein, 1984; Kohut, 1978). They write that empathy can be sufficient, without the aid of illuminating insight, to cause meaningful and lasting psychological change. Kohut (1971) initially expressed apprehension at going beyond his original, narrower concept of empathy as "a tool for the gathering of psychological data" (p. 300), but subsequently wrote: "I must now, unfortunately, add that empathy per se, the mere presence of empathy, has also a beneficial, in a broad sense, a therapeutic effect – both in the clinical setting and in human life, in general" (1984b, p. 85).

While empathy may help an analyst ascertain what it is that the patient needs, empathy should not be confused with the satisfaction of those needs. This is not to say that analysts should not be warm or sensitive toward their patients – certainly they should. But it is incorrect to refer to such behavior as "empathic" or to consider such tenderness sufficient to produce substantial psychological change. Basch (1983) emphasized this point when he wrote: "Empathic understanding is not curative in the psychoanalytic sense; cure is the function of interpretation. By the same token, empathic understanding is not a substitute for interpretation; rather, it lays the groundwork that makes interpretation appropriate and effective" (pp. 123–124).

All of this leads to a definition of empathic failure as "a failure to understand accurately either how or why individuals feel as they do." Though such misunderstanding needs only to exist in the analyst's mind, empathic failures usually are not detected until the analyst's *actions* demonstrate to the patient whether she or he has been well understood. This occurs either when analysts act on an inaccurate understanding of their patients or when analysts fail to take into account what they accurately understand about their patients in their interactions with them. Such empathic failures become evident either through "faulty" interpretations (ones that are overly inaccurate or poorly timed) or through some mismanagement of the relationship (i.e., by expecting the patient to be able to tolerate what, for them, is intolerable). Empathic failures may also develop when an analyst's understanding of a patient fails to have any effect on her/his affective responses to that patient.

Conveying one's empathic "findings" to a patient, who is then jarred by such an interpretation, may be referred to by some as "unempathic." This usage of the term *unempathic* seems to run counter to the definition proposed above. However, it is not the intervention's effect on the patient per se that determines whether empathy is lacking. A patient's being jarred or disturbed by an intervention is not, by itself, grounds for calling that intervention "unempathic." However, if the analyst is unable to anticipate how a patient will react upon hearing a given interpretation and therefore is surprised by the intensity of that patient's reaction, then one can call this lack of understanding a lack of empathy.

Bacal (1985) writes of how an analyst has "to consider what response will be optimal in relation to the current level of his patient's specific developmental capacity to utilize empathic understanding of his selfobject needs for human relatedness" (p. 224). Offering interpretations about what the patient's behavior means, even when those interpretations are empathically derived, can be experienced by the patient as the analyst thinking about the patient at a distance (observing), rather than being with the patient (participating). Feeling distanced by the analyst may disrupt the patient's sense of having been with the analyst in a way that felt containing and reassuring. Interpretations about the unconscious meaning of latent content about which the patient is unaware may be experienced by the patient as "intrusive" rather than "holding" or "containing" – especially when such interpretations are at odds with how patients understand themselves (Reed, 1984). Such interpretations may be experienced as the intrusion of foreignness, which represents the "otherness" of the analyst.

The causes of empathic failures

While empathic failures are most often thought to result from the *analyst's* failure to properly understand the patient, empathic failures may occur for other reasons as well. What follows is a discussion of the various factors which may contribute to empathic failure: (1) the analyst's contributions to empathic failures; (2) the patient's contributions to his or her failure to be understood by the analyst; and (3) instances when empathy cannot be achieved simply because it is impossible to empathize with different aspects of another's experience when those aspects conflict with one another.

The analyst's contribution to empathic failures

Psychoanalysts are considered "particularly empathic" when they understand a wide variety of patients a high percentage of the time. But even "particularly empathic" analysts are subject to instances when they fail to understand their patients empathically. All psychoanalysts are susceptible to finding a patient's experience so foreign that they are unable to call upon their own analogous experiences and, as a result, are unable to achieve empathic understanding (Freud, 1915; Kohut, 1959, 1971). Basch (1988) describes occasions in which "a patient's appearance, viewpoints, life style, and/or background are so foreign that one feels less curious and interested in the person and more in the grip of 'stranger anxiety'" (p. 168).

Some psychoanalysts are generally inhibited in their ability to empathize. Greenson (1960) points out how some analysts may be "unconsciously unwilling to leave the isolation of the position of the uninvolved observer" (p. 420), because they feel threatened by the temporary decathexis of their self-image which is necessary for them to feel another's feelings or put themselves in another's place.

One important source of empathic failure is the analyst's tendency to rely too heavily upon his/her own experience in order to understand patients. While some consider the analyst's own experiences to be faulty grounds upon which to base empathic understanding of patients, Freud felt otherwise. He wrote that making the behavior of others intelligible requires that we draw analogues between their experiences and our own. "[W]e attribute to everyone else our own constitution and therefore our consciousness as well, and...this identification is a *sine qua non* of our understanding" (1915, p. 169).

Constructs about patients that are primarily based on the analyst's own experience run counter to the contemporary concept of empathy, which eschews projecting oneself into the other as a way of understanding. For instance, Schwaber (1981) emphasizes the importance of being open to how the other person feels, regardless of how we might feel or react under similar circumstances. She and others feel that accurate empathy requires putting oneself aside in order to function as a kind of pure receiver, an instrument that resonates in keeping with the experiences of another without contaminating that resonance with one's own experience. Renik (1993) takes issue with Schwaber's position when he refers to the impossibility of "isolating or subtracting" an analyst's personal responses from the rest of his or her analytic activity:

> Instead of saying that it is *difficult* for an analyst to *maintain* a position in which his or her analytic activity objectively focuses on a patient's inner reality, I would say that it is *impossible* for an analyst to be in that position *even for an instant*...Everything an analyst does in the analytic situation is based upon his or her personal psychology. This limitation cannot be reduced, let alone done away with; we have only the choice of admitting it or denying it. (pp. 560–561)

Stolorow (1994) also takes issue with the idea of the analyst "banishing his own psychological organization" (p. 45) in order to be empathic. He argues that doing so defies the intersubjective nature of the analytic process.

Identification permits us to understand how another person feels without actually having to experience that person's feelings. We remember having had experiences like those which the other is now having, and based on our own experiences we make assumptions about what it must be like for the patient. Those who relish thinking of empathy as an experience-near phenomenon might take issue with any definition that places the empathizer at a distance from the patient's experience as it is happening. But many feel that such a distance is a necessary precondition for the analyst to be able to do something with the affect that is different from what the patient is doing with it. Little (1951) writes of how:

> ...[t]he analyst necessarily identifies with the patient, but there is for him an interval of time between himself and the experience which for the patient has the quality of immediacy – he knows it for past experience, while to the patient it is a present one. That makes it at that moment the patient's experience, not his. (p. 35)

Basch (1983) states:

> ...[t]o be empathic an individual must be able to separate himself sufficiently from his feelings and emotions so that instead of simply reacting

> to them he can establish their genesis and the significance they have in the context in which they are experienced. (p. 119)

The patient's contribution to empathic failures

Even though empathy is considered by some to constitute "emotional manna" or sustenance, patients may nonetheless resist being empathized with (Buie, 1981; Kohut, 1971; Olinick, 1984). Some patients, Greenson (1960) notes, "consciously and unconsciously want to remain ununderstood; they dread being understood. For them, to be understood may mean to be destroyed, devoured, unmasked, etc." (p. 422). Buie (1981) states that such patients "withhold or distort cues which would enable others to gain the empathic understanding of them which they fear would make them vulnerable" (p. 302). Grotstein (1984) writes of patients who "seem immune to or contemptuous toward any demonstration of empathy by the analyst" and, as a result, must first be "made safe for empathy" (p. 207).

One reason patients resist being lured by the promise of empathy is that feeling deeply understood can reactivate childhood wishes and longings that the patient may hope will be satisfied by the analyst. The dread of being retraumatized by hoping for and again failing to have these needs met "may *heighten* the conflictual and resistive aspects of transference" (Stolorow, Brandchaft, & Atwood, 1987, p. 102). A second reason for resisting empathy is that the analyst's empathy threatens some patients because it endangers the security afforded by "the protection which the narcissistic isolation affords the personality" (Kohut, 1971, pp. 306–307). Some patients take comfort in thinking of themselves as unique and incapable of being understood by others. Feeling understood may jeopardize some patients' ability to continue thinking of themselves as unique and hence superior, thus robbing them of a much-needed compensation for their fragile selves.

Inherent difficulties due to conflicting needs or self states

Some empathic failures result not because of the analyst's failure to understand or because of the analysand's resistance to being understood, but as the result of something inherent to the situation. Empathizing with one aspect of a patient may preclude the analyst from being able to establish empathic contact with other aspects.

For example, there are times when patients need to feel that they have had an emotional impact on their analyst. At times like these, it is not the analyst's empathy patients are primarily seeking. For instance, analysts' enjoyment in, or celebration of, their patients' ability to be angry with them can act as a kind of barrier which protects analysts from directly experiencing the full force of their patients' rage. Such an analytic stance may be heard by the patient as the analyst saying, "You cannot get to me." Such a message will leave patients feeling that the analyst is "out of reach" and that their efforts to have an emotional impact have fallen short. Recent literature on "enactments" emphasizes the importance of instances when analysts become so drawn in by their patients that they momentarily lose their rational objectivity as they spontaneously and emotionally react to patients before realizing they are doing so.

While such experiences may prove pivotal in analysis, reacting emotionally to the patient in this manner can just as easily prove traumatic. By operating at a distance from the emotional reactions aroused by the patient, the analyst often increases her/his ability to be useful to the patient. Sharing our understandings of the patient *with* the patient may prove reassuring because it teaches the patient how we avoid taking their attacks personally. The patient may then feel free to vent anger without worrying we will be destroyed or driven off in the process. Sometimes patients want us to maintain distance so that we do not get caught up in their emotions while at the same time requiring that we be close enough for them to be able to affect us sufficiently to cause a visible reaction. Satisfying both needs inevitably leads to empathic failures, no matter how carefully and thoughtfully we position ourselves.

Attempting to empathize simultaneously with different aspects of the patient can prove to be an impossible task. How do we as analysts decide which of the patient's current experiences deserves foremost attention? Do we empathize with patients who need us to be emotionally drawn in to the point of enactment or with patients who need the reassurance that we have not been injured by their behavior? Do we empathize with patients as they are, or with the patients that they could become (Loewald, 1960)? Do we empathize with patients who are grandiose (and feel so different as to be unfathomable to others), or with patients who yearn to be fathomed but fear becoming ordinary as a result (Kohut, 1971; Tuch, 1993)? And do we empathize with patients who want to kill themselves and want others to understand such a wish, given their circumstances, or with patients who want to live and fear that another's empathic understanding of their situation will decrease their resistance to act on such impulses?

A case illustration

Mr. O. is a married executive in his early forties who sought treatment for depression. He felt no joy in life. Though usually a hard worker, he began sitting in his office with the door shut, unable to work. Everything was an effort. He had become fixated on the idea of suicide and had begun cutting himself. The patient felt empty inside and sought stimulation to fill his inner void. He experienced his father as a tyrannical, manipulative, and controlling man who demanded that his children recognize how great a dad he was. The patient thought that his inability to see how great his dad was meant that there was something wrong with *him*. "Father had to be right and told us all how to think. Disagreeing with him was not tolerated." Now that Mr. O. was about to become a father, he wondered how he would ever be able to think for himself so that he might be a good parent for his son.

Mr. O. described his mother as self-centered: "She just goes on and on about herself. She sucks everything out of people by making conversations be just about her." His mother seemed concerned only with appearances and not with who the patient was as a person.

Mr. O. had never felt he had any control over his life. He was forever conceding to others' wishes, expectations, or demands. He would accede to his wife's ultimatums rather than deciding on matters for himself. In general, he was passively aggressive. He refused to act, shrank from confrontation, and got others to make decisions for him.

Making his own decisions became impossible because it threatened to reveal the patient's "secret self" – a self he felt sure that others could neither understand nor tolerate. Experience had taught Mr. O. that others did not even think it was necessary to try to understand him. While others could demand to be understood and accommodated, he could not. Experience had also taught him that others would not tolerate his emotions. If he became excited, he could anticipate his father bursting his bubble. If he complained to his father that he had been hurt by him in some way, he could expect his father to tell him he was wrong for feeling that way – and selfish for putting him down.

The patient feared that his true self would be minimized or destroyed if revealed in therapy. He feared bringing any "good" feelings into sessions out of fear that I would be disinterested. He came in hoping that I would join in his excitement, but anticipated only disappointment because of how things had played out for him in the past. He felt that all I wanted was a "pathology" we could work on – material to prove my brilliance as an analyst.

The patient was quick to become confused about what he wanted and how he felt. This confusion protected him from having to expose his true self. "If someone starts to question me as to why I feel as I do, I begin to lose my mind – I can't offer logical explanations to support my position so I conclude I must be mistaken – the other person must be right. I have a hard time sticking to what I feel is true. Confusion defines me. I can't imagine being without it."

Mr. O.'s confusion was typically followed by him accepting the other's position as correct. "I'd be lost if it wasn't for others who help determine who I am by what they expect of me." Yet he felt angry at others for not letting him be himself and live his own life.

When the patient was angry with me, he feared that I would not understand why he was angry, and that I would try to talk him out of his anger by questioning the legitimacy of his feelings. "You'll throw your hands up and tell me you've had it with me." In fact, the patient felt his relationships were in jeopardy whenever his own opinions differed from those he depended on. Becoming confused dissolved these differences, thus protecting his object ties. In this way, Mr. O. became "mush in other people's hands."

After some months in treatment, the patient began to talk about how he hated coming to treatment. "It's like cod liver oil, something that must be good for me but tastes terrible." The patient wondered, "Can you tolerate my feeling this way about coming to see you?" Sometimes, when the patient had been particularly depressed throughout a session, he would apologize as he left the session for having been a "drag." He needed to be able to leave sessions depressed and to believe that I would allow him to feel this way, but he feared that I wanted him to leave uplifted on account of the time we had spent together.

The patient imagined that my other patients could not wait to see me, loved every minute they spent with me, and got depressed at the session's end. "If I can't feel that way about therapy, it makes me feel like I'm doing this wrong and letting you down. I'm not a good patient because I don't relish coming and I've yet to lay down on the couch."

Facing the couch

The prospect of using the couch was upsetting to the patient because he did not know if he could "do it right" – that is, "do it the way everyone else does it." He wanted to be accepted, but hid behind "conventional behavior," all the while understanding that this brought him no closer to feeling understood by me since his secret self remained hidden. To be seen by me was to be naked and open to ridicule.

The patient was conflicted about using the couch. He felt I expected him to comply and feared he would "cave in" to my wishes to avoid my ire. For him, the couch became yet another "mold" he was to adapt to. He viewed his "trip to the couch" as something he would be doing just for me. He felt my watching him walk to the couch would fill me with triumph at his expense, since all he could imagine feeling was defeat. He could not imagine being allowed to take the credit for getting on the couch, assuming instead that I would want the credit.

For weeks the patient was in an obsessional quandary over whether to try the couch. He experienced the chair as a kind of prison he wished to break out of, while getting himself to the couch meant that he was electing to do something, rather than being directed to do it. Being exposed as someone who had wishes and goals left the patient feeling emotionally naked. Doing something on his own also meant being abandoned, being totally responsible for the consequences of his actions. The patient feared that if things did not work out, he had only himself to blame. He wished not to be left on his own to make that decision. If only I could give him a push – tell him to try the couch next session – then maybe he could feel we were in this thing together – that we shared the responsibility for however it turned out.

In a misguided attempt to encourage the patient off his ambivalent "fence," I placed a napkin on the couch prior to the following session. I had momentarily abandoned my typical analytic stance and succumbed to the urge one often feels to help the obsessional patient by siding with one side of the conflict. I had committed the regrettable error that Anna Freud (1936) had cautioned about when she spoke of the need for analysts to remain "equidistant" (p. 28), and by so doing, I had enacted something from the patient's past.

My action failed to have the desired effect. The following session I sensed that the patient was angry with me for what I had done. He felt pushed by what he experienced as my need and expectation that he "lie down now." But this was not what he expressed. The patient justified my behavior as having been "well intended." I understood that the patient was upset that I had failed to anticipate correctly how my preparing the couch would make him feel. But I had not anticipated how intensely he would react upon hearing that I understood how upsetting this had been for him.

I interpreted that he felt I was insensitive. He responded by saying he felt conflicted about having been angry with me. He anticipated that if he expressed his anger, I would just get angry in return, and then he would feel sorry that he had gotten angry in the first place. To circumvent this problem, the patient turned his anger back on himself for resenting the very person who was trying so hard to help him. At the same time, he wondered why it was that I hadn't been more sensitive and understanding about how the napkin would make him feel. He supported this defense by admitting that these feelings of anger were "really meant" for past objects who had treated him in the way he now "assumed" I was treating him. Through explorations of this kind, the patient ultimately decided to try the couch and now feels comfortable with it.

Facing suicide

At other times in the analysis, the patient felt so miserable that he considered suicide his only way out. "Anything has to be better than what I'm going through," the patient reasoned. He regarded suicide as the only choice left to him that was totally his own. "To be myself, to live for once, requires that I act to end my life." The patient fixated on the idea of suicide. He "cruised" gun shops in search of an implement. I feared for his life and felt forced to take measures to protect him from acting on these impulses. I placed him on medication and suggested hospitalization once I became convinced he intended to act.

The patient's reaction to my alarm was twofold. He felt encouraged that, for once, someone was taking him seriously – that I was not dismissing his feelings as nothing more than crying wolf. Maybe he had finally found in me someone who could believe him when he spoke of how miserable his life was, rather than telling him, as others had, that "things can't be that bad" and that "nothing could be so bad as to justify suicide." But as much as he felt encouraged by my reaction to his suicidal ideas, he also felt unsettled. Did my taking him seriously mean that he had more to worry about than he thought? How close *was* he, he wondered, to killing himself?

Case discussion

This case illustrates several points about how empathy is used in the psychoanalytic setting. The patient often left sessions dejected and worried that I felt let down by his not loving every minute we spent together. I understood that the patient was also saying that he feared growing dependent on me and that needing the sessions made him feel too vulnerable. It was as if he said, "You'll have to buy my contention that I don't like being here because if you rip that mask off, it will be intolerable." Ultimately, the patient did come to understand his need to hide his attachment and dependency on me, but only after being allowed to deny that fact for some time. He felt that he had no model for getting close to men – interpreting such feelings as homosexual. For him, feeling understood had the meaning of seduction.

In my handling of the "couch" issue, I failed to understand how strongly the patient would react to what I considered the "gentle nudge" of laying a napkin on the couch. My wish to be helpful to the patient by acceding to his wish that I would share in the responsibility of his moving to the couch led to the first of two empathic failures. Empathy helped me see through the patient's contentions that he was not upset in the least by what I had done. But by insisting on interpreting the patient's reaction to my empathic failure, I created yet another empathic failure.

I interpreted that he felt I was insensitive in how I had handled the issue of the couch. This was understood by the patient as demonstrating that I, unlike his father, was someone who did not always have to be right and who could tolerate his criticism and anger. However, by prematurely offering that interpretation, I seemed once again to be insensitive to the patient. I had been out of touch with his need to get "good and angry" with me so that he could, once and for all, risk revealing that side of himself. He felt that I had taken the wind out of his sails by "apologizing prematurely." He was also worried that my seeming to take responsibility was not genuine, but my way of cutting off his anger by preempting it.

Attempting to empathize with the patient's suicidal impulses created other problems. I wondered how I could show the patient that I understood just how miserable he felt without seeming to support this solution for his problems. Might not expressing my understanding to the patient tip the balance in favor of the patient acting out suicidal impulses which ran counter to another part of him? Which patient was I to empathize with? Was the only way back to life to enter into the patient's suicidal world and risk what might result? Ultimately, I concluded that this was the case, and I believe that this decision has proved to be in the patient's best interest.

Beyond empathy

Empathy implies that the analyst understands the patient's current affective state, ego state, or self state. Going beyond how patients currently experience or think of themselves is considered by some to be tantamount to an empathic failure. In particular, some consider it "unempathic" to add something of ourselves to our interpretations because doing so introduces our "otherness" into what it is about the patient that we are presently trying to understand.

Whether it is possible or even desirable for analysts to keep themselves out of their interpretations is a matter of great debate. Such an "intrusion" of the analyst's personality may prove to be just what it takes to get patients beyond how they are currently experiencing themselves. This may prove quite helpful in breaking the closed system that the patient had maintained. Introducing new elements in this way may provide a nidus for change within the patient. Bacal (1995) refers to a seemingly unnoticed "lacuna" in self psychology theory when he notes how that theory "has neglected the fact that people suffer not only from self-depletion but also from self-distortion" (p. 355).

Empathic mothering includes empathizing both with the side of the child that feels himself/herself incapable and the child who is, in fact, capable but does not yet believe it. Loewald (1960) speaks about how:

> ...[t]he parent ideally is in an empathic relationship of understanding the child's particular stage in development, *yet ahead in his vision of the child's future and mediating this vision to the child in his dealings with him.* This vision...is, ideally, a more articulate and more integrated version of the core of being which the child presents to the parent. This "more" that the parent sees and knows, he mediates to the child so that the child in identification with it can grow. (p. 20, italics added)

In psychoanalysis, addressing the patient's "potential self" may go beyond how the patient is currently experiencing herself or himself. This must be done in such a way that the patient does not experience this as something expected or needed but, instead, as the faith the analyst has in the patient. Some feel that even this, representing as it does a part of the analyst which is separate from the patient, may be considered tantamount to an unempathic stance and a rupture of selfobject functioning. Believing in a patient's ability to overcome adversity may paradoxically feel unempathic to a patient who cannot locate such hope from within. Some believe we fail at being empathic if we go beyond who the patient experiences herself/himself to be at any given time. Schafer (1959) points out how psychoanalysts must be able to empathize with the patient's experience of feeling utterly helpless while, at the same time, conveying the sense that they have the capacity to handle the situation.

In conclusion, providing optimal selfobject functioning is considered by some analysts to be necessary for the maintenance of an analysand's narcissistic equilibrium. They believe that disruptions of a patient's narcissistic equilibrium indicate a lack of empathy on the analyst's part since they equate empathy and optimal selfobject functioning. However, saying something to a patient which the analyst knows will prove to be jarring is sometimes favored over the continued maintenance of optimal selfobject functioning when it is done for the sake of the patient's development. Must doing this be considered "unempathic"?

Bacal (1995) writes:

> ...the maintenance of an empathic stance may or may not, however, be experienced as a therapeutic response by the analysand. Analysts of all theoretical persuasions encounter instances in which the invalidation of the patient's experience will be experienced as more therapeutic than its empathic tracking or validation...Sometimes a confrontation is more effective than an empathic echo or empathically elaborated interpretation. (p. 358)

Kohut's work promoted the development of psychoanalysis by emphasizing how empathy could and should be used as a tool to better grasp the patient's experience. Since the introduction of his ideas, some have elevated the role of empathy to one of being the essential curative agent in any psychoanalytic venture. According to this view, empathy is considered something that will promote development at any given time. If this is so, one would reason that, at times, it is "unempathic" to be satisfying certain selfobject needs. I believe that defining empathy as whatever will best promote development at any given point claims too much territory for the term.

It is sometimes necessary for the analyst to go beyond empathy for change to occur. The analyst's view of what the patient may be capable of becoming may not reflect how the patient sees himself/herself. Nevertheless, this situation may be the very one the patient needs to change. Kohut's work forced the pendulum to swing in favor of a deeper appreciation for the role and power of empathy in the psychoanalytic setting. Since then, the pendulum has swung toward an overvaluation of empathy's powers. Appreciating the limitations of empathy should help correct this overvaluation by emphasizing what empathy is and is not, what empathy can and cannot achieve.

Chapter 9

Learning from Middle School theorists

Technique from a Middle School perspective

Psychoanalysts hailing from the British Middle School have had a profound effect on the development of psychoanalytic thinking and practice. If one were to limit oneself to just three of its chief contributors – W.R.D. Fairbairn, Donald Winnicott, and John Bowlby – one would begin to appreciate the extent to which their emphasis on the *environmental impact on psychological development* has influenced psychoanalytic thinking in general: Fairbairn's model essentially outlines his belief that we are all destined to rely upon schizoid defenses to help us cope with the ravages of less than ideal parenting; Winnicott's model outlines how one can best parent a child so as to avoid damaging the child in the process; and Bowlby's model of attachment outlines how parenting styles may leave one feeling securely or insecurely attached throughout life. In each instance, the field of psychoanalysis benefitted from the employment of a perspective that lay outside the confines of traditional psychoanalytic thinking: Fairbairn was theologically trained; Winnicott was a practicing pediatrician; Bowlby studied ethology. Considering from whence these Middle School analysts came leads to an appreciation of the beneficial effects of the independent thinking of outsiders on the development of mainstream psychoanalysis.

The Middle School earned its name chiefly because its members did not have allegiance to the two alternate schools of thought – led by Anna Freud on the one hand and Melanie Klein on the other. Members of the Middle School were not solely united by their refusal to pledge allegiance to either of these theorists; they were also united by shared beliefs about development – in particular, the role the environment played in the creation of psychopathology. Many from the Middle School believed that actual experiences with early caregivers (the "environment") have a profound molding effect on psychic structure (Fairbairn, Balint), on the individual's sense of self and his capacity to be "real" – true to himself (Winnicott) – and on his capacity to feel safely and securely attached to others (Bowlby). This emphasis on "real experiences" is in opposition to the thinking of Melanie Klein, who tended to de-emphasize actual experience in favor of experience *as it is colored by phantasy* – which, in turn, is colored by the infant's innate aggression.

In this chapter, we examine aspects of the theories advanced by Fairbairn, Winnicott, and Bowlby. These theories not only outline a path by which individuals become psychologically impaired, but also suggest ways in which such conditions can be psychoanalytically ameliorated. Lessons learned from the likes of these Middle School theorists suggest modifications in how classically trained analysts might approach treatment.

W.R.D. Fairbairn

Ogden (2010) refers to Fairbairn's theory of internal object relations as "one of the most important contributions to the development of analytic theory in its first century" (p. 102). Fairbairn's theories represent a radical departure from classic psychoanalytic theorizing. For example, while Klein considered fantasy primary and actual experience secondary, Fairbairn saw it the other way around; while Freud saw object seeking as driven secondarily by the pleasure principle – by the need for objects that can lessen bodily tension that wells up as a consequence of mounting physiologic need – Fairbairn insisted that object seeking was primary; and while Klein and Freud saw aggression as a primary, innate biological drive, Fairbairn envisioned it as arising more from the frustration of the infant's needs. Greenberg and Mitchell (1983) sum up Fairbairn's position, noting:

> ...he is suggesting that human experience and behavior derive fundamentally from the search for and the maintenance of contact with others... [that] psychopathology is understood not as deriving from conflicts over pleasure-seeking impulses, but as reflective of disturbances and interferences in relations with others...[which makes psychotherapy] a process through which the capacity for making direct and full contact with real other human beings is restored. (p. 156)

Fairbairn (1952d) envisioned psychic structure (which he termed "endopsychic structure") as developing as a result of the infant's need to find ways to cope with actual traumatic experiences the child had endured at the hands of his caregivers – experiences that were not merely of his own making (via fantasy, interpretation). Given that every infant realizes there are limits to a mother's loving ministration, argued Fairbairn, every infant must find ways to psychically cope with this reality, and how the infant does just that has a profound effect on the *structure* of his mind. Fairbairn described how infants utilize *schizoid mechanisms*,[1] as he called them, which help the infant split off (sequester, dissociate) awareness of certain traumatic, developmental memories of how he'd been treated by his caregivers in order to come to a tenuous peace with such unbearable memories/realizations about which the infant alternately (depending on his state of mind) knows and does not know. As Fairbairn sees the matter, at our core we all evidence schizoid tendencies (Fairbairn, 1952d); the only difference is the extent to which any given individual relies upon these mechanisms to cope with "failure on the part of the mother to convince the child that she really loves him as a person" (p. 13). "It becomes too painful to long for and depend on an object which is physically or emotionally absent a good deal of the time," note Greenberg and Mitchell (1983), "therefore the child establishes internal objects inside himself, which act as substitutes and solutions for unsatisfying relationships with real external objects…internal objects within his theory [that] are by definition psychopathological structures" (p. 159).

While Fairbairn emphasized the behavior of early caregivers, he noted individual differences in how infants experience the inevitable deprivations that result from the inability of real objects to function as ideal objects, which leaves the child painfully dissatisfied with how his primary caregivers had behaved. Infants are forced to contend with a range of experiences that challenge their ability to cope: feeling unloved and unlovable, leaving the child with a life-long yearning to, and a belief in his ability to, somehow elicit the hoped-for unequivocal love and help of others; feeling rejected, which the infant may come to think was the result of his innate "badness"; and feeling teased into expecting, only to be let down time and again. For Fairbairn (1944), frustration of the infant's needs begets a sense of a lack of love that, in turn (depending in part on how the individual infant imagines the situation), begets a sense of having been purposefully rejected by the "teasing" mother.

Coming face to face with the realization of the limits of the mother's love is a matter the infant cannot take in stride, because it is "an affective experience which is singularly devastating" (Fairbairn, 1952c, p. 84) – one that can greatly affect both the infant's sense of self as well as his sense of being. Believing one sees evidence of the mother's lack of love can lead to a diminution of the infant's self-worth – his capacity to maintain a belief in his essential goodness as he feels "reduced to a state of worthlessness, destitution or beggardom" (p. 84). He feels inferior, believing he'd demanded too much of the mother; he feels powerless to affect change (p. 84). More disturbing is the possibility that perceived evidence of his mother's lack of love will, at the deepest level, create a sense of "disintegration and of imminent psychical death" (p. 84).

To cope with such devastating effects, the child splits off awareness of the two ways in which the mother had failed him – either through a wholesale rejection of him (failing to be loving and failing to appreciate/accept the infant's love and/or level of need) or by enticing the infant into believing that his yearning for love is about to be satisfied at any moment as he patiently and desperately hopes it will be. To cope with these two faces – the "rejecting mother" and the "exciting/enticing/tantalizing mother" (who stimulates the hope of being loved), the infant internalizes these "objects," turning them into "bad" (non-gratifying) internal objects. Identification with these objects then makes them seem to be a part of the infant, thus granting him greater control.

These two internal objects – the rejecting and the exciting object – elicit corresponding "ego" responses within the infant, each of which represents a split-off part of the infant's "central ego," which produces "subsidiary egos" (Fairbairn, 1952c, p. 79) – more accurately, segments of the self: the *exciting mother* (instances of actual maternal indulgence combined with fantasies of the same) gets linked with the loving, perpetually longing "libidinal ego" (1958, p. 374), while the *rejecting mother* becomes affectively linked with the enraged, potentially destructive "antilibidinal ego," originally referred to as "the internal saboteur" (1944, p. 78). Endopsychic structure is then composed of two self-with-other pairs (antilibidinal ego/rejecting object; libidinal ego/exciting-teasing object) linked by powerful emotions (the former with disappointment, a sense of impotence and betrayal, mixed with anger and hate; the latter infused with hope, longing, and shameless yet shameful begging). The hateful feelings stimulated by frustration are effectively kept apart from the loving feelings stimulated by the hope of satisfaction – hence, ambivalence is eliminated as a pure split between good and bad prevails.

The child comes to feel that he is bad on many counts. He questions his innate goodness, believing "the reason for his mother's apparent lack of love towards him is that he has destroyed her affection and made it disappear... [proving that] his own love is destructive and bad" (Fairbairn, 1952a, p. 25).[2] Hence, the infant isn't bad solely because he's become identified with the bad behavior of his objects, who he's internalized and hence become like; the infant also experiences himself as bad because he believes that his libidinal (loving) ego is inherently bad. By virtue of having his love/need rejected, the child is left feeling shunned, unworthy of having his love accepted and his needs properly addressed. The child's sense of badness is reinforced by his use of a "moral defense" (1952a, p. 65) – blaming himself for the failure of his objects – which sustains the illusion of the caregiver's goodness. Fairbairn, who'd received theological training, explains this mechanism with the help of a religious-based analogy:

> It is better to be a sinner in a world ruled by God than to live in a world ruled by the Devil. A sinner in a world ruled by God may be bad; but there is always a certain sense of security to be derived from the fact that the world around is good...In a world ruled by the Devil the individual... can have no sense of security and no hope of redemption. The only prospect is one of death and destruction. (pp. 66–67)

The infant goes on to become strongly attached to these bad internal objects because the alternative is worse – to live without any objects whatsoever. Somewhat paradoxically, infants attach more tightly to objects that frustrate their needs – prolonging their dependency on the object – than to objects that gratify their needs. Fairbairn (1952a) notes:

> If a child's parents are bad objects, he cannot reject them, even if they do not force themselves upon him; for he cannot do without them. Even if they neglect him, he cannot reject them; for, if they neglect him, his need for them is increased. (p. 67)

Paradoxically, the infant clings ever more tightly to the unloving mother, meaning that the infant grows into an adult who'll be inclined, in repetition compulsion fashion, to seek out and recreate frustrating-type relationships, not only because they are dearly familiar, but because such adults hope against hope that things might actually turn out differently this time around. The same can be said for the patient's search for enticing objects (e.g. "unavailable men"). Either way, the patient is at risk of chasing after rejecting objects, resulting, for example, in a well-known pattern for some men to only be attracted to women who want to be "friends," lacking any interest whatsoever in women who truly desire them. A pursuit of enticing objects can similarly give rise to stalking behavior that is predicated on the delusional belief that the enticing object must certainly feel likewise toward the pursuer:

> Love objects are selected for and made into withholders and deprivers so as to personify the exciting object, promising but never fulfilling. Defeat is orchestrated again and again to perpetuate the longing and need of the libidinal ego for the fulfillment of the promise of the exciting object. (Greenberg & Mitchell, 1983, p. 174)

Given the four potential roles that a patient can either assume or assign to others in "doer/done to" fashion (Benjamin, 2004), one can imagine a wide variety of possibilities depending on who's assigned the role of rejecter or "rejectee," enticer or "enticee." Celani (2010) notes:

> Fairbairn's structural model aids the therapist by providing him with four basic possibilities that are relatively easy to sort through and then identify which ego or internalized object is dominating the patient's consciousness, as well as the reciprocal ego structure and role that is being forced on the analyst. (p. 124)

For example, the patient can play the role of the rejected child just as he can assign that role to the analyst, leaving the patient to then assume the role of the rejecting mother. In a similar fashion, either the patient or the analyst may play the role of the enticing/teasing object who has what the other wants, but will never give it. As an adult, individuals who remain deeply attached to rejecting and exciting objects will be attracted to, and will be motivated to evoke in others these sorts of relational configurations, which we'd expect to manifest through the patient's transference reactions (and corresponding countertransference enactments) during the course of analysis.

Hope springs eternal: the individual keeps returning to the scene of the crime in the hope that, this time around, the matter will play out differently and – should that be the case – the core problem of the patient's childhood will accordingly be solved. Ogden (2010) notes:

> ...the infant's effort to transform unsatisfactory objects into satisfactory objects – thus reversing the imagined toxic effect on the mother of the infant's love – is the single most important motivation sustaining the structure of the internal object world. And that structure, when externalized, underlies all pathological external object relationships. (p. 107)

Besides difficulties recognizing and relating to real objects as distinct from pathological internal objects, a second significant outcome of the depletion of the central ego by virtue of the creation of substantial subsidiary egos (libidinal and antilibidinal) is the tendency to turn to "substitutive satisfactions" (Fairbairn, 1952a, p. 261) that arise from fixations of infantile sexuality, leading to autoerotic and addictive-type psychopathology.

To the extent the two specified configurations (antilibidinal ego/rejecting object; libidinal ego/exciting-teasing object) are both isolated from the real world and remain powerful forces shaping the individual's attractions and perceptions, they form a "closed system" (Fairbairn, 1958, p. 380) that becomes very hard for the analyst to penetrate or reconfigure. Ogden (2010) notes how "internal objects interact with the external world only in the form of narcissistic object relationships, that is, externalizations of internal object relationships (which are necessarily narcissistic in nature)" (p. 113). Greenberg and Mitchell (1983) write how "psychopathology results from this fragmentation of the ego and the devotion of the resulting portions of the ego to their internal objects at the expense of relations with real people" (p. 165), and "the degree of pathology depends on how much of the [central] ego is still available for real and potentially fulfilling relations with others" (p. 171). By contrast, Ogden (2010) notes:

> The central ego includes no dynamically repressed (unsatisfactory) internal object relationships; rather, the central ego consists exclusively of good enough (as opposed to idealized) object relationships such as identifications with people whom one has loved and by whom one has felt loved, recognized and accepted. Such identifications underlie feelings that include a sense of internal security, as well as background feelings of solidity and integrity. (p. 113)

The goal of treatment is to increase the domain of the central ego that had been diminished in the process of ceding territory to these "subegos," which became dissociated from the whole of the individual's conscious psyche. The therapist aims to return these split-off subegos to the realm of the central ego, to whatever extent that is possible. Ogden (2010) is of the opinion that psychotherapeutically facilitated change comes about as a function of the extent to which treatment helps the patient come to genuinely accept himself and, by extension, to accept others, resulting in a patient:

> ...discovering a world of people and experiences that exists outside of oneself...a world in which one feels no compulsion to transform the realities of one's human relationships into something other than what they are, i.e. to change oneself or "the object" (who is now a whole and separate subject) into other people. (p. 114)

This includes the realization that it is not the analyst's job, nor is it even a desirable or necessary goal, to be transformed by the analyst into something other than who one is. This establishes the intended goal of treatment, as outlined by Ogden (2010), to help the patient come to terms with, and accept, who and what he is:

> With psychological growth, one comes to know at a depth that one's early experiences with one's unloving and unaccepting mother will never be other than what they were. It is a waste of life to devote oneself to the effort to transform oneself (and others) into the people one wishes one were (or wishes they were). In order to take part in experience in a world populated by people whom one has not invented, and from whom one may learn, the individual must first loosen the unconscious bonds of resentment, addictive love, contempt and disillusionment that confine him to a life lived principally in his mind. (pp. 116–117)

Ogden imagines this happening largely on account of the analyst's ability to truly accept the patient for who he is, rather than harboring fantasies of turning the patient into something of the analyst's making in accordance with the analyst's wish or desire.

Fairbairn's (1958) model of therapeutic action involves the integration of split-off (dissociated) parts, which results in the expansion of the central (reasonable, reality-oriented) ego: to accept one's childhood for what it was; to experience and mourn the loss of what never was, what "should" have been, but will never be; and to cease the endless search for the sorts of infantile needs and wishes that can never be satisfied in the here-and-now by another individual. Celani (2010) sees this taking place, in part, as a result of the patient coming to realize that the analyst is a good object, which requires the patient to work through tendencies to assign roles and misperceive the analyst in accordance with one of his endopsychic structures (libidinal ego, antilibidinal ego, rejecting object, exciting object). While Fairbairn repeatedly asserted that his theory does not allow for the internalization of good objects, only bad objects (because internalization, in Fairbairn's eyes, is a distinctively defensive act), Celani repeatedly insists (in concert with Greenberg & Mitchell, 1983) that the internalization of the analyst as a good object is an essential development that leads to the patient's improvement to the extent it provides an alternate attachment, thus loosening the patient's vice-like attachment to pathologic introjects and corresponding libidinal and antilibidinal positions. Fairbairn (1952a) writes that "there can be no room for doubt that the obstinate attachment of the libidinal ego to the needed object and its reluctance to renounce this object constitute a particularly formidable source of resistance" (pp. 85–86).

Celani (2010) describes Fairbairn's model of how the analyst helps a patient work though his attachment to such endopsychic structures by noting a two-step procedure whereby "the analyst must first break through the 'closed system' of the patient's inner world of transference projections and, when that is accomplished, must use the 'real relationship' with the patient to restart the patient's thwarted emotional development" (p. 73). To this, Celani adds a third step, disallowed by Fairbairn, involving internalization of the analyst as a good object. Without requiring that the patient internalize the analyst as a good object, Fairbairn (1958) nevertheless acknowledged the mutative function of the analyst in the role as good object:

> The actual relationship existing between the patient and the analyst as persons must be regarded as in itself constituting a therapeutic factor of prime importance. The existence of such a personal relationship in outer reality not only serves the function of providing a means of correcting the distorted relationships which prevail in inner reality and influence the reactions of the patient to outer objects, but provides the patient with an opportunity, denied to him in childhood, to undergo a process of emotional development in the setting of an actual relationship with a reliable and beneficent parental figure…in my opinion, such a psychology [of object relations] not only promotes therapeutic aims more effectively than the predominantly "impulse-psychology" formulated by Freud, but actually corresponds more closely to the psychological facts and possesses a greater explanatory value from a purely scientific standpoint. (p. 377)

Fairbairn's sophisticated theory provides analysts with a way to understand the patient's "narrative" storyline in order to both help the analyst withstand the patient's projections (contain, not react to) and resist the impulse to enact, which "nails" the analyst for a time with some imagined crime. The end goal of such a treatment is to integrate aspects of the psyche that heretofore could not be integrated and, as a result, to widen the field of influence of the central ego, which necessarily requires that the analyst finds ways not to become hopelessly lost in the maze created by the patient's expectation-laden projections. Levenson (1991) pinpoints the anxiety of analysts who imagine being transformed by the patient in accordance with the patient's projections:

> That is, that in his experience with the patient he will be converted into an object in the patient's world. This transformation is not merely a fantasy of the patient, it is a genuine threat to the therapist, and his reality… Therapy proceeds not so much by virtue of the therapist's capacity to provide the patient with a *de novo* experience, as by his capacity to *resist being converted into an old and familiar experience*. (p. 20, italics added)

Celani (2010) is careful to note that the danger of losing oneself in a patient's projection doesn't mean that the analyst doesn't or shouldn't, for a time, allow himself to experience himself as he is being experienced by the patient – to "wear the attribution" (Lichtenberg, Lachmann, & Fosshage, 1992, 1996) – by taking care to not prematurely challenge the transference by "saying it isn't so." Interpretations may prove helpful, but finding ways to gracefully tolerate then transcend a projected role assignment might, in the final analysis, prove to be the more mutative of the two clinical strategies.

Donald Winnicott

Most analysts associated with the Middle School share in common certain beliefs about development in general and about treatment in particular. For example, both Fairbairn and Winnicott emphasized the environmental impact on the developing child's psyche – how caregivers could behave in ways that negatively impacted development. Furthermore, each of these authors conceptualized aggression as reactive – as the result of a thwarting of essential, developmentally based needs – and not as a core, innate drive likely to push for expression no matter what the child had experienced at the hands of his caregivers. While Fairbairn's relationship with the classic analytic canon was downright iconoclastic, being unapologetic about his disagreements with certain of the essential beliefs and theories of Freud and Klein, Winnicott took care not to flagrantly challenge the central tenets of the field. Greenberg and Mitchell (1983) describe Winnicott's approach as a more surreptitious subversiveness, advancing his ideas in ways designed to avoid a head-on challenge of classic theory by making it appear as if his contributions were a continuation, and not a departure from, Freudian thinking. Greenberg and Mitchell quote Guntrip as noting that while Winnicott privately acknowledged his approach's difference from Freud's drive-based model, he took great pains "to proclaim himself at one with Freud in all respects" (p. 205). Winnicott accomplished this sleight of hand by acting as if Freud didn't quite mean what he said. Winnicott engaged in a "systematic misreading of Freud's formulations," doing so by redefining terms Freud used as if "Freud did not really mean what he said" (pp. 205–206), and – by so doing – making it appear as if his own theories did not take leave of Freud's theories, which was not at all the case.

As much as they shared in common, there is a major, unacknowledged difference in the underlying attitudes of Fairbairn and Winnicott: the former was pessimistic while the latter was relatively optimistic when it came to the question of whether a caregiver could conduct himself in ways that would prove "good enough" so as to free a child's development from being encumbered by pathogenic neglect, which Fairbairn considered a standard, unavoidable consequence of an across-the-board parental inability to even approximate treatment that would *not* leave each and every human schizoid to the core. Winnicott's theory essentially outlines a model of how parents might optimally operate so as to successfully guide their child through the narrow straits of development, avoiding the ever-present pitfall of raising a child who is overly compliant to the views and needs of others – a child whose true self is cast into the shadows, potentially lost even to himself, as he masquerades through the presentation of a false self that is meant to represent who he actually is – leaving aside his core being that never has to show up because doing so is far too risky a venture. In this regard, Winnicott is hopeful to the extent he sees a plateau atop the mountain upon which parents can stand, which provides them a way to avoid slipping down either side of the slope, which Fairbairn sees as inevitable. Winnicott sees the slippery slopes as either prematurely confronting the child with realities he is not yet ready or prepared to face, or by failing to require the child to face facts when the time is developmentally right for him to do so. Just so long as these twin dangers are avoided, notes Winnicott, the child's development might prove successful, minimizing the chances he will become neurotic.

Winnicott's model of development involves three basic stages: the first involving the child's inability to differentiate self from other; the second involving his recognition of the separate existence of "not me," need-satisfying others (Winnicott, 1965) over whom he nevertheless believes he has total control; and a third stage in which he grows to accept his objects as distinct and separate from himself – as having lives and needs of their own. At the core of Winnicott's model is a theory that young children cannot tolerate the premature realization that they are separate beings who are relatively powerless over the adults upon whom they totally depend for the longest period of time. While it is now generally accepted that infants know and accept the essential difference between self and other in a physical sense – casting doubt on the concept of infantile symbiosis – it remains the case that young children need their illusions – in particular, the illusion that they have more control over their environment than they actually have.

During Winnicott's first stage of development, ending at roughly eight weeks of age, the idea of a standalone baby is inconceivable to the baby, who experiences himself as indistinguishable from the requisite maternal matrix (the idea that there is no such thing as a baby separate and apart from its mother; Winnicott, 1971). The mother's attuned provisions help maintain the illusion that infant and mother are one. The illusion of oneness keeps the infant in the dark about such matters as "need" or a "need-providing other." The infant's needs are more or less seamlessly met by the good-enough mother and are, by and large, kept from developing into desire (the experience of "wishing for," along with the terrifying realization "this need may go unmet"). Experiencing desire (wishing for) can cause the child to have to prematurely contend with the reality of the mother's otherness. Ideally, the mother does what she can to forestall the infant's traumatic realization of separateness, working all the while to help ready the infant for a time when he will be better able to face reality. In this way, she provides a "benign environmental matrix" that the child will then internalize as a "good object." This readies the child for the realization and acceptance of separateness, seeing it as survivable given the existence of goodness both in the world (the remembered maternal ministrations) and within oneself (the internalized good object). Ogden (1985) emphasizes that it is the matrix that becomes internalized/appropriated, not the object itself: "The mother must not make her presence as object too important," he notes, "for this would lead the child to become addicted to her as omnipotent object" (p. 357). In the end, it is more important that the mother be known for what it is she can do/has done (her function; her role in creating the matrix; the fact that another could just as easily have provided the same) rather than for who she is – the idea that she alone can provide for the infant in such an effective and caring fashion.

Being confronted with the sudden and overwhelming awareness of his own needs, notes Winnicott (1965), generates unthinkable ("annihilation") anxiety experienced as "going to pieces, falling forever, having no relationship with the body [and] having no orientation" (p. 58). The mother's well-timed and accurately attuned provisions help to defend against the outbreak of annihilation anxiety by supporting the illusion of oneness, satisfying the infant's needs before he even realizes he has needs, keeping him from realizing he relies on a need-providing object over whom he has little control. All that the child need do is *begin* to imagine something he needs and – voila! – it's delivered to his door post-haste. It's a bit like being a servant – the kind of "perfect" servant described in the movie *Gosford Park* (Fellows & Altman 2001) – a servant that knows, even before his master knows, what it is the master will be wanting. Such absolute attentiveness is reassuring just so long as it has its limit and the child is eventually made to realize the world outside will not satisfy his needs indefinitely.

At around eight weeks of life, the infant enters a new developmental stage – the transitional stage – which is characterized by the infant's growing awareness that he has needs and depends on the need-satisfying other (mother/mothering figure) to satisfy those needs. Having more or less dedicated herself completely to the infant in the first several weeks of his life, the mother is now ready to reclaim her life as she becomes increasingly less preoccupied with the baby's welfare and a bit more concerned about getting her own needs met. By so doing, the mother plays midwife, delivering the child from the once-comforting illusion of oneness. Ideally, the infant's own biologically programmed developmental timetable is more or less ready for, even needing, such help from the mother.

While the infant is on the verge of being able to differentiate external from internal reality – what he objectively perceives from what he subjectively conceives (Winnicott, 1965, p. 45) – he still tends to blur, is even *encouraged* to blur, fantasy and reality. A mother who's attuned to her infant's needs will take care not to confront and confuse him with the facts: that fantasy and reality are not the same; that transitional objects are provided for, not created by the infant; that the infant hasn't the kind of control he prefers to believe he has over his objects. In order to defend against the emergence of traumatic helplessness, the infant needs to believe he has more control over the environment than he actually has. In his fantasy, the infant has absolute control over the object, which keeps him from becoming overwhelmingly anxious at the thought that his needs might go unmet. And, for the time being, the child is to be permitted to believe what he momentarily needs to believe: that adults exist to serve him, that adults function at his behest, that all the infant need do is imagine wanting, and – as the genie in the bottle says – "Your wish is my command!"

Development can go awry during this stage in two different ways. If the mother isn't ready, when the infant is ready, to let the infant begin to experience degrees of separateness that usher in the transitional stage of mother and infant living together, she will impede his development. Alternately, if the mother impatiently hastens development by prematurely rupturing the child's transitional illusion of control over the object that ushers in the next developmental stage, the child is at risk of becoming prematurely mature – of creating a "false self" – in response to the mother's needs, forgoing satisfaction of his wish to be permitted to linger a bit longer in this stage of transition.

During this transitional period, the mother comes to realize her baby no longer needs or expects her to magically know precisely what he needs. Winnicott (1960) observes: "The mother seems to know that the infant has a new capacity, that of giving a signal [a "spontaneous gesture"] so that she can be guided towards meeting the infant's needs" (p. 593). While development is sometimes thought to progress in a steady, uphill fashion, infants actually fluctuate between needing the mother's magical knowing and needing to be left alone long enough to reach some understanding about who they are and what it is they want and need. Winnicott captures this fluctuation when he writes: "One minute they are merged with their mothers and require empathy, while the next they are separate from her, and then if she knows their needs in advance she is dangerous, a witch" (p. 594).

The fluctuation Winnicott refers to is particularly well illustrated in the children's picture book *Runaway Bunny*, written by Margaret Wise Brown (1942), author of the classic *Goodnight Moon*. The story tells a tale of a baby rabbit who announces its intention to run away. In response, the mother declares her plan to run after him wherever he may go, no matter how persistent his efforts to escape might be. The little bunny tells the mother that if she chases after him, he will become a fish in a trout stream and swim away from her. Undaunted, the mother responds saying she will then become a fisherman and fish for him. In succession, the baby rabbit comes up with scheme after scheme to evade the mother's reach, but each time the mother invents a way to stay close on his tracks: if he becomes a sailboat and sails away from her, the mother answers that she will turn into the wind and blow him where she wants him to go. Eventually, the baby rabbit figures there is no way out, so he succumbs, resolving that he may as well just stay where he is and be her little bunny. Depending on the age of the child being read this story, it will either be experienced as reassuring, by actively negating states of separateness, or as terrifying, a macabre tale of maternal intrusion, of imprisoning oneness from which the child will never be able, or be permitted, to escape.

During this transitional stage of development, the infant begins to develop a capacity to be alone in the presence of the mother/another (Winnicott, 1958). This means the infant feels no pressure from the other to have to react. A space of relative isolation is carved out that facilitates the emergence of the infant's own impulses and desires. "It is only under these conditions that the infant can have an experience that feels real" (p. 34), writes Winnicott. Such an experience forms the basis of a true self – the discovery of the infant's own personal life, one borne not out of reactivity, but out of a state of calm and quiet that permits the discovery of the infant's own emerging inclinations, proclivities, and so on. Here, external impingement doesn't so greatly threaten the child's psychic existence as it once had during the first stage of development. Instead, it impedes the infant's developing ability to learn what it means to be himself.

During the third and final stage of development, the mother is recognized as an object in her own right. Dependency is now understood as a matter of being at the other's mercy, as opposed to seeing the object as one who can't help but satisfy the infant's needs, seeing that the infant is either merged with the mother (stage one) or imagining the object as being under his control (stage two). This is the dawn of the depressive position, with all that entails. At this point in development, the young child has a greater capacity to do without actual care. When frustrated, he falls back on the memory of maternal provision and draws upon the built-up sense of a good internal object that he projects, generating a belief in the environment as essentially benign. As a rule, separateness is no longer the menace it had once been, and actually enriches the individual's experience of life, as well as his ability to make it in the world. When separated from the mother for too long a time, the infant experiences more pedestrian separation anxiety – a welling up of need that the mother (or a mothering figure) knows best how to satisfy – rather than annihilation anxiety. If frustration becomes too great, the child develops a capacity to hate the absent mother. Whether the mother responds to the child's hate by attempting to reinstate the idealized and glorified sense of merger or, alternately, by struggling with the consequences of separateness makes all the difference in the world.

The clinical applications of Winnicott's theories are twofold: one educates therapists about how to be good-enough clinicians, cautioning therapists about the dangers of interacting with patients in ways that encourage the patient's continued reliance on a false self; the other sets a goal for treatment in terms of enticing the patient's true self to dare to emerge, to be recognized and known. The model of the transitional space in which the infant's creation of reality goes unchallenged is clinically mirrored in the realization that analysts must, if but for a time, conduct themselves in ways that allow the patient the illusion that his transference is accepted as such – that the analyst can live, for a time, within the confines created by the patient's construction of who he is and what motivates him to do the things he does. The concept of "wearing the attribution" is but one of many ways that analysts have characterized the task of permitting the patient to live out the transference until such a time as the patient is ready to accept a different view of the matter, in the same way children grow to a point where their separateness is tolerable and the child is ready to accept the separable subjectivity of the other, who is distinctly different from who the child/patient had imagined them to be.

Besides helping to specify a way for the analyst to conduct himself, Winnicott's theory also establishes a tangible goal for treatment. What "schizoid" is to Fairbairn, "false self" is to Winnicott, and while these two types of defense mechanisms differ markedly in the ways in which they operate, they nevertheless have in common the fact that both aim to protect the child from a traumatic realization of the reality of the environment. Fairbairn's schizoid mechanisms work to split off/sequester the memory of terrible parenting – the experience of feeling unloved, rejected, and the like. Treatment then entails helping reintegrate these dissociated experiences, expanding the domain of the central ego in the process as the patient comes to terms with the fact that his parents had mortal flaws and he'd best abandon all efforts to undo the damage by seeking out experiences that might "make up for" what he'd missed out on. Winnicott's "false self" also results from an absence of a good-enough mother that forces the child to adapt by hiding his true self, leading him to send in a false self in its place. Therapy then entails helping the patient recover his true self, which requires conditions be met that make that task achievable. This, in part, requires the analyst not prematurely challenge the transference. But it also requires him to function along the lines outlined by Winnicott about what constitutes "good-enough mothering" – which means the therapist must be carefully attuned to what the patient can and cannot presently tolerate, that the therapist does not intrude upon the patient by covertly insisting he think, or be, or act in accordance with the therapist's needs, and that the therapist accepts whatever ends up emerging as the patient's true self.

Winnicott's ideas about transitional space readily can be applied in the clinic setting. Some analysts believe that the act of interpreting risks leaving certain patients feeling misunderstood and, as a result, alienated from an analyst. They fault practitioners who not only insist on interpreting but, additionally, insist on their interpretations. These critics recommend de-emphasizing the use of interpretation in order to protect patients who aren't yet ready to face the reality of separateness arising from prematurely having to cope with the realization that they and the analyst are not of like mind as they had once imagined. For such patients, realization of the analyst's otherness shatters the favored illusion of closeness/oneness, leaving them grappling with the unsettling sense of separateness.

An analyst may stumble his way into such a calamity by failing to heed the patient's unspoken plea to be permitted to cling to the fantasy of oneness a bit longer, implying that the analyst's chief responsibility is to safeguard the sustaining fantasy and to dare not speak its name lest he bring down the house of cards before it's been glued in place. An analyst who blindly upsets the apple cart in this fashion will be taken off guard by the intensity of the patient's reaction that may seem inexplicable. At other times, an analyst will strategically decide it is high time the patient contends with the reality of differences, come what may, thus ushering in a heroic, and potentially foolhardy, new phase of treatment. Instances when such a clinical shift represents an enactment of the analyst having tired of being relegated to the position of mute witness to the patient's life need to be acknowledged as such and worked through accordingly.

John Bowlby

Over the course of the last half-century, the work of John Bowlby on attachment theory has mushroomed into a full-fledged movement predicated on the identification and study of various types of attachment styles that can have a determining effect on the quality of one's object relations. Bowlby was chiefly interested in the formation of intimate social bonds between parent and child – though he emphasized that attachment issues play an important role throughout an individual's lifespan. Bowlby studied the reciprocal behavioral processes involved in bringing about such bonds, describing such attachment behaviors as innate, biologic, and evolutionarily based. He insisted that attachment serves a basic survival function, which accordingly granted it status as a *primary motive*, rather than it being a means to an end (Bowlby, 1988a), contradicting Freud (1926), who saw the infant's object-seeking behavior as primarily motivated by a drive that aims to ensure the satisfaction of the infant's most basic biologic needs. For example, Freud explained the normal development of stranger anxiety (in the ninth month of life) as being the result of the infant's uncertainty about whether a stranger will be as adept and inclined as the mother to service the *child's bodily needs*. Contradicting this assertion are studies demonstrating that infants cry in the presence of strangers ("stranger anxiety") not out of fear that their oral needs might go unmet but, instead, because they feel unsafe and insecure when they are not in the proximity of attachment figures with whom they have worked out *a repertoire for procuring a sufficient modicum of security* (attachment behaviors; Ainsworth, 1969; Hesse & Main, 1999).

Bowlby described the process of human attachment as involving an inborn capacity to seek out, establish bonds with, and elicit protection from an adult caregiver (the "attachment figure"). The process by which this occurs – termed the "attachment behavioral system" – involves the attaching individual's (e.g., infant) emitting behavioral attachment signals that communicate his need for proximity, which are then read and responded to – optimally or less than optimally – by the attachment figure. This whole system (the attachment-seeking individual nonverbally transmitting his attachment needs to the selected attachment figure) functions like a homeostatic feedback loop. For example, the infant experiences a state of alarm caused by unnerving conditions (hunger, fear, etc.). He nonverbally signals his distress to the attachment figure (e.g., by crying), sometimes specifying what it is he wants the attachment figure to do (e.g., indicating a wish to be picked by stretching his arms out and up). Ideally, the attachment figure responds in a timely and accurate manner to the infant's "SOS" – drawing near, picking the child up, comforting the child in whatever manner he chooses, verbalizing awareness of the child's internal state sufficient to contribute to the child's developing ability to articulate his inner states, and the like.

Caregivers who are better able to respond accurately, consistently, and in a reasonably timely manner to the infant's signals contribute to the infant's developing capacity to feel secure in his object world; alternately, less than optimal sorts of responses result in the infant becoming more anxiously attached to his objects. The responses of the attachment figure also help establish the infant's "internal working model" (Bowlby, 1969; Bretherton & Waters, 1985), which determines how the infant expects other human beings to respond when he signals his distress and need for some reassuring response from his objects. Children whose caregivers routinely and predictably are insensitive and/or unresponsive to the infant's needs will lose faith in the utility of sending out such signals and may accordingly cease to engage in attachment-seeking behaviors – becoming seemingly self-sufficient, need-denying, and attachment-avoidant in the process. Other children raised by such caregivers may become anxiously attached – exhibiting either a clingy, demanding, beseeching, even coercing pattern of behavior or tendencies to become excessively caregiving in their interactions with others – providing the sorts of supplies they themselves had needed but had not been able to successfully entice their original caregivers to provide.

A brief clinical example

It would be misleading to suggest a unity in the way in which Middle School analysts work clinically, though it is not unreasonable to conclude that many are on the lookout for clinical signs that the patient's difficulties, as they manifest through the transference, issue – at least in part – from the experience of faulty parenting of whatever sort. One may see evidence of this in the way in which the patient experiences and reacts to the analyst's interventions – for example, seeing them as unempathic, as uncaring, as unloving, as misunderstanding, as misattuned, as reflective of the analyst's need to use the patient, and so on and so forth. It is not uncommon to find analysts who work from different theoretic perspectives using different terms to refer to the same psychological situation, so while we will be talking in terms of faulty mirroring in this section, other analysts might call the same clinical phenomenon by a different name.

What follows is a clinical example provided to illustrate the way in which a Middle School orientation leads the analyst to understand the patient's material in a particular light, leading the analyst to address the transference or talk with the patient in particular ways. Enid Balint (1993) addresses the pathogenic effect of a child not having experienced sufficient "feedback" (read, "mirroring") from her caregivers to enable her to know her own mind. In this case, the lack thereof led to the patient being "empty of herself" (lacking a sense of self). When the analysis began, Sarah was a severely disturbed, twenty-four-year-old woman who could barely function beyond getting herself to sessions. She could not hold a job or otherwise be productive. Sessions tended to be primitive in nature – generally characterized as flat in tone, marked with long silences punctuated with violent outbursts, and containing interactions she considered "meaningless." The patient, who was the youngest of three children, had been sexually molested by her two older brothers from the ages of seven to twelve. The mother seemed oblivious not just to this ongoing situation, but also to most of what the patient experienced. Sarah saw herself as scorned by her family but – more importantly – as not being recognized, not being seen.

Balint came to believe that the patient's development was so lacking that she seemed "troubled more by a lack of a sense of self than of objects good or bad inside of herself" (p. 41). Balint considered it premature, early in the treatment, to conceptualize her case in terms of the projection of parts of herself into her object, which might then give rise to persecutory anxiety. Rather, the patient's pervasive anxiety seemed to arise from a complete lack of a sense of self, and it was not until late in the analysis, when she'd developed more of a sense of herself, that she then became terrified of her aggression or that of the analyst. "Before this discovery," noted Balint, "her relationship to me and her expectations of me was of an empty and lifeless person. Her anger was despairing and aimless" (p. 47).

Balint came to understand the essence of the transference as the patient's efforts to communicate her own experience to the analyst in the hope the analyst might come to know – might recognize – what it was that was going on inside of her. This need to be known became glaringly evident intermittently when the analyst failed to see the patient's experience for what it was:

> ...when I appeared to think she was exaggerating or pretending to be iller than she was, or the reverse, when I took her condition more seriously than it actually warranted. By the material that followed these episodes I learned that she felt deserted by me...*the void [that developed] was caused by my presence when I did not understand her*. (p. 46)

The patient would also feel deeply misunderstood "when I was ever carried away by my 'understanding' of some material which at that time was quite irrelevant to Sarah's real communication" (p. 46) – illustrating Britton's (2004) concept of "malignant misunderstanding"[3] that has a disintegrating effect on certain sorts of patients. Since Sarah's mother found it hard to tolerate unresolved internal states in her daughter, Sarah feared her analyst would try to "extinguish" her feelings rather than recognize them for what they were without *feeling* a need or – worse – *acting on a need* to "put out" such feelings as the mother had.

Balint summed up the patient's psychodynamic situation by noting: "Sarah's mother was impervious to any communication which was different from the picture she had of her daughter and, in consequence, Sarah could not understand her mother's communications and felt that her mother never saw her as she was" (p. 51). Balint wrote about the patient's need to find an echo of herself coming from the mother – reflecting "the mother accepting her child's as yet unorganized feelings and emotions and, by her reactions to them, *enabling the child to organize them into a self*" (p. 51, italics added). This is what Balint refers to as "feed-back," which seems no different from what others call mirroring. Balint concluded by noting: "A proper feed-back is when the mother receives the [child's communication of] hurt, recognizes it, does not make too much fuss over it ["marked mirroring"], but just accepts its reality" (p. 52).

Final comments about technique

Knowing that one has a mind of one's own should not be taken for granted. It is easy to assume that individuals come to know their minds independently of the mirroring function of others, but this claim seems dubious, and it stands to reason that development requires the help of caregivers who mirror back – on a continuum from somewhat accurately to questionably accurately – who they see the growing individual as being. Such mirroring can take place on multiple levels: verbal as well as nonverbal, involving affect attunement, mediated by empathy or mentalization, and so on. The particulars are not nearly as important as is the awareness that mirroring – or whatever one chooses to call it – plays a vital role in the growing individual's capacity to know his own mind, to feel recognized and seen for who he is.

There are a host of other sorts of environmental effects that caregivers can have on the psychological and emotional development of young individuals. Mirroring should be considered one among these many ways in which caregivers assist development, meaning that there are many ways in which environmental input can go awry. Winnicott spoke of the need for caregivers to help a child maintain the illusion of control over the object until such a time as the developing child can realize this to be an illusion. Bowlby speaks of the need for adult attachment figures to respond to the infant's attachment signals in a timely and sensitive manner. The list goes on and on, and one could fashion treatments that address problems associated with each of these potentially problematic areas of development. What Middle School analysts have in common is a focus on these sorts of environmental factors in the course of development.

If one felt obliged to distinguish the overall orientation of analysts who think along the lines of those from the Middle School from those who practice more in accordance with Kleinian tradition, it would entail noting the difference between seeing the patient as largely affected by his environment – for better or for worse (the potential traumatogenic effect of less than optimal caregiving on whatever basis that occurs) – versus seeing the patient from a more solipsistic, one-person psychological perspective involving the patient's internal objects, his struggle with his innate (versus reactive) aggression, which causes him to split and to rid himself of his hostility by projecting it into his objects, begetting persecutory anxiety in the process. Such matters are not of the sort the Middle School analyst concerns himself with; he searches instead for signs of environmental traumas that result from a failure of the environment – caregivers – to be optimally attuned to the internal world of the developing child, leading to the patient's expectation that the same may happen or will happen (or one hopes won't happen) in the transference, where misattunements of many sorts, signs of malignant misunderstanding, failures to facilitate attachment, premature ruptures of the patient's need to engage in the transitional maintenance of the illusion of control, and the like become enacted in the course of the treatment. This notably differs from a more Kleinian focus on intrapsychic conflict between aggressive and libidinal drives, struggles to arrive at and remain in the depressive position (reconciling the wish to bite the hand that feeds you), and healing splits between internal good and bad objects as a means of developing a more solid identity.

Notes

1 Fairbairn introduced Melanie Klein to this term, resulting in her modifying the "paranoid" position by renaming it the "paranoid–schizoid position."

2 If the child feels that *his love* has destroyed the mother's feelings for him, then the child is in the schizoid state; if the child feels *his hate* has destroyed the mother's feelings for him, then he's then in the depressive state (Rayner, 1991).

3 Britton (2004) defines this as "an experience of being so *misunderstood*, in such a fundamental and powerful way, that one's experience of oneself would be eliminated, and correspondingly, the possibility of the self's establishment of meaning would be annihilated" (p. 59).

Section IV

Passing the baton

From generation to generation

Chapter 10

Learning how to think like an analyst

Teaching technique to psychotherapy students

Over the last few decades, most US-based psychoanalytic institutes have taken to teaching psychodynamic psychotherapy, expanding their original mission of training the next generation of psychoanalysts. This development is a sign of the times; psychoanalysis proper has largely fallen out of favor with consumers in the States – it is no longer as trendy or as "sexy" as it had been a half-century ago when patients clamored to be analyzed and often had to wait months until another patient vacated the couch in order to make room in the analyst's schedule for a new initiate. There is no getting around the fact that psychoanalysis is costly, time-consuming, and contrary to the modern pace of life, filled with sound bites and 140-character tweets, that leaves some people seeking a quick fix, particularly if they are unsettled by the task of opening themselves up and permitting a powerful, mutative relationship to take hold. Hearing about the virtues of cognitive behavioral treatments that are touted to be quicker, more affordable, and equally efficacious drive some of these patients to pursue this method of treatment, though some may nevertheless end up, when all is said and done, in the analyst's office having discovered the limitations of such an approach.

Given the state of psychoanalysis in the 21st century, one might think our analytic institutes would be shuttering their doors right about now. However, psychotherapists have been streaming through those very doors in impressive numbers seeking help to further their education and hone their skills, motivated by the wish to have something more to offer their patients that might, in turn, make the practicing of their craft more personally satisfying. What's more, many of these psychotherapy students become so intrigued by what they've learned that a number decide to go on and pursue formal psychoanalytic training.

This chapter addresses two sets of readers: those interested in learning more about psychodynamic psychotherapy, and analysts who are interested in teaching these clinicians about the psychodynamic approach to treatment. To that end, this chapter outlines some of the topics worth covering in a psychodynamic psychotherapy curriculum, along with suggested reading that might be assigned to students wishing to learn more about psychodynamic techniques, often listed in footnote form.[1] These readings, cherry-picked from amongst the scores of volumes published over the last half-century on the topic, represent the best of what is presently available in the way of teaching materials.

Psychodynamic technique

Sigmund Freud was relatively reluctant to write about the matter of technique, doing so sparingly and resisting earlier calls on the part of his colleagues that he do so sooner than later. When Freud finally got around to writing about the subject, he framed his ideas as "suggestions," steering clear of spelling out hard and fast rules that might make it appear that there was but one way to conduct analysis. Taking our cue from Freud, we must take care not to convey the impression that there is but one way in which analytically based treatments should be conducted. Students may be seeking guidance along these lines – hoping that a clear-cut template might spare them the anxiety associated with employing a less directive approach – but while we are in a position to provide broad brushstrokes about what analytically based treatments look like, it is imperative that teachers resist the pressure to provide anything like a watered down, cookbook-type approach.

As outlined in Chapter 3, how one conducts an analytically oriented treatment varies widely and is, at least in part, a function of the therapist's personality. Whether one's inclined to be engaging or self-disclosing; whether one relies more on interpreting or more on the quality of the therapeutic relationship to fuel the therapeutic process and promote therapeutically facilitated psychic change doesn't matter as much, I submit, as does the therapist's ability to approach treatment with a depth of understanding about how minds work, about what causes psychological impairment, and about the range of therapeutic maneuvers that might help the patient improve. Accordingly, my emphasis is on how analysts think more than on how analysts act, though technique will also be covered in this chapter.

All analytically based treatments (analysis proper, short-term dynamic psychotherapy, long-term dynamic psychotherapy) share certain features, focuses, and goals in common. The component parts of such treatments include, first and foremost, a belief in the influence of unconscious factors (memories, wishes, hopes, fears, and so forth) that might contribute to a patient's grief, dissatisfaction with life, symptoms, self-defeating behaviors, and so forth, which have driven him to seek treatment. These unconscious factors are often revealed in the here-and-now relationship with the therapist in the form of "transference reactions" that, if noted and interpreted, stand a chance of heightening the patient's self-awareness to degrees that make him less prone to the effects of these unconscious forces. Analyzing a patient's transference is complicated by the existence of powerful resistances to the realization of these repressed or dissociated factors, making the recognition and management of resistance a major focus of psychodynamic treatments. Resistance can make itself known, for example, when the patient fails to be able to say whatever comes to mind in accordance with the "fundamental rule" of free association. Failure to be able to free associate, evidenced in gaps in the patient's stream of consciousness, hints at underlying resistances, and addressing these resistances is part of a therapeutic process known as "working through." The psychodynamic therapist does not limit himself, however, to noting and analyzing such gaps; he takes full advantage of the information that is being transmitted through multiple channels, whether they be verbal (e.g., what the patient verbally conveys to the therapist in the way of "content"), nonverbal (e.g., body posture, tone of voice, and the like), relational (the nature of relationship the patient is in the process of forming with his therapist), or aspects of process, of which difficulties free associating are but one example.

A frequently lodged complaint about psychodynamic psychotherapies is that they focus too much attention on the patient's past, which – some argue – makes little sense, seeing that patients typically seek treatment for present-day difficulties they believe are unrelated to the past. The analytic position challenges this notion by noting the extent to which the root of our everyday problems typically can be found in the patient's past. Therapists who subscribe to a psychodynamic perspective believe in the following proposition: unconscious aspects of one's past – in particular, the patient's past relations with others – can have a determining effect on what the patient presently expects from people in general, presently perceives about others, is presently looking for from others, or how he is presently interacting with others, and so on. Freud referred to this as "*the repetition compulsion*"[2] – in line with the notion that those who fail to study history (in this case, one's own history) are doomed to repeat it. This explains why past experiences can have a determining effect not just on present events, but – if things don't change – will continue to do so in the future. Arlow (1987) describes the process in this manner:

> The analyst helps the patient grasp the concept of how the past is *dynamically active* in the present. Treatment, then, becomes a matter not of recollecting and purging one's self of a noxious memory from the past; it becomes instead a matter of knowing and mastering a *persistently disturbing influence* in the present. (p. 75, italics added)[3]

Patients are often unaware of the degree to which they may be reliving a piece of their history by either perceiving the therapist as being like an important transference figure from the past or interacting with the therapist in ways unconsciously designed to draw the therapist into acting like that transference figure had acted (by the therapist accepting a role assigned to him by the patient or by him engaging in a "countertransference enactment" that ostensibly "acts out" what the patient had anticipated or suspected).

One belief that likely distinguishes practitioners who employ a psychodynamic method from those who use a different modality is the belief that resistance is not something a therapist can merely power through or easily get around. Rather, resistance is something that must be analyzed if one ultimately hopes to help lessen the patient's ongoing tendency to fend off such psychic content. Resistances exist for good reason – they are, in effect, self-protective to the extent they strive to prevent a recurrence of a past trauma. However, when conditions change and past dangers recede, it isn't always the case that the individual notices that things have in fact changed. Accordingly, a patient may feel a continued need to rely on outdated methods of self-protection, which proves costly to the extent this limits one's options – preventing the individual from recognizing novel situations *as* novel rather than reacting to them as if they are continuations of the past – with the patient vowing "screw me once, shame on you; screw me twice, shame on me." This iteration of the well-known saying leaves aside a third concern: "shame on me for missing out on a new opportunity because I mistakenly saw it as nothing more than a repetition of a bad experience I long ago learned to avoid."

Psychodynamic theory posits that resistance is driven by deep defenses that cannot simply be circumvented without first addressing and working through the underlying defensive need to protect the patient from having to experience or realize feelings, memories, drives, and thoughts that the patient feels are beyond his capacity to bear. Therapy then becomes focused on the identification and working through of the patient's defenses. Learning about the workings of one's mind – recognizing instances when one is defending and learning about why one continues to feel the need to do so – is now seen as a prerequisite to the final step of facing the psychic contents one had been working so hard to avoid. This, then, represents the central task of defense analysis.[4]

How psychoanalysis and psychodynamic psychotherapy differ

Learning about psychodynamic psychotherapy begins with an understanding of how this psychoanalytically based treatment differs from psychoanalysis proper. Certain generalizations can be made in this regard, and it is important to keep in mind that they are just that – generalizations. It has often been noted that these two modalities overlap like circles in a Venn diagram – with the depth achieved in the most fruitful psychodynamic treatments exceeding that achieved in the least favorable psychoanalyses. All in all, in comparison to psychodynamic psychotherapy, psychoanalysis usually proves to be the more intense process of the two given: (a) its typical duration (lasting several years); (b) its frequency (meeting four to five times weekly,[5] which deepens the patient's reliance upon, and feelings about, the therapist); (c) the use of a variety of regression-promoting devices – the use of the couch (a regular though not invariant component of analysis, which promotes regression by virtue of the fact the analyst's feet remain firmly planted on the ground and his perspective isn't limited in the way the analysand's vision is limited); (d) the analyst's tendency to react in a less immediate, gratifying, or involved fashion; and (e) a stance of anonymity that closets, to some degree, the analyst's reactions and emotions, requiring the analysand to fill in the gap by relying upon his intuition and fantasies about who the analyst is – how he thinks, analyzes, and so on and so forth. All combined, these factors favor regression that translates into the analysand's tendency to re-experience feelings, needs, modes of thinking (primary versus secondary processes – described in greater length further along in this chapter), and styles of relating (recognizing the analyst as a separate entity with his own feelings and needs versus treating him as if he exists exclusively to serve the patient's needs) that had characterized the analysand's younger years. The analyst's dedication to the task of paying rapt attention to and addressing the transference at every turn highlights and furthers the regression, intensifying the transference wishes that come into focus and are addressed through the therapist's interpretations, whether those interpretations are articulated to the patient or merely serve to inform how the analyst goes about interacting with the patient.

One begins to differentiate psychoanalysis from psychodynamic psychotherapy by first considering how psychoanalysis historically has been defined by prominent leaders in the field – in particular, Merton Gill and Leo Rangell. Gill (1954) defines psychoanalysis as "*that technique which, employed by a neutral analyst, results in the development of a regressive transference neurosis and the ultimate resolution of this neurosis by techniques of interpretation alone*" (p. 775, italics added). Note the extent to which Gill insists that interpretation alone brings about psychoanalytically facilitated psychic change, thus ruling out interpersonal interactions between analyst and analysand that are often thought to play an important mutative role in treatment. Gill's emphasis on neutrality is also controversial given that many analysts currently interpret that term as synonymous with a studied indifference on the analyst's part that could easily be experienced by the analysand as cold and distancing, and at risk of replicating the way the analysand had been treated early on by caregivers, which had proven to be pathogenic. Those who promote neutrality, on the other hand, consider it a proper and responsible therapeutic attitude that affords the analyst an *objective* perspective. While conceding that the analyst's perspective might be tinged by his own subjectivity,[6] these analysts argue that it nevertheless remains "objective" if by that term one does not mean "more truthful or reality based," but instead one takes it to mean "a perspective that lies outside the bounds of the patient's subjectivity."[7] Cavell (1988) writes:

> The superordinate goal of analysis – to know one's own mind – can be achieved *only in relation to the mind of another*, since "only a person who is or has been in communication with at least one other creature can know his or her own mind." (p. 877, italics added)

A final aspect worth noting about Gill's definition is how it emphasizes the centrality of regression and interpretation – hallmarks of psychoanalysis proper. While one sometimes sees signs of regression in psychodynamic psychotherapy, and transference interpretations are offered both in analysis and in psychodynamic psychotherapy, regression is typically limited in psychotherapy, as is the offering of deep interpretations that get to the heart of the matter, which requires a profound reliving of the past in order for the transference to come to life, which more typically requires the support provided by daily sessions.

Leo Rangell (1954) defines psychoanalysis in a somewhat different fashion, referring to it as:

> a method of therapy *whereby* conditions are brought about favorable for the development of a transference neurosis, in which the past is restored in the present, *in order that*, through a systematic interpretative attack on the resistances which oppose it, there occurs a resolution of that neurosis (transference *and* infantile) *to the end* of bringing about structural changes in the mental apparatus of the patient to make the latter capable of optimum adaptation to life. (pp. 739–740)

Rangell's definition emphasizes *restoration of the past in the here and now*, while Gill merely alludes to "regression." Rangell also emphasizes the centrality of *addressing the resistances* (an emphasis on "defense analysis"), which Gill's definition overlooks.

Psychodynamic psychotherapy typically is conducted on a less frequent basis than psychoanalysis. And while some are willing to refer to treatments that take place on a once-a-week basis as psychodynamic psychotherapy, Kernberg (1999) disagrees to the extent he defines that modality as needing to take place on no less than a twice-a-week basis. In my opinion, trying to teach psychodynamic psychotherapy using material from once-a-week treatments is a fool's errand, because less frequent visits translate into a less intense involvement with, and reliance upon, the therapist that, in turn, works against the past becoming convincingly restored in the present. Transference in psychodynamic psychotherapy is typically less intense and less apparent to the extent its manifestations are usually subtle and easily missed when sessions don't take place on consecutive days, and particularly if they take place on a once-a-week basis. Since attachment isn't nearly as strong as it tends to be in more intensive treatments, separations aren't experienced intensely, making interpretations of separation reactions less relevant. And while transference can be addressed in psychodynamic psychotherapy, transference is not nearly the same or as deep as it often ends up being in psychoanalysis proper. Trying to address transference in psychodynamic psychotherapy as if it is as evident and as strong as it tends to be in psychoanalysis often proves unrealistic and can be experienced by patients as "a stretch," even if the therapist is technically correct in what he's surmised. In other terms, relatively infrequent visits collude with resistance.

Gunderson and Gabbard (1999) write:

> There is a broad consensus among practitioners today that the therapeutic action of psychoanalytic/psychodynamic therapy involves two major

> factors: (1) the acquisition of insight via interpretation of unconscious conflicts, defenses, and their associated internal object relations, especially as they emerge in the transference relationship to the therapist, and (2) the internalization of the therapeutic relationship, which involves careful attention to the management of the therapeutic interaction. (p. 684)

Multiple studies support the claim that "accurate interpretations consonant with a patient's core issues are predictive of treatment outcome" (Gunderson & Gabbard, 1999, p. 684). It may, in fact, prove easier to distinguish analytic psychotherapies (psychoanalysis and psychodynamic psychotherapy) from other forms of psychotherapy than to draw clear-cut lines between different forms of analytically based therapies that share in common certain distinctive features. In an extensive meta-analysis of studies that described the clinical focus of a variety of different psychotherapies, Blagys and Hilsenroth (2000) were able to generate a list of features that distinguish a psychodynamic approach to psychotherapy from other psychotherapies:

> Focus on affect and expression of patient's emotions; exploration of patient's attempts to avoid topics or engage in activities that hinder the progress of therapy; the identification of patterns in patient's actions, thoughts, feelings, experiences and relationships; emphasis on past experiences; focus on patient's interpersonal experiences; emphasis on the therapeutic relationship; exploration of patient's wishes, dreams, fantasies. (p. 185)

The types of tools used by therapists who practice psychodynamic psychotherapy are similar to those employed by psychoanalysts conducting formal psychoanalyses. These therapists consider it their duty to offer interpretations (explanations) – that is, the therapist's "take" on what ails the patient, what psychic content lies hidden from the patient's view, why he repeats self-defeating patterns of behavior, and so on and so forth. The analytic therapist holds a mirror up and reflects what the therapist believes he sees as coming chiefly from the patient, all the while remaining alert to the possibility that his perceptions may be unduly influenced (distorted) by his own subjectivity born of his own past experiences along with his hopes, expectations, and fears. Oftentimes, there is little harm in offering an interpretation *as a hypothesis*, knowing that it may prove to be "off base" from the patient's perspective. A therapy-threatening condition develops if the therapist insists on the veracity of his interpretation and refuses to back down – in which case there is the distinct possibility that the treatment has reached an impasse that cannot be resolved.[8]

Thinking like an analyst: adopting an analytic attitude or stance

Therapists endeavoring to conduct psychodynamic psychotherapy can benefit from adopting an "analytic stance" or "analytic attitude" (Schafer, 1982) toward the emerging material, whether that material is verbalized (associations, reported dreams, *expressed* transference reactions, etc.), nonverbally transmitted (e.g., by body posture, facial expressions, breathing patterns, *unconsciously enacted* transference reactions, etc.), or something that is reflected in the process (e.g., breaks in the patient's associations). The analytic stance is composed of several different beliefs, positions, and perspectives that combine to shed considerable light on the underlying meanings of the patient's material. Analytically oriented therapists pay close attention to both content-type material (both verbalized and nonverbally manifesting) as well as process-type material (the patient's train of thought as well as how topics or themes shift from one to the other). The psychodynamic stance includes a belief in the unconscious motivations and unconscious processes that underlie manifest behavior and operate in accordance with the principle of *psychic determinism* – the belief that most everything we do *happens for a reason* or, more precisely, for *reasons* (since analysts believe in *multi-determinism*, a principle that stipulates that reasons – plural – typically work in concert to bring about behaviors, symptoms, and the like). Such unconscious reasons are often not readily apparent and may need to be investigated if one wishes to arrive at a full (conscious) accounting of why one acted as one had.

The analytic stance is alerting insofar as it keeps analytically oriented therapists on the lookout, perennially searching to discover the underlying complexities of human motivation, which protects therapists from lapsing into simplistic, reductionist thinking evidenced by the use of the word *just* – as in: "He is just doing that to get attention." Schafer (1982) addresses the need for analysts (and, by extension, psychodynamically oriented therapists) to avoid either-or thinking, noting:

> ...if there is anything that consistently characterizes psychodynamic interpretation it is the analyst's recognition that multiple and often contradictory meanings and consequences may be usefully ascribed to one phenomenon...much time in analysis is spent interpreting the analysand's need to see things as either black or white...[all of which aims to] increase complexity and tolerance of contradiction. (pp. 7–8)

One might wonder about the extent to which patients may sometimes fall ill because of tendencies to think in simplistic, either-or terms about their internal worlds – leading them to form a view of their psyches that is out of keeping with how their mind is actually working.

For a psychotherapist to be thinking like an analyst means, in part, that he possesses a healthy respect for the power of unconscious forces, reinforced not just through repeated clinical demonstration of this principle in action, but by research findings in *the science of unconscious motivation* (for a review, see Custers & Aarts, 2010). A plethora of studies and meta-studies have now scientifically established the efficacy of psychodynamic psychotherapy (see

Chapter 12 in this volume), and it behooves students interested in conducting psychodynamic psychotherapy to acquaint themselves with this literature that clearly establishes the scientific basis and efficacy of this form of treatment.

An awareness of primary process thinking, distinguished from rational-type, everyday thinking known as secondary process thinking, is also part of the analytic stance. While primary process thinking typically makes no sense given the extent to which it tends to be irrational, the principle of psychic determinism predicts that a concerted effort to make sense of such nonsense stands a fair chance of ultimately revealing how such thinking makes a different kind of sense – one in keeping with the rules of primary process thinking whereby, for example, contradictory beliefs can co-exist, and conflicting feelings need not be reconciled in an effort to establish which of the two feelings represents how the patient "really" feels. Many who enter treatment lack a firm grasp of the fact that one can – for example – hold diametrically opposed feelings toward the same person or simultaneously possess seemingly mutually exclusive desires or have contradictory feelings. Such individuals may try to enlist the therapist in a futile attempt to help them decide, for example, whether they love or hate a given individual, ignoring the fact that seemingly contradictory feelings can and do co-exist, making it impossible to discard one set of feelings in favor of another set. Other forms of treatment – such as cognitive behavioral treatment – may take advantage of such disparities by using one set of feelings against the other. Analytically oriented therapists do the exact opposite by helping patients accept and appreciate the complexities of emotions that often lie below the surface, so that the individual can incorporate these repressed or split-off parts into his conscious awareness, helping him become more psychically integrated. Therapists who work analytically understand that they themselves are likewise required to use their minds in a somewhat unusual fashion – setting aside a strict reliance on a linear-type fashion that simplifies the relationship between cause and effect and treats time as if it extends from "back when," to "now," to "later" (in the future).

There are many other components of the analytic stance, such as the maintenance of an *unknowing attitude* on the therapist's part that balances tendencies to prematurely arrive at conclusions that lead him to believe he knows precisely why the patient is doing what he is doing. Analytic therapists cannot help but form conclusions about patients; however, it is essential that they not become wedded to those assumptions, keeping in mind that they are, in fact, mere "hypotheses," not hard fact – hypotheses in need of further testing to see if they are supported or refuted by additional information. Therapists do their patients a service by modeling open-mindedness, taking care to keep in mind the fact that their theories are just that – theories – which means they may prove to be true or not true.

While analysis is often thought to be fueled, first and foremost, by the offering of interpretations meant to alert the patient to repressed or dissociated psychic content that is being kept from the patient's conscious awareness, McWilliams (2004) reminds us:

> ...psychotherapy technique has more to do with how one listens than with how one talks...listening in a professional capacity is a disciplined, meditative, and emotionally receptive activity in which the therapist's needs for self-expression and self-acknowledgement are subordinated to the psychological needs of the client. (p. 133)

Therapists who feel obliged to "earn their keep" by providing the patient with plenty of food for thought may fail to appreciate how much is provided by listening with undivided attention to everything the patient communicates, whether verbally, nonverbally, or through the process of the patient's thinking. That level of attentiveness and attunement not only helps instill trust in the therapist, but also captures the patient's attention to the extent he feels listened to on a profound level. Hence, the quality of the therapist's listening plays at least as much of a role in fueling treatment as do the things he ends up offering the patient in the way of reflections on what his listening reveals about the operations of the patient's mind.

It is important that therapists who undertake such treatment be humble about their overall role in the therapeutic process. It is probably most helpful for the therapist to imagine his role as that of facilitator – midwife to the therapeutic process that is set in motion by the therapist establishing conditions that facilitate the process. These conditions constitute an index of the topics underlying this form of treatment: establish the frame, elucidate the basic rule, provide one's undivided attention, be curious, keep an open mind, resist tendencies to jump to conclusions, reach a reasonable understanding of the patient, test that hypothesis, and be respectful, compassionate, empathic, and non-judgmental toward the patient. Approximating these goals can go a way toward creating an environment that is conducive to the patient opening himself up to the process – even though doing so scares him.

What's required of the therapist

To be able to conduct psychodynamic psychotherapy, a therapist must possess a well-developed, innate capacity for empathy that operates on a gut level and doesn't rely solely or chiefly on an intellectual understanding of the patient. Most likely, empathy is inherent and not something that can be taught or learned in the process of one's therapy. Mentalization, on the other hand, is something that one can likely be taught and may in fact be a measurable result of therapy. Mentalization[9] is an essential component of, and may even constitute the essence of, what is known as "psychological mindedness" – the capacity to think on a complex level about hidden or opaque motives underlying human behaviors based on a relatively accurate "read" of the other's beliefs, desires, and intentions. Beyond capacities to empathize and mentalize, therapists must be capable of thinking *complexly*, remembering there are many possible motives that together can account for a patient's manifest behavior. The therapist must also be able to think *abstractly* rather than concretely, so that he can appreciate symbolic thinking of the sort reflected in dreams. Therapists wishing to conduct analytically based treatment should strive to resist the urge to succumb to the distraction of verbal content, which can seduce the therapist into listening too closely to what the patient is verbalizing, paying insufficient attention to what is left unsaid or what is being said in an indirect, nonverbal, or roundabout fashion, which requires the therapist "read between the lines" or "listen with the third ear" (Reik, 1948). Therapists must also forgive themselves when they "fall for" content, momentarily ceasing to search beyond what is merely being said, just as they must forgive themselves when they discover they had become unwittingly swept up in an enactment without realizing as much at the time.

Affect recognition also plays a large role in the dynamic psychotherapies – accordingly, a clinician who wishes to work with patients analytically had best be in touch with his own affects and, furthermore, be keenly attuned to the subtle affects emanating from the patient. Affects serve as critical information that helps redirect the therapist's attention in a clinically useful direction. When words lie, affects often become the sole reliable indication of the direction in which the treatment needs to head. Affect education is also an important goal of treatment, particularly for patients who need help parsing their varied affects on a more nuanced basis. Evidence suggests that individuals who have not been raised by caregivers who helped them learn words to describe and help them communicate a wide range of feelings do not fare as well in later life as those who had parents who assisted them in this regard. Therapists employing a psychodynamic approach had also best know themselves well enough to be adept at using an awareness of their countertransference reactions as vital information about the patient, so that he doesn't become blindly lost in the maze of a countertransference enactment, unable to find his way out.

Psychodynamic psychotherapy takes considerable time, which requires the therapist be patient and less inclined to offer shortcut suggestions or provide advice or "answers" meant to accelerate the therapeutic process. The therapist must also be patient with the time it takes for him to grasp the meaning of the patient's material, which requires that he tolerate states of not knowing longer than he might like, sometimes for an extended period.

The initial tasks of the patient and therapist

The patient's initial task: showing up and attempting to free associate

Therapists attempting to conduct psychodynamic psychotherapy should give due consideration to making explicit what Freud referred to as "the fundamental rule" or "the basic rule,"[10] which calls upon the patient to try as hard as he can to "free associate" by committing himself to say whatever comes to mind regardless of whether he deems it irrelevant, believes it too personal too mention, feels it will insult the therapist, imagines his "insides" to be repulsive or off-putting, and so on and so forth. Free associating permits signs of the patient's unconscious material to begin to materialize – signs of what lies hidden, which begins to peak through the cloud cover. Free association is also needed to facilitate an ongoing "process" – the flow of material (the stream of consciousness) that is permitted to unfold – per the fundamental rule – without being interrupted by the patient's plan to break in and take over – to regain the reins and direct the flow of his thoughts in directions he feels best suits his conscious desire. And while such a maneuver may be, in the patient's view, the best way to proceed, there is ample reason to doubt the proposition that conscious, willful decision-making will lead the treatment toward a more productive outcome than will be achieved by "merely free associating."

When the patient "opens up" by free associating, he provides access to material the therapist needs to know if he hopes to help the patient. Free associating entails a level of honesty and candor that asks the patient to risk "playing his cards face up," which no level-headed person would ever elect to do under any other circumstance, given that it places one at a distinct disadvantage while simultaneously advantaging the other. By sharing his innermost thoughts, the patient provides the therapist with a glimpse of the inner workings of his mind – his train of thought as well as instances when he resists daring to share what typically turns out to be repressed content about which the patient himself is loath to know. The therapist closely monitors the patient's associations (Gray, 1994), taking note of instances when the patient's associations reveal an unconscious effort to veer from travelling down a given path, then addresses this breach in free association with an aim toward learning the causes of the resistance.

Many patients haven't a clue about what therapy requires of them unless the basic rule is spelled out in advance at the onset of treatment. If they'd previously been in treatment, the patient may assume he knows what he is expected to do, but even patients who've previously been psychoanalyzed sometimes express dismay when their present psychoanalyst explains the basic rule, which the patient had no memory of being told at the outset of his first analysis. Knowing that they are expected to say whatever comes to mind – that they must eschew tendencies to avoid topics for whatever reasons – makes therapy easier for the therapist because it relieves him of the responsibility of having to come up with topics for the patient to talk about each session. If the therapist believes it is his job to "keep the ball in the air," the patient accordingly will feel relieved of the responsibility of sharing everything that comes to mind – which he might find a relief, thought it greatly limits what can be accomplished in a treatment that requires more of him.

Sometimes patients assume there is value in "picking up where we last left off," but just because the patient had been grappling with a new and important issue the session before does not mean he will, or even should for that matter, return to that topic when the next session begins. Sometimes patients begin a session by asking the therapist, "What were we talking about last time?" explaining that they did not remember, though they had a sense it had been important. There are two problems with this development: first, it isn't the patient who is being asked to do the remembering; and second, it may even prove to be a test to see how carefully the therapist had been listening by seeing if he can remember the last session if put on the spot. Furthermore, the premise that one session should follow the next like chapters of a book runs counter to the goal of free associating. The patient may naturally find himself thinking about the previous session during the current session, and if that be the case, there is nothing wrong with his freely associating across the gap that separates the two sessions. In fact, doing just that sometimes reveals a wish to obliterate the intervening time between sessions as if it didn't exist. Otherwise, the material from the last session may in fact have remained very much alive in the patient's mind, in which case returning to the topics touched on in the session before may genuinely be a function of free association.

One problem with requiring the patient to free associate is the impression it may create that he is expected to be able to do just that on an ongoing basis. In fact, nothing could be further from the truth. Patients sometimes believe that therapy won't work if they cannot reliably and consistently free associate, highlighting the utility of sometimes making clear to patients that the fundamental rule is something the patient is expected to *try* to do, not necessarily something he will actually be expected to be able to do – at least not on a continuous basis. The basic rule establishes a goal that is, in fact, often achieved during treatment, though more often intermittently and never continuously. Whatever trouble the patient has free associating is "grist for the mill" – is thought to reflect evidence of his defenses at work protecting him from "who knows what"; that "who knows what" is what patient and therapist are to take up as their joint task on the way toward the working through of the discovered impediments to free association – impediments that may well be related to the underlying issues that drove the patient to treatment in the first place. Individuals who are already capable, on a more or less regular basis, of free associating aren't likely to run into the sorts of trouble that land people in treatment. A gross though instructive simplification of psychoanalysis could be offered in a condensed fashion (quoting from the first chapter of this book): recommend the patient free associate; see the extent to which he can't; work to discover what is getting in his way; help the patient see what is limiting his ability to freely associate; see how he becomes much better able to free associate (assuming one's correctly identified the "blocks"); then, when he seems to be much more freely associating, discharge him from treatment having accomplished one's end goal.[11]

The therapist's initial task: establishing the frame

Analytically oriented therapists place great weight on establishing and maintaining what is known as "the frame" (Langs, 1990): conditions thought to create a safe and facilitating treatment environment thought to encourage patients to open up and take risks they might otherwise be disinclined to take fearing judgment, fearing rejection, fearing being misunderstood, fearing...God knows what – fears the patient fears could become actualized if they don't take care to protect themselves from such imagined eventualities. While the analytic stance contributes to establishing the frame, it is but one of the many elements that together constitute the frame. Articulated "ground rules" spell out the essential nature of the "arrangement": the maintenance of proper boundaries, making sure the patient knows what is expected of him as well as of the therapist, and stipulating how certain things are to be handled. Over the course of treatment, the therapist acts in a consistent fashion relative to time and money. He makes sure that sessions begin and end on time, which means he takes care not to allow the patient to hold him over just because the patient "decides" to raise an important point just as the session is ending, or the therapist wants to demonstrate his flexibility, to make up for the feeling he'd not done enough for the patient during the session, or to communicate his fondness for a patient by permitting him a bit more time than he'd been allotted. Granted, there may be instances when deciding against rigidly ending on time is in the therapy's best interest, but these would need to be exceptions rather than the rule. The therapist's handling of money also communicates a degree of honesty and reliability. Freud made clear the value of speaking without false modesty when talking about the fee – making clear when payment is due, how much sessions will cost, and how the therapist plans to handle cancellations relative to the agreement to pay for missed sessions under certain circumstances.[12] In order to allow himself to say whatever comes to mind, the patient must understand that what he shares will be treated and respected as material worth exploring, not information that will be acted upon by either party.

Part of establishing a frame involves the therapist spelling out expectations and boundaries that define how the patient is to act – the fact he's required to say whatever comes to mind and, furthermore, is expected to put his thoughts and feelings into words rather than acting them out. The freeing aspect of treatment, which develops when one is invited and welcomed to say whatever comes to mind, does not imply permission for the patient to engage in extreme forms of acting out, such as literally destroying the therapist's office. There are, after all, limits to the therapist's tolerance, and each therapist differs with regard to how much they can put up with before either lapsing into an enactment or resorting to warning the patient that certain behaviors *will not be permitted*! Sometimes good-enough parenting involves saying "yes," at other times it involves saying "no," and therapists who see limitless tolerance or non-stop gratification as their assigned task misunderstand development in general, misunderstand this form of treatment in particular, and will eventually run into trouble when they permit and engage in contortions of the frame. Try as some patients might to pull the therapist across a line by enticing him to engage in some sort of unprofessional, boundary-crossing behavior, the therapist establishes himself as ready and able to resist the pull, which patients may find frustrating though, at the same time, reassuring. Tragic are instances when boundary crossings prove to be the complete undoing of what had seemed to be, up to that time, a promising treatment.

The patient is not the only one bounded by rules of conduct that constitutes the frame. The therapist has rules that govern his behavior as well – rules that respect the patient's vulnerability. Therapists must act in ways that reassure the patient that the therapist will not take advantage of him, though he is positioned to do just that given the patient's reliance and dependence on the therapist, as well as the therapeutically induced tendency for the patient to question his judgment and perceptions, which places him at considerable risk by quieting the alarm bells that might have otherwise gone off when the therapist does something that should alert the patient about the need to institute self-protective measures.

Here, we are butting up against matters of ethical behavior – in particular with regard to the question of what gratifications a therapist can reasonably expect from conducting therapy. Patients should feel confident that the therapist won't use them in ways that might leave the patient feeling he'd been taken advantage of by virtue of the therapist's unique role and position – which means the therapist must safeguard the treatment by reining in any questionable tendencies on his part that might negatively impact the treatment by causing the patient to distrust his motives. Even when the therapist is operating optimally, a patient may nevertheless distrust the therapist, but it is best that distrust issues from the patient's reliving of the past – his transference reactions – rather than from the therapist's questionable behavior.

Cultivating the treatment should be the patient's and the therapist's shared motive and chief concern, which requires the therapist to be scrupulously vigilant about the intrusion of his own personal needs into the treatment setting. He is not to ask a patient for favors of any sort, nor is he to materially benefit from information gleaned from the session (e.g., he cannot trade stock on insider information). Treatment is to take place solely within the confines of the clinical setting, with purposeful extra-analytic contact being a rare exception that is permitted under extraordinary circumstances with due consideration given to analyzing its meaning both before and after the event. The same can be said for physical contact. Keeping sessions confidential is essential; mentioning patient-related material outside of session should be strictly limited to the use of such material for educational purposes only (e.g., for publication of papers and presentation in case conferences), with extreme care dedicated to effectively disguising the patient's identity. The matter of when and whether a therapist discloses aspects of his personal life (his own experiences – lived events as well as feelings that arise in the course of treating the patient) has been widely debated, and while no absolute prohibition against such disclosures seems warranted, every therapist must give considerable thought to whether such disclosures are in the patient's best interest.[13]

Of particular concern is the gratification of the therapist's narcissistic needs to have his cleverness, intelligence, breadth of experience, facility of understanding, the depth of his capacity to love, and so on and so forth validated by the patient. Sometimes therapists like to play the role of the all-knowing guru to whom the patient can turn for sage advice about how best to live their lives, which Lacan (1949) refers to as "*le sujet suppose savoir*" – the one who is supposed to know. Some therapists find it enticing to be treated as if, and to act as if, they have all the answers. Wishing to be seen by the patient in this light not only reinforces the patient's fantasy that such people exist, but also supports the patient's view of himself as not being knowledgeable enough or capable enough to figure out his "next move." Patients who lack confidence in their ability to decide how they should proceed in life may directly or covertly appeal to the therapist to provide them with answers, believing this to be the therapist's job – what it is he gets paid to do. If a therapist takes the bait – buying into the patient's expectation and contention that the therapist is an expert in how to live life – he ignores the fact that his chief expertise primarily lies in knowing how to conduct treatment,[14] with his opinions about the patient's life decisions amounting to little more than that – opinions.

The therapist's narcissistic needs must be kept sufficiently in check so that he does not seek gratification of such needs through his treatment of patients – by, for example, taking pride in having a famous patient or covertly asking a patient to validate his wish to be seen as brilliant or clever, or requiring the patient to support the therapist's favored self-image, whatever that may be. Even expecting one's patients to feel that they are well understood by the therapist, in the service of validating the therapist's wish to be seen as such, can interfere with the therapist being available to a patient who may, for a time, need to see the therapist as someone who is incapable of understanding them. However, being assigned such a role will prove challenging for therapists who very much like to be seen, and see themselves, as a healer who is more than capable of understanding all who seek their help.[15]

Seeking gratification of needs beyond those that constitute the sorts of recognizable, legitimate professional needs that accompany the practice of psychotherapy can be seen as a betrayal of one's solemn oath to, first and foremost, safeguard the patient's interests. The therapist's reasonable professional needs include the need to practice his craft, to earn a living, and to be of assistance to others, though this last need can sometimes gum up the works of treatment as outlined above. Friedman (1988) spells out the sorts of expectations that therapists implicitly feel as they go about conducting treatment:

> Expectations of discovery, a promise of intellectual mastery, anticipations of intense emotional experience; there is an opportunity to exercise practical expertise...[these] shade off into subtler but no less important motives, such as the wish to see an anticipated change or feel a hidden relationship, which are also stimulated and certified by theory. (p. 431)[16]

Therapists undertake this sort of work for a host of different reasons, though it might be reasonable to assume that many wish to get a chance – really, a privilege – of being able to get really close to the raw reality of who another person is at the deepest and most elemental level – having shed (ideally) the mask the patient regularly employs on an everyday basis. Therapists hope to create an environment that helps their patients feel safe enough to risk letting themselves be known deeply without the need of a façade; it may even be argued that patients themselves yearn for, yet are terrified by, the chance of having just such an experience. Many therapists also yearn for this degree of connection – an awe-inspiring connection that attests to a level of closeness one knew could exist between individuals, even though it is a relatively rare occurrence; one that, ideally, is at least approximated – if not achieved – in the therapeutic setting.

Additional tasks of patient and therapist

The patient's second task: understanding how his mind works

Patients are typically unaware of the extent to which their perceptions are determined by their hopes and expectations, believing instead that what they see is what is there to be seen – nothing more, nothing less. Put another way – even if they can intellectually acknowledge the extent to which the mind *represents* reality rather than *identically replicating* it in the mind's eye, they nevertheless tend to forget this truism of perception in the process of insisting that what they saw, remembered, heard, sensed is *precisely* how events had literally played out beyond a shadow of a doubt. This failure to remember the essential representational/constructivistic nature of the mind – that the mind tends to construct reality in accordance with one's beliefs and desires, in accordance with what one expects, hopes, or fears will happen – is not limited to patients alone; therapists are also at risk to the extent awareness of this truism slips in and out of the therapist's consciousness. Difficulty separating "what is" from "what something looks like" – an essential developmental achievement – can be intermittently lost, particularly when under duress. Magritte's famous painting *The Treachery of Images* drives home the point: a painting of a smoking pipe is featured, beneath which, written in French, are the words: *This is not a pipe*. Some viewers cannot figure out what the artist means since – clearly – what is pictured is undeniably a pipe given that pipe-like quality of the rendering, which is Magritte's point – that this is a realistic rendering but a rendering nevertheless, just as our perceptions – our psychic renderings – often appear veridical and not at all representational approximations of what is there to be seen.

The therapist's second task: establishing a working alliance

Establishing and maintaining the frame is the first step toward accomplishing this goal, but there are other things that therapists do that help ensure that patient and therapist are "on the same page" about their shared goals for treatment, their shared understanding of what constitutes therapeutic activity on the therapist's part, and their shared conception of how therapy will bring about change – though this last issue is one about which there is often covert disagreement that becomes evident and, ideally, is worked through in the course of treatment. In the process of conducting psychodynamic psychotherapy, therapists conduct themselves in ways designed to heighten the strength and quality of the alliance between the therapist and the patient – what's referred to as the "therapeutic alliance" (Zetzel, 1956) or the "working alliance" (Greenson, 1967). This alliance is predicated on the patient's ongoing belief that the therapist is chiefly motivated by benign intentions and acts in session in ways the therapists hopes and expects will prove helpful to the patient *over the long haul*, even though the patient may question this assumption when he is suffering through a painful phase of treatment during which he's remembering and reliving past traumas or his alliance with the therapist seems on shaky ground, which may cause the patient to question the therapist's motives. In fact, not all patients consistently interpret the therapist's motives as benign, and some patients can go on to become frankly paranoid about what the therapist is up to when he challenges the patient's understanding of himself, as well as his perceptions of the therapist or of others – challenges that may strike certain patients as adversarial, as motivated by a wish to defeat the patient, to make him dependent on the therapist, to prove that the therapist is witty or clever or brilliant or sensitive or loving or trustworthy, and so on and so forth. Fostering a strong therapeutic alliance requires the therapist works to restore the alliance when it is in jeopardy, using the tools of interpretation, empathy, and mentalization in an effort to effect change.[17]

The transferential aspect of the patient's relationship with the therapist – the extent to which his experiencing of the therapist is greatly colored by his past relationships – can cause the patient to overlook "the real relationship" – an insulated, reality-based aspect of the therapeutic relationship that is not contaminated by the transference.[18] It is the real relationship that keeps the patient coming and working even when the transference heats up and the patient feels in the full grip of it – when he questions his view, for example, that the therapist has his best interest at heart. Having one foot firmly planted in the real relationship helps the patient keep firmly in mind the "as if" quality of the transference,[19] which protects the patient from seriously losing track of the fact (or losing track of the fact for a prolonged period of time) that the transference is but an illusion that alludes to something beyond the particulars of what is presently happening in the room. The real relationship helps the patient keep an eye on the ultimate goal of treatment – why he and the patient continue to meet. In the case of patients suffering from borderline pathology, the loss of just such a perspective becomes a common feature of the treatment.

Shared tasks of patient and therapist

Forming, sustaining, exploring, and evolving the therapeutic relationship

What is most unusual about the experience of conducting psychodynamic psychotherapy, or being in psychotherapy, is how quickly therapist and patient learn the extent to which *each affects the other* in ways that can prove surprising, unsettling, and – ultimately – enlightening. Patients who are unfamiliar with what the therapist has up his sleeve may recoil when the therapist "starts in" by addressing the transference. Patients unfamiliar with this approach to treatment not infrequently question what the therapist is up to – why he keeps returning to the topic of how the patient is reacting to, feeling about, or understanding him. Some patients express the view that such an approach feels unprofessional, uncalled for, and even inappropriate or completely beside the point, given that the topic of treatment is to be about the patient and not the therapist. Such a patient may go so far as to charge the therapist with being unduly self-centered, wishing to turn the therapy into something that is "about him" rather than centering the treatment on its rightful and proper subject – the patient. Naturally, patients who'd been raised by narcissistic parents will be particularly prone to view the situation in this fashion. Given such circumstances, it is best that the therapist makes explicit why he focuses such attention on what the patient "makes" of him – with "make" being the operative concept, the unavoidable and therapeutically helpful reality that patients construct the therapist in accordance with transference expectations. The transference has the patient seeing the therapist alternately as being very much like original transference objects, very much like the ideal parent the patient had always hoped to have, or very much how the patient himself had felt or acted when he was young and was being treated by his parents in ways he now is treating the therapist. Explaining that the therapist sees great value in examining the transference may help the patient be a bit more comfortable with this highly unusual practice of focusing on qualities of the relationship, which is a conversation that typically is limited solely to intimate relationships. Ideally, the patient slowly comes to realize that the therapeutic relationship is, in fact, another type of intimate relationship – though it fails to share certain specific features of other such relationships (e.g., mutuality and an absence of boundaries) while, at the same time, proving – in certain ways – more intimate than any previous intimate relationship had been, given the degree of risk and naked candor involved.

As surprised as many patients are about how touched and affected they are by the therapist, therapists can be equally shocked by how affected they are by certain of their patients. Seasoned therapists accept this circumstance as a necessary and inevitable (even a welcomed and helpful) aspect of analytic treatment, though they too can sometimes feel sheepish when they are caught off guard by the strength of their countertransference reactions, as well as the degree to which they end up acting on their emotions as they engage in a countertransference enactment that has them acting before they think. An analytic treatment that fails to pull the therapist emotionally into the mix may be considered, by some, not analytic at all, as illustrated in Boesky's (1990) often quoted remark: "If the analyst does not get emotionally involved sooner or later in a manner that he had not intended, the analysis *will not proceed* to a successful conclusion" (p. 573, italics added). Some therapists even insist that a test of whether an analysis has gone well is whether the therapist has also changed in the process.[20]

Treatment goals: what to expect

Many different factors – some having to do with the patients, others having to do with the therapist – combine to help determine how far the treatment might get in helping the patient resolve his presenting complaints and, furthermore, in helping him grow in ways he might not even have expected were possible when he first sought treatment. Naturally, psychoanalysis would be expected to result in more thorough and far-reaching changes in a patient's psyche, with the potential goals of psychodynamic psychotherapy being more modest. Kernberg (1999) writes:

> ...the objective of psychoanalysis is *fundamental structural change*, the integration of repressed or dissociated unconscious conflict into the conscious ego. In expressive or psychodynamic psychotherapy, the objective is a *partial reorganisation of psychic structure* in the context of significant symptomatic change. (p. 1078, italics added)

Here, we see the difference to be a matter of degree relative to how profound a change can be effected with less integration of unconscious psychic content coming about during psychodynamic psychotherapy.

Regardless of one's favored theory about how therapy brings about change, all psychodynamic therapies share in common particular goals:

a) Promote psychological growth (facilitate development that's become blocked or fixated);
b) Help ameliorate symptomatic behaviors;
c) Lessen self-limiting and self-destructive tendencies;

d) Improve one's sense of self (one's core identity, with a heightened capacity to maintain reasonably good, reality-based self-esteem, improve one's sense of self-agency, and so on and so forth);
e) Facilitate character development;
f) Facilitate improvement in one's object relations (how one relates to others);
g) Help a patient acquire certain psychological skills – a heightened capacity to be self-reflective and to be able to mentalize the minds of others;
h) Help patients parse their emotions – to be able to appreciate the nuances of one's emotions beyond simple distinctions of being, say, mad, sad, or glad;
i) Promote "structural change" – helping patients soften their harsh superegos, develop more realistic ego ideals by which they measure themselves, and strengthen ego capacity to help withstand frustration and utilize more mature types of defenses;
j) Improve psychological integration by recovering split-off parts of the self and/or recovering repressed memories;
k) Help patients feel "more alive" by heightening the fullness of their experience.

No doubt, this list is incomplete to the extent it cannot do justice to the myriad of ways in which analytically based treatments can promote change, but it hopefully should serve as a summary and guide to help one think in broad brushstroke terms about what psychodynamic psychotherapy is all about.

Finally, it should be noted that it is essential that therapists are able to establish realistic expectations of what might be therapeutically accomplishable when working with a particular patient – given the patient's own psychopathology as well as the therapists own limitations that make it easier for him to treat certain sorts of patients and harder to treat others. Psychoanalysts speak about "working through the transference," which is misleading to the extent transference reactions can never truly be "dispensed with" once and for all. Studies clearly demonstrate that analytic treatment does not *eradicate* transference – rather, in the best-case scenario, it helps the patient be better at identifying transference reactions when they first emerge, which means the patient is much less likely to get carried away believing in the veracity of the reaction rather than seeing it for what it is. While some may bemoan this to be an overly modest gain, it is in fact a remarkable achievement that goes a long way toward improving a patient's quality of life.

While the patient's suffering, combined with his wish to get better, drives him to treatment, he soon learns he's gotten more than he'd initially bargained for when he lands in the hands of an analytically oriented therapist who ends up addressing the patient's transference-readiness that reveals latent wishes combined with perception-altering expectations, which the therapist believes will prove helpful for the patient to realize if only the patient would permit them to surface so that they then can be meaningfully addressed…and tested.

In the end, discovering underlying meanings is what this form of treatment is all about – however the analytic couple arrives at that meaning.

Before we conclude, it is important that something be said about "therapeutic action"—theories offered to explain how psychoanalytic-facilitated psychic damage comes about. It is essential that students have a solid grasp not just about their own implicit theories, but also the multitude of theories that have been proposed to explain how psychoanalysis "cures"—if we dare use that word. Freud's initial belief, which remains a guiding light for many psychoanalysts, posits that insight or knowledge about oneself is what is essential in order to bring about change worthy of being called "psychoanalytic"—in particular, "making the unconscious conscious". As has been noted in various spots throughout this volume, plenty of psychoanalysts are skeptical that the imparting of knowledge (or its discovery in a patient's eye-opening "A Ha!" moment) is sufficient to change basic intrapsychic structure, to lessen the need to rely upon primitive defenses, to ameliorate tendencies to act out—to repeat rather than remember the past, and the like. Some analysts suggest that instances when the therapist acts in ways that directly counter the patient's transference-based expectations is what proves the most therapeutic. Others speak about the analyst providing a "new relationship"—one that either makes up for, or demonstrates what the patient has been needing from important caregivers during his formative years that was woefully missing. The list of potential "mutative agents" is extensive—and includes softening the patient's harsh superego through an identification with the analyst's more humane superego; helping patients learn more about how their mind works, rather than learning about the specifics of what they have been trying to keep repressed; providing words with which patients might then be better able to communicate their nuanced affects; modification of primitive or unformulated experiences into experiences that can be communicated without having to be acted out (e.g., retrieve split-off dissociated aspects of oneself); lessening the patient's reliance on primitive defenses; heightening a patient's capacity to think symbolically and to be self-reflective. This is not meant to be an exhaustive list the theories offered to explain the mutative effects of psychoanalytically-informed treatments, it is only to demonstrate the wide variety of ideas that have been circulated to explain the beneficial effects of analysis. Every student should familiarize himself with these theories and should compare them with what the student himself believes about how therapy brings about change. Everyone who conducts psychotherapy should be able to speak with authority about why they do the things they do in the course of treatment, and they should have a firm grasp on how those interventions relate to their core theory about therapeutic action.

Notes

1 This chapter does not address the initial assessment, nor the task of arriving at a dynamic formulation that serves as a metapsychological theory about the origins

of the patient's presenting complaint. Volumes by McWilliams (1999, 2004), Thompson and Cotlove (2005), Gabbard (2010), and Cabaniss et al. (2011) cover these topics quite thoroughly.

2 Suggested reading on the repetition compulsion: Freud (1914).
3 Suggested reading: Greenson (1967, pp. 295–319).
4 Suggested readings on resistance: Cabaniss et al. (2011, pp. 242–258), Gabbard (2010, pp. 115–133), Greenson (1967, pp. 59–71), McWilliams (1999, pp. 85–101), and Thompson and Cotlove (2005, pp. 135–147).
5 Arguments have been made that psychoanalysis proper can be conducted on a three-day-a-week basis, with certain institutes having adopted this as an acceptable frequency. As we go to press, the International Psychoanalytic Association has argued that a three-day-a-week analysis constitutes a bona fide analysis.
6 Renik (1993) calls the analyst's subjectivity "irreducible" – meaning that his perspective must, to whatever extent, be so contaminated by his subjectivity as to render him, essentially, incapable of being objective (see Chapter 4, this volume).
7 Suggested reading on neutrality: Cabaniss et al. (2011, pp. 90–97).
8 Suggested reading: Cabaniss et al. (2011, pp. 149–157, 158–185).
9 The essential difference between empathy and mentalization is that the former requires one to feel a bit of what the other is feeling; by contrast, mentalization does not require this, nor does it even require we care about the other's experience – only that we are adept at accurately reading what is going on in the other's mind.
10 The first chapter of this book addresses this topic in great detail.
11 Suggested reading on the topic of free association: Cabaniss et al. (2011, pp. 203–216; see also Chapter 1 in this volume).
12 Suggested reading regarding time and money: Freud (1913).
13 For a good illustration of the effective use of therapist disclosure, see Ehrenberg (1982).
14 This isn't to suggest that the therapist's expertise is solely limited to knowledge about how to conduct treatment (given his knowledge about development, human nature, and the like); it is only to alert the therapist that his wisdom about how one goes about living a life is necessarily limited.
15 Suggested reading on the topic of what is required of the therapist: Cabaniss et al. (2011, pp. 116–125, 143–148) and Greenson (1967, pp. 364–388).
16 Suggested reading on "the frame": Cabaniss et al. (2011, pp. 72–83), Freud (1912), Gabbard (2010, pp. 60–69), Greenson (1967, pp. 271–281), Langs (1990, pp. 305–323), and McWilliams (2004, pp. 277–284).
17 Suggested reading on the therapeutic alliance: Cabaniss et al. (2011, pp. 84–89) and Greenson (1967, pp. 190–216).
18 Some argue no such thing actually exists, seeing that one cannot artificially separate off an uncontaminated part of the relationship.
19 That it feels to the patient as if certain aspects of the therapist's behavior "prove" that the therapist is thinking or feeling about the patient in accordance with certain (e.g., negative) views he has formed about the patient, though the patient is willing to question the absolute veracity of this belief and accordingly remains open to considering the possibility that things merely appear "as if" they are this way when, in fact, the situation is considerably more complex.
20 Suggested reading on countertransference: Cabaniss et al. (2011, pp. 107–115).

Chapter 11

The effect of style on the quality of supervision

Should the details of treatment be left to the treating clinician?

While the educational value of supervision remains largely undisputed, the same cannot be said about the question of whether certain styles of supervision serve supervisees'/candidates' needs better than others, which remains a hotly debated topic. In this chapter, we define the tasks and goals of supervision, raise questions about whether the task of student evaluation conflicts with the task of facilitating the supervisee's professional development, study stylistic differences in the way supervisors go about supervising, outline the potential pitfalls of these stylistic differences, and raise questions about which aspects of the treatment supervisors might have a right to claim authority. Finally, we explore the value of helping supervises learn how to make the most of their countertransference reactions by respecting them and considering them data on par with others sorts of clinical data that emerges in the course of the analysis.

A supervisor whose stance may be summed up by the phrase: "If *I* were you I would have done...or said...this or that," may inadvertently imply not only that the supervisee had erred but that the supervisor knows best how treatment should be conducted. Such an attitude may ultimately manifest in the supervisor's offering interpretations for the supervisee to "try out" in session with the patient. If the supervisee is being difficult, ignoring the possibility that the supervisee has sound reasons that may be hard for him to articulate because they represent an intuitive-based sense of what may or may not fly with the patient at this point in time. I believe that supervisors had best be respectful of the supervisee's sense that the clinical approach advocated by the supervisor might not be one the supervisee can presently implement.

Some supervisors believe that they are in a position to be able to speak definitively not just about the dynamics of the case, but also about how treatment should proceed. I think otherwise; while I believe that supervisors are uniquely positioned to be able to formulate the case and shed light on what is taking place in the consulting room, they may not be comparably situated to be able to speak authoritatively about how the treatment should be conducted or about the types of interpretations that are most likely to prove clinically productive. I further argue that certain supervisory styles are more likely than others to benefit a given supervisee's educational development and that certain ways of supervising may even negatively impact the treatment – for example, when a supervisor's certainty about his formulations of the case cascades down, manifesting in the supervisee becoming closed-minded about the theories he is laboring to get his patient to accept.

This chapter is predicated on a bold assertion that constitutes my central thesis: much of the time, the supervisor is better situated than the supervisee to be able to make out the dynamics of the case and to ascertain the nature of what is going on between the supervisee and his patient; on the other hand, the supervisor is poorly positioned to know how to make the best use of this knowledge in the actual treatment setting. If my thesis is correct, it would then require that the supervisor leave it to the supervisee to decide how best to translate the case formulation into palatable and productive clinical maneuvers that move the treatment forward.

Supervisors oftentimes see the case more clearly because they are unencumbered by the sorts of distractions that can interfere with the treating analyst's (supervisee's) ability to devote his full attention to a reflective consideration of the unfolding material. The supervisee's need to be available to the patient by being fully present in the room, in combination with the distractions created by a multitude of subtle interactions and varied affects flying about the room, takes a toll on the supervisee's ability to maintain sufficient presence of mind to be able to fully dedicate himself to the task of figuring out what is going on in the room on multiple levels – to see the forest for the trees. Ideally, an analyst ought to be able to accomplish both tasks at the same time – but that often amounts to an unachievable ideal. Try as he or she may, it is hard for therapists in general, and neophytes in particular, to be able to observe and consider the meaning of experienced events whilst simultaneously working to be emotionally present in the room as they are happening.

The tasks and goals of supervision

To seriously consider the topic of supervision requires we consider the tasks and goals of supervision as seen from varying perspectives. A position statement issued mid-century by the Board of Professional Standards (BOPS) of the American Psychoanalytic Association (reported in Fleming & Benedek, 1966) stipulates four tasks:

(1) To instruct the student in the use of the psychoanalytic methods;
(2) To aid him in the acquisition of therapeutic skill based upon an understanding of the analytic material;
(3) To observe his work and determine how fully his personal analysis has achieved its aim;

(4) To determine his maturity and stability over an extended period of time. (p. 16)

Striking is the degree to which the evaluative task of supervision appears to be emphasized (items 3 and 4), which is *problematic for the field* to the extent the profession's need to assess competence may discourage supervisees from being reasonably candid, honest, and forthcoming about their work (Fleming & Benedek, 1966; Jaffe, 2000; Lebovici, 1970).[1] Speaking from his own experience, Baudry (1993) notes:

> Many candidates expressed reluctance to be really open about what went on in their work, and they searched for "what the supervisor was looking for." Other students expressed their concern about voicing disagreement with their supervisor for fear of hurting his or her feelings or damaging their own reputations or their proper progression within the organization. (pp. 595–596).

More recent attempts to pen a mission statement about supervision downplay the goal of evaluation in recognition of the likelihood that an over-emphasis on evaluation may weigh heavily on the supervisee's freedom to honestly admit how he thinks and how he had conducted himself in the course of conducting treatment.[2] A very different perspective on supervision emerged out of work conducted by the COPE[3] Study Group on Supervision (described in Wallerstein, 1981). This group pictured supervisors as ideally engaging in a process they called "evocative questioning" (DeBell, 1981, p. 54), which helps "catalyze the student's own associative processes" (DeBell, 1981, p. 50). The study group believed that supervision is facilitated by the supervisor's demonstration (modeling) his own ability to maintain an open mind as he reflects on the presented clinical material. Evocative questioning was seen to stimulate the supervisee's thinking about the case (why the patient feels and/or acts the way he does, why the supervisee feels and/or acts as he does, and how these two factors come to define a process known as "the analytic third" – Aron, 2006; Ogden, 1994 – which is more than the sum of the parts). Another identified task of supervision is that of consistently reminding the supervisee to allow his theories about the patient and about how therapy promotes change to remain in the background during the session, implicitly influencing the supervisee's perception of the emerging data, as well as helping him decide on how best to intervene in treatment.

The COPE Study Group concluded that supervision works best when it constitutes an "enabling process" (Schlesinger, 1981, p. 31).

> The supervisor, both by his way of studying the analytic material and his method of conducting supervision, serves as a model for: (1) a mode of listening, (2) a method of weighting and thinking while suspending

> judgment and action, and (3) in periods of emergency or crisis, a way of getting out of a regressive jam and back to a constructive course. (DeBell, 1981, p. 57)

This description ties the importance of continued, open-minded listening with the task of making sure to avoid drawing conclusions prematurely, then acting on those conclusions by offering them in the form of interpretations. This description is also noteworthy in that it addresses the need for supervisors to sometimes help rescue a supervisee who has become lost in a countertransference enactment that is bogging down the treatment or may even be jeopardizing the treatment as an ongoing venture – illustrated in a supervisory vignette presented further along in this chapter. In the end, supervision ideally culminates in the supervisee's ability to operate independently without needing to rely on the supervisor on an ongoing basis.

To help the supervisee develop the capacity to work independently requires that the supervisor conducts himself in accordance with the adage: "If you give a man a fish you may feed him for a day; if you teach him how to fish you feed him for a lifetime." The supervisor "gives a fish" when he makes standard practice of providing sample interpretations that aren't chiefly offered to demonstrate the *analyst's reflective thinking in action*, but rather are interpretations the supervisor literally expects the supervisee to repeat or paraphrase while working in session with his patient.[4] The same can be said about the practice of *offering formulations* about the case rather than working to stimulate the supervisee to think about why the treatment under consideration is taking shape as it is, why he chooses to intervene in the way he does, what he believes such interventions are meant to accomplish, what he makes of the patient's responses to his interventions, and so on and so forth. Whether there's danger in a supervisor sharing his formulation with the supervisee can only be determined on a case-by-case basis, which means the supervisor needs to be alert for instances when his offered formulations may be experienced by the supervisee as relieving him of the need to come up with formulations of his own, which would be a most unfortunate outcome.

More recent attempts to specify the essential tasks of supervision have tended to focus more heavily on processes designed to facilitate the candidate's professional development. For example, Wolf (1995, p. 255) downplays the tasks of *imparting information* and of overseeing and directing the treatment in favor of a *facilitating a process* aimed at strengthening the student's self-confidence and self-esteem. Lachmann (2003) thinks along similar lines when he envisions supervision as helping the supervisee "evolve a unique style of working" (p. 342), which requires the supervisor be aware of and work to try to circumvent the ever-present danger of interacting with the supervisee in ways that leave him feeling "repeatedly outclassed, criticized, shamed and constricted" (p. 343). Ogden (2005) writes about the need for the supervisor to supervise in a way that helps "create a 'fiction' that is true to the supervisee's emotional experience with the analysand" (p. 1265), facilitated by the creation of an environment that:

> ...affords the supervisee a sense of security that his efforts at being honest in the presence of the supervisor will be treated humanely, respectfully and confidentially...In return, the supervisor shows the supervisee what it is for him to be (and to continue to become) an analyst through the way he thinks and dreams, the way he formulates and expresses his ideas and feelings, the way he responds to the supervisee's conscious and unconscious communications, the way he recognizes the supervisee as a unique individual for whom the supervisory relationship is being freshly invented. (p. 1269)

Naturally, the tasks of supervision are intimately related to *the ultimate goals* of the supervisory process. Slavin (1998) refers to one desirable outcome whereby supervisees learn to "trust themselves" by coming to the realization "that what emerges spontaneously from them will indeed be therapeutically relevant and useful" (p. 236), which Slavin sees as requiring the supervisee to get more comfortable with the experience of becoming completely lost in a moment with the patient. Slavin sees a need for the supervisor to provide the supervisee with "a sense of safety and the feeling that their needs, their agenda, and their capacity to have an influence will be recognized" (p. 236), which – he points out – *precisely parallels* what the supervisee needs to provide for his patient. Here, we see Slavin touching on an important factor – the way in which a supervisor treats the supervisee may cascade down as aspects of the supervisory relationship take shape in how the supervisee ends up treating and interacting with his patient. If, for example, the supervisor is overly certain and/or overly insistent about his formulation of the case, such attitudes stand a fair chance of spilling over into the consulting room, potentially leading the supervisee to adopt similar attitudes, which would likely have a therapeutically stifling effect.

Additional goals of supervision include the supervisee's heightened ability to tolerate uncertainty, keeping an open mind rather than rushing to judgment by prematurely settling on a comforting formulation that provides an illusion – not recognized as such by the supervisee – that he knows more about the patient than he actually does. A corollary to the supervisee's ability to sustain an "unknowing" stance is his ability to rethink matters – to reconsider his hypotheses or formulations in the light of newly emerging data. A capacity to think analytically – to be self-reflective enough of the time – is an essential, and possibly *the* essential, goal of supervision, which doesn't come about through the imparting of information, but rather by the supervisor modeling his own reflective process as he works to stimulate such thinking in the supervisee.

My proposal about the tasks and goals of supervision

I will now offer some thoughts of my own about the tasks and goals of supervision. First, supervision helps a supervisee identify what constitutes *salient* (relevant) *data* from amongst the vast amount of data streaming in through multiple channels (e.g., verbally conveyed content, nonverbal communications, affects emanating from both parties, emerging transference and countertransference reactions, a host of different behaviors, symptoms and signs, dreams, features of the unfolding process – the list goes on and on).[5] The supervision then parlays the selected data into hypotheses that hopefully expand the supervisory team's understanding about a host of matters, including such big picture questions as: what caused the patient to get sick in the first place and what will it take to help him get better? A "formulation" is generated by the supervisor and/or by the supervisee, sometimes arising through the process of collaboration or, alternately, by the independent thinking of either party. Disagreements may arise and a debate may ensue if either party feels strongly enough about their own formulation and, additionally, the supervisee feels safe enough and courageous enough to dare disagree with the supervisor. If outright competition develops between the two, tensions may develop that will somehow need to be worked through to ensure the ongoing maintenance of a good-enough supervisory alliance. A breakout of contentiousness might also be reflective of a contentious process taking place in the consulting room between the supervisee and his patient, which is unconsciously transferred to the supervisee's relationship with the supervisor through "parallel processes" (Doehrman, 1976; Brown & Miller, 2002; Eckstein & Wallerstein, 1958; Caligor, 1981).

Formulations are hypotheses that must consistently be recognized as such. But "consistently" is a tall order, insofar as supervisors and/or the supervisees may intermittently lose track of the fact that their hypotheses are just that – theories that must be tested to see if they continue to fit with newly emerging data. Problems can develop if the supervisor and/or the supervisee become too wedded to a given formulation, in which case it may become an "overvalued idea" (Britton & Steiner, 1994). Such an idea may seem to tie up loose ends and "explain all" – creating the illusion that the job of formulation has been completed and now all the supervisee need do is drive home the point (indoctrinate the patient) in session. To mitigate such dangers, the supervisor demonstrates and advocates for the maintenance of an open-minded, curious, "unknowing" stance to counter his own tendencies as well as those of the supervisee to draw unwarranted or premature conclusions or to be overly insistent about their formulations.

Another task of supervision is to help supervisees decide how best to handle the case by strategically intervening in the treatment. While there are generic guidelines about how an analysis is to be conducted (e.g., the patient's use of free associations, the analyst's use of evenly suspended attention, and so on and so forth), the supervisee must customize his treatment approach in accordance with what he's concluded about what his patient can tolerate in the way of interpretations and/or interventions (detailed in Chapter 5). Supervisors should feel comfortable challenging supervisees: (1) to explain why they'd chosen to intervene in the treatment in the fashion they had; (2) to take stock of how the patient had responded to his interventions; and (3) to account for why the patient had responded to the supervisee's interventions in the way he had. This may be expecting a lot of the supervisee, and it may sometimes leave the supervisee feeling as if he'd been put on the "hot seat" – which may generate so much anxiety that it becomes hard for him to come up with answers on the spot. Knowing when to push, how to push, and whether it might be best to back off is a measure of the supervisor's ability to tailor supervision to the particulars of a given supervisee. Just as analysts learn that they must adapt to who their patient actually is, rather than expecting him or her to behave in accordance with a model of how the ideal analysand should behave, Slavin (1998) describes the need for supervisors to "learn form a particular supervisee how to be the supervisee's teacher" (p. 241).

Supervisors also provide didactic education by educating the supervisee about a host of "tricks of the trade" (Lewin & Ross, 1960, p. 258), which a supervisee can collect in his quiver to be used at appropriate points in the course of treatment. This includes such matters as how silences might be handled, how a patient's failure to pay the bill might be approached, how questions posed as the patient exits the room might be managed, and the like.

Seeing things from a distance and the variable presence of mind model

Just as supervision can place the supervisee "on the hot seat," conducting treatment can comparably stress the supervisee, making it hard for him to think in the moment in a reflective fashion in order to be able to say something meaningful about the unfolding process. Schlesinger (1981) suggests that supervision serves:

> ...to help the candidate experience the analytic situation more deeply in an affective sense as well as to help him *take sufficient distance from it* to conceptualize better what is going on, and from that conceptualization to develop a rational approach to the patient based both on his own intuition and on a sound psychoanalytic understanding. (p. 32, italics added)

This statement contains two noteworthy aspects. First, it identifies the need for the supervisee to do much more than merely conceptualize or intellectually formulate the case – he must also be acutely attuned to affects emanating from the patient as well as those stirring within him. Furthermore, the supervisee must gain "sufficient distance" from the affective experience to then be able to *think about it* in a more dispassionate fashion. It is this capacity to gain sufficient distance from the presented material that constitutes one of the supervisor's chief advantages – providing him with a forest-for-the-trees perspective on the events taking place in the session under discussion. This from-a-distance perspective is one the supervisee might *intermittently* be able to muster, but there are plenty of times when this task will prove exceedingly difficult, and may even become nearly impossible given the amount of attention the supervisee must dedicate to the dual tasks of riding the wave of powerful affects and being fully present in the room with the patient on a moment-by-moment basis. This requirement to "show up" and be "fully engaged" oftentimes precludes the treating analyst from being able to reflect on the material to the extent the supervisor *is* typically able to do, given that he is not comparably encumbered by these same tasks and accordingly considers the presented material at a comfortable distance from the action under discussion.

Early in my professional career, I had an experience during supervision that drove home this point in a most convincing fashion. I was a second-year psychiatric resident and was sitting across from my analytic supervisor. I flipped open the steno pad containing my process notes, read the first line, and broke into laughter. My supervisor looked at me with a quizzical expression and inquired about what I'd found so funny. I explained that I'd suddenly realized what the session had been about after reading the opening line of the session, though I hadn't had a clue at the time about the matter. It was then that I realized one great advantage supervisors enjoy over supervisees – that of being freed of the burden of needing to relate to the patient, which positions the supervisor to be able to reflect on the material as I now found myself able to do as I sat reading my notes at a now-comfortable distance from what had earlier been a lived experience. Being in the room with the patient can routinely diminish an analyst's capacity to think about the situation at hand. No doubt, every supervisor realizes as much. But the same cannot be said universally of neophyte therapists, which is why I now make it my standard practice to demystify the process of supervision by letting my supervisees in on this "little secret" that explains the supervisor's advantage, which could equally be the supervisee's advantage were the tables to be turned, with the supervisor being the one presenting material from a session that he had conducted. This advantage, I submit, is why supervisors are uniquely positioned to be able to see the expanse of the process, which then positions them to be able to note and offer a somewhat more comprehensive view of the matter than the treating therapist is able to muster. Schlesinger (1981) summed up this advantage when he wrote about the supervisor's vista:

> From this uninvolved position, above the fray and after-the-fact, the supervisor can more easily remain objective and see things in their proper perspective. The advantage of this somewhat detached position vastly

> enhances the probability of his being the more correct in his assessment of the analytical process. (p. 31)

Levenson (1992) also noted this phenomenon when he observed:

> People whom I've supervised, who seem confused to me at the time, seem to be perfectly clear when they're supervising other people; and I've had the experience, at a White Institute seminar, of presenting my own adumbrated clinical material and having a class of seven or eight candidates seeming perfectly lucid about what's wrong with what I'm doing, and what I should be doing instead. (pp. 1–2)

The variability of the analyst's reflective capacity

One might expect that the experience of being psychoanalyzed combined with that of having one's clinical work supervised should necessarily translate into a heightening of an analyst's capacity to be able to think reflectively in the moment. This, however, is not *consistently* the case. While it is reasonable to expect such experiences to heighten an analyst's capacity to think reflectively, reflective capacity waxes and wanes throughout an analyst's day as a result of factors that either have solely to do with the analyst or are created by the rigors associated with treating certain types of patients – in particular, those who make effective use of projective identification, those who are unusually adept at drawing the analyst into becoming unwittingly swept up in countertransference enactments, or those with whom strong affects rule the day. Remaining fully conscious of what's taking place in the room at all times is more than we can expect of analysts – a lesson that's been driven home over the course of the last quarter-century by our mounting realization of the ubiquity of countertransference enactments. While being psychoanalyzed may (should?) heighten one's overall level of conscious awareness, one's moment-to-moment ability to be able to do so proves to be highly variable, and fretting about the matter or feeling ashamed that such are the conditions under which we work is unhelpful at best, and can further burden one's ability to do the work.

Let's consider in greater depth the matter of an analyst's incapacity to be aware of his countertransference reactions at all times or, if not, at least a respectable amount of the time. One needn't go to the extreme that Renik (1993) went – declaring emphatically that an analyst's countertransference awareness is *always* after the fact[6] – in order to recognize a shade of truth in Renik's clear-cut overstatement. If one "dials back" the absoluteness of Renik's assertion, one begins to recognize that his statement casts doubt on the extent to which analysts sometimes believe themselves capable of being self-aware – a daunting realization that undermines our ability to feel as "in command" of treatment as we would like to think we are. The fact that most analysts can attest to instances when they had been *very much aware* of their countertransference reactions, particularly when those reactions had not been particularly strong and accordingly could be easily contained rather than acted out, doesn't completely negate Renik's point, which serves to alert us to the fact that we are nowhere near as aware as we might like to think we are, and we often don't realize as much until we become more completely aware of something about which we'd been only dimly aware before.

In writing about the recovery of forgotten memories, Freud made a statement that had, for the longest time, confused me: "When the patient talks about these 'forgotten' things he seldom fails to add: 'As a matter of fact I've always known it; only I've never thought of it'" (p. 148). I now have a much better handle on what Freud was alluding to: once one becomes fully aware of something about which they'd previously only been dimly aware, they come to the realization – in retrospect – that they *had* in fact known such a thing all along – that they had been "kind of" aware, though not aware enough to have been able to declare that they knew such a thing at the time. Psychic content that lies on the border of awareness cannot be declared "known" until such a time as awareness intensifies, leading an individual to then realize, only in retrospect, that they had known about the matter all along, though they hadn't known enough about it to know that they had known it – meaning that they had been in no position to declare at the time, even to themselves, that they knew about the existence of such thoughts, feelings, impulses, memories and the like. Recognizing this to be the case leads to the humbling realization that things we recognize in retrospect to have been in our perceptual field (if but at the periphery – in the preconscious) were not things we'd been able to see or know at the time, even though – looking back on the matter – we now see clearly – indisputably – that it *had* been there to be seen all along, if only we'd been in a position to be able to see it.

The variable presence of mind model

This brings us to a consideration of the variable *presence of mind model*, which posits that an individual often loses presence of mind when immersed in a powerful emotional experience, making it hard, if not impossible, for him to think reflectively about the situation as if from a distance. In order to best illustrate this principle, we turn to the consideration of another hyperbolic situation.[7] In a paper I had written about exhibitionism (Tuch, 2008), in which I had noted how frequently such an experience momentarily disables the victim – rendering her speechless, without a sense of what to do or where to turn – I quoted Siegman (1964), who'd described the effect that exhibitionism had on the observer:

> We speak of being under the spell of such an experience... We become frozen, immobile, 'rooted to the spot' – we feel that the entire experience

> is not under our control, that we cannot cause it to cease at will. The outside object is perceived as controlling us…the omnipotence is granted the object, since internally perceived sensations are experienced as having been induced by the object, and the omnipotence, in large measure, rests in just this ability. (pp. 321–324)

Now, if one considers the act of exhibitionism from the comfort of merely imagining such an event rather than actually becoming swept up in one, then one will typically find it hard to imagine how one could become completely, psychically indisposed, even though that is precisely what most women report – sometimes with a bit of shame for having lost their capacity to act in a self-protective manner – and it is this loss of a capacity to empathize with the extreme experiences of others that proves, to my way of thinking, deeply troubling and centrally problematic.[8]

Sometimes such conditions arise in the clinical setting, particularly when the analyst is under the sway of projective identification or swept up in an enactment but blind to the fact. Britton (1989) describes his treatment of a difficult patient (described in Chapter 5) – Miss A. – who made it extremely hard for him to think in her presence:

> It seemed impossible to disentangle myself sufficiently from the to-and-fro of the interaction to know what was going on…What I felt I needed desperately was a place in my mind that I could step into sideways from which I could look at things. If I tried to force myself into such a position by asserting a description of her in analytic terms, she would become violent, sometimes physically, sometimes by screaming. (p. 88)

Honoring intuition

Let's return to my original assertion: that supervisors are better situated to making out what is going on between the candidate and his patient, *yet poorly positioned to precisely know what to do with this knowledge.* What about the second half of this assertion? I would submit that it is terribly presumptuous for a supervisor to think he knows how best to intervene at a specific point in time with a given patient. The supervisor may think he substantially grasps the nuances of the case – and well he might – but that does not translate into his knowing how the supervisee should proceed, since the supervisor lacks essential knowledge that he would need to be able to claim authority to direct the treatment from where he sits. When a supervisor comes to believe that an interpretation he's fashioned is precisely what the supervisee "ought to have said," that supervisor has ventured on to shaky ground and may, furthermore, be oblivious to the fact that he is claiming greater authority than circumstances allow.

It is vital to recognize that the therapist who is in the room with the patient knows infinitely more than he can possibly convey in words to his supervisor, captured in Ogden's (2005) observation that "all of the ways that the analyst consciously and unconsciously brings to the supervision his experience with the analysand do not add up to the actual presence of the patient" (p. 1267). Levenson (1992) notes that there is something "ineffable (or beyond words) in the process of doing therapy" (p. 1); the treating analyst is privy to an immense amount of data about the patient – much of which he "knows" without being able to declare as much. Since the treating analyst knows more about the patient than he can verbally transmit to the supervisor, the supervisor lacks an in-depth model of what the patient can and cannot tolerate – an internal model of the patient that the supervisor would need to have in order to be in a position to accurately predict how the patient would handle a given interpretation or intervention. Notwithstanding the fact that data is transmitted back and forth on an unconscious basis from supervisee to supervisor, I believe the treating analyst knows his patient on a gut level that is hard to wholly convey, one which the supervisor can't come close to replicating.

Now, what about the matter of the supervisor suggesting interpretations for the supervisee to offer his patient? While the supervisor is uniquely positioned to come up with interpretations that may prove to be "spot on," that says nothing about whether the time is right to announce such a thing to the patient – particularly if the supervisee isn't completely sold on the supervisor's notions about the patient as reflected in his suggested interpretations. If a supervisee doesn't see the merits of a suggested interpretation, he should think twice about repeating the interpretation to the patient. If the supervisor is truly "on" to something about the patient – encapsulated in his suggested interpretation – mounting evidence should surface over time that proves it so – which might, in turn, help the supervisee recognize the interpretation as being more than mere conjecture, which is how it may have seemed to him when it was initially articulated by the supervisor. Allowance must be made by the supervisor for instances when the supervisee insists that a supervisor-suggested intervention doesn't feel like something that the supervisee can comfortably implement for reasons he may be unable to articulate, seeing as this impression is intuition-based. Under such conditions, it would be an error, I submit, for the supervisor to blithely conclude that the supervisee is resisting – that his personal issues are getting in the way of his being able to appreciate the value of the supervisor's recommendation. Discounting intuition as weak justification for either believing in or rejecting a suggested interpretation or intervention ignores the fact that intuition isn't nearly as unscientific as the term might seem to imply, seeing as it likely results from theories operating implicitly in the background of the supervisee's mind, which grounds his intuition-based conclusions on something considerably more substantial and – dare we say – scientific that the term "intuition" implies.

Consider the example of a supervisor who'd pressed his supervisee to get the patient to talk more openly about her sexual habits (DeBell, 1981). Knowing the patient as he did, the supervisee felt it was too early in the game to make such inquiries or to press the patient to explore her reticence to discuss such matters:

> The supervisor insisted, and the candidate protested that he could confront the patient with her reticence, but that pressing for details was wrong. The supervisor ended this exchange with, "I can see that you don't want to learn anything from me. You had better take this problem up in your analysis." (p. 48)

Styles of supervising and the corresponding pitfalls of supervision

DeBell (1981) describes two types of supervisors that constitute extreme ends of a spectrum[9]: on the one hand are supervisors who adopt a forward-leaning, hands-on approach that has them formulating the case for the supervisee's edification, and may even go so far as involving themselves in the treatment itself by fashioning interpretations the supervisee is then expected to offer to his patient; on the other hand are supervisors who take a much more "laid-back," laissez-faire approach, taking care to neither judge nor critique the supervisee's work or pre-empt the supervisee's thinking by sharing his formulations of the case with the supervisee. Such supervisors believe they are providing a facilitating environment that will naturally culminate on its own accord in the optimal development of the supervisee's clinical abilities. Between these two extremes lie supervisors who offer a hybrid approach, fluidly shifting their method depending on what they think might work for a given supervisee or what is required at different points during a given candidate's supervision.

The COPE Study Group came to the conclusion that certain styles of supervising are associated with less than optimal supervisory outcomes. In particular, the Group faulted overbearing, authoritarian-like supervisors – those who expected the supervisee to adopt the supervisor's point of view and to implement his suggested interventions. Evidence culled by the Study Group led to the conclusion that such supervisions not only produce less than optimal results, but may be associated with a multitude of potential pitfalls, some of which may negatively impact the treatment itself. The Study Group also faulted laissez-faire-type supervisors, who were seen as not being active enough to lead the supervisee to feel they were actually being helped.

Submitting to supervision renders one markedly vulnerable to the supervisor's feedback; one untoward effect of supervision is the diminution of the supervisee's confidence in his handling of cases. Granted, awakening a supervisee to the possibility that his understanding about or approach to the treatment may be problematic runs the risk of narcissistically injuring the supervisee, and supervisors must find ways to provide feedback that minimize the hurt their critical assessments might generate. This does not mean, however, that the supervisor must abandon the task of providing feedback altogether. Of particular concern are supervisors who undermine a supervisee's self-confidence by suggesting that he'd erred to the extent he'd failed to pursue a course of action that "obviously" would have proven much more fruitful had the supervisee been talented enough to realize as much and acted accordingly.

Beside undermining the supervisee's self-confidence and making him feel worse about himself, such a style of supervision might also have a direct detrimental effect on the treatment itself, particularly if the supervisee mimics the supervisor's overly certain manner, to the point of becoming overbearing in session to the same extent that the supervisee feels that the supervisor had been with him (another example of a parallel process, this time traveling from the supervisor's office back to the supervisee's consulting room). A supervisee may become overly compliant in supervision, and there are clear-cut risks associated with a supervisee tacitly agreeing with most everything the supervisor says. The supervisee may adopt such a strategy because: (1) he idealizes the supervisor; (2) he feels that acceptance of the supervisor's formulations and suggested interventions relieves him of the need to go out on a limb by sharing his own formulations and/or honestly sharing what he is actually doing in the consulting room; and/or (3) he feels that to do otherwise is too risky, given the supervisee's fear that the supervisor's negative assessment might translate into him having trouble advancing in the analytic training program. Many have written about how some supervisees fear that they must hide what they are actually doing with the patient (Balint, 1948; Cabaniss, Glick, & Roose, 2001; Fleming & Benedek, 1966; Lebovici, 1970; Weiss & Fleming, 1975) out of fear that the supervisor will disagree with his handling of the case given the supervisor's theoretic bent and/or his strongly expressed formulations or interpretations. Such fears may be heightened to the extent the supervisee has come to believe that the supervisor's narcissism[10] requires the supervisee's adulation and will brook no challenge or disagreement.

Another aspect of supervision that can prove problematic is the fact that the work typically involves a retrospective assessment of what had taken place, which is inherently problematic for a host of reasons. To begin with, one must keep in mind that the patient has moved on ("you can't step into the same river twice"), and may well be relatively unconcerned about what had very much concerned him in the session before (Fleming & Benedek, 1966). For a supervisee to carry back to the next session what he and the supervisor had talked about during the intervening supervision runs counter to Bion's advice that one enter sessions without memory or desire, and doing so runs the risk of diverting the natural course of the session by imposing the supervisee's agenda, which disrupts the free flow of the patient's associations. In an effort to avoid this situation, I make a practice of cautioning candidates against actively applying what we'd discussed in supervision in the following session unless the patient's associations naturally bring to mind what the supervisee and I had been talking up in supervision. Looking back on a session that has already taken place and suggesting what the supervisee ought to have said or done makes little sense not only because the supervisor's ability to speak authoritatively about such matters is questionable, given the reasons previously outlined, but also because the clinical moment has already played out and is now history, making whatever "better" intervention suggested by the supervisor moot. The opportunity to have done it differently has passed; whether a comparable clinical situation will develop going forward – one that gives the candidate a "shot" at trying out the supervisor's suggested approach – is doubtful. Slavin (1998) addresses the question of the relevance of looking back on an interaction that has already taken place:

> We rarely ask how it is that a retrospective examination of clinical work is useful...Do we hope that a parallel situation will come up with this or another patient so that, somehow, we can use similar techniques again? In my view, the point of looking back is not to critique a particular interaction or to learn how to conduct oneself more effectively should a similar situation arise. Rather, the point is that the supervisor can find – and help the supervisee find – how his or her personal responsiveness and vulnerability were therapeutically relevant...Looked at in this way, it becomes less important whether the specific manner in which the supervisee responded in a prior hour was as useful as, in the abstract, it might have been. What matters is that the supervisor can find – and the supervisee can learn – that what she or he brought personally to that moment was responsive not simply to her or his own inner urgencies but to the impact of the patient and to finding that, in fact, her or his "inner urgencies" are highly influenced by the patient. In learning this, supervisees will be in a better position, subsequently, not to believe that they have a model or technique for a specific response to a specific situation but, rather, that they can have increased trust in themselves and in their own essential responsiveness. If new therapists are to believe in themselves, their supervisors must believe in them (Yerushalmi, 1994). And the process of fostering such belief by both is accomplished by the retrospective examination that is the hallmark of supervision (pp. 241–242).

"Treat or teach": addressing countertransferences of various sorts

Aside from the varied tasks and goals of supervision previously outlined in the above section of this chapter, there is a final task of supervision that requires the supervisor's active involvement and may require him to confront the supervisee with evidence that the supervisee's personal issues or reactions are interfering with the optimal management of the case. Early in the history of psychoanalysis, supervision was chiefly seen as providing candidates another avenue to learn about and work through their "complexes" – making supervision more akin to treatment, in distinction from how we generally think about supervision these days. Max Eitingon (1926), credited with introducing the use of supervision in the mid-1920s, described how the supervisor is expected to help the trainee understand "why he makes mistakes, that is to say, in what complexes in himself they originate" (p. 134). Distinguishing whether the chief goal of supervision was to "treat or teach" supervisees (Lewin & Ross, 1960) has clearly moved in favor of the latter over the former. By the time the COPE Study Group convened in 1981, supervisors were much less comfortable thinking in terms of "treating" the supervisee. DeBell (1981) summed up the Group's sentiment:

> It is difficult to find proponents of the explicit "treatment" of candidates during supervision; certainly no one in the group advocates analyzing the supervisee. Still, every member of the group agrees that it is sometimes necessary to point out to the analyst certain obstructive behavior patterns, and even on occasion to comment about and even inquire into their possible motivation...To state the matter in extreme terms, everybody appears to oppose "treatment" of the supervisee and yet everyone does it. (pp. 42–43)

Supervisors often feel reluctant to "get into it" with a supervisee even when the supervisor believes that the supervisee's issues or complexes are interfering with his optimal treatment of the patient. Many factors contribute to the tendency to shy away from confronting supervisees with their "faults," succinctly outlined by Baudry (1993):

> Supervision during training might be the logical time for bringing to the analyst's attention the impact of his or her character on technique. However, we usually fail to touch on this vital issue for multiple reasons. (1) The supervisor is reluctant to tread on what he or she considers to be the domain of the analysis. (2) The supervisor may not conceptualize the problem in characterologic terms. (3) The supervisor may see the way the candidate's character intrudes on the treatment but may not be able to find a useful way to communicate this to the candidate. (4) The supervisee's character may intrude on the supervisor/supervisee relationship but, again, there may seem to be no clear way to deal with this. (pp. 604–605)

Difficulties confronting supervisees notwithstanding, DeBell concludes by noting in no uncertain terms that it is:

> ...the supervisor's responsibility to detect and deal with these problems, at least to the point of bringing them unambiguously to the supervisee's

> attention, lest the analysts remain forever handicapped...[In this regard] it is not necessarily a favor to the analyst to be overly considerate of his feelings. It can indeed be a disservice to him to fail to confront him with his mistakes or his ignorance. (p. 46)

The following instance, reported by Baudry (1993), illustrates the dangers of failing to note and address a candidate's issues because her tacit agreement with the supervisee belied more serious and problematic tendencies that only surfaced years later:

> In her training [a female candidate] had been considered a model supervisee: she seemed to grasp the intent of her supervisor and carry it out with sensitivity...Some years later [after graduation], she experienced some difficulties in dealing with demanding patients. She felt an urge to be excessively accommodating, and she experienced anger when the patients, instead of being grateful, seemed to demand more. This time, however, she sought help from a supervisor who...instead of passively acquiescing in the repetition of the same pattern – the supervisee's compliance with his suggestions – raised the question of whether the supervisee was always in total agreement with him, which was most unlikely. He also suggested an analogy between the problem presented by the supervisee in her work (her compliance with the patient) and in her relationship with him. Fortunately, the gifted supervisee was able to do some self-searching. She soon realized that she had been intimidated by the previous supervisors and had been inhibited in challenging their views and thinking for herself. She felt she had learned relatively little from her student experience – or at least less than she could have learned had her attitude been pointed out to her. (pp. 606–607)

Dealing with countertransference reactions has become exponentially more common as the field has come to appreciate and embrace the ubiquity and centrality of countertransference enactments. This does not represent a shift back to the "treat" end of the "treat or teach" continuum,[11] given that such enactments, while predicated on something that is particular to the analyst, are nevertheless representative – to some degree – of the average expectable reaction (rather than an idiosyncratic reaction) that most analysts would have had, given the circumstances. Hence, such a reaction isn't something that needs to further be worked through, but rather constitutes important data worth attending to with the expectation that doing so will prove therapeutically beneficial for the patient to the extent the supervisee's reactions serve as commentary about the patient's situation (Brown & Miller, 2002; Slavin, 1998; Szecsody, 2008).

Dealing with countertransference: a supervisory vignette

Consider the example of a bright, psychoanalytically oriented psychiatric resident who relayed the following circumstances about a patient named Peter S., a single man in his forties who the resident had been treating in psychodynamically oriented psychotherapy for the last several months. The resident told me that this was the second time that he'd forgotten his scheduled session with the patient. Only after receiving an irritated voicemail message from the patient shortly after their appointment was scheduled to take place did the resident realize what he'd done (yet again). He quickly called the patient, but all he received in response was a text message in which the patient mentioned he was too angry to talk right then, though he wanted the resident to contact him so that they could talk about the matter. Six days had passed since the resident had received that message; he had yet to respond, and he and I were exploring the situation in supervision.

I asked the resident if he had any idea what might be behind his forgetting the patient's appointments. In response, the resident admitted that he did not like how this patient treated him. The patient was 15 years his senior, an academic, and treated the supervisee like he was "an amateur" – made all the worse to the extent the resident was undeniably a beginner, though I would never have considered him amateur. Still, his status as neophyte left him vulnerable to the stinging charge that he was an amateur. His admission provided us with a window through which he and I could begin discussing his aversion to feeling treated by the patient in what felt to him like a contemptuous and dismissive manner, as well as the possible reasons the patient could have for interacting with him in ways that left the supervisee feeling that way. "Could this be an instance of projective identification?" I wondered. Might the patient be feeling a need to avoid the possibility that he himself was at risk for feeling such feelings in the course of treatment, so he unconsciously arranged for his doctor to experience them in his stead? And was the patient able to pull off this feat without providing much in the way of evidence other than the fact that someone in the room was feeling those feelings?

The supervisee was intrigued by the possibility that the gears of such a mechanism might actually be turning behind the scenes. The resident had felt dismissed and was now acting dismissively toward the patient not only by forgetting to show up for his sessions, but by failing to respond back in a timely fashion to the patient's request that he do so. I wondered if the treatment might be in jeopardy if the resident didn't do something to help rectify the matter.

When I asked the resident if he knew why he had yet to respond to the patient's text message, I was yet again relieved by his willingness to be forthcoming about his feelings. He explained that he hadn't called the patient back because he was scared he might get rejected, thus supporting and extending my suspicion of projective identification, which led me to wonder whether the resident might also be containing the patient's fear of rejection. It seemed quite possible that the patient had in fact felt rejected – really doubly rejected – first by his doctor's missing of the appointment and now by his doctor's failure to respond in a timely manner. This way of thinking about my supervisee's reactions not only provided us with what I regarded as indirect data about the patient, it furthermore got us around the potentially sticky problem of finger-wagging the resident for having acted out his feelings in this manner. Might another therapist have felt just as my supervisee had? The possibility seemed likely. But my supervisee had acted out those feelings when another therapist might have been able to resist the pull to do so. Yes, that was true. But – then again – another therapist might succumb to enactments that my supervisee would *not* have been vulnerable to – so, *there you go*! Who amongst us can say their roots are so deep that their tree never bends but a bit when gale-force winds ensue?

I asked the resident whether he'd considered the possibility that failing to contact the patient in a timely fashion, as the patient had requested, might have added insult to injury – heightening the patient's growing conviction that the resident wasn't all that keen about treating him. I told the resident I understood he hadn't any intention of causing the patient to feel such feelings (at least no conscious intention, but I left that aside) – that he had acted in a self-protective manner, given how it pained him to be treated by the patient in what he experienced as a shabby fashion. But there were two people involved in the room and there were two stories being told by the two of them.

I then began to wonder whether the patient might already have concluded that it was no longer safe to permit himself to care about whether he and the resident would ever met again. Maybe he had already written off the resident and was in the process of moving on. I then imagined my way into the patient's mind, which is always perilous to the extent it is quite presumptuous for a supervisor to believe himself in a position to do so with any degree of accuracy. Still, this is where my thoughts went. I imagined thinking: "How long do I have to wait to hear back from him? What more has to happen before I finally 'get the message' that this guy just doesn't want to see me anymore? If he calls me now – it's too little too late. I am *over* it. I'm done! I *hope* he calls! He'll want to make another appointment and I relish being positioned to reject him."

After all, the resident was fearfully anticipating just such a rejection, causing him to feel extraordinarily reluctant to reach out to the patient. Again, these were my thoughts and thinking them didn't make them so. What I did have to go on were my supervisee's feelings, which I was now assuming were not solely nor strictly about him. I went out of my way to make clear to the resident that I was not at all sure that my construction of the patient held water. I was engaged in the process of hypothesis creation, and I had to admit that the patient might not be feeling the feelings I was in the process of attributing to him.

Having arrived at a point of worry that the treatment might be in jeopardy, with a bit of information in hand that led me to believe that the patient might fear being treated in a dismissive and rejecting fashion by his doctor who himself might be experiencing this countertransference enactment to represent just that, I felt the need to move into action by making a direct suggestion, which runs counter to much of what I have written thus far in this chapter. I suggested that the resident call up the patient, apologize for not having gotten back to him sooner, and express some concern for how his actions may have caused the patient to feel. Then I made it clear that he needn't do anything of a sort unless – of course – what I had said genuinely stirred him to have similar concerns, in which case he might feel so inclined to call, but it was best he find his own words rather than repeat what I had said in the way in which I had said it. Furthermore, he was free to disagree with my construction of the situation. After all, I could be "off" about how I imagined the patient might be feeling.

I continued to think about the situation and to keep my supervisee abreast of the sorts of things I was thinking. If the patient felt as hurt and rejected as I imagined he might, I thought he might be more inclined to "lead" with anger as his expressed emotion rather than hurt, since admitting to feeling hurt could reveal that he cares more than he cares to let on that his doctor's actions had "mattered" to him. So even if the supervisee was thinking about mustering up some empathy in reaction to our now joint belief that the patient felt hurt, how the patient would end up acting in response was hard to predict, though he might well be wishing to keep his vulnerability hidden from view.

At our next supervisory session, the resident described how he had more or less followed my suggestions. He had contacted the patient shortly after leaving the supervision, apologized for not having contacted him sooner, and imagined aloud how the patient might be feeling – that he might have felt that the resident had treated him in an insensitive manner. The patient agreed to meet at their normal appointment time the following day. When they met, the patient expressed feeling angry about the matter, though he had "gotten over it days ago." No, he hadn't been hurt in the least by the resident forgetting his session and by him failing to return his call for almost a week because – and herein lie the clues – he had come to wonder whether something was wrong with the resident – maybe he was having problems of his own – that accordingly called for sympathy and pity in place of feeling any upset at the resident for acting as he had. In retrospect, I realized that I'd had enough information to have imagined it playing out in just this way, rather than its playing out with the patient copping either to feeling hurt or angry – both of which would have entailed an admission that he cared about how he'd been treated by his doctor. The way in which the patient did act seemed very much in keeping with his subtly contemptuous attitude toward the resident for being an "amateur." Now, not only was he an amateur, but an injured and compromised amateur as well! In place of the calamitous possibility of feeling hurt or injured, the patient now erected a sense of superiority that cast the resident in the role of the one who was vulnerable.

Conclusion

The task of teaching through supervision is not as simple as it may seem at first glance, and it's been the goal of this chapter to elaborate upon this theme, to offer reasons to explain why this might be so, and to suggest styles of supervision that stand a greater chance of proving more fruitful for supervisees. This leads to an important question: what do supervisees themselves say they find most helpful about supervision? What do they value most about the process of being supervised? In a large study, Cabaniss, Glick, and Roose (2001) studied the responses of candidates at the Columbia University Center for Psychoanalytic Training and Research (Columbia Supervision Project) and found that the candidates considered discussions about transference and countertransference most helpful, followed by "support" and "encouragement," which were ranked a bit lower. It was particularly noteworthy that only half of the respondents found discussion of theory "very useful," while "explicit directions" as to how to clinically intervene were judged to be *least helpful of all.* This research graphically supports some of the essential points that have been made in this chapter – the fact that a style of supervision that is best summed up in the phrase "If I were you I would have done this or that" is one that candidates find least helpful.

It's essential that supervisors find ways to maintain a genuine sense of humility about what they think they know. They must also find ways to guard against the seduction of the "overvalued idea" that can lead one to believe that one has found an explains-all explanation that then allows them to coast their way toward the finish line with little more to do but bang the drum repeatedly in order to drum such ideas into the supervisee's (or patient's) mind. Needless to say this would be a poor excuse for analysis, and teaching supervisees about such dangers constitutes a substantial supervisory task.

Besides the task of helping stimulate the supervisee's thinking about the case, one other essential task of supervision is to help the supervisee get comfortable sharing his inner processes – not only his intellectual formulations, but his gut-level experiences that arise in the course of conducting the analysis. It is essential that supervisees develop a deep acceptance and appreciation of the extent to which their own personal reactions constitute data on par with other types of data they might be more inclined to consider "legitimate." Exploring the supervisee's countertransference reactions can be done in a way that shields him from feeling shame about his all too human emotional reactivity to patients. Supervision can be a deeply gratifying experience just so long as the supervisor remains aware of the complexities of the process and the pitfalls.

The candidate's compelling need to quickly settle on a theory that might help direct his handling of the case makes him particularly vulnerable to prematurely settling on a particular hypothesis. If the supervisor: (1) models patience and open-mindedness, (2) reassures the candidate that he need not have a full understanding of the material to be able to make helpful interventions, and (3) takes care to avoid acting as if he or she knows "for sure" what the material means and how best to clinically intervene, he or she provides the candidate with a model of professional security and sincere humility that will tend to play best in the consulting room. We expect candidates to perennially make educated guesses about what the clinical material means. These hunches should neither be embraced nor dismissed, but instead should be kept in mind – waiting for the emergence of data that might validate or negate the hypothesis. How such guesses come to mind – the study of epistemology – is one useful approach to supervision.

Notes

1 I believe that the definition BOPS offered also proved problematic for BOPS to the extent an apparent over-concern with evaluation relative to the educational needs of candidates hints at one important factor that may have contributed to the ultimate demise of BOPS and its replacement by the Department of Psychoanalytic Education, which is charged solely with enhancing psychoanalytic education, having been relieved of the task of student or institute evaluation.

2 The task of evaluation, while thorny, cannot entirely be dismissed, and ways must be found to adequately satisfy the profession's requirement to identify candidates who need more time to ripen.

3 Committee on Psychoanalytic Education, American Psychoanalytic Association.

4 Concluding that this was the supervisor's intent could either be of the supervisor's making (actually, even if covertly directing the supervisee to do as much) or of the supervisee's making (misunderstanding the supervisor's demonstration of reflective thinking by concluding that the conclusion the supervisor had tentatively reached was actually the last word on the matter of what the presented material means).

5 The topic of the analyst's search for data was addressed in Chapter 2.

6 "Everything I know about my own work and that of my colleagues leads me to the conclusion that an analyst's awareness of his or her emotional responses as they arise in the course of an analysis *necessarily* follows translation of those responses into action – i.e., awareness of countertransference is always retrospective, preceded by countertransference enactment" (Renik, 1993, p. 556).

7 This may strike the reader as a questionable exercise, given that the extreme nature of the example provided disqualifies its use to make a point about a much less intense (and accordingly less obvious) phenomenon. I believe such an exercise *has* merit because there is benefit to considering the most extreme case then *dialing it back* to note subtle aspects of the process that might have gone unnoticed had one not considered the more extreme example.

8 Incidentally, this applies to so many other traumatic experiences – ones that prove hard for "outsiders" to be able to fathom.

9 This dichotomy need not be reduced to one of activity versus passivity, since a supervisor can be very actively involved, though not in a way that feels to the supervisee like the supervisor is intruding into the actual treatment setting.

10 It may sometimes be hard to tell if the supervisee's assessment of the supervisor represents a projection of the supervisee's own psychology that reflects an overinvestment in his own need to have his work praised by the supervisor, rather than subjected to what ideally amounts to constructive criticism.

11 Many analysts may not approach the matter in an either-or fashion and may adjust their approach given the circumstances of the supervision and the specific nature of the supervisee.

Chapter 12

What is scientific about psychoanalysis?

Truth comes in many colors

From the outset, Freud was concerned that psychoanalysis be seen as scientific. He sensed that an emphasis on hermeneutics could prove problematic, and noted that the narrative nature of psychoanalytic case histories lacked "a serious stamp of science" (Breuer & Freud, 1895, p. 160). He took great care to frame his thinking in the science of the day – the energetics of Helmholtzian physics and the unearthing metaphor provided by the then-burgeoning field of archeology – and he was greatly relieved when his clinically derived theories were supported by scientific studies carried out by Carl Jung (1906) on word associations. "Psychology is a natural science like any other," noted Freud (1940) at the end of his life:

> The processes with which it is concerned are just as unknowable as those dealt with by the other sciences, by chemistry or physics, for example; but it is possible to establish the laws which those processes obey and to follow over long and unbroken stretches their mutual relations and interdependences – in short, to gain what is known as an understanding of the sphere of natural phenomena in question. (p. 39)

Early doubt about the field's legitimate scientific status was tied, in part, to the fact that its initial popularity didn't so much issue from an acceptance by the scientific establishment so much as it did from it having become, first and foremost, a cultural phenomenon popularized by discussions taking place in coffee houses throughout *fin de siècle* Vienna and a revolutionary fervor to overthrow the lingering restraints imposed by Victorians against which Freud's theories proved a powerful weapon (Makari, 2008). Only later would the scientific community slowly and somewhat grudgingly accept Freud's hypotheses, pushed no doubt by a tidal wave of popular support.

Decades passed, during which time psychoanalysis remained more or less safely entrenched within medicine and somewhat beyond the reach of its detractors. Challenges were intermittently mounted, but psychoanalysis was generally able to keep a few steps ahead – particularly aided in the US by the scientific-sounding ego psychological theories advanced mid-century by Hartmann, Kris, and Loewenstein (1946, 1949). Questions about the scientific validity of psychoanalysis nevertheless have dogged the field from its inception. For the last half-century, the scientific basis of psychoanalysis repeatedly has been called into question (e.g., Nagel, 1959; Popper, 1963), most recently and persistently by Adolf Grünbaum (1976, 1977, 1981, 1984, 1993, 2006), a widely respected philosopher of science who has made a career of "proving" that psychoanalysis fails to meet the standards required for any field of study to earn the right to be considered truly "scientific." Mills (2007) notes:

> Grünbaum pulls no punches in attempting to discredit the notion of repression, a dynamic unconscious, the nature of transference, and the free associative therapeutic process. The corollary of his implications is that dynamic mental processes such as unconscious conflicts, relational patterns of repetition, and defensive maneuvers do not actually occur. (p. 541)

While not questioning whether the clinical practice of psychoanalysis is efficacious, Grünbaum (1981) attributed whatever clinical gains were achieved during psychoanalysis to the combined effects of placebo or suggestion, and he further argued that there was inadequate evidence to substantiate what he identified as the core Freudian assumption: that individuals fall ill due to repression and improve with the lifting of repression. Grünbaum identified the "tally argument"[1] – that "proof" of core psychoanalytic theories and practice rests solely on empiricism, the clinical demonstration that correct interpretations (those that truly tally with the analysand's unconscious psychic reality) are alone clinically efficacious to the extent that only interpretation can lift repression, thus rendering the patient cured. Grünbaum's accounting of the tally argument, which differs markedly from Freud's later views about how psychoanalysis can be validated (see Brunell, 1999), posits the following: only the psychoanalytic method can yield correct interpretations, and only correct interpretations can resolve repression sufficiently to effect a cure, but since "cures" are likely a function of suggestion or placebo, they don't count for anything[2] – meaning the validity of psychoanalysis cannot be scientifically established merely on the basis of what happens in the consulting room.

In practice, Grünbaum's theory proves overly simplistic and out of keeping not only with the complexities encountered during actual treatment (e.g., when repression may solve one problem while creating another, or one symptom gives way to another), but also to the extent that therapeutic action is portrayed by Grünbaum as completely hinging on the lifting of repression, which is out of keeping with present-day thinking and is furthermore out of keeping with how Freud viewed the matter early on. Grünbaum also refused to grant scientific status to the method of free association, believing it was inevitably (across the board) contaminated by the analyst's subjectivity, with rare exception. In the end, reasoned Grünbaum, the only way that psychoanalysis can be validated sufficiently for it to be deemed truly scientific is for it to be supported by "extra-clinical validation" – data that would be free of personal contamination of the analyst's being and beliefs, data coming from outside of the psychoanalytic procedure.

Grünbaum's arguments have received considerable attention, generating scores of papers written in response that take up and address the arguments he puts forth, which will be discussed in detail further along in this chapter. The point of mentioning his effect on the field is to establish context for a series of events that took place in the spring of 2015, when the often-embattled field of psychoanalysis again fell under attack, this time from a different group of doubters. In short order, two substantial critiques appeared in the press repeating the often-made claim that psychoanalysis lacks scientific backing – one lodged by Jeffrey Lieberman, Chairman of Psychiatry at Columbia University College of Physicians and Surgeons, the other by Edward Shorter, Professor of Medical History at the University of Toronto's Department of Psychiatry. In his book *Shrinks: The Untold Story of Psychiatry* (2015), Lieberman lambastes psychoanalysis as a "plague on American medicine that infected every institution of psychiatry with its dogmatic and anti-scientific mindset" (p. 69). The *New York Times* review of *Shrinks*, penned by a female science writer who admits her own analysis was "one of the most miserable experiences of my young adulthood," challenged the field by asking: "Where is the evidence that this excruciating and expensive ordeal really works?" (Angier, 2015). A more scathing critique, published in *Psychiatric Times*, was Shorter's (2015) commentary that likens psychoanalysis to "witchcraft" and calls upon psychiatric training programs to "abolish psychoanalysis from the psychotherapy training of residents," seeing that psychoanalytic instruction was "like making a course in astrology requisite for the training of astronomers." The gauntlet has been thrown down, and it yet again fell to psychoanalysts to address the charge that psychoanalysis is anything but scientific. An emphasis on "hard science" was beginning to catch up with the lead psychoanalysis had earlier established through the better part of the 20th century. Sooner or later, psychoanalysis was bound to become caught up in the avalanching demand that psychiatric treatments be evidence-based. Such an environment provided fertile ground for the critiques of Lieberman and Shorter, whose ideas resonated with those who demanded more from reimbursable treatments financially supported by government-based and insurance-based payments.

Scientific evidence

Were there, in fact, a dearth of empirical studies validating the effectiveness of psychoanalytic treatments (psychodynamic therapies and psychoanalysis proper), such critiques would seem in order. This is hardly the case, however, given the countless studies that provide substantial empirical support documenting the effectiveness of psychoanalytic treatments. Such studies are notably reviewed in such works as *An Open Door Review of Outcome Studies in Psychoanalysis*, prepared by the Research Committee of the International Psychoanalytic Association (Fonagy et al., 1999), and the often-quoted paper "The Efficacy of Psychodynamic Psychotherapy" (Shedler, 2010).

In a review of the second edition of *An Open Door…*, Ablon (2004) speculates that the reason no one's listening to the wealth of empirical data now supporting the effectiveness of psychoanalytic treatment is "the lack of a central, easily referenced source of information about systematic research efforts in psychoanalysis" (p. 605), which, he notes, has hereby been solved by a handful of worldwide leaders in psychoanalytic research who collectively performed the monumental task of gathering and analyzing the research contained in that volume. Given the amount of support that's amassed, one's left to wonder what continues to give such critics as Lieberman and Shorter the right to claim authority to speak in no uncertain terms about the lack of science backing psychoanalytic practice and theory. In Orwellian fashion, such critics ignore science in the name of science. In the end, the politics of science are enough to cause one to shudder.

While an overview of empirical outcome research is included in this paper, no attempt is made to engage in an exhaustive review of the multitude of such studies and meta-analyses of such studies conducted to date, given the fact that this task has already been carried out successfully by others (see Fonagy et al., 2005). Rather, this paper endeavors to grapple with the question of why such research goes ignored. The solution Ablon (2004) suggests – to find better ways to get the word out – strikes me as naive. We kid ourselves if we believe answers lie in finding practical solutions for such underlying prejudices. It seems more likely that "turning a deaf ear" will ultimately prove psychologically based, the product of resistances that won't simply yield to a mere recitation of the facts. Such maneuvers don't work clinically, so it is curious psychoanalysts who would believe a clear-cut, easily accessible review of the data could conceivably circumvent historic trends on the part of some to steadfastly deny not just the utility of psychoanalytic treatment in general, but psychoanalytic knowledge *in particular* – which is the central focus of this chapter.

To this end, we will briefly review outcome studies, move on to explore neuroscientific research that soundly supports psychoanalytic theory, and then consider the potential sources of resistances to the acceptance of psychoanalytic concepts. The chapter concludes with a brief discussion of what can reasonably be considered science's proper domain – whether science has a legitimate right to speak in global terms about the universe or, more reasonably, must acknowledge a more limited ability to speak with authority about a *circumscribed* domain, one defined by the limits of the tools it employs (O'Donnell, 2015).

While many consider randomized controlled studies ("efficacy studies") to be the gold standard by which efficacy can solely be measured (see Chambless & Hollon, 1998), for a host of reasons, such studies aren't always possible when it comes to psychoanalytic treatment proper. Seligman (1995) notes that "the efficacy study is the wrong method for empirically validating psychotherapy as it is actually done, because it omits too many crucial elements of what is done in the field" (p. 966), to which Leichsenring et al. (2005) add: "The alleged strengths of controlled studies, especially randomization, can turn out to be their central weakness, because they create artificial conditions that are not representative of clinical practice" (p. 435). So, right from the start, we see controversy about how outcome is to be optimally measured, with certain researchers favoring "naturalistic" studies (Seligman, 1995) that take into consideration how things operate in the real world with reference to the ways actual patients end up in treatment in the first place.

Enough outcome studies have now been conducted on short-term and long-term psychodynamic psychotherapies (Anderson & Lambert, 1995; Crits-Christoph, 1992; Leichsenring, 2001, 2005; Leichsenring & Leibing, 2003), as well as on psychoanalysis proper (de Maat et al., 2009; Leichsenring et al., 2005), to permit them to be grouped together and studied in meta-analyses. The outcome metric typically used in these studies is the "effect size" (Cohen, 1988), with an effect size greater than 0.8 being considered statistically significant.[3] A meta-analysis conducted by Leichsenring and Rabung (2008) of outcome studies of patients treated in long-term psychoanalytic psychotherapy, for example, calculated an effect size of 1.03 involving five outcome domains (overall effectiveness, target problems, psychiatric symptoms, personality functioning, and social functioning). Another, by Leichsenring and Leibing (2003) – who conducted a meta-analysis of fourteen studies of mostly time-limited psychodynamic psychotherapies published between 1974 and 2001 – discovered a large overall effect size (1.46), with patient self-reports yielding an average effect size of 1.08 and observer-rated measurements of 1.79.

There are other ways of measuring treatment outcome besides effect size. Various scales measure the rate of "improvement of target symptoms" (e.g., the Beck Inventory for Depression), while others look beyond symptomatic improvement by considering a broader array of positive life changes. Leichsenring and Leibing (2003), for example, take into consideration the overall improvement in the quality of a patient's life, measured in terms of his capacity to have more meaningful relationships, to effectively capitalize on his strengths and abilities, to tolerate a wider range of affects, and the like – illustrating the short-sighted effect of zeroing in on a patient's "chief complaint," which often proves to be but one of many problems contributing to the patient seeking help, though it may be the one he's most comfortable admitting to as he makes his way to the therapist's door.

A more recent meta-analysis (Gerber et al., 2011) that eliminated problematic outcome studies, thus narrowing the field to twenty-five "high-quality" studies, yielded ample results to deem psychodynamic psychotherapy "empirically validated" (in accordance with American Psychological Association standards published by Chambless & Hollon, 1998), save for the fact that additional stipulations were subsequently added requiring the treatments studied to be manualized and conducted with a cohort of like-diagnosed patients.

Particularly encouraging studies that address the twin needs for empirical research to employ manualized treatment approaches applied to like-diagnosed patients are presently underway, conducted by teams led by Otto Kernberg and Peter Fonagy. Kernberg's *transference-focused psychotherapy* (Diamond et al., 2013; Kernberg et al., 2008) and Peter Fonagy's *mentalization-based treatment* (Bateman & Fonagy, 2004) have repeatedly been shown to be highly effective in the treatment of personality disorders (borderline and narcissistic). When compared against other treatment modalities (dialectical behavioral therapy and supportive psychotherapy), for example, transference-focused psychotherapy proved superior in many respects (Clarkin et al., 2007).

Several studies have documented that patient improvement continues to take place months to years after treatment has ended (Abbass et al., 2006; Anderson & Lambert, 1995; de Maat et al., 2009; Leichsenring & Rabung, 2008; Leichsenring et al., 2005). The "dose effect" (the longer the patient's in treatment, the more probable it is he'll improve) was noted in several studies (Howard et al., 1986; Kordy et al., 1988; Leichsenring, 2005). Certain symptoms (character pathology, interpersonal difficulties, disorders of self-regard) were consistently found to improve only after the first year of treatment (Kopta et al., 1994; Leichsenring, 2005), and the efficacy of employing interpretations was demonstrated by Silberschatz et al. (1986), Crits-Cristoph et al. (1988), and Joyce and Piper (1993).

Moving from studies focused on psychodynamic psychotherapy to rarer ones that study the outcome of *psychoanalysis proper* includes such studies as Leichsenring et al. (2005), which involved 36 patients and demonstrated statistically significant improvement in *symptoms*, *interpersonal problems*, and *quality of life* as measured by different checklists, symptom inventories, and questionnaires. After one year, 77% of the patients showed improvement, documented by a large effect size, and an even larger percentage of patients reported improvements at the one-year follow-up.[4]

Evidence supporting psychoanalytic theory

Not only does empirical evidence support the effectiveness of psychoanalytic therapies, but neuroscience also validates basic psychoanalytic assumptions about how the mind works. Such core psychoanalytic tenets as the existence of unconscious/non-conscious psychic content (Dijksterhuis & Nordgren,

2006; Halford et al., 2005; Westen, 1998), the power of unconscious motivation (Bargh & Chartrand, 1999; Custers & Aarts, 2010; Mlodinow, 2012; Solms, 1997; Wegner, 2003), and expectation-based selective perception (transference-based pattern recognition; Pally, 2000) have all received substantial neuroscientific backing (Berlin, 2011).

"A century after Freud introduced his many radical and counter-intuitive ideas into psychology," observe Turnbull and Solms (2007), "several of his most basic claims appear to stand on surprisingly firm neuropsychological ground" (p. 1088). These authors note: "One would be hard pressed to find a cognitive neuroscientist who did not consider mental activity outside of conscious awareness to be a well-established fact" (p. 1083). Not only has the existence of unconscious mental activity irrefutably been established, the fact that humans are motivated to act in accordance with forces outside their conscious awareness has likewise been proven, as has the fact that individuals delude themselves into believing things that aren't true in order to evade unpleasant aspects of reality, just as Freud had suggested.

In a review article published in *Science*, Custers and Aarts (2010) offer noteworthy examples of how non-conscious forces help shape one's behavior, referencing studies on subliminal (below perceptual threshold) "priming":

> Upon entering an office, people become more competitive when seeing a leather briefcase placed on a desk, talk more softly when looking at library pictures on the wall, and clean their table more when there is a vague scent of cleaning agent in the air. (p. 48)

The subjects of these sorts of studies hadn't a clue why they'd acted as they had, and some hadn't even taken note that they were acting in any particular way. Based on such studies, Dijksterhuis and Aarts (2010) conclude: "People have long assumed that consciousness plays a leading role in guiding volitional behavior, but we contend that the lead role is actually for goals and for attention [neither of which need be conscious to exert their affect]" (p. 469). Such findings suggest it's reasonable to think in terms of *unconscious will* and *unconscious intention*, in opposition to the widespread tendency to see volition (choice, decision-making) strictly as a function of conscious thought. Hence, "deliberate" behavior need not be *consciously* deliberate, nor need we consider the process of "deliberation," which leads to choice, something that necessarily requires a conscious weighing of alternatives. It should be noted that these types of studies establish the existence of the *descriptive* unconscious and not the *dynamic* unconscious – the latter having to do with psychic conflict and the existence of factors that generate forces that render psychic content out of one's awareness.

Besides priming, another basic neuroscientific principle – that of top-down versus bottom-up neural processing – provides a neuroscientific basis for tendencies to unconsciously avoid (defend against attending to) disturbing internal and/or external stimuli – whether it be thoughts, affects, impulses, memories, or the like. Given the conscious mind's limited capacity to process data (Halford et al., 2005), selectively attending to one stimuli or group of stimuli necessarily entails being selectively *inattentive* to (ignoring) other stimuli that compete for conscious recognition (Mack & Rock, 1998). Seeing that top-down regulation of the perceptual system can either be conscious or unconscious/non-conscious implies that an individual may automatically avoid an unpleasant bit of data without being aware he is actively trying not to see that which he wishes not to see.

The power of the wish not to know can be likened to a magic trick or sleight of hand, whereby attention is drawn to one stimulus and, hence, away from another – namely, the trick that's presently underway. The invisible gorilla experiment (Chabris & Simons, 2010) – a study in selective inattention and the manifestation of the phenomena of scotoma (blind spots) and "negative hallucination" – illustrates the principle to a tee: one watches a video clip where two teams of men pass a basketball back and forth. If the observer pays close attention and follows the instruction to count the number of times men with black shirts pass the ball, most viewers fail to notice a man in a gorilla suit who ambles across the screen in full view. This eye-opening experiment about this eye-closing exercise drives home our ability to not see things that are right before our eyes. By extension, defensive operations work comparably to draw one's attention away from the proverbial "man behind the curtain," who's not to be noticed lest havoc reign.

Research shows the extent to which input from the brain (top-down neural activation) readies the doors of perception (the organs of perception – eyes, ears, etc.) to be on the lookout for what one is hoping, expecting, or fearing to find – an anticipated pattern, an expected outcome, a predicted event, or the like. When the anticipated stimulus appears in the perceptual field, the now-readied, bottom-up perceptual neurons react "more quickly and vigorously" (Grossberg, 1999, p. 13) when such stimuli come into view, thus accounting for the *selective perception* of stimuli deemed salient on an unconscious/non-conscious basis (Becklen & Cervone, 1983; Neisser & Becklen, 1975). The implications of such neural processes lead to the following conclusion:

> Even *before* events happen, the brain has already made a prediction about what is *most likely* to happen, and sets in motion the perceptions, behaviors, emotions, physiologic responses and interpersonal ways of relating "that best fits with what is predicted"...in a sense, we learn from the past what to predict for the future and then live the future we expect. (Pally, 2007, pp. 861–862)

Top-down regulation not only plays a role in attentiveness/inattentiveness, it also helps account for the processes of anticipation, prediction, and pattern recognition – providing the neural basis for the commonly recognized phenomenon that one tends to see what one's looking to find, and it's corollary, that it's hard to see what one wishes to avoid seeing. Even though our eyes and ears are detecting stimuli and sending sensory information to the brain (bottom-up), the brain won't consciously attend to such input if the cerebral cortex (top-down) is, for whatever reasons, consciously or unconsciously disinclined to take note. In other words, the *lack of expectation* can make it hard to see what is right before one's eyes due to an *inadequate level of attentiveness*.

Top-down regulation of the perceptual process supports the twin psychoanalytic principles of transference and repetition compulsion. How a child's been treated by important figures in his life primes/prepares him for comparable present-day interactions that are reminiscent of those he'd experienced during his childhood. Specific elements of a given childhood interaction (e.g., a look, a tone of voice, etc.) are tagged as salient, are scanned for in the present, and – when found – can trigger a re-experiencing as if the past interaction is taking place in the here and now. The individual is "on his toes" – prepared to handle the experience he's predicted into existence – demonstrating the power of transference and repetition compulsion.

The overlapping neuroscientific concepts of "connectionism," "neural networks," and "parallel distributed processing" (Rumelhart & McClelland, 1986) further support basic analytic concepts about unconscious mental processes, demonstrating the extent to which consciousness can be considered more of *an afterthought* than a way in which the brain primarily operates – along the lines of how things subjectively seem to most everyone, reality aside. Researchers working in these areas envision the lion's share of thinking to reside outside of conscious awareness, and Berlin (2011) suggests "people have little or no direct introspective access, and have only inferential access, to their higher order cognitive processes and casual links of their mental states" (p. 11).

Returning to Grünbaum's grumble

Though some analysts take issue with Grünbaum's style of arguing, and others comment about the audacity of an academic completely lacking in first-hand knowledge of a method nevertheless authoritatively critiquing it, the power of Grünbaum's intellect combined with his command of Freud's corpus – "Here at last is a philosopher who has done his homework before criticizing Freud," quipped Holt (1985, p. 293) before he realized he was escorting the Trojan Horse through the gates – led many analysts to step up to the challenge, willing to roll up their sleeves and rise to the occasion by seriously considering Grünbaum's provocatively delivered arguments rather than dismissing them out of hand. In fact, an entire issue of *Behavioral and Brain Science* (June 1986, Vol. 9, No. 2), containing responses from forty-one authors representing a wide spectrum of viewpoints, took up and addressed Grünbaum's challenge.

A number of excellent articles have appeared over the years (Aguillaume, 2001; Ahumada, 1997; Berger, 1995; Brunell, 1999; Eriksson, 2010; Fourcher, 1996; Lothane, 2001, 2007; Mills, 2007; Richards, 2002; Rosenblatt, 1989; Wallace, 1989; Wallerstein, 1986) that effectively refute many of Grünbaum's arguments, and neuroscientific research has now been completed that provides irrefutable extra-clinical evidence proving the existence of unconscious processes, intrapsychic conflict, and the effect of repression. Whereas previous experimental research had only gotten as far as to prove the existence of the descriptive unconscious, we now have research clearly proving the existence of the dynamic unconscious. Specifically, research conducted by Shevrin and his collaborators (Shevrin et al., 1996, 2013) used psychoanalytic techniques to determine the nature of intrapsychic conflict harbored by experimental subjects, which resulted in the generation of a subject-specific list of conflict-related words and phrases that were then subliminally (below the threshold of perception) presented in order to determine whether a neurological effect could be measured in the form of event-related potentials. These studies "found a cause-and-effect relationship between the existence of an unconscious conflict and it inhibitory repressive effect" (Barry & Fisher, 2014, p. 1093), leaving Grünbaum to declare, when confronted with the evidence, "I am convinced" (p. 1093), thus satisfying the essential requirement he had previously set forth to deem psychoanalysis scientific (quoted in Barry & Fisher, 2014, in which they reference the work of Shevrin et al., 1996, 2013).

While it is beyond the scope of this chapter to present a thorough review of the literature challenging Grünbaum's arguments, I will touch upon some of the more crucial arguments that effectively have been mounted to counter Grünbaum's reasoning. Of concern is Grünbaum's lamentable failure to accurately represent Freud's clear-cut intention evidenced in Grünbaum's noted tendency (Lothane, 2007; Richards, 2002) to quote Freud out of context by, for example, failing to consider the entirety of Freud's position by quoting only the first part of his argument. Richards identifies one such example in which Grünbaum accurately quotes Freud as having said "Psychology, too, is a natural science. What else can it be?" (Freud, 1938, p. 282). This statement follows Freud's reasoning that physicists are not held back from provisionally presupposing the existence of electricity, and proceeding accordingly, even in the absence of complete knowledge about the nature of electricity: "What we are ignorant of is precisely the most important and interesting part of the whole business, but for the moment that does not worry us. It is simply how things happen in the natural sciences" (p. 282). The inclusion of his prefacing remark helps clarify Freud's intent, as does the very next sentence in which Freud goes on to clarify the point he is making:

> Psychology, too, is a natural science. What else can it be? *But its case is different. Not everyone is bold enough to make judgments about physical matters; but everyone – the philosopher and the man in the street alike – has*

> *his opinion on psychological questions and behaves as if he were at least an amateur psychologist.* (pp. 282–283, italics added)

Noting this to be a pattern in Grünbaum's writing rather than a single, excusable incident, Richards (2002) opines:

> [W]hether Grünbaum's omissions are due to deliberate bad faith or simply to inadvertent carelessness, they deal a death blow to his project of trying to turn Freud's own definitions of psychoanalysis against him by showing that psychoanalysis fails to live up to the scientific claims that he allegedly made for it. (p. 399)

Lothane (2007) directly calls out Grünbaum for comparable instances of what he deems "misdepictions" (p. 580):

> Here is your tactic: you cite a truncated sentence from page 528 in Freud (1953), and use it to claim that "in short, Freud adduces *therapeutic success* to vouch for the 'correctness of our method' of free association as causally probative for etiologic research in *psychopathology*" (Grünbaum, 1993, pp. 24–25). But you are short-changing Freud, for etiologic research in psychopathology is not his focus here, only the method per se. To further drive your point home you aver that the "original German text contains a confusing slip of the pen" (p. 268): but there is no slip here, only your faulty reading of it. (p. 582)

While many analysts had initially been dazzled by Grünbaum's intellect – believing, as had Holt (1985), that Grünbaum had "done his homework" (p. 293) – a more careful reading of Grünbaum's writings proves otherwise. If readers are inclined to consider the above-mentioned misdepictions as mere nitpicking, they'd best consider the unsettling critique lodged by Brunell (1999) – in line with Wallerstein (1986) and Rosenblatt (1989) – which calls into question the core assumption of Grünbaum's (1984, 1993) thesis: that Freud's core belief was that repression causes illness and the lifting of repression accordingly resolves repression-based symptoms. Brunell notes that this was but one of Freud's theories – not his sole theory of psychopathology and therapeutic action. For Grünbaum to base his case on this assumption, noted Brunell, is to ignore the expanse of Freud's thinking, as well as all that has transpired in the field since Herr Professor put pen to paper, leaving Brunell to wonder, "why does Grünbaum base his reading of Freud on the version of his writings from the 1890s and not on those from the 1930s which succinctly express the post-1923 structural model?" (p. 92). All one need do is consider the central thesis put forth by Weiss and Sampson (1986) – control mastery theory – that posits therapeutic action based not on a lifting of repression but on the effective challenging of a patient's pathogenic beliefs by presenting contradictory evidence that, while not providing the patient with the right answers, at least serves to throw into question the adequacy and accuracy of his pathogenic belief as the sole and sufficient explanation of his life circumstances, including the repetition of pathological patterns. In his review of Ahumada's (2001) book *The Logics of the Mind: A Clinical View*, Fisher (2003) notes:

> The aim of the psychoanalytic method is to disprove key examples of the analysand's unconscious certainties by providing empirical falsification in individual concrete instances (ostensive refutation). The patient's unconscious certainties are expressed in the analysis as enacted relational propositions that the patient takes to be universal. (p. 325)

This is a very different model of psychopathology and therapeutic action than the repression model upon which Grünbaum bases the entirety of his argument. Brakel (2007) notes:

> Few contemporary psychoanalytic theorists hold that the central task in psychoanalysis is overcoming repression such that patient and analyst agree upon the reconstructed contents. To the extent that this aim is not central to psychoanalysis, the attempt to use the tally argument against psychoanalysis rests on a faulty premise. (pp. 273–274).

It has been noted and lamented that many psychoanalysts seem to have been mesmerized by the sheer power of Grünbaum's formidable intellect. Mills (2007) notes:

> Grünbaum's critique is notably intimidating and erudite and likely to be overwhelming to those not learned in his discipline. There is a logical acumen to his specific criticisms despite his blanket generalizations and categorical abnegation of Freud's theoretical corpus. But there is also an overall straw man to his sweeping dismissal: by ruminating on the minutia of specific aspects of Freud's theories, he generates the false impression that the whole Freudian edifice is precarious, when Grünbaum is actually focusing on a select set of problematics and then making an unwarranted generalization – as if his criticisms debunk the entire body of psychoanalytic knowledge and practice. (p. 540)

And yet, notes Brunell (1999), "Grünbaum's critique – so impressive in its scholarship and internal logic – quickly entrenched itself as fundamentally accurate in its understanding of Freud's writings" (p. 87), in spite of the fact that he was playing fast and loose with the facts of what Freud had said and meant. The attractiveness of pure logic is seductive even for individuals trained in psychoanalysis, who ought to know better – though knowing doesn't immunize one against the dangers of becoming swept away in a world where reason reigns when, in fact, that which is unreasonable – beyond reason – typically plays a larger role in the everyday functioning of our emotional lives. This we know, yet forget time and again.

Grünbaum subscribes to a particular type of thinking (positivism) that leads him to a particular *brand of science*, a statement some will likely find confusing, even blasphemous, given the hierarchical position afforded science since the onset of the Age of Enlightenment, the Age of Reason. This brand of science, based on the Galilean method (see von Wright, 1957), stipulates that science involves variables that can be measured and whose outcomes can be reliably predicted, and it stands in contrast with Aristotelian science (better suited to the study of biology), which relies heavily on observation by which complex patterns and arrangements can be ascertained. Grünbaum will undoubtedly argue that his brand of Galilean science is *the* science, real science – the sole science worthy of the name ("natural science" or "exact science") – the kind of science used by real scientists like physicists. Positivism places complete faith in the scientific method to establish cause–effect relationships in the world: if it can't be proven scientifically, it doesn't exist. Writing to and about Grünbaum, Lothane (2007) notes:

> As a philosopher of science you are in the company of the *quondam* sect called logical positivists...Common to this system of logic was a denial of all metaphysics, commonsense psychology, and the life of the emotions. These logicians dealt predominantly with things in the external world, and only *cognitively* with the internal world of thoughts, images, and feelings... Logical positivism is thus unsuited as a critique of the psychoanalytic method that encompasses both modes, cognitive and imaginative. Such logicians press the richness of lived life into a Procrustean bed of a circumscribed, artificial, theoretical scientifico-philosophical language. (p. 579)

Mills (2007) sees Grünbaum aligned with a conservative, Anglo-American philosophical tradition (philosophy of science) that fully and singularly embraces the scientific method, which then allows its adherents to believe they'd cornered the market on truth and objectivity, in contrast with the European tradition of philosophy, "where the nature of subjectivity and culture is both celebrated and deconstructed from within competing contexts of individual experience, society, and linguistic order" (p. 541). While philosophers of science might think otherwise, all scientific endeavors are a least a little tainted by the subjectivity of those seeking to find answers in keeping with what they desire to find. Furthermore, philosophers of science aren't scientists per se and accordingly are at risk of believing:

> ...that pure objectivity can be achieved through rigorous control of experimental methods, when even the most hard-core natural scientists

> like experimental physicists would denounce this assumption…In his introduction to Richard Feyman's (1995) book on the elementary principles of physics, Paul Davies writes: There is a popular misconception that science is an impersonal, dispassionate, and thoroughly objective enterprise. Whereas most other human activities are dominated by fashions, fads, and personalities, science is supposed to be constrained by agreed upon rules of procedure and rigorous tests. It is the results that count, not the people who produce them. (p. 542)

While such reasoning led Ahumada (1997), on the one hand, to conclude, "Mind is not an apt subject for the kind of reduction demanded by a Galilean science built on the regularities displayed by inanimate nature" (p. 508), he equally took issue with those who "retreat to hermeneutics" (Blight, 1981) – who take comfort in solely seeing psychoanalysis as a hermeneutically based activity (a "human science," if you will), ignoring the *empirical* qualities of psychoanalytic practice.

When I previously asked "which science" ought to be *the* science used to assess the psychoanalytic venture, I was seeking to distinguish between three alternatives: natural science, of the sort arguably applicable to the hard sciences; human science, of the sort best suited to the soft sciences – the social sciences like ethology, anthropology or psychology; or neither – advocated by those who strictly adhere to the argument that the hermeneutic nature of psychoanalysis excuses it from having to participate in the exercise. In fact, truth comes in many colors, and to think otherwise – to imagine a monolithic truth rather than imagining facets of the truth – reflects a sort of monotheism that may work in religion but makes for bad science. Freud's mission aimed at getting at truth, but he himself wasn't so simple-minded as to imagine the existence of a solitary truth – the brass ring, a discoverable truth that trumps all other truths. Yes, getting at the truth was Freud's mission, but no, arriving at that theoretical end point was forever elusive, given the extent to which Freud never believed he'd arrived, once and for all, at a final answer. Friedman (1997) succinctly sums up the analytic venture in the following fashion:

> The injunction to confront objective truth gave the patient an endless task by which he could endeavor to win the analyst's favor…If you don't offer one demand, the patient will perceive another. Freud provided a demand: let up on your yearnings and aim for objective truth! And that, in turn, would free the patient. The patient could please Freud only by seeking the truth. And the truth would then make the patient free, because he would be putting himself into a position where he could *choose*, instead of being compelled automatically…We welcome what the patient is revealing, but we think he's revealing it in order to conceal something more important. Nothing is more characteristic of

> psychoanalysts than their inclination to *see through* everything...[the analyst keeps a balance] between analytic credulity and analytic skepticism...[he] rebuffs advances to "buy" any picture of the patient or his fate, waves away comforting roles, and says to everything, in effect, "No; something else." Adversarialness deconstructs the patient's presentation and frees the analyst's imagination. It eyes appearances skeptically and keeps looking for a reality beyond. (pp. 29–30)

Friedman's statement reflects the nuances of psychoanalytic treatment, about which Grünbaum assuredly knows little to nothing – a fact that bankrupts his argument to the degree it is predicated on an unfaithful picture of what actually goes on in the consulting room. A celibate priest ought not to be offering marital advance when he knows not of what he speaks.

Mills (2007), echoed by Thomä and Kächele (2007), faults Grünbaum for committing a categorical error when he lumps psychoanalysis, which is a "human science," in with the physical sciences, thus applying a standard and method of scientific inquiry that is unsuited to the subject matter of psychoanalysis. But the situation is even more complicated than this schema makes it seem, leading Ahumada (1997), who remains committed to an empirical perspective, to observe:

> There is no consensus on the definition of science, that not even so-called "exact sciences" can meet Grünbaum's criteria, and it is high time for the great scientific myth of the twentieth century, that physics is the model of all science, to be finally put to rest...I will argue that Grünbaum rejects the evidential value of psychoanalysis because the complex observational variables of its clinical method are neither homogeneous nor discrete and cannot be incorporated into formal deductive systems or subjected to John Stuart Mill's rules of experimental manipulation. They are therefore judged to lack predictive power. Though their general structure may be subject to repetition, this repetition is not linear; hence, being insufficiently "specific," they are deemed neither cogent nor probative. (pp. 509–510)

Ahumada goes on to conclude:

> A philosophy of science approach that forsakes observational contexts and becomes the judge of observationally based arguments has in the case of clinical psychoanalysis no baseline to ground itself but only a personal brand of commonsense psychology (not to mention such outright prejudices as the idea of conscious logic as a primary mental function). Accordingly, the philosopher of science should try to remember what Russell, a more open-minded inductivist, stated in 1948, that "even the

> words that we most desire to render scientifically impersonal require for their interpretation personal experiences of the interpreter" (p. 104): it is futile for the philosopher of science to try to hold himself to arguments in observational terrains of which he knows little. (p. 526)

The limitations of science

Some individuals exhibit religious-like tendencies to unquestioningly believe in the findings of science – evidence of the phenomenon of "scientism" (Bloom, 1996; Habermas, 1972; Knight, 1986; Rorty, 1982). "'Scientism' means science's belief in itself," notes Habermas (1972), "that is, the conviction that we can no longer understand science as one form of possible knowledge, but rather must identify knowledge with science" (p. 4). "It is important to distinguish science from scientism," notes Mitchell (1998), "the former referring to the accumulation of certain kinds of knowledge, the latter referring to the belief that accumulating scientific knowledge will tell us all we need to know about human experience, meaning, and values" (p. 3).

Science isn't all it's cracked up to be. Still, some continue to place undue faith in its findings, which to my way of thinking represents a misunderstanding of what science has to offer, which often overlooks its limitations. While science can help fend off tendencies to give undue weight to our innate and unavoidable tendencies to believe in our prejudices – some of which stem from unconscious tendencies to engage in wishful thinking as Freud suggested – accepting science as our ultimate salvation is dangerous to the extent we may become blinded by the glare of its supposed illumination of the truth and its claim to be able to speak with absolute authority about objective reality – whatever that is.

Proper respect for science must be accompanied by a proper sense of its limitations. In her paper, "What's the Matter with Psychoanalysis?" O'Donnell (2015) plays with words by first alarming the prospective reader into imagining they are about to get an earful about the shortcomings of the field, only to end up treated to a treatise about the need to make clear what sort of "matter" psychoanalysis aims to deal with – meaning the field needs to be clear about what it takes as its realm of authority, what it believes it has a right to address:

> The epistemology of psychoanalysis should begin with the unapologetic admission that the "matter" in question is not *matter* at all. Its proponents should not flounder when asked whether psychoanalytic knowledge is real...Do we really care whether it is *real*?...Might we consider things to have *being* – and to admit to systematic inquiry – even if they are not material (and therefore not tractable within the *particular* system of science)?...The biological sciences restrict their study to matter – but in doing so, they do not deny the *reality* of force; they simply do not consider it to lie within their epistemological domain. (p. 3)

Here, O'Donnell puts her finger on the final point I wish to make in this chapter. O'Donnell understands the nuanced nature of science in a way that others, who bandy about science in support of their contention that psychoanalysis lacks a scientific basis, seem oblivious to. O'Donnell notes:

> Many such crusaders have little direct experience or understanding of the practice, philosophy, and proper objects of scientific inquiry...Instead, a florid scientism underlies much of the rhetoric...[These weapons] are wielded by such a loud and boisterous army that any defense might sound feeble by comparison. (p. 5)

O'Donnell concludes by quoting Leo Rangell (1967), who encourages analysts to "remain secure in our science" (p. 430) as the antidote to becoming swept away by pseudo-arguments lodged by critics who deem psychoanalysis to be a pseudo-science. O'Donnell (2015) notes:

> To be secure in our science we must see that psychoanalysis is a form of empirical – albeit not experimental – research that can, when applied to the proper object, produce knowledge. But I would argue the proper object – the *matter* – of psychoanalytic knowledge is not *matter* itself. The object of psychoanalytic inquiry – the *matter* not of *science*, but of "our science" – is interiority...*Science* is not a threat to psychoanalysis because *science restricts its objects and methods; it makes no assertions about what lies outside its scope.* Scientism, by contrast, is a threat. Not because it has intellectual power, but because it has captured the contemporary imagination, generating arguments with little content that are nevertheless loudly expressed. (pp. 5–7)

Notes

1 Referring to Freud (1917): "After all, [the patient's] conflicts will only be successfully solved and his resistances overcome if the anticipatory ideas he is given tally with what is real in him. Whatever in the doctor's conjectures is inaccurate drops out in the course of the analysis; it has to be withdrawn and replaced by something more correct" (p. 452).
2 With Grünbaum willingly assuming this is how most analytic patients improve.
3 It is beyond the scope of this chapter to explicate the way in which effect size is measured.
4 Other studies of psychoanalysis proper include Brockmann et al. (2001), Dührssen and Jorswieck (1965), Heinzel et al. (1998), Rudolf et al. (1994), and Sandell et al. (1999, 2001).

References

Abbass, A., Kisely, S., & Kroenke, K. (2006). Short-term psychodynamic psychotherapy for somatic disorders: Systematic review and meta-analysis of clinical trials. *Psychother. Psychosom.*, *78*, 265–274.

Ablon, S. (2004). Research: An open door review of outcome studies in psychoanalysis (2nd ed.). *J. Am. Psychoanal. Assoc.*, *52*, 605–609.

Abram, J. (2008). Donald Woods Winnicott (1896–1971): A brief introduction. *Int. J. Psychoanal.*, *89*, 1189–1217.

Aguillaume, R. (2001). Epistemology and psychoanalysis. *International Forum for Psychoanalysis*, *10*, 97–101.

Ahumada, J. (1997). Toward an epistemology of clinical psychoanalysis. *J. Am. Psychoanal. Assoc.*, *45*, 507–530.

Ahumada, J. (2001). *The Logics of the Mind: A Clinical View*. London: Karnac.

Ainsworth, M. (1969). Object relations, dependency and attachment: A theoretical review of the infant-mother relationship. *Child Dev.*, *40*, 969–1025.

Alexander, J., Carr, M., & Schwanenflugel, P. (1995). Development of metacognition in gifted children: Directions for future research. *Dev. Rev.*, *15*, 1–37.

Anderson, E., & Lambert, M. (1995). Short-term dynamically oriented psychotherapy: A review and meta-analysis. *Clin. Psychol. Rev.*, *15*, 503–514.

Angier, N. (2015). *Shrinks*, by Jeffrey A. Lieberman with Ogi Ogas [book review]. *New York Times*, p. BR17. March 26, 2015.

Appelbaum, S. (1973). Psychological-mindedness: Word, concept and essence. *Int. J. Psychoanal.*, *54*, 35–46.

Arlow, J. A. (1987). The dynamics of interpretation. *Psychoanal. Q.*, *56*, 68–87.

Arlow, J. A. (1993). Training for psychoanalysis and psychotherapy. *Psychodynamic Review*, *80*, 183–197.

Arlow, J. & Brenner, C. (1990). The psychoanalytic process. *Psychoanal. Q.*, 59, 678–692.

Aron, L. & Benjamin, J. (1999). The development of intersubjectivity and the struggle to think. Presented at Meeting of Division 39 of Psychoanalysis, American Psychological Association, April 17, 1999, New York City, NY.

Aron, L. (1990). One-person and two-person psychologies and the method of psychoanalysis. *Psychoanalytic Psychology*, *7*, 475–485.

Aron, L. (1995). The internalized primal scene. *Psychoanalytic Dialogues*, *5*, 195–237.

Aron, L. (1996). *A Meeting of Minds: Mutuality in Psychoanalysis*. Hillsdale, NJ: Analytic Press.

Aron, L. (2000). Self-reflexivity and the therapeutic action of psychoanalysis. *Psychoanal. Q.*, *17*, 667–689.
Aron, L. (2006). Analytic impasse and the third: Clinical implications of intersubjectivity theory. *Int. J. Psychoanal.*, *87*, 349–368.
Astor, J. (1998). Some Jungian and Freudian perspectives on the Oedipus myth and beyond. *Int. J. Psychoanal.*, *79*, 697–712.
Atwood, G. & Stolorow, R. (1984). *Structures of Subjectivity: Explorations in Psychoanalytic Phenomenology*. Hillsdale, NJ: The Analytic Press.
Bacal, H. (1985). Optimal responsiveness and the therapeutic process. In *Progress in Self Psychology*, ed. A. Goldberg. New York, NY: Guilford, pp. 202–227.
Bacal, H. (1995). The essence of Kohut's work and the progress of self psychology. *Psychoanalytic Dialogues*, *5*, 353–366.
Bach, S. (1985). *Narcissistic States and the Therapeutic Process*. New York, NY: Jason Aronson.
Bach, S. (1994). *The Language of Perversion and the Language of Love*. Northvale, NJ: Jason Aronson.
Balint, E. (1993). On being empty of oneself. In *Before I was I: Psychoanalysis and the imagination*. New York, NY: Guildford Press, pp. 470–480.
Balint, M. (1948). On the psychoanalytic training system. *Int. J. Psychoanal.*, *29*, 163–173.
Bargh, J. & Chartrand, T. (1999). The unbearable automaticity of being. *Am. Psychol.*, *54*, 462–479.
Barry, V. & Fisher, C. (2014). Research on the relation of psychoanalysis and neuroscience: Clinical meaning and empirical science. *J. Am. Psychoanal. Assoc.*, *62*, 1087–1096.
Basch, M. (1974). Interference with perceptual transformation in the service of defense. *Ann. Psychoanal.*, *2*, 87–97.
Basch, M. (1983). Empathic understanding: A review of the concept and some theoretical considerations. *J. Am. Psychoanal. Assoc.*, *31*, 101–126.
Basch, M. (1988). *Understanding Psychotherapy*. New York, NY: Basic Books.
Bass. A. (1997). The problem of "concreteness". *Psychoanal. Q.*, *66*, 642–682.
Bass, A. (2003). "E" enactments in psychoanalysis. *Psychoanalytic Dialogues*, *13*, 657–675.
Bateman, A. & Fonagy, P. (2004). *Psychotherapy for Borderline Personality Disorder: Mentalization-based Treatment*. Oxford: Oxford University Press.
Baudry, F. (1993). The personal dimension and management of the supervisory situation with a special note on the parallel process. *Psychoanal. Q.*, 62, 588–614.
Becklen, R. & Cervone, D. (1983). Selective looking and the noticing of unexpected events. *Memory & Cognition*, *11*, 601–608.
Benjamin, J. (1988). *The Bonds of Love*. New York, NY: Pantheon Books.
Benjamin, J. (1992). Recognition and destruction: An outline of intersubjectivity. In *Relational Perspectives in Psychoanalysis*, eds. N. J. Skolnick & S. C. Warshaw. Hillsdale, NJ: The Analytic Press, pp. 43–60.
Benjamin, J. (1995). *Like Subjects, Love Objects: Essays on Recognition and Sexual Difference*. New Haven, CT: Yale University Press.
Benjamin, J. (2004). Beyond doer and done to: An intersubjective view of thirdness. *Psychoanal. Q.*, *1*, 5–46.
Beres, D. & Arlow, J. (1974). Fantasy and identification in empathy. *Psychoanal. Q.*, *43*, 26–50.

Berger, L. (1995). Grünbaum's questionable interpretation of inanimate systems. *Psychoanalytic Psychology, 12*, 439–449.
Berlin, H. (2011). The neural basis of the dynamic unconscious. *Neuropsychoanalysis, 13*, 5–31.
Berman, E. (2000). Psychoanalytic supervision: The intersubjective development. *Int. J. Psychoanal. 81*, 273–90.
Bion, W. R. (1977). *Two Papers: The Grid and the Caesura*. London: Karnac.
Bion, W. R. (1957). Differentiation of the psychotic from the non psychotic personalities. *Int. J. Psycho-Anal., 38*, 3–4.
Bion, W. R. (1959). Attacks on linking. *Int. J. Psychoanal., 40*, 308–315.
Bion, W. R. (1962). *Learning from Experience*. London: Heinemann.
Bion, W. R. (1962). The psycho-analytic study of thinking. *Int. J. Psychoanal., 43*, 306–310.
Bion, W. R. (1963). *Elements of Psychoanalysis*. London: Karnac Books.
Bion, W. R. (1967a). Notes on memory and desire. *Psychoanalytic Forum, 2*, 271–286.
Bion, W. R. (1967b). *Second Thoughts*. New York, NY: Jason Aronson.
Bion, W. R. (1979). Making the best of a bad job. In *Clinical Seminars and Four Papers*, ed. F. Bion. Abingdon: Fleetwood Press, pp. 247–257.
Bion, W. R. (2011). *Clinical Seminars and Other Works*. London: Karnac Books Ltd.
Blagys, M. & Hilsenroth, M. (2000). Distinctive features of short-term psychodynamic interpersonal psychotherapy: A review of the comparative process literature. *Clinical Psychology, 7*, 167–188.
Blight, J. (1981). Must psychoanalysis retreat to hermeneutics? *Psychoanalysis & Contemporary Thought, 4*, 147–205.
Blitzsten, L. & Fleming, J. (1953). What is supervisory analysis? *Bull. Menninger Clin., 17*, 117–129.
Bloom, H. (1996). *Omens of Millennium*. New York, NY: Riverhead Books.
Boesky, D. (1990). The psychoanalytic process and its components. *Psychoanal. Q., 59*, 550–584.
Boesky, D. (1990). The psychodynamic process and its components. *Psychoanal. Q., 59*, 550–584.
Bohleber, W., Fonagy, P., Jiménez, J. P., Scarfone, D., Varvin, S., & Zysman, S. (2013). Towards a better use of psychoanalytic concepts: A model illustrated using the concept of enactment. *Int. J. Psychoanal., 94*, 501–530.
Bowlby, J. (1969). *Attachment and Loss, Volume 1: Attachment*. London: Hogarth Press.
Bowlby, J. (1988a). Developmental psychology comes of age. *Am. J. Psychiatry, 145*, 1–10.
Brakel, L. (2007). The placebo effect: Can psychoanalytic theory help explain the phenomenon? *American Imago, 64*, 273–281.
Bretherton, I. & Waters, E. (eds.) (1985). *Growing Points in Attachment Theory and Research*. Chicago, IL: University of Chicago Press.
Breuer, J. & Freud, S. (1895). *Studies on Hysteria* (J. Strachey, ed. & trans.). London: Hogarth Press.
Britton, R. (1989). The missing link: Parental sexuality in the Oedipus complex. In *The Oedipus Complex Today: Clinical Implications*, eds. R. Britton, M. Feldman, E. O'Shaughnessy, & J. Steiner. London: Karnac, pp. 83–102.
Britton, R. (1998). *Belief and Imagination: Explorations in Psychoanalysis*. London: Routledge.

Britton, R. (2004). Subjectivity, objectivity, and triangular space. *Psychoanal. Q.*, *73*, 47–61.

Britton, R. & Steiner, J. (1994). Interpretation: Selected fact or overvalued idea? *Int. J. Psychoanal.*, *75*, 1069–1078.

Britton, R., Chused, J., Ellman, S., & Likierman, M. (2006). Panel I: Contemporary views on stages versus positions. *Journal of Infant, Child, and Adolescent Psychotherapy*, *5*, 268–281.

Brockmann, J., Schlüter, T., & Eckert, J. (2001). The Frankfurt–Hamburg study of psychotherapy – Results of the study of psychoanalytically oriented and behavioural long-term therapy. In *Long-term Psychotherapy: Perspectives for Therapists and Researchers*. Stuttgart: Kohlhammer, pp. 271–276.

Bromberg, P. (1998). *Standing in the Spaces: Essays on Clinical Process, Trauma, and Dissociation*. Hillsdale, NJ: Analytic Press.

Bromberg, P. (2003). One need not be a house to be haunted: On enactment, dissociation, and the dread of "not-me" – A case study. *Psychoanalytic Dialogues*, *13*, 689–709.

Bromberg, P. (2011). *The Shadow of the Tsunami and the Growth of the Relational Mind*. New York, NY: Routledge.

Bronstein, C. (2004). On free association and psychic reality. *Br. J. Psychiatry*, *18*, 477–489.

Brown, L. & Miller, M. (2002). The triadic intersubjective matrix in supervision: The use of disclosure to work through painful affects. *Int. J. Psychoanal.*, *83*, 811–823.

Brown, J., Donelan-McCall, N., & Dunn, J. (1986). Why talk about mental states? The significance of children's conversations with friends, siblings and mothers. *Child Dev.*, *67*, 836–849.

Brown, M.W. (1942). *Runaway Bunny*. New York, NY: Harper.

Brunell, C. (1999). How accurate is Grünbaum's reading of Freud? *Psychoanalysis & Contemporary Thought*, *22*, 85–110.

Buie, D. (1981). Empathy: Its nature and limitations. *J. Am. Psychoanal. Assoc.*, *29*, 281–307.

Busch, F. (1994). Some ambiguities in the method of free association and their implications for technique. *J. Am. Psychoanal. Assoc.*, *42*, 363–384.

Busch, F. (1995). *The Ego at the Center of Clinical Technique*. Northvale, NJ: Jason Aronson.

Busch, F. (1996). The ego and its significance in analytic interventions. *J. Am. Psychoanal. Assoc.*, *44*, 1073–1099.

Busch, F. (1997). Understanding the patient's use of the method of free association: An ego psychological approach. *J. Am. Psychoanal. Assoc.*, *45*, 407–423.

Busch, F. (1999). *Rethinking Clinical Technique*. Northvale, NJ: Jason Aronson.

Busch, F. (2009). "Can you push a camel through the eye of a needle?" Reflections on how the unconscious speaks to us and its clinical implications. *Int. J. Psychoanal.*, *90*, 53–68.

Cabaniss, D, Glick, R., & Roose, S. (2001). The Columbia Supervision Project: Data from the dyad. *J. Am. Psychoanal. Assoc.*, *49*, 235–267.

Cabaniss, D., Cherry, S., Douglas, C., & Schwartz, A. (2011). *Psychodynamic Psychotherapy: A Clinical Manual*. Oxford: Wiley-Blackwell.

Caligor, L. (1981). Parallel and reciprocal processes in psychoanalytic supervisor. *Contemporary Psychoanalysis*, *17*, 1–27.

Caper, R. (1997). A mind of one's own. *Int. J. Psychoanal.*, *78*, 265–278.

Carpy, D. (1989). Tolerating the countertransference: A mutative process. *Int. J. Psychoanal.*, *70*, 287–294.

Cassorla, R. (2012). What happens before and after acute enactments? An exercise in clinical validation and the broadening of hypothesis. *Int. J. Psychoanal.*, *93*, 53–80.

Cavell, M. (1988). Interpretation, psychoanalysis, and the philosophy of mind. *J. Am. Psychoanal. Assoc.*, *36*, 859–879.

Cavell, M. (1988). Interpretation, psychoanalysis, and the philosophy of mind. *J. Am. Psychoanal. Assoc.*, *36*, 859–879.

Celani, D. (2010). *Fairbairn's Object Relations Theory in the Clinical Setting*. New York, NY: Columbia University Press.

Chabris, C. & Simons, D. (2010). *The Invisible Gorilla: And Other Ways Our Intuitions Deceive Us*. New York, NY: Crown Books.

Chambless, D. & Hollon, S. (1998). Defining empirically supported therapies. *J. Consult. Clin. Psychol.*, *66*, 7–18.

Chandler, M. (1988). Doubt and developing theories of the mind. In *Developing Theories of Mind*, eds. J. W. Astington, P. L. Harris, & D. R. Olson. New York, NY: Cambridge University Press, pp. 387–413.

Chessick, R. (1999). Contingency and the unformulated countertransference: A case presentation. *J. Am. Psychoanal. Assoc.*, *27*, 135–149.

Chmiliar, L. (1997). Metacognition and giftedness. *Agate*, *11*, 28–34.

Chused, J. (1991). The evocative power of enactments. *J. Am. Psychoanal. Assoc.*, *39*, 615–639.

Chused, J. (1996). The therapeutic action of psychoanalysis: Abstinence and informative experiences. *J. Am. Psychoanal. Assoc.*, *44*, 1047–1071.

Chused, J. (2003). The role of enactments. *Psychoanalytic Dialogues*, *13*, 677–687.

Clarkin, J., Levy, K., Lenzenweger, M., & Kernberg, O. (2007). Evaluating three treatments for borderline personality disorder: A multiwave study. *Am. J. Psychiatry*, *164*, 922–928.

Coburn, W. (2001). Subjectivity, emotional resonance, and the sense of the real. *Psychoanal. Psychol.*, *18*, 303–319.

Cohen, J. (1988). *Statistical Power Analysis for the Behavioral Sciences* (2nd ed.). Hillsdale, NJ: Lawrence Erlbaum Associates.

Coltart, N. (1988). The assessment of psychological-mindedness in the diagnostic interview. *Br. J. Psychiatry*, *153*, 819–820.

Crits-Christoph, P. (1992). The efficacy of brief dynamic psychotherapy: A meta-analysis. *Am. J. Psychiatry*, *149*, 151–158.

Crits-Christoph, P., Cooper, A., & Luborsky, L. (1988). The accuracy of therapists' interpretations and the outcome of dynamic psychotherapy. *J. Consult. Clin. Psychol.*, *56*, 490–495.

Custers, R. & Aarts, H. (2010). The unconscious will: How the pursuit of goals operates outside of conscious awareness. *Science*, *239*, 47–50.

Davies, J. (1999). Getting cold feet, defining "safe-enough" borders: Dissociation, multiplicity, and integration in the analyst's experience. *Psychoanal. Q.*, *68*, 184–208.

de Maat, S., de Johghe, F., Schoevers, R., & Dekker, J. (2009). The effectiveness of long-term psychoanalytic therapy: A systematic review of empirical studies. *Harv. Rev. Psychiatry*, *17*, 1–23.

DeBell, D. (1981). Supervisory styles and positions. In *Becoming a Psychoanalyst: A Study of Psychoanalytic Supervision*, ed. R. S. Wallerstein. New York, NY: International Universities Press, pp. 39–60.
Dennett, D. (1978). Beliefs about beliefs. *Behavioral and Brain Sciences*, *1*, 568–570.
Deutsch, H. (1942). Some forms of emotional disturbance and their relationship to schizophrenia *Psychoanal. Q.*, *11*, 301–321.
Diamond, D., Yeomans, F., Stern, B., Levy, K., Horz, S., Doering, S., Fisch-Kern, M., Delaney, J., & Clarkin, J. (2013). Transference focused psychotherapy for patients with comorbid narcissistic and borderline personality disorder. *Psychoanalytic Inquiry*, *33*, 527–551.
Diamond, M. (2014). Analytic mind use and interpsychic communication: Driving force in analytic technique, pathway to unconscious mental life. *Psychoanal. Q.*, *83*, 525–563.
Dijksterhuis, A. & Aarts, H. (2010). Goals, attention, and (un)consciousness. *Ann. Rev. Psychol.*, *61*, 467–490.
Dijksterhuis, A. & Nordgren, L. (2006). A theory of unconscious thought. *Perspectives on Psychological Science*, *1*, 95–109.
Doehrman, M. (1976). Parallel process in supervision and psychotherapy. *Bull. Menninger Clin.*, *40*, 1–104.
Donnet, J.-L. (2009). *Precious Ambiguities: The Analyzing Situation* (A. Weller, trans.). London: Karnac.
Dover, A. & Shore, B. (1991). Giftedness and flexibility on a mathematical set-breaking task. *Gifted Child Quarterly*, *35*, 99–107.
Dührssen, A. & Jorswieck, E. (1965). Eine empirisch-statistische Untersuchung zur Leistungsfähigkeit psychoanalytischer Behandlung [An empirical-statistical study of the effectiveness of psychoanalytic treatment]. *Nervenarzt*, *36*, 166–169.
Eagle, M. (2003). Clinical implications of attachment theory. *Psychoanalytic Inquiry*, *23*, 27–53.
Eckstein, R. & Wallerstein, R. (1958). *The Teaching and Learning of Psychotherapy*. New York, NY: International Universities Press.
Edelman, G. (1987). *Neural Darwinism: The Theory of Neuronal Group Selection*. New York, NY: Basic Books.
Ehrenberg, D. (1982). Psychodynamic engagement: The transaction as primary data. *Contemporary Psychoanalysis*, *18*, 535–555.
Ehrenberg, D. (1992). *The Intimate Edge*. New York, NY: Norton.
Ehrenberg, D. (1996). On the analyst's emotional availability and vulnerability. *Contemporary Psychoanalysis*, *32*, 275–286.
Eitingon, M. (1926). Preliminary discussion of the question of analytic training 1925. *Int. J. Psycho-Anal.*, *7*, 129–135.
Elliott, A. & Spezzano, C. (1996). Psychoanalysis at its limits: Navigating the post-modern turn. *Psychoanal. Q.*, 65, 52–83.
Ellman, S. (2010). *When Theories Touch: A Historical and Theoretical Integration of Psychoanalytic Thought*. London: Karnac.
Elms, A. (2001). Apocryphal Freud: Sigmund Freud's most famous "quotations" and their actual sources. *Ann. Psychoanal.*, *29*, 83–104.
Epstein, M. (1990). Beyond the oceanic feeling: Psychoanalytic study of Buddhist meditation. *International Review of Psychoanalysis*, *17*, 159–165.

Epstein, M. (1995). Thoughts without a Thinker: Psychotherapy from a Buddhist Perspective. New York, NY: Basic Books.

Eriksson, J. (2010). The epistemological status of the case history and the play-character of clinical psychoanalysis. *Scandinavian Psychoanalytic Review*, *33*, 40–46.

Etchegoyen, R. (1991). *Fundamentals of Psychoanalytic Technique*. London: Karnac.

Fabozzi, P. (2012). A silent yet radical future revolution: Winnicott's innovative perspective. *Psychoanal. Q.*, *81*, 601–626.

Faimberg, H. (1992). The countertransference position and the countertransference. *Int. J. Psychoanal.*, *73*, 541–546.

Fairbairn, W. R. D. (1944). Endopsychic structure considered in terms of object-relationships. In *Psychoanalytic Studies of the Personality*. London: Tavistock, pp. 82–132.

Fairbairn, W. R. D. (1952a). Schizoid factors in the personality. In *Psychoanalytic Studies of the Personality*. London: Routledge & Kegan Paul, pp. 3–27.

Fairbairn, W. R. D. (1952b). A revised psychopathology of the psychoses and psychoneuroses. In *Psychoanalytic Studies of the Personality*. London: Routledge & Kegan Paul, pp. 28–58.

Fairbairn, W. R. D. (1952c). The repression and the return of bad objects (with special reference to the "war neuroses"). In *Psychoanalytic Studies of the Personality*. London: Routledge & Kegan, pp. 59–81.

Fairbairn, W. R. D. (1952d). Endopsychic structure considered in terms of object-relationships. In *Psychoanalytic Studies of the Personality*. London: Routledge & Kegan Paul, pp. 82–132.

Fairbairn, W. R. D. (1958). On the nature and aims of psychoanalytical treatment. *Int. J. Psychoanal.*, *39*, 374–385.

Farber, B. (1985). The genesis, development and implications of psychological-mindedness in psychotherapies. *Psychotherapy*, *22*, 170–477.

Feldman, M. (1997). Projective identification: The analyst's involvement. *Int. J. Psycho-Anal.*, *78*, 227–241.

Feldman, M. (2004). Supporting psychic change: Betty Joseph. In *In Pursuit of Psychic Change*, eds. E. Hargreaves & A. Varchevker. New York, NY: Brunner-Routledge, pp. 20–36.

Fellow, J. & Altman, R. (2001). *Gosford Park* (a movie).

Fenichel, O. (1945). *The Psychoanalytic Theory of Neurosis*. New York, NY: W. W. Norton.

Feyman, R. (1995). *Six Easy Pieces*. Reading, MA: Addison Wesley Publishing Co.

Fine, S. & Fine, E. (1990). Four psychoanalytic perspectives: A study of differences in interpretive interventions. *J. Am. Psychoanal. Assoc.*, *38*, 1017–1048.

Fink, B. (1997). *A Clinical Introduction to Lacanian Psychoanalysis: Theory and Technique*. Cambridge, MA: Harvard University Press.

Fink, B. (2007). *Fundamentals of Psychoanalytic Technique*. New York, NY: Norton.

Fink, B. (2014). *Against Meaning: Commentary and Critique in a Lacanian Key*. London: Routledge.

Fisher, C. (2003). The logics of the mind: A clinical view [book review]. *J. Am. Psychoanal. Assoc.*, *51*, 323–330.

Flavell, J. (1979). Metacognition and cognitive monitoring. A new area of cognitive developmental inquiry. *Am. Psychol.*, *34*(10), 906–911.

Flavell, J. (1988). The development of children's knowledge about the mind: From cognitive connections to mental representations. In *Developing Theories of Mind*, eds.

J. W. Astington, P. L. Harris, & D. R. Olson. New York, NY: Cambridge University Press, pp. 244–267.

Fleming, J. & Benedek, T. (1966). *Psychoanalytic Supervision*. New York, NY: Grune & Stratton.

Fonagy, A., Roth, A., & Higgitt, A. (2005) Psychodynamic psychotherapies: Evidence-based practice and clinical wisdom. *Bull. Menninger Clin.*, *69*, 1–58.

Fonagy, P., Redfern, S., & Charman, T. (1997). The relationship between belief-desire reasoning and a projective measure of attachment security (SAT). *Br. J. Dev. Psychol.*, *15*, 51–61.

Fonagy, P. & Target, M. (1998). Mentalization and the changing aims of child psychoanalysis. *Psychoanalytic Dialogues*, *8*, 87–114.

Fonagy, P. (1991). Thinking about thinking: Some clinical and theoretical considerations in the treatment of a borderline patient. *Int. J. Psychoanal.*, 72, 639–656.

Fonagy, P. (2008). The mentalization-focused approach to social development. In *Mentalization: Theoretical Considerations, Research Findings, and Clinical Implications*, ed. F. N. Busch. New York, NY: The Analytic Press, pp. 3–56.

Fonagy, P., Steele, M., Steele, H., Leigh, T., Kennedy, R., Mattoon, G., & Target, M. (1995). Attachment, the reflective self, and borderline states: The predictive specificity of the Adult Attachment Interview and pathological development. In *Attachment Theory*, eds. S. Goldberg, R. Muir, & J. Kerr. Hillsdale, NJ: The Analytic Press, pp. 233–278.

Fonagy, P., Steele, M., Steele, H., Moran, G. S., & Higgitt, A. C. (1991). The capacity for understanding mental states: The reflective self in parent and child and its significance for security of attachment. *Infant Mental Health Journal*, *12*, 201–218.

Fonagy, P., Gergely, G., Jurist, E., & Target, M. (2002). *Affect Regulation, Mentalisation, and the Development of the Self*. New York, NY: Other Press.

Fonagy, P., Kächele, H., Krause, R., Jones, E., & Perron, R. (1999). *An Open Door Review of Outcome Studies in Psychoanalysis*. London: International Psychoanalytical Association.

Forguson, L. & Gopnik, A. (1988). The ontogeny of common sense. In *Developing Theories of Mind*, eds. J. W. Astington, P. L. Harris, & D. R. Olson. New York, NY: Cambridge University Press, pp. 226–243.

Fourcher, L. (1996). The authority of logic and the logic of authority: The import of the Grünbaum debate for psychoanalytically informed psychotherapy. *Psychoanalytic Dialogues*, *6*, 515–532.

Freud, A. (1936). *The Ego and the Mechanisms of Defense*. New York, NY: International Universities Press.

Freud, S. (1900). *The Interpretation of Dreams* (J. Strachey, ed. & trans.). London: Hogarth Press.

Freud, S. (1912). *Recommendations to Physicians Practicing Psycho-analysis* (J. Strachey, ed. & trans.). London: Hogarth Press.

Freud, S. (1913). *On Beginning the Treatment* (J. Strachey, ed. & trans.). London: Hogarth Press.

Freud, S. (1914). *Remembering, Repeating and Working-through* (J. Strachey, ed. & trans.). London: Hogarth Press.

Freud, S. (1915). *The Unconscious* (J. Strachey, ed. & trans.). London: Hogarth Press.

Freud, S. (1916). *Some Character-types Met With in Psycho-analytic Work: Those Wrecked by Success* (J. Strachey, ed. & trans.). London: Hogarth Press.

Freud, S. (1917). *Introductory Lectures on Psycho-analysis* (J. Strachey, ed. & trans.). London: Hogarth Press.

Freud, S. (1918). From the history of an infantile neurosis. In *The Standard Edition of the Complete Psychological Works of Sigmund Freud, Volume XVII (1917–1919): An Infantile Neurosis and Other Works*, pp. 1–124.

Freud, S. (1925). *Negation* (J. Strachey, ed. & trans.). London: Hogarth Press.

Freud, S. (1926). *Inhibitions, Symptoms and Anxiety* (J. Strachey, ed. & trans.). London: Hogarth Press.

Freud, S. (1930). Civilization and its discontents. In *Standard Edition, 21*. London: Hogarth Press, pp. 64–145.

Freud, S. (1933). *New Introductory Lectures on Psycho-analysis. Recommendations to Physicians Practising Psycho-analysis* (J. Strachey, ed. & trans.). London: Hogarth Press.

Freud, S. (1937). *Constructions in Analysis* (J. Strachey, ed. & trans.). London: Hogarth Press.

Freud, S. (1938). *Some Elementary Lessons in Psycho-analysis* (J. Strachey, ed. & trans.). London: Hogarth Press.

Freud, S. (1940). An outline of psycho-analysis. *Int. J. Psychoanal.*, *21*, 27–84.

Freud, S. (1953). The interpretation of dreams. In *The Standard Edition of the Complete Psychological Works of Sigmund Freud (Volumes 4 and 5)* (J. Strachey, ed. & trans.). London: Hogarth Press.

Friedman, H. (2000). A discussion of the presented paper: "Challenges to the analyst's authority to interpret," (Richard Tuch). Presented at the Spring Meeting of the American Psychoanalytic Association, May 2000, Chicago, IL.

Friedman, L. (1988). *The Anatomy of Psychotherapy*. Hillsdale, NJ: Analytic Press.

Friedman, L. (1997). Ferrum, ignis, and medicina: Return to the crucible. *J. Am. Psychoanal. Assoc.*, *45*, 20–36.

Friedman, L. (1999). Why reality is a troubling concept. *J. Am. Psychoanal. Assoc.*, *47*, 401–425.

Friedman, L. (2002). Symbolizing as abstraction: Its role in psychoanalytic treatment. In *Symbolization and Desymbolization: Essays in Honor of Norbert Freedman*, ed. R. Lasky. New York, NY: Other Press, pp. 204–330.

Fromm-Reichmann, F. (1950). *Principles of Intensive Psychotherapy*. Chicago, IL: University of Chicago Press.

Gabbard, G. (1995). Countertransference: The emerging common ground. *Int. J. Psychoanal.*, *76*, 475–486.

Gabbard, G. (1997). A reconsideration of objectivity in the analyst. *Int. J. Psycho-Anal.*, *78*, 15–26.

Gabbard, G. (2007). "Bound in a nutshell": Thoughts on complexity, reductionism, and "infinite space." *Int. J. Psycho-Anal.*, *88*, 559–574.

Gabbard, G. (2010). *Long-term Psychodynamic Psychotherapy*. Arlington, VA: American Psychiatric Publishing.

Gabbard, G. & Westin, D. (2003). Rethinking therapeutic action. *Int. J. Psycho-Anal.*, *84*, 823–841.

Gerber, A., Kocsis, J., Milrod, B., Roose, S., Barber, J., Thase, M., Perkins, P., & Leon, A. (2011). A quality-based review of randomized controlled trials of psychodynamic psychotherapy. *Am. J. Psychiatry*, *168*, 19–28.

Gergely, G. & Watson, J. (1996). The social biofeedback theory of parental affect-mirroring: The development of emotional self-awareness and self-control in infancy. *Int. J. Psycho-Anal.*, *77*, 1181–1212.

Gill, M. (1979). The analysis of the transference. *J. Am. Psychoanal. Assoc.*, *27*, 263–288.
Gill, M. (1954). Psychoanalysis and exploratory psychotherapy. *J. Am. Psychoanal. Assoc.*, *2*, 771–797.
Glover, E. (1931). The therapeutic effect of inexact interpretation. *Int. J. Psycho-Anal.*, *12*, 397–411.
Gonzalez, F. J. (2013). Movement requires nothing: Commentary on Paper by Becker and Shalgi. *Psychoanalytic Dialogues*, *23*, 439–444.
Gray, P. (1973). Psychoanalytic technique and the ego's capacity for viewing intrapsychic conflict. *J. Am. Psychoanal. Assoc.*, *21*, 474–494.
Gray, P. (1982). "Developmental lag" in the evaluation of technique for psychoanalysis of neurotic conflict. *J. Am. Psychoanal. Assoc.*, *30*, 621–655.
Gray, P. (1986). On helping analysands observe intrapsychic activity. In *Psychoanalysis, the Science of Mental Conflict: Essays in Honor of Charles Brenner*, eds. A. D. Richards & M. S. Willick. Hillsdale, NJ: Analytic Press, pp. 245–262.
Gray, P. (1994). *The Ego and Analysis of Defense*. Northvale, NJ: Jason Aronson.
Green, A. (2000). The central phobic position. *Int. J. Psycho-Anal.*, *81*, 429–451.
Greenberg, J., & Mitchell, S. (1983). *Object Relations in Psychoanalytic Theory*. Cambridge, MA: Harvard University Press.
Greenson, R. (1960). Empathy and its vicissitudes. *Int. J. Psycho-Anal.*, *41*, 418–424.
Greenson, R. (1967). *The Technique and Practice of Psychoanalysis*. New York, NY: International Universities Press.
Greenspoon, J. (1955). The reinforcing effect of two spoken sounds on the frequency of two responses. *Am. J. Psychology*, *68*, 409–416.
Grossberg, S. (1999). The link between brain learning, attention, and consciousness. *Conscious. Cogn.*, *8*, 1–44.
Grossman, L. (1996). "Psychic reality" and reality testing in the analysis of perverse defenses. *Int. J. Psycho-Anal.*, *77*, 509–517.
Grotstein, J. (1984). Some perspectives on empathy from others and toward oneself. In *Empathy I*, pp. 201–215.
Grotstein, J. & Franey, M. (2008). Conversations with clinicians. *Fort Da*, *14*, 87–116.
Grünbaum, A. (1977). How scientific is psychoanalysis? In *Science and Psychotherapy*, eds. R. Stern, L. Horowitz, & J. Lynes. New York, NY: Haven Press, pp. 219–254.
Grünbaum, A. (1981). The placebo concept. *Behav. Res. Ther.*, *19*, 157–167.
Grünbaum, A. (1984). *The Foundations of Psychoanalysis*. Berkeley, CA: University of California Press.
Grünbaum, A. (1993). *Validation in the Clinical Theory of Psychoanalysis*. New York, NY: International Universities Press.
Grünbaum, A. (2006). Is Sigmund Freud's psychoanalytic edifice relevant to the 21st century? *Psychoanalytic Psychology*, *23*, 257–284.
Grünbaum. A. (1976). Is falsifiability the touchstone of scientific rationality? Karl Popper versus inductivism. In *Essays in Memory of Imre Lakatos*, eds. R. S. Cohen, P. K. Feyerabend, & M. W. Wartofsky. Dordrecht: D. Reidel, pp. 215–229.
Gunderson, J. & Gabbard, G. O. (1999). Making the case for psychodynamic therapies. *J. Am. Psychoanal. Assoc.*, *47*, 679–704.
Habermas, J. (1972). *Knowledge and Human Interests*. Boston, MA: Beacon Press.
Halford, G., Baker, R., McCredden, J., & Bain, J. (2005). How many variables can humans process? *Psychol. Sci.*, *16*, 70–76.

Hansell, J. (2008). Psychoanalytic aims and attitudes. *Psychoanal. Q.*, *77*, 1179–1192.

Hartmann, H., Kris, E., & Loewenstein, R. (1946). Comments on the formation of psychic structure. *Psychoanal. Study Child*, *2*, 11–38.

Hartmann, H., Kris, E., & Loewenstein, R. (1949). Notes on the theory of aggression. *Psychoanal. Study Child*, *3/4*, 9–36.

Heimann, P. (1950). On countertransference. *Int. J. Psycho-Anal.*, *31*, 81–84.

Heinzel, R., Breyer, F., & Klein, T. (1998). Ambulante analytische Einzel-und Gruppenpsychotherapie in einer bundesweiten katamnestischen Evaluationsstudie. [Outpatient individual and group psychoanalytic therapy in a Germany-wide follow-up study]. *Gruppenpsychotherapie und Gruppendynamik*, *334*, 135–152.

Herzog, J. (2001). *Father Hunger: Explorations with Adults and Children*. Hillsdale, NJ: Analytic Press.

Hesse, E. & Main, M. (1999). Second-generation effects of unresolved trauma in non-maltreating parents: Dissociated, frightened, and threatening parental behavior. *Psychoanalytic Inquiry*, *19*, 481–540.

Hirsch, I. (1998). The concept of enactment and theoretical convergence. *Psychoanal. Q.*, *67*, 78–101.

Hoffer, A. & Youngren, V. R. (2004). Is free association still at the core of psychoanalysis? *Int. J. Psycho-Anal.*, *85*, 1489–1492.

Hoffman, I. (1983). The patient as interpreter of the analyst's experience. *Contemporary Psychoanalysis 19*, 389–422.

Hoffman, I. (1992). Some practical implications of a social constructivist view of the psychoanalytic situation. *Psychoanalytic Dialogues*, *2*, 287–304.

Hoffman, I. (1994). Dialectical thinking and therapeutic action in psychoanalysis. *Psychoanal. Q.*, *63*, 187–218.

Hoffman, I. (1996). The intricate and ironic authority of the psychoanalyst's presence. *Psychoanal. Q.*, *65*, 102–136.

Hoffman, I. (2006). The myths of free association and the potentials of the analytic relationship. *Int. J. Psycho-Anal.*, *87*, 43–61.

Holt, R. (1985). The current status of psychoanalytic theory. *Psychoanalytic Psychology*, *2*, 289–315.

Howard, K., Kopta, S., Krause, M., et al. (1986). The dose–response relationship in psychotherapy. *Am. Psychol.*, *41*, 159–164.

Isaacs, S. (1943). The nature and function of phantasy. In *Developments in Psychoanalysis*, eds. M. Klein, P. Heimann, S. Isaacs, & J. Riviere. London: Hogarth Press, pp. 67–121.

Ivey, G. (2008). Enactment controversies: A critical review of current debates. *Int. J. Psycho-Anal.*, *89*, 19–38.

Jacobs, T. (1986). On countertransference enactments. *J. Am. Psychoanal. Assoc.*, *34*, 289–307.

Jacobs, T. (1991). *The Use of Self: Countertransference and Communication in the Analytic Situation*. Madison, CT: International Universities Press.

Jacobs, T. (1993). The inner experiences of the analyst: Their contribution to the analytic process. *Int. J. Psycho-Anal.*, *74*, 7–14.

Jacobson, E. (1957). Denial and repression. *J. Am. Psychoanal. Assoc.*, *5*, 61–92.

Jaffe, L. (2000). Supervision as an intersubjective process: Hearing from candidates and supervisors. *J. Am. Psychoanal. Assoc.*, *48*, 561–570.

Jorgensen, C. (2004). Active ingredients in individual psychotherapy: Searching for common factors. *Psychoanalytic Psychology*, *21*, 516–540.
Joseph, B. (1985). Transference: The total situation. *Int. J. Psycho-Anal.*, *66*, 447–454.
Joseph, B. (1989). *Psychic Equilibrium and Psychic Change*. London: Tavistock/Routledge.
Joseph, B. (2003). Ethics and enactment. *European Journal of Psychoanalysis*, *57*, 147–153.
Josephs, L. (1989). The world of the concrete: A comparative approach. *Contemporary Psychoanalysis*, *5*, 477–500.
Josephs, L. (1992). The timing of an interpretation: A comparative review of an aspect of the theory of therapeutic technique. *Psychoanal. Rev.*, *79*, 31–54.
Joyce, A. & Piper, W. (1993). The immediate impact of transference in short-term individual psychotherapy. *Am. J. Psychotherapy*, *47*, 508–526.
Jung, C. G. (1906). Psychoanalysis and association experiments. In Collected *Papers on Analytic Psychology* (C. Long, trans.). New York, NY: Kessinger Publishing.
Kernberg, O. (1993). Convergences and divergences in contemporary psychoanalytic technique. *Int. J. Psycho-Anal.*, *74*, 659–673.
Kernberg, O. (1996). The analyst's authority in the psychoanalytic situation. *Psychoanal. Q.*, *65*, 137–157.
Kernberg, O. (1999). Psychoanalysis, psychodynamic psychotherapy and supportive psychotherapy: Contemporary controversies. *Int. J. Psycho-Anal.*, *80*, 1075–1091.
Kernberg, O. (2015). Narcissistic defenses in the distortions of free association and their underlying anxieties. *Psychoanal. Q.*, *84*, 625–642.
Kernberg, O., Yeomans, F., Clarkin, J., & Levy, K. (2008). Transference focused psychotherapy: Overview and update. *Int. J. Psycho-Anal.*, *89*, 601–620.
Killingmo, B. (1989). Conflict and deficit: Implications for technique. *Int. J. Psycho-Anal.*, *70*, 65–79.
Klein, M. (1930). The impact of symbol formation in the development of the ego. *Int. J. Psycho-Anal.*, 11:24–39.
Knight, D. (1986). *The Age of Science: The Scientific World-view in the Nineteenth Century*. Oxford: Basil Blackwell.
Kohut, H. (1959). Introspection, empathy, and psychoanalysis: an examination of the relationship between mode of observation and theory. *J. Am. Psychoanal. Assoc.*, *7*, 459–483.
Kohut, H. (1971). *The Analysis of the Self: A Systematic Approach to the Psychoanalytic Treatment of Narcissistic Personality Disorders*. New York, NY: International Universities Press.
Kohut, H. (1977). *The Restoration of the Self*. New York, NY: International Universities Press.
Kohut, H. (1978). The psychoanalyst in the community of scholars. In *The Search for the Self: Selected Writings of Heinz Kohut, 1950–1978, Volume 2*, ed. P. H. Ornstein. New York, NY: International Universities Press, pp. 685–724.
Kohut, H. (1984a). *How Does Analysis Cure?* Chicago, IL/London: University of Chicago Press.
Kohut, H. (1984b). Introspection, empathy, and the semicircle of mental health. In *Empathy*, Vol*ume* I, ed. J. Lichtenberg, M. Bornstein, & D. Silver. Hillsdale, NJ: Analytic Press, pp. 81–99.

Koller, M. (1992). More from the water jars. Master's thesis. Montreal: McGill University.
Kopta, S., Howard, K., Lowry, J., & Beutler, L. (1994). Patterns of symptomatic recovery in psychotherapy. *J. Consult. Clin. Psychol.*, *62*, 1009–1016.
Kordy, H., von Rad, M., & Senf, W. (1988). Time and its relevance for successful psychotherapy. *Psychotherapy and Psychosomatics*, *49*, 212–222.
Kris, A. (1996). *Free Association: Method and Process*. Hillsdale, NJ: Analytic Press.
Lacan, J. (1949). The mirror stage as formative of the function of the I as revealed in psychodynamic experience. In *Écrits: A Selection* (A. Sheridan, trans.). New York, NY: W. W. Norton & Co., pp. 1–7.
Lacan, J. (1971). Seminar XVIII, January 13, 1971, *Écrits* 106/13 and 588/228; Scilicet 4 (1973) 37; and Scilicet 5 (1975): 16.
Lacan, J. (1975). Discourse on analysis and ego analysis: Anna Freud or Melanie Klein? In *The Seminars of Jacques Lacan: Freud's Writings on Technique*, ed. J.-A. Miller & trans. J. Forrester. Cambridge: Cambridge University Press, pp. 63–70.
Lacan, J. (2001). *Autres* Écrits [Other writings] (J.-A. Miller, ed.). Paris: Seuil.
Lachmann, F. (2003). Supervision: The devil is in the details. *Psychoanalytic Dialogues*, *13*, 341–353.
Langs, R. (1990). *Psychotherapy: A Basic Text*. Northvale, NJ: Jason Aronson.
Leavy, S. (2005). *Questioning Authority: Essays in Psychoanalysis 1970–1996*. New York, NY: Trafford.
Lebovici, S. (1970). Technical remarks on the supervision of psychoanalytic treatment. *Int. J. Psycho-Anal.*, *51*, 385–392.
Lecours, S. (2007). Supportive interventions and nonsymbolic mental functioning. *Int. J. Psycho-Anal.*, *88*, 895–915.
Leichsenring, F. (2001). Comparative effects of short-term psychodynamic psychotherapy and cognitive-behavioral therapy in depression: A meta-analytic approach. *Clin. Psychol. Rev.*, *121*, 401–419.
Leichsenring, F. (2005). Are psychodynamic and psychoanalytic therapies effective? A review of empirical data. *Int. J. Psycho-Anal.*, *86*, 841–868.
Leichsenring, F. & Leibing, E. (2003). The effectiveness of psychodynamic therapy and cognitive behavioral therapy in the treatment of personality disorders: A meta-analysis. *Am. J. Psychiatry*, *160*, 1223–1232.
Leichsenring, F., Biskup, J., Kreische, R., & Staats, H. (2005). The Göttingen study of psychoanalytic therapy: First results. *Int. J. Psycho-Anal.*, *86*, 433–455.
Leichsenring, S. & Rabung, S. (2008). Effectiveness of long-term psychodynamic psychotherapy: A meta-analysis. *J. Am. Med. Assoc.*, *300*, 1551–1565.
Leslie, A. (1988). Some implications of pretense for mechanisms underlying the child's theory of mind. In *Developing Theories of Mind*, eds. J. W. Astington, P. L. Harris, & D. R. Olson. New York, NY: Cambridge University Press, pp. 19–46.
Levenson, E. (1991). *The Purloined Self*. New York, NY: Contemporary Psychoanalysis Books.
Levenson, E. (1992), Follow the fox. *Contemporary Psychoanalysis*, *18*, 1–15.
Levenson, E. (2001). Freud's dilemma. *Contemporary Psychoanalysis*, *37*, 375–390.
Levenson, E. (1972). *The Fallacy of Understanding*. New York, NY: Basic Books.
Levenson, E. (2006). Response to John Steiner. *Int. J. Psycho-Anal.*, *87*, 321–324.
Levey, M. (2006). Questioning authority: Essays in psychoanalysis, 1970–1996. By Stanley A. Leavy [book review]. *J. Am. Psychoanal. Assoc.*, *54*, 1426–1431.

Levine, H. & Friedman, R. (2000). Intersubjectivity and interaction in the analytic relationship: A mainstream view. *Psychoanal. Q.*, *69*, 63–92.

Levy, S., & Inderbitzin, L. (1997). Safety, danger, and the analyst's authority. *J. Am. Psychoanal. Assoc.*, *45*, 377–394.

Lewin, B. (1954). Sleep, narcissistic neurosis, and the analytic situation. *Psychoanal. Q.*, *23*, 487–510.

Lewin, B. (1955). Dream psychology and the analytic situation. *Psychoanal. Q.*, *24*, 169–199.

Lewin, B. & Ross, H. (1960). *Psychoanalytic Education in the United States*. New York, NY: Norton.

Lichtenberg, J. (1999). Discussion. *Psychoanalytic Inquiry*, *19*, 922–937.

Lichtenberg, J., Lachmann, F., & Fosshage, J. (1992). *Self and Motivational Systems: Toward a Theory of Psychoanalytic Technique*. Hillsdale, NJ: Analytic Press.

Lichtenberg, J., Lachmann, F., & Fosshage, J. (1996). *The Clinical Exchange: Techniques Derived from Self and Motivational Systems*. Hillsdale, NJ: Analytic Press.

Lieberman, J. (2015). *Shrinks: The Untold Story of Psychiatry*. New York, NY: Little Brown and Company.

Linehan, M. (1993). *Cognitive-behavioral Treatment of Borderline Personality Disorder*. New York, NY: Guilford Press.

Little, M. (1951). Counter-transference and the patient's response. *Int. J. Psycho-Anal.*, *32*, 32–40.

Loewald, H. (1960). On the therapeutic action of psychoanalysis. *Int. J. Psycho-Anal.*, *41*, 16–33.

Lothane, Z. (2001). A response to Grünbaum's "A century of psychoanalysis critical retrospect and prospect" (and other texts). *International Forum of Psychoanalysis*, *10*, 113–132.

Lothane, Z. (2007). Response to Professor Adolf Grünbaum. *Psychoanalytic Psychology*, *24*, 577–585.

Mack, A. & Rock, I. (1998). *Inattentional Blindness*. Cambridge, MA: MIT Press.

Mahony, P. (1979). The boundaries of free association. *Psychoanalysis & Contemporary Thought*, *2*, 151–198.

Main, M. (1991), Metacognitive knowledge, metacognitive monitoring, and singular (coherent) versus multiple (incoherent) model of attachment: Findings and directions for future research. In: *Attachment Across the Life Cycle*, eds. C. M. Parkes, J. Stevenson-Hinde & P. Marris. London: Tavistock-Routledge, pp. 127–159.

Makari, G. (2008). *Revolution in Mind: The Creation of Psychoanalysis*. New York, NY: HarperCollins.

Mayer, E. (1996). Changes in science and changing ideas about knowledge and authority in psychoanalysis. *Psychoanal. Q.*, *65*, 158–200.

McCallum, M. & Piper, W (1997). *Psychological Mindedness: A Contemporary Understanding.* Mahway, NJ: Lawrence Erlbaum Associates.

McCallum, M. & Piper, W. (1997). The psychological mindedness assessment procedure. In *Psychological Mindedness: A Contemporary Understanding*, eds. M. McCallum & W. Piper. Mahwah, NJ: Lawrence Erlbaum, pp. 27–58.

McGaughey, C. (2008). To be or not 2 bee: An examination of the breaking set. In *Meta-cognition: A Recent Review of Research, Theory and Perspective*, eds. M. F. Shaughnessy, M. V. J. Veenman, & C. Kleyn-Kennedy. Hauppauge, NY: Nova Science Publishers, pp. 85–108.

McLaughlin, J. (1991). Clinical and theoretical aspects of enactment. *J. Am. Psychoanal. Assoc.*, *39*, 595–614.
McWilliams, N. (1999). *Psychodynamic Case Formulation*. New York, NY: Guilford Press.
McWilliams, N. (2004). *Psychodynamic Psychotherapy: A Practitioner's Guide*. New York, NY: Guilford Press.
Meins, E., Fernyhough, C., Russell, J., & Clark, C. (1998). Security of attachment as a predictor of symbolic and mentalising abilities: A longitudinal study. *Social Development*, *7*, 1–24.
Mermelstein, J. (2000). The role of concordance and complementarity in psychoanalytic treatment. *Psychoanalytic Psychology*, *17*, 706–729.
Mills, J. (2007). A response to Grünbaum's refutation of psychoanalysis. *Psychoanalytic Psychology*, *24*, 539–544.
Mitchell, S. (1998). The analyst's knowledge and authority. *Psychoanal. Q.*, *67*, 1–31.
Mlodinow, L. (2012). *Subliminal: How Your Unconscious Mind Rules Your Behavior*. New York, NY: Pantheon.
Modell, A. (1984). *Psychoanalysis in a New Context*. New York, NY: International Universities Press.
Modell, A. (1991). A confusion of tongues, or whose reality is it? *Psychoanal. Q.*, *60*, 227–244.
Moore, B. & Fine, B. eds. (1968). *A Glossary of Psychoanalytic Terms and Concepts*. 2nd ed. New Haven, CT/London: American Psychoanalytic Association and Yale University Press.
Moss, E., Parent, S., & Gosselin, C. (1995), Attachment and theory of mind: Cognitive and metacognitive correlates of attachment during the preschool period. Paper presented at the biennial meeting of the Society for Research in Child Development, March 1995, Indianapolis, IN.
Mukaidono, M. (2001). *Fuzzy Logic for Beginners*. River Edge, NJ: World Scientific.
Murray, E. (1956). *A Content-analysis Method for Studying Psychotherapy*. Washington, DC: American Psychological Association.
Murray, E. & Jacobson, L. (1971). The nature of learning in traditional and behavioral psychotherapy. In *Handbook of Psychotherapy and Behavior Change: An Empirical Analysis*, eds. A. E. Bergin & S. L. Garfield. New York, NY: John Wiley & Sons, pp. 909–950.
Nagel, E. (1959). Methodological issues in psychoanalytic science. In *Psychoanalysis, Scientific Method and Philosophy*, ed. S. Hook. New York, NY: New York University Press, pp. 38–56.
Neisser, U. & Becklen, R. (1975). Selective looking: Attending to visually significant events. *Cognitive Psychology*, *7*, 480–494.
O'Donnell, K. (2015). What's the matter with psychoanalysis? Paper presented at the University of California Los Angeles, May 20, 2015.
Ogden, T. (1985). The mother, the infant and the matrix: Interpretations of aspects of the work of Donald Winnicott. *Contemporary Psychoanalysis*, *21*, 346–371.
Ogden, T. (1994). The analytic third – Working with intersubjective clinical facts. *Int. J. Psycho-Anal.*, *75*, 3–20.
Ogden, T. (1997). Reverie and interpretation. *Psychoanal. Q.*, *66*, 567–595.
Ogden, T. (2005). On psychoanalytic supervision. *Int. J. Psycho-Anal.*, *86*, 1265–1280.

Ogden, T. (2010). Why read Fairbairn? *Int. J. Psycho-Anal.*, *91*, 101–118.

Ogden, T. (2016). On language and truth in psychoanalysis. *Psychoanal. Q.*, *85*, 411–426.

Olinick, S. (1984). A critique of empathy and sympathy. In *Empathy*, Volume I, eds. J. Lichtenberg, M. Bornstein, & D. Silver. Hillsdale, NJ: Analytic Press, pp. 137–165.

Pally, R. (2000). *The Mind–Brain Relationship*. London: Karnac Books.

Pally, R. (2007). The predicting brain: Unconscious repetition, conscious reflection and therapeutic change. *Int. J. Psycho-Anal.*, *88*, 861–881.

Perner, J. (1988). Higher-order beliefs and intentions in children's understanding of social interaction. In *Developing Theories of Mind*, eds. J. W. Astington, P. L. Harris, & D. R. Olson. New York, NY: Cambridge University Press, pp. 271–294.

Perner, J. (1991). *Understanding the Representational Mind.* Cambridge, MA: MIT Press.

Piaget, J. & Inhelder, B. (1969). *The Psychology of the Child.* New York, NY: Basic Books.

Pine, F. (2011). Beyond pluralism: Psychoanalysis and the workings of the mind. *Psychoanal. Q.*, *80*, 823–856.

Piper, W., de Carufel, F., & Szkrumelak, N. (1985). Patient predictors of process and outcome in short-term individual psychotherapy. *Journal of Nervous and Mental Diseases*, *173*, 726–733.

Poland, W. (1984). On the analyst's neutrality. *J. Am. Psychoanal. Assoc.*, *32*, 283–299.

Poland, W. (1992). Transference: "An original creation." *Psychoanal. Q.*, *61*, 185–205.

Popper, K. (1963). *Conjectures and Refutations*. London: Routledge & Kegan Paul.

Premack, D. & Woodruff, G. (1978). Does the chimpanzee have a theory of mind? *Behavioral and Brain Sciences*, *1*, 515–526.

Quinodoz, J.-M. (1993). *The Taming of Solitude: Separation Anxiety in Psychoanalysis*. London: Routledge.

Quinodoz, J.-M. (1996). The sense of solitude in the psychoanalytic encounter. *Int. J. Psycho-Anal.*, *77*, 481–496.

Racker, H. (1957). The meanings and uses of countertransference. *Psychoanal. Q.*, *26*, 303–357.

Rangell, L. (1954). Similarities and differences between psychoanalysis and dynamic psychotherapy. *J. Am. Psychoanal. Assoc.*, *2*, 734–744.

Rangell, L. (1967). Psychoanalysis: A current look. *J. Am. Psychoanal. Assoc.*, *15*(Suppl.), 423–431.

Rangell, L. (1997). At century's end: A unitary theory of psychoanalysis. *Journal of Clinical Psychoanalysis*, *6*, 465–484.

Raphling, D. (1992). Some vicissitudes of aggression in the interpretive process. *Psychoanal. Q.*, *61*, 352–369.

Raphling, D. (1995). Interpretation and expectation: The anxiety of influence. *J. Am. Psychoanal. Assoc.*, *43*, 95–111.

Raphling, D. (1997). Interpretation as comparison. *Psychoanal. Q.*, *66*, 242–258.

Rayner, E. (1991). *The Independent Mind in British Psychoanalysis*. Northvale, NJ: Jason Aronson.

Reed, G. (1984). The antithetical meaning of the term "empathy" in psychoanalytic discourse. In *Empathy*, Volume I, ed. J. Lichtenberg, M. Bornstein, & D. Silver. Hillsdale, NJ: Analytic Press, pp. 7–23.

Reed, G. (1997). The analyst's interpretation as fetish. *J. Am. Psychoanal. Assoc.*, *45*, 1153–1181.

Reich, W. (1949). *Character Analysis* (3rd ed.). New York, NY: Orgone Institute Press.
Reik, T. (1948). *Listening with the Third Ear: The Inner Experience of a Psychoanalyst*. New York, NY: Grove Press.
Reisman, D. (1950). *The Lonely Crowd*. New Haven, CT: Yale University Press.
Renik, O. (1992). Use of the analyst as a fetish. *Psychoanal. Q.*, *61*, 542–563.
Renik, O. (1993). Analytic interaction: Conceptualizing technique in light of the analyst's irreducible subjectivity. *Psychoanal. Q.*, *62*, 553–571.
Renik, O. (1995). The ideal of the anonymous analyst and the problem of self-disclosure. *Psychoanal. Q.*, *64*, 466–495.
Renik, O. (1996). The analyst's self-discovery. *Psychoanalytic Inquiry*, *16*, 390–400.
Renik, O. (1998a). The analyst's subjectivity and the analyst's objectivity. *Int. J. Psycho-Anal.*, *79*, 487–497.
Renik, O. (1998b). Getting real in analysis. *Psychoanal. Q.*, *67*, 566–591.
Richards, A. (2002). How new is the "new American psychoanalysis"? The example of Irwin Z. Hoffman. *Journal of Clinical Psychoanalysis*, *11*, 379–401.
Richards, A. & Richards, A. (2015). Benjamin Wolstein and us: Many roads lead to Rome. In *Psychoanalysis: Critical Conversations (Selected Papers by Arnold Richards, Volume 1)*. New York, NY: International Psychoanalytic Press, pp. 213–246.
Richards, A. (2015) A.A. Brill and the politics of exclusion. In *Psychoanalysis: Critical Conversations (Selected Papers by Arnold Richards, Volume 1)*. New York, NY: International Psychoanalytic Press, pp. 25–43.
Rorty, R. (1982). Philosophy in America today. In *The Consequences of Pragmatism*. Minneapolis, MN: University of Minnesota Press, pp. 211–230.
Rosegrant, J. (2005). The therapeutic effects of the free-associative state of consciousness. *Psychoanal. Q.*, *74*, 737–766.
Rosenblatt, A. (1989). Reinspecting the foundations of psychoanalysis. *Psychoanalysis & Contemporary Thought*, *12*, 73–96.
Rosenfeld, H. (1952). Notes on the psychoanalysis of the superego conflict in an acute schizophrenic patient. *Int. J. Psychoanal.*, 33, 111–131.
Roughton, R. (1994). Repetition and interaction in the analytic process: Enactment, acting out, and collusion. *Annual of Psychoanalysis*, *22*, 271–286.
Rudolf, G., Manz, R., & Öri, C. (1994). Ergebnisse psychoanalytischer Therapie [Results of psychoanalytic therapy]. *Zeitschrift fur Psychosomatische Medizin und Psychotherapie*, *40*, 25–40.
Rumelhart, D. & McClelland, J. (1986). *Parallel Distributed Processing*. Cambridge, MA: MIT Press.
Sandell, R., Blomberg, J. & Lazar, A. (1999). Wiederholte Langzeitkatamnesen von Langzeitpsychotherapien und Psychoanalysen [Repeated long-term follow-ups of long-term psychotherapy and psychoanalysis]. *Zeitschrift fur Psychosomatische Medizin und Psychotherapie*, *45*, 43–56.
Sandell, R., Blomberg, J., Lazar, A., Carlsson, J., Broberg, J., & Schubert, J. (2001). Unterschiedliche Langzeitergebnisse von Psychoanalysen und Langzeitpsychotherapien. Aus der Forschung des Stockholmer Psychoanalyse-und Psychotherapieprojekts [Different long-term outcome in psychoanalyses and long-term psychotherapies. From the Stockholm Research Project of psychoanalysis and psychotherapy]. *Psyche*, *55*, 273–310.
Sandler, J. (1976a). Countertransference and role-responsiveness. *International Review of Psychoanalysis*, *3*, 32–37.

Sandler, J. (1976b). Actualization and object relationships. *Philadelphia Association for Psychoanalysis, 3*, 59–70.
Sandler, J. (1993). On communication from patient to analyst: Not everything is projective identification. *Int. J. Psychoanal., 74*, 1097–1107.
Sandler, P. (2006). The origins of Bion's work. *Int. J. Psychoanal., 87*, 179–201.
Schafer, R. (1959). Generative empathy in the treatment situation. *Psychoanal. Q., 28*, 342–373.
Schafer, R. (1976). *A New Language for Psychoanalysis* New Haven, CT: Yale University Press.
Schafer, R. (1982). *The Analytic Attitude*. New York, NY: Basic Books.
Schafer, R. (1991). Book review of *Psychic Equilibrium and Psychic Change: Selected Papers of Betty Joseph* (E. Spillius & M. Feldman, 1989). *Int. J. Psychoanal., 72*, 169–171.
Schafer, R. (1992). *Retelling a Life*. New York, NY: Basic Books.
Schafer, R. (1996). Authority, evidence, and knowledge in the psychoanalytic relationship. *Psychoanal. Q., 65*, 236–253.
Schlesinger, H. (1981). General principles of psychoanalytic supervision. In *Becoming a Psychoanalyst: A Study of Psychoanalytic Supervision*, ed., R. Wallerstein. New York, NY: International Universities Press, pp. 29–38.
Schoenhals, H. (1995). Triangular space and the development of a working model in the analysis. *Int. J. Psychoanal., 76*, 103–113.
Schwaber, E. (1981). Empathy: A mode of analytic listening. *Psychoanalytic Inquiry, 1*, 357–392.
Schwaber, E. (1983). A particular perspective on analytic listening. *Psychoanal. Study Child, 38*, 519–546.
Schwaber, E. (1992a). Countertransferences: The analyst's retreat from the patient's vantage point. *Int. J. Psychoanal., 73*, 349–361.
Schwaber, E. (1992b). Psychoanalytic theory and its relation to clinical work. *J. Am. Psychoanal. Assoc., 40*, 1039–1057.
Schwaber, E. (1996). The conceptualisation and communication of clinical facts in psychoanalysis: A discussion. *Int. J. Psycho-Anal., 77*, 235–253.
Schwaber, E. (1997). Reflections on the concept "the patient's psychic reality." *Psychoanal. St Child, 52*, 42–53.
Searles, H. (1962). The differentiation between concrete and metaphorical thinking in the recovering schizophrenic patient. *J. Am. Psychoanal. Assoc., 10*, 22–49.
Segal, H. (1973). *Introduction to the Work of Melanie Klein*. London: Hogarth Press.
Segal, H. (1978). On symbolism. *Int. J. Psychoanal., 59*, 315–319.
Segal, H. (1957). Notes on symbol formation. *Int. J. Psychoanal., 38*, 391–397.
Seligman, M. E. (1995). The effectiveness of psychotherapy: The Consumer Reports study. *Am. Psychol., 50*, 965–974.
Shane, M., Shane, E., & Gales, M. (1997). *Intimate Attachment: Toward a New Self Psychology*. New York, NY: Guilford Press.
Shapiro, D. (1965). *Neurotic Style*. New York, NY: Basic Books.
Shapiro, D. (1981). *Autonomy and Rigid Character*. New York, NY: Basic Books.
Shapiro, T. (1974). The development and distortions of empathy. *Psychoanal. Q., 43*, 4–25.
Shaughnessy, M., Veenman, M., & Kleyn-Kennedy, C. (2008). *Metacognition: A Recent Review of Research, Theory and Perspectives*, ed. M. F. Hauppauge, New York, NY: Nova Science Publishers, pp. 207–220.

Shedler, J. (2010). The efficacy of psychodynamic psychotherapy. *Am. Psychol.*, *65*, 98–109.

Shevrin, H., Bond, J., Brakel, L., Hertel, R., & Williams, W. (1996). *Conscious and Unconscious Processes: Psychodynamic, Cognitive, and Neurophysiologic Convergences*. New York, NY: Guilford Press.

Shevrin, H., Snodgrass, M., Brakel, L., Kuschwaha, R., Lailada, N., & Basan, A. (2013). Subliminal unconscious conflict alpha power inhibits supraliminal conscious symptom experience. *Front. Hum. Neurosci.*, *7*, 544.

Shorter, E. (2015, March 19). Commentary: Improving the mental health system by addressing core problems. *Psychiatric Times*. Retrieved from http://www.psychiatrictimes.com/cultural-psychiatry/improving-mental-health-system-addressing-core-problems

Siegman, A. (1964). Exhibitionism and fascination. *J. Am. Psychoanal. Assoc.*, *12*, 315–335.

Siegel, D. (2007). *The Mindful Brain: Reflection and Attunement in the Cultivation of Well-Being*. New York, NY: WW Norton.

Silberschatz, G., Fretter, P., & Curtis, J. (1986). How do interpretations influence the process of psychotherapy? *J. Consult. Clin. Psychol.*, *54*, 646–652.

Slavin, J. (1998). Influence and vulnerability in psychoanalytic supervision and treatment. *Psychoanalytic Psychology*, *15*, 230–244.

Sloane, P. (1957). Panel report: The technique of supervised analysis. *J. Am. Psychoanal. Assoc.*, *5*, 539–547.

Slochower, J. (1996). *Holding and Psychoanalysis: A Relational Perspective*. Hillsdale, NJ: Analytic Press.

Solms, M. (1997). What is consciousness? *J. Am. Psychoanal. Assoc.*, *45*, 681–703.

Spence, D. (1982). *Narrative Truth and Historical Truth: Meaning and Interpretation in Psychoanalysis*. New York, NY: Norton.

Spillius, E. (1992). Clinical experiences of projective identification. In *Clinical lectures on Klein and Bion*, ed. R. Anderson. London: Tavistock/Routledge, pp. 59–73.

Spillius, E. & Feldman, M. (1989). *Psychic Equilibrium and Psychic Change: Selected Papers of Betty Joseph*. London: Tavistock/Routledge.

Stanicke, A. & Killingmo, B. (2013). Object trust: A specific kind of analytic change. *Psychoanalytic Psychology*, *30*, 423–437.

Stark, M. (1999). *Modes of Therapeutic Action*. Northvale, NJ/London: Jason Aronson.

Steiner, J. (2000). Containment, enactment and communication. *Int. J. Psychoanal.*, *81*, 245–255.

Steiner, J. (2006). Interpretative enactments and the analytic setting. *Int. J. Psychoanal.*, *87*, 315–320.

Sterba, R. (1934). The fate of the ego in analytic therapy. *Int. J. Psychoanal.*, *15*, 117–126.

Stern, D. (1997). *Unformulated Experience: From Dissociation to Imagination in Psychoanalysis*. Hillsdale, NJ: Analytic Press.

Stern, D. (2003). The fusion of horizons: Dissociation, enactment, and understanding. *Psychoanalytic Dialogues*, *13*, 843–873.

Stern, D. (2004). The eye sees itself: Dissociation, enactment, and the achievement of conflict. *Contemporary Psychoanalysis*, *40*, 197–273.

Stern, D. (2009). Partners in thought: A clinical process theory of narrative. *Psychoanal. Q.*, *78*, 701–731.
Stern, D. (2017). Personal communication.
Stern, D. N. (1985). *The Interpersonal World of the Infant: A View from Psychoanalysis and Developmental Psychology*. New York, NY: Basic Books.
Stolorow, R. & Atwood, G. (1979). *Faces in a Cloud: Subjectivity in Personality Theory*. Northvale, N.J.: Aronson.
Stolorow, R. (1988). Intersubjectivity, psychoanalytic knowing, and reality. *Contemporary Psychoanalysis*, *24*, 331–337.
Stolorow, R. (1994). The nature and therapeutic action of psychoanalytic interpretations. In *The Intersubjective Perspective*, eds. R. D. Stolorow, G. E. Atwood, & B. Brandchaft. Northvale, NJ/London: Aronson, pp. 43–55.
Stolorow, R., Brandchaft, B., & Atwood, G. (1987). *Psychoanalytic Treatment: An Intersubjective Approach*. Hillsdale, NJ/London: Analytic Press.
Strachey, J. (1934). On the nature of the therapeutic action of psycho-analysis *Int. J. Psychoanal.*, *15*, 127–159.
Strachey, J. (1958). Editor's introduction. In The Case of Schreber, Papers on Technique and Other Works, pp. 83–88.
Sugarman, A. (2006). Mentalization, insightfulness, and therapeutic action: The importance of mental organization. *Int. J. Psychoanal.*, *87*, 965–987.
Szecsody, I. (2008). Does anything go in psychoanalytic supervision? *Psychoanalytic Inquiry*, *28*, 373–386.
Teasdale, J., Moore, R., Hayhurst, H., Pope M. Williams, S., & Segal, Z. (2002) Metacognitive awareness and prevention of relapse in depression: Empirical evidence. *J. Consult. Clin. Psychol.*, *70*, 275–287.
Thomä, H. & Kächele, H. (2007). Comparative psychoanalysis on the basis of a new form of treatment report. *Psychoanalytic Inquiry*, *27*, 650–689.
Thompson, J. M. & Cotlove, C. (2005). *The Therapeutic Process*. New York, NY: Jason Aronson.
Tower, L. (1956). Countertransference. *J. Am. Psychoanal. Assoc.*, *4*, 224–255.
Truax, C. (1966). Reinforcement and nonreinforcement in Rogerian psychotherapy. *J. Abnorm. Psychol.*, *71*, 1–9.
Tuch, R. & Kuttnauer, L. (2018). *Conundrums and Predicaments in Psychotherapy and Psychoanalysis: The Clinical Moments Project*. London: Routledge.
Tuch, R. (1993). Blocks to creativity: Writer's block as seen from the self psychological perspective. In *The Widening Scope of Self Psychology: Progress in Self Psychology, Volume 9*, ed. A. Goldberg. Hillsdale, NJ/London: Analytic Press, pp. 243–257.
Tuch, R. (1999). The construction, deconstruction and reconstruction of memory in the light of social cognition. *J. Am. Psychoanal. Assoc.*, *47*, 153–183.
Tuch, R. (2001). Questioning the psychoanalyst's authority. *J. Am. Psychoanal. Assoc.*, *49*, 491–513.
Tuch, R. (2007). Thinking with, and about, patients too scared to think: Can non-interpretive maneuvers stimulate reflective thought? *Int. J. Psychoanal.*, *88*, 91–111.
Tuch, R. (2008). Unravelling the riddle of exhibitionism: A lesson in the power tactics of perverse interpersonal relationships. *Int. J. Psychoanal.*, *89*, 143–160.
Tuch, R. (2015). The analyst's way of being: Recognizing separable subjectivities and the pendulum's swing. *Psychoanal. Q.*, *84*, 363–388.

Tuch, R. & Kuttnaver, L. (in press). *Precarious Predicaments: working with clinical conundrums in psychotherapy and psychoanalysis*. Routledge.

Turnbull, O. & Solms, M. (2007). Awareness, desire, and false beliefs: Freud in the light of modern neuropsychology. *Cortex*, *43*, 1083–1090.

Varga, M. (2006). A clinical approach to transforming enactment. *Psychoanalytic Review*, *93*, 411–435.

Veenman, M. (2008). Giftedness: Predicting the speed of expertise acquisition by intellectual ability and metacognitive skillfulness of novices. In *Meta-Cognition: A Recent Review of Research, Theory and Perspective*, eds. M. F. Shaughnessy, M. V. J. Veenman, & C. Kleyn-Kennedy. Hauppauge, NY: Nova Science Publishers, pp. 207–220.

Vida, J. (2002). The indispensable "difficult event." In *Failures in Psychoanalytic Treatment*, eds. J. Reppen & M. Schulman. Madison, CT: International Universities Press, pp. 17–36.

von Wright, G. (1957). *The Logical Problem of Induction*. New York, NY: Macmillan.

Wallace, E. (1989). Pitfalls of a one-sided image of science: Adolf Grünbaum's foundations of psychoanalysis. *J. Am. Psychoanal. Assoc.*, *37*, 493–529.

Wallerstein, R., ed. (1981). *Becoming a Psychoanalyst: A Study of Psychoanalytic Supervision*. New York, NY: International Universities Press.

Wallerstein, R. (1986). Psychoanalysis as a science: A response to the new challenges. *Psychoanal. Q.*, *55*, 414–451.

Wallerstein, R. (1988). One psychoanalysis or many? *Int. J. Psychoanal.*, *69*, 5–21.

Wallerstein, R. (1992) (ed.). *The Common Ground of Psychoanalysis*. Northvale, NJ: Jason Aronson.

Wegner, D. (2003). *The Illusion of Conscious Will*. Cambridge, MA: MIT Press.

Weiss, J. & Sampson, H. (1986). *The Psychoanalytic Process*. New York, NY: Guilford Press.

Weiss, S. & Fleming, J. (1975). Evaluation of progress in supervision. *Psychoanal Q.*, *44*, 191–205.

Wellman, H. (1988). First steps in the child's theorizing about the mind. In *Developing Theories of Mind*, eds. J. W. Astington, P. L. Harris, & D. R. Olson. New York, NY: Cambridge University Press, pp. 64–92.

Wellman, H. (2002). Understanding the psychological world: Developing a theory of mind. In *The Blackwell Handbook of Childhood Cognitive Development*, ed. U. Goswami. Oxford: Blackwell, pp. 167–187.

Westen, D. (1998). The scientific legacy of Sigmund Freud: Toward a psychodynamically informed psychological science. *Psychol. Bull.*, *124*, 333–371.

Westen, D. & Garrard, G. (2002). Development in cognitive neuroscience: II. Implications for theories of transference. *J. Am. Psychoanal. Assoc.*, *50*, 99–134.

Wheelis, A. (1973). *How People Change*. New York, NY: Harper & Row.

Whitaker, C. & Malone, T. (1953). *The Roots of Psychotherapy*. Philadelphia, PA: Blakiston.

Winnicott, D. W, (1958). The capacity to be alone. *Int. J. Psychoanal.*, *39*, 416–420.

Winnicott, D. W. (1958), The capacity to be alone. In: *The Maturational Process and the Facilitating Environment*. New York, NY: International Universities Press, pp. 29–36.

Winnicott, D. W. (1960). Ego distortion in terms of the true and the false self. In *Maturational Process and the Facilitating Environment*. New York, NY: International Universities Press, pp. 140–152.

Winnicott, D. W. (1965). *The Maturational Processes and the Facilitating Environment: Studies in the Theory of Emotional Development.* London: Hogarth Press.

Winnicott, D. W. (1968). Playing: Its theoretical status in the clinical situation. *Int. J. Psychoanal., 49,* 591–599.

Winnicott, D. W. (1969). The use of an object. *Int. J. Psychoanal., 50,* 711–116.

Winnicott, D. W. (1971). Mirror-role of mother and family in child development. In *Playing and Reality.* New York, NY: Basic Books, pp. 111–118.

Wolf, E. (1995). How to supervise without doing harm: Comments on psychoanalytic supervision. *Psychoanal. Inq., 15,* 252–267.

Yerushalmi, H. (1994). A call for change of emphasis in psychodynamic supervision. *Psychotherapy,* 31, 137–145.

Zetzel, E. R. (1956). Currents concepts of transference. *Int. J. Psychoanal., 37,* 369–376.

Index

AAI *see* Adult Attachment Interview
active mode of cognition 23–6
Adult Attachment Interview (AAI) 124
affect education 203
affect recognition 203
aggression 93
Ahumada, J. 250
alpha elements 104
alternate modes of cognition 24
alternate modes of thinking, accessing and utilizing 27–9
alternate states of consciousness 29
American Psychoanalytic Association 217
analyst-initiated enactments 145–7
analyst's activity 49–50; clinical theory 42; effects of concrete thinking 129–31; general psychology theory 42; observing *vs.* interpreting 52–3; patient-specific theory 42, 54, 58; patient's subjectivity 43; therapeutic action theories 50–2
analyst's inherent susceptibility 147
analyst's otherness: aspects of 107; intolerance of 110–11
analyst's use of authority: discounting 80; experience-distant interpretations 80, 83–4; feigned perspectivelessness 89–90; interpretation aspects 82–6; irreducible subjectivity 79; lessening regression 87–8; objectifying perspective 86; objectivity debate 84–6; other concerns 86–7; patient's mind 79, 90–1; patient's perspective 88–9; regression aspects 80–2; styles of interpreting 91–2
analyst's use of interpretations 58–9
analyst's way of being 66–7
analytic attitude 200–2
analytic stance 200–2
annihilation anxiety 181
antilibidinal ego 174
antilibidinal, ego-rejecting object 176
"as if" personality 29, 30
assured conviction 6, 83
attachment behavioral system 186
attachment figure 186
attachment style: secure attachment 171; insecure attachment 124, 171; anxious attachment 186
Atwood, G. 9

bad object 175, 177, 189
Balint, Enid 187
benign environmental matrix 181
beta elements 104
biofeedback training procedure 103
Bion, W. R. 16, 41, 44, 45, 46, 102, 103, 126, 130
Board of Professional Standards (BOPS) 217
BOPS *see* Board of Professional Standards
Bowlby, John 185–6; attachment behavioral system 186; infant's internal working model 186; primary motive 185; stranger anxiety 186
brand of Galilean science 251
"breaking set" 48, 120, 133
British Middle School 12, 14, 171
Bromberg, Phillip 150
Bronstein, Catalina 36–7
Brown, Margaret Wise 182

Carpy, Denis 138
cause-and-effect relationship 248

central ego 176–7
"chance thoughts" 22
clinical theory 42
closed-minded concrete thinkers 126–7
close process monitoring 52
cognition modes 23–6
cognitive regression 81
Columbia Supervision Project 236
Columbia University 15
common ground 1, 7
complementary reactions 69
concordant reactions 69
concrete attitude 97
concrete thinkers 12, 116–18, 120, 126–7
concrete thinking: compelling feature of 129–31; as developmental arrest 123–4; differentiation 121–22; effects on analysts 129–31; environmental factors 124–6; limitations of 117; perspectives 117; symbolic thought *vs.* 116; symbolization 121–22; symptoms of 116; theory of mind and 123–4; transference interpretations 126–9
conjunctive reactions 75
conjunctive relationship 69
connectionism 247
constructivistic model of mind 101
containment, container-contained 4, 72, 103, 126, 142, 143
Contemporary Psychoanalysis (Wolstein) 12
contentiousness 2, 221
control mastery theory 249–50
COPE Study Group on Supervision 218, 220
core transference 61
countertransference; *see also* transference: complementary reactions 69; concordant reactions 69; mutuality 71; Racker's contribution to 69; supervisory vignette 233–6; "treat or teach" continuum 230–2
countertransference enactments 5, 62, 137; as demonizing 138; Sigmund Freud and 195; as transformative 138
countertransference reactions 4–5, 61–2; determination of role 75; patient's behaviors 72; as primary evidence 42
cultural shift 86–7

Davies, Jody 9
Davies, Paul 252
"dead mother" transferences 20
defense analysis 8, 196, 198
deliberation process 245
depressive position 105, 126, 183, 189
developmental lag 36
differentiation 121–22
disavowal 121
disjunctive intersubjectivity 72
disjunctive reactions 75
disjunctive relationship 69
dissociation 19, 152
dissociative model of enactments 152–3
doer/Done to 138–9
developmental arrest 121, 123–4

efficacy studies 243
ego psychologists 52–3
Eitingon, Max 231
emotional manna 163
emotional self-awareness 103
empathic failures: analyst's contribution to 161–3; case illustration and discussion 164–8; conflicting needs/self states 163–4; definition of 160; patient's contribution to 163; selfobject failures and 156–7
empathic mothering 169
empathy: beyond 168–70; definitions of 158–61; psychological nutriment 157–8
enactment-emerging transferences 20
essentialism 85
evocative questioning 218
exciting object 174–7
executive functioning 23
experience-distant interpretations 80, 83–4
extra-clinical validation 241
extracting oneself from enactment 153–5

Faces in a Cloud (Atwood and Stolorow) 9
Fairbairn, W.R.D. 14, 172–9; antilibidinal, ego-rejecting object 176; early caregivers behaviors 173; endopsychic structure 172; enticer/enticee 175; exciting mother 174; internal saboteur 174; libidinal, ego-exciting object 175–6; mutative function of analyst 178; rejecter/rejectee 175; rejecting mother 174; religious-based analogy 174; schizoid mechanisms 172; structural model 175; subegos 176–7; theory of internal object relations 172; therapeutic action model 177

false belief test 111
"false self" notion 30
feed-back 188
Feyman, Richard 252
first-order representations 100
Fonagy, Peter 244
formal regression 81
frame establishment 206–9
free association: active mode of cognition 23–6; alternate modes of cognition 24; alternate modes of thinking, accessing and utilizing 27–9; finding mind of one's own 29–33; fundamental rule 26–7, 195; inaction *vs.* action 27; intervention and 28–9; link between play and 34–5; objective self-awareness 28–9; passive mode of cognition 23–6; passive nature of 22; patients other reasons 33–4; showing up and attempting to 204–6; Sigmund Freud and 21–3; subjective self-awareness 28–9; targeted goals of 35–8; therapeutic benefits of 19–39
Freud, Anna 167, 171
Freud, Sigmund: countertransference enactment 195; ego as object 102; free associative method 21–3; impulse-psychology 178; narcissism and 2; psychology and 239; repetition compulsion 195; therapeutic success 249; way of being 67
Friedman, Henry 79
Friedman, Lawrence 81
Fromm-Reichmann, Frieda 34, 39n2
fundamental rule, difficulties following 26–7
fuzzy logic 25, 155

general psychology theory 42
giftedness 49, 120
Gill, Merton 197
good-enough mothering 184
Goodnight Moon (Brown) 182
good object 177–8, 181
Gosford Park movie 181
Gray, Paul 36
Grünbaum, Adolf 15

hallucination, negative 246
hallucinatory wish fulfillment 121, 132
harvesting enactments: dissociative model of 152–3; informational content of 148–9; interpersonal perspective 149–52; serviceable definition of 148
hermeneutics 239, 252
higher-order thinking: concrete attitude 97; constructivistic model of mind 101; first-order representations 100; less tolerant of instances 97; psychic functioning mode 98; Rashomon phenomenon 101; second-order representations 100

impulse-psychology 178
inaction *vs.* action 27
inexact interpretations 45, 60n5
infantile symbiosis concept 180
infant's internal working model 186
internal saboteur 174
internal working model 186
interpersonalist enactments: analyst-initiated 145–7; analyst's inherent susceptibility 147; doer/done perspectives 139–42; general consensus 139; mutual recognition 140; refusal to wear the attribution 142–5; two-way directionality 138–9
interpersonal psychoanalysts 150
interpretations: experience-distant 80, 83–4; observing *vs.* 52–3; patient's inner life 82; patient's mind 84–6; problems with 53–6; Procrustean bed argument 82–3
interpretive enactments 146
interpretive interventions 54
intrapsychic conflict 153
irreducible subjectivity 79, 86
Isaacs, Susan 121

Jacobs, Ted vignette: core countertransference reaction 66; implications of 64–6; manifest countertransference reaction 66; meta-reaction 66; self-restraint 63–4
Joseph, Betty 55–6
Jung, Carl 239

Kernberg, Otto: Hanna Segal and 6; projective identification 5; psychodynamic psychotherapy 198, 212; transference-focused psychotherapy 244

Klein, Melanie 125, 171, 189n1
Kohut, H. 89, 156, 157, 158, 159, 170

Lacan, Jacques 51, 56
le sujet suppose savoir 56, 208
Levey, Mark 37
libidinal ego 174
libidinal, ego-exciting object 175–6
Lieberman, Jeffrey 15, 241
The Logics of the Mind: A Clinical View 250

malignant misunderstanding 188
manifest transference 61
"marked mirroring" 33
mentalization 119, 203
mentalization-based treatment 244
metacognition 12; basis of therapeutic action 120; definition of 132; mentalization 119; mindfulness 119; psychological mindedness 119; reflective function 119; self-reflective thought 119; theory of mind and 118–19
metacognitive activities 118
metacognitive knowledge 118
meta-reaction 66
mindfulness 119
mirroring 156, 187, 188
multi-determinism 200
mutative effect of articulation 51
mutuality 71
mutual recognition 140

narcissism 2; analysand's 64; analyst's 55, 58, 82; self psychology and 156
negative therapeutic reaction 10
neural networks 247
neuroscience 2, 244
New York Psychoanalytic Institute 13
New York Times review 241
non-interpretive intervention 54
non-self-disclosing analyst 33

objective self-awareness 28–9
object relations, 81, 178, 185
observing *vs.* interpreting, analyst's activity 52–3
obsessive–compulsive character type 28
Ogden, T. 50, 51, 76, 172, 176, 177, 181, 219, 227
one-person psychology 62, 65
An Open Door Review of Outcome Studies in Psychoanalysis 242
open-minded, open-mindedness 92, 101
optimal frustration 157
optimal responsiveness 157
optimal selfobject functioning 169–70
outcome studies 242–4
overcoming resistance 35–6
overvalued idea *vs.* selected facts 43–9

Pally, Regina 49
paranoid-schizoid position 104, 189n1
passive mode of cognition 23–6
pathogenic beliefs 249–50
patient's initial task 204–6
patient-specific theory 42, 54, 58
patient's second task 209–10
patient's shared task 211–12
patient's subjectivity 43
pattern recognition 43
persecutory anxiety 125, 129, 187, 189
Piaget, Jean 12
play *vs.* free association 34–5
pleasure principle 172
Poincaré, Jules- Henri 45
positivism 85
postmodern, postmodernism 79, 85
potential self 169
projective identification 5, 13, 65, 70, 99, 103, 125, 137, 140, 147–8, 153, 224, 226, 233–4
prereflective intervention 54
primary process thinking 201
Procrustean bed argument 82–3
Psychiatric Times 241
psychic determinism 200
psychic functioning mode 98
psychic reality 111
psychic structure 171–2, 212
psychoanalysis: clinical practice of 240; definition of 198; fundamental structural change 212; partial reorganisation of psychic structure 212; therapeutic action of 199; *vs.* psychodynamic psychotherapy 196–200
psychoanalytic third 218
Psychoanalytic Training and Research (Columbia Supervision Project) 236

psychoanalytic war 58
psychodynamic psychotherapy: therapeutic action of 199; transference in 198–9; *vs.* psychoanalysis 196–200
psychodynamic technique 194–6; analytic attitude/stance 200–2; goals of 213; initial task of patient and therapist 204–6; psychoanalysis *vs.* psychodynamic psychotherapy 196–200; repetition compulsion 195; second task of patient and therapist 209–10; shared task of patient and therapist 211–12; therapist requirements 202–3; treatment goals 212–14
psychodynamic therapy goals 213
psychological mindedness 102, 119, 203
psychological nutriment 157–8

Racker, H. 69
radical relativism 85, 89
randomized controlled studies 243
Rangell, Leo 197, 198, 255
Rashomon phenomenon 101
rationalization 151
reflective function 119
reflective thought: biofeedback training procedure 103; clinical development of 111–13; emotional self-awareness 103; open-mindedness 101; psychological-mindedness and 102; self-reflection 103, 104; self-reflexivity 104–5; sense impressions 103; triangular space 103
regression: cognitive/formal 81–2; lessening 87–8
regression-promoting devices 196–7
Reisman, David 30
rejecting object 177
relational-based analysts 60n12
repetition compulsion 195
Research Committee of the International Psychoanalytic Association 242
resistance 75
role responsiveness 69, 70
Runaway Bunny (Brown) 182

Sampson, H. 249
Sandler, J. 70
Schafer, Roy 56
schizoid mechanisms 172
Science 245
scientific evidence 241–4; brand of Galilean science 251; Carl Jung and 239; cause-and-effect relationship 248; deliberation process 245; effect size 243; empirical outcome research 242; extra-clinical validation 241; mentalization-based treatment 244; misdepictions and 249; negative hallucination 246; neural processes 246; randomized controlled studies 243; supporting psychoanalytic theory 244–7; top-down regulation 246–7; transference-focused psychotherapy 244
scientific limitations 254–5
scientism 254–5
second-order representations 100
Segal, Hanna 6
selected facts *vs.* overvalued idea 43–9
selective attention 41–2
selective inattention, 42, 246
selfobjects 156; failures 156–7; transferences 20
self psychology 156
self-reflection 97, 103, 104
self-reflective functioning 112
self-reflective thought 119
self-reflexivity 104–5
semiotic method 53
sense impressions 103
separation anxiety: clinical case studies 107–10; experiencing to observing mode 106; patient's realization 97
Shafer, Roy 15
shame 33, 91, 130, 196, 226
Shorter, Edward 15, 241
Shrinks: The Untold Story of Psychiatry (Lieberman) 241
split: horizontal 19, 121; vertical 19, 121
spontaneous gesture 182
"spontaneous thoughts" 22
Stark, Martha 50
states of consciousness 24
Stern, Donnel 150
Stolorow, Robert 9, 13
stranger anxiety 186
subegos 176–7
subjective self-awareness 28–9
supervisee *see* supervision
supervision: analyst's reflective capacity 224–5; challenges 222; COPE

Study Group on 218, 220; dealing with countertransference 233–6; evocative questioning 218; facilitating process 219; formulations 221; honoring intuition 226–8; imparting information 219; pitfalls of 228–30; position statement 217–18; seeing from distance 222–4; strategically intervention 221–2; styles of 228–30; tasks and goals of 217–22; "treat or teach" continuum 230–2; trust themselves 220; variable presence of mind model 222–6
supervisor *see* supervision
sustenance 163
symbolic equation 122
symbolization 121–22

teach metacognition 120
theory-based (intended) interventions 58
theory of internal object relations 172
theory of mind 12; concrete thinking and 123–4; definition of 100; in metacognition 118–19; research 99
therapeutic action: Fairbairn's model of 177; metacognitive basis of 120; of psychoanalysis 199; of psychodynamic psychotherapy 199; theories 50–2
therapeutic alliance 210
therapeutic zeal 146
therapist's initial task 206–9
therapist's shared task 211–12
Thompson, Clara 39n2
top-down regulation 246–7
total transference 146
transference; *see also* countertransference: clinical illustrations 71–7; core 61; dimensions of 67–8; interpretations on concrete patients 126–9; manifest 61; psychoanalytic practice 20; in psychodynamic psychotherapy 198–9
transference-focused psychotherapy 244
transmuting internalization 156–7
transmuting internationalizations 13
treatment goals 212–14
"treat or teach" continuum 230–2
triangular space 103
two-person psychology, 62, 67–8, 65, 84

unconscious intention 245
unconscious will 245
unempathic intervention 160
unformulated experience, 154
unitary theory 19
University of Toronto 15
"unwilled thoughts" 22

variable presence of mind model 222–6

wear the attribution 4, 71, 75, 115, 142–5, 179, 184
Weiss, J. 249
Winnicott, Donald 14, 34, 179–85; annihilation anxiety 181; benign environmental matrix 181; clinical applications of 184; clinical calamities 184; developmental stages of 180; good-enough mothering 184; infantile symbiosis 180; spontaneous gesture 182; transitional period 182–3
without memory or desire 41
Wolstein, Benjamin 12
working alliance 210–11